HINDU RELIGION, CUSTOMS AND MANNERS

HINDU RELIGION CUSTOMS AND MANNERS

Describing the Customs and Manners, Religious, Social and Domestic Life, Arts and Sciences of the Hindus

P. THOMAS

D. B. TARAPOREVALA SONS & CO. PRIVATE LIMITED
210 Dr. Dadabhai Naoroji Road, Bombay 400 001

TO MY DAUGHTER

COPYRIGHT © 1969 D. B. TARAPOREVALA SONS & CO. PRIVATE LTD.

PRINTED IN INDIA

Printed and published by Russi J. Taraporevala for D. B. Taraporevala Sons & Co. Private. Ltd., 210 Dr. Dadabhai Naoroji Road, Bombay 400 001. at their Electrographic Industries Division, Apte Industrial Estate, Worli, Bombay 400 018.

PREFACE

WHILE there is no dearth of scholarly works on the religion, philosophy or sociology of the Hindus, a popular work dealing with the Hindu way of life is difficult to find. Probably the only book of its kind, still widely read, is the Abbe Dubois' well known work written in the first half of the nineteenth century. Excellent as his work undoubtedly is, the Abbe was a zealous missionary and many of his observations were coloured by a horror of the heathen; further his experience was confined to South India and what he wrote of the Hindus of the north was based mainly on hearsay. Above all, what was true of the Hindus in the first half of the nineteenth century is not all true now.

Besides the Abbe's book there are, it is true, a few travellers' tales available to foreigners. These were written by Europeans at the time when the Portuguese, the Dutch, the French and the British had begun to take an active interest in the destiny of India. What these travellers saw and reported was not Hinduism but the ruins of medieval Brahminism.

The Hindus have suffered much as a nation. With the loss of political power to Muslims and later to the British, they had been, for centuries, persecuted and treated as an inferior race. Their national independence gone, their culture, civilisation and traditions misunderstood and actively suppressed, the spirit of Hinduism was cowed and nearly smothered to death.

But Hinduism did not die. Under the impact of modern conditions, a strange and new vigour animated it and like a dried up tree putting forth new shoots on the outbreak of the monsoon, Hinduism sprang to life again. With surprising rapidity it regained its characteristic power of adaptation, and discarding the accretions of medieval superstition and bigotry started a vigorous new life. But this new life is still in its infancy.

The religion, customs and manners of the Hindus, a race as ancient as the Assyrians yet modern, cannot but rouse interest especially at this juncture of their history when, after centuries of foreign domination, the Hindus have at last gained complete political freedom. The customs of the Hindus will, no doubt, be found to be different from those of Europeans and Americans, but this in itself does not constitute superiority or inferiority. In a heterogeneous community like the Hindus whose traditions are lost in remote antiquity, it is easy to find practices among certain sections of the people that may revolt modern conceptions; on the other hand, from the sacred literature of the Hindus it can be seen that they are heirs to institutions and schools of thought which have elicited admiration from all. Few writers, however, view both together and draw a balanced picture of the Hindus, the general tendency being either to exaggerate their misfortunes or idealize their way of life.

In this work, as in my previous book "Epics, Myths and Legends of India", my main effort has been to help the reader see the Hindus as they are. It may, however, be mentioned that the modernism of the few cosmopolitan Hindus of the cities, which may strike casual foreign observers as remarkable, has not been allowed, in this work, to shadow the profound conservatism of the Hindus of the villages who form the bulk of the population.

P. THOMAS

CONTENTS

PREFACE V

LIST OF ILLUSTRATIONS IX

I. MYTHICAL ORIGIN, ANTIQUITY AND HISTORY 1

Hindu Theories of Creation—Cyclic Conception of the Universe—Legend of the Flood—Prehistoric India—Dravidian Civilisation of Mohen-Jo-Daro—Aryan Conquest—Racial Theories of Aryans—Religious Synthesis and Social Rigidity—Alexander's Conquest and Greek Influence—Chandra Gupta Maurya—Megasthenes on India—Asoka—Kanishka—The White Huns—Harsha—Hiuen Tsang's Visit—South India—The Chera, Pandyan and Chola Kingdoms—Muslim Conquest—Campaigns of Mahmud of Ghazni—Mohammad Ghori—Kutub-ud-din Aibek—The Moghuls—Aurangzeb—Rise of the Mahrathas—British Occupation—Muslim and British Influence on Hindus,

II. THE CASTE SYSTEM .. 10

Origin of the Word Caste—The Five Castes—Brahmins and Their Sub-divisions—The Kulins of Bengal—Nambudiris of Malabar—The Kshatriyas or Warrior Caste—War of Annihilation between Brahmins and Kshatriyas—Genocide by Parasurama—The Rajputs—Vaisyas or the Trader and Farmer Caste—The Banias of the North and Chettiars of the South—The Sudras or Servile Caste—The Mahrathas—The Panchamas or Outcastes—Working of Caste System Generally—Story of Viswamitra and Vasishta—Some Advantages of Caste System—Caste in Modern India.

III. RELIGION .. 22

Hinduism a Growth and not Founded by a Single Person—Its Synthesis—Essential Characteristics—Vedic Religion—The Upanishads—Puranic Religion—Principal Deities of the Hindu Pantheon—Six Orthodox Hindu Sects—Ritual at Home and in Temple—Description of a Regular Puja—Hindu Method of Religious Instruction—Animism—Tree and Serpent Worship—Ancestor Worship—Demonology—Importance of Pilgrimages—Centres of Pilgrimage—The Doctrine of Metempsychosis.

IV. PHILOSOPHY 37

The Materialists of India—The Six Orthodox Systems—Nyaya—Vaisheshika—Sankhya—Yoga—Purva Mimamsa—Uttara Mimamsa—Advaita as Propounded by Sankara—Vivekananda's Song of the Sanyasin—Vishishta Advaita as propounded by Ramanuja—The Bhagavad Gita.

V. BUDDHISM, JAINISM, SIKHISM, BRAHMO SAMAJ AND ARYA SAMAJ .. 45

Buddhism, a Revolt against Brahminism—Life of the Buddha—His Teachings—Buddhism under Asoka and Kanishka—Its Disappearance from India—Jainism—Life of Varddhamana—His Teachings—The Schism in Jainism—Jain View of Sanctity of Life—Sikhism—Kabir—Nanak—Gurus—Granth—The Manly Philosophy of the Sikhs—Brahmo Samaj—Rām Mohan Roy—Devendra Nath Tagore—Keshub Chandra Sen—Muslim and Christian Influence on Hinduism—Arya Samaj—Militant Nationalism of Swami Dayanand—His Teachings—Dissentions in Arya Samaj—Present Position of the Samaj.

VI. SOCIAL LIFE 56

Caste Panchayat—Its Functions and Powers—The Temple as a Centre of Social Life—Temple Festivals—Feasting—Social Calls—Games and Amusements—Status of Hindu Women in Society—The Lot of the Widow—Beauty Culture—Craze for Ornaments.

CONTENTS

VII. DOMESTIC LIFE .. 64

The Joint Family System—Daily Life in the Joint Family—The Head of the Family and His Domestic Tyranny—The Mother-in-Law and Her Age Old Functions—Advantages and Disadvantages of the Joint Family System—The Daily Routine Life of the Mother-in-Law and Her Husband—Children's Lot in Joint Families—The Ties of Blood—Hindu Domestic Life in the Great Cosmopolitan Cities of India.

VIII. CUSTOMS, MANNERS, COSTUMES, POPULAR SUPERSTITIONS, ETC. .. 71

Methods of Greeting—Rules of Etiquette Between Sexes—Men's Dress—Women's Dress—Ornaments—Hair-dressing—Popular Superstitions—The Evil Eye—The Black Tongue—Darsan—The Science of the Wall Lizard.

IX. CEREMONIES .. 78

The Twelve Samskaras—The Name Giving Ceremony—Upanayanam or Investiture with Sacred Thread—Marriage and Connected Ceremonies—Funeral Ceremonies—Shraddhas or Ceremonies for the Manes of Ancestors—Bone Gathering Ceremony—Sacrifices—Asvamedha or Horse Sacrifice—Yagas of the Present Day.

X. LITERATURE AND LANGUAGES .. 87

Two Divisions of Sanskrit Literature—Smritis and Srutis—The Epics—The Puranas—Dharma Sastras or Law Books—Smartha Sutras—Vedangas—Niti Sastras—Buddhist Literature—Secular Literature—Kalidasa—Bhavabhuti—Bharavi—Bhatti — Kumaradasa—Magha—Mricchakatika—Mudra Rakshasa—Sanskrit Prose Works—Historical and Scientific Works—Modern Indian Languages—The Aryan Group—The Dravidian Group.

XI. MUSIC AND DANCING .. 99

Indian Music—Some Musical Instruments—Bharata Natyam, the Classical Dance of India—Popular Dances—Kathakali—Garba—Manipuri Dances—Orissan Dances—War Dances of Wild Tribes—Devil Dances of the South.

XII. ARCHITECTURE, SCULPTURE AND PAINTING .. 105

Early Buddhist Shrines—Stupa at Sanchi—Rock cut Architecture and Sculpture—Some North Indian Temples—Temples of South India and the Deccan—Sculpture—Painting—A Portrait of Shakuntala as Described in Kalidasa's Shakuntala—Ajanta Caves and Paintings—The Mogul School—Abul Fazal on Painting—The Rajput Schools.

XIII. ART AND SCIENCE OF LOVE .. 114

The Four Objects of Life—Ancient Hindu Sexologists—Vatsyayana and His Kama Sutra—Courtship and Love—Mystic Love—Gita Govinda—Venal Love—Damodara Gupta and Kshemendra, Two Bards of Venal Love—The Courtesan and Her Wiles.

XIV. HINDU CALENDAR AND HOLIDAYS .. 123

The Lunar and Solar Reckonings in India—The Different Hindu Eras—Hindu Holidays—All Days are Holy Days—Vratas—Ekadasi—Feasts and Festivals—Divali—Dasara—Mahashivaratri—Ganesha Chaturthi—Janmashtami—Cocoanut Day—Ramnavami—Hanuman Jayanti—Naga Panchami or The Feast of Serpents—Gudi Parwa—Vaman Dwadasi—Vasanta Panchami.

XV. CONCLUSION .. 132

Author's Personal Observations—The Burden of the Past—Pseudo Spirituality—The Virtues of the Villagers.

GLOSSARY AND INDEX .. 135

LIST OF ILLUSTRATIONS

Vishnu, Lakshmi, Saraswati (Colour) — **Frontispiece**

Between pages 8 and 9
1. Ganesha
2. Shiva Symbols and Images
3. Ancient Hindu Coins
4. Carved Brackets
5. Fort of Chitor
6. Kathiawar Shepherd
7. Rajput Nobleman

Between pages 16 and 17
8. Beggars on a Temple Step
9. Party of Brahmins
10. Ring of Sacred Kusa Grass
11. A Festival
12. Hindu Mendicant
13. Folk Dance
14. Feasting Brahmins
15. Demon
16. Vaishnava Brahmin
17. Image of Ramanuja
18. Child Rama
19. Nandilinga
20. Rama & Sita
21. Surya
22. Bhairava
23. Sarasvati
24. Indra
25. The Linga
26. Vase of Copper
27. Agni
28. Kamala
29. Kali
30. Gomatesvara
31. Shiva & His Wife
32. Vishnu with His Wives

Between pages 24 and 25
33. Garuda
34. Birth of Brahma
35. Sacrificial Utensil
36. Rama winning Sita
37. Sacrificial Implement
38. Shiva, Destroyer
39. Radha & Krishna
40. Mahakali
41. Virabhadra
42. Hindu Sectarian Marks
43. Vaishnava Symbols
44. Vishnu Sleeping on Ananta
45. Matsya
46. Kurma
47. Varaha
48. Vamana
49. Narasimha
50. Parasurama

Between pages 32 and 33
51. Rama destroying Ravana
52. Krishna
53. Buddha

54. Kalki
55. Worshipping the Banyan Tree
56. Paintings on walls
57. Gangotri
58. Balkrishna
59. Serpent Symbols
60. Dhanurasana
61. Padmasana
62. Padmasana
63. Sarvangasana
64. Bhagirathasana
65. Young Girl
66. Mayurasana
67. Gomukhasana
68. Vrischikasana

Between pages 40 and 41
69. Jain Sanctuary
70. Gomatesvara Statue
71. Jain Pilgrim
72. Procession of Jain Women
73. Image of Goddess
74. Jain Temple, Calcutta
75. Images of Thirthankaras
76. Thirthankara
77. Sea Bath
78. Religious Procession
79. Mendicants
80. Marriage Procession
81. Sati

Between pages 48 and 49
82. Collection of Brasses
83. Sandalwood Box
84. Ivory
85. Bracelets
86. Anklet
87. Toe Ring
88. Hanuman
89. Ornaments
90. Arm Ornaments
91. Ornaments
92. Peasant Ornaments
93. Ear-Rings
94. Armlet
95. Rajput Crown
96. Head Ornaments

Between pages 56 and 57
97. Anklets
98. Hair Pendent
99. Foot & Toe Ornaments
100. Sarangi
101. Sarbati
102. Jala Tarang
103. Sitar Player
104. Sarangi Player
105. Abhisarika
106. Pictorial Vasant

LIST OF ILLUSTRATIONS

107 Tansen
108 Megha Raga
109 Hindola Raga
110 The Trumpeter
111 Trumpets
112 Rajput Musician
113 Tabla Player
114 Dancers

Between pages 64 and 65

115 Kathakali Dancers
116 Folk Dance During Holi
117 Temple Procession
118 Worship of Sea
119 A Vow of Silence
120 Girl in Neem
121 Sculptures of Deities
122 Indra
123 Ganesha
124 Statue of Chandra Gupta
125 Royal Group
126 Fall of Ganges
127 Vishnu as the Sun God
128 Surya the Sun God
129 Kulu
130 Hindu Temple

Between pages 72 and 73

131 1000 Pillared Hall
132 Kesava Temple
133 Ornamental Architrave
134 Carvings in Jain Temple
135 Birla Mandir
136 Temple of Mahadeva
137 Dwaraka Temple
138 Shiva Temple
139 Halabid Temple
140 Carving on Wall

Between pages 80 and 81

141 Shiva Dancing
142 Temple Tower
143 Shiva Temple
144 Sculpture in a Cave Temple
145 Interior
146 Rama's Temple
147 Temple of Jagannath
148 Ablutions
149 Vaishnava Brahmin
150 Spinning Yarn
151 Ceremonial Shaving
152 Thread Ceremony
153 Ablutions
154 Wedding of Tulsi
155 God Maker
156 Villagers Offering Flowers & Cocoanuts
157 Worship of Sankara

Between pages 88 and 89

158 Facade of Temple
159 Haridwar
160 Jugglers
161 Indian Boxing

162 Snake Gods, Goddesses
163 Image of Ganesha
164 Vishnu
165 Varaha
166 Sarasvati & Ganesha
167 Naganandi Linga
168 Khandehrao
169 Hanuman
170 Shiva, Parvati & Kartikeya
171 Brahma
172 Krishna
173 The Bell
174 Idols of Jagannatha
175 Krishna Riding on Elephant
176 Cocoanut Day
177 Rangoli

Between pages 96 and 97

178 Bhima Drinking the Blood of His Enemy
179 Yudhishtira's Feast
180 Bhishma
181 Triumphal Procession
182 Effigies of Demons Being set fire to
183 Image of Bhima
184 Yudhistira
185 Battle Array of Kauravas
186 Battle Array of Pandavas
187 Religious Dance
188 Upakarma Ceremony
189 Divali Celebrations
190 Temple Priest on Ceremonial Ride
191 Worship of Good King Bali
192 Tree Worship
193 Sculpture of Hindu Deities
194 Lakshmi Temple

Between pages 104 and 105

195 Stick Fighting
196 Meditation
197 Ceremonial Oil Bath
198 Bangle Ceremony
199 Ganesh being Worshipped
200 Exhibition of Dolls in Home for Navaratri Festival
201 Brahmin Boy learning Sacrificial Duties
202 Durga Procession
203 Sadhu at Wayside Shrine
204 Naga
205 Nagpanchami
206 Mendicant with lemon Garlands
207 Cartman Worshipping his Bullocks
208 Nayar Girl
209 Sandhya Prayers
210 Ganesh Procession for Immersion
211 Rati
212 Decorated Images Procession
213 Changing Sacred Thread
214 Brass Lamp
215 Making Cakes of Cow Dung
216 White Clay for Sale
217 Domestic Worship
218 Village God
219 Giving Alms

LIST OF ILLUSTRATIONS

Between pages 112 and 113

220 Hindu Mendicant
221 Heralding Temple Procession
222 Painting on Elephant
223 State Elephant
224 Bangle & Bracelet
225 Shiva Dancing
226 Mendicant Shiva
227 Signs of Zodiac
228 Car Festival
229 The Earth
230 Guardians of Universe
231 Worship of Books
232 Hindu Girl Adorning Her Forehead
233 A Sacred Cow
234 Breaking a White Pumpkin
235 Ganesha

CHAPTER I
MYTHICAL ORIGIN, ANTIQUITY AND HISTORY

LIKE all the great races of mankind whose traditions go back to prehistoric times, the Hindus believe that they are of divine origin. They claim descent from the person of Brahma, the creator; the Brahmins (the priestly caste) from his head, the Kshatriyas (the warrior caste) from his arms, the Vaisyas (the trading and agricultural caste) from his thighs, and the Sudras (the menial caste) from his feet. The other races of men are believed to have sprung out of the darkness which Brahma, in the process of creation, "cast away".

This is not, however, the only account of creation found in Hindu sacred books. The mythical sage Manu, for instance, claims, in his code, that he created mankind though not the universe. He acknowledges, however, the superiority and precedence of Brahma, whom he recognizes as his father. "This universe," says Manu, "was enveloped in darkness, unperceived, undistinguishable, undiscoverable, unknowable, as it were entirely sunk in sleep. Then the irresistible, the self-existent Lord, undiscerned, causing this universe with the five elements and all other things to become discernible, was manifested. He who is beyond the cognizance of senses, subtle, undiscernible, and eternal, and is the essence of all beings, and inconceivable, shone forth. He desiring, seeking to produce various creatures from his own body, first created the waters, and deposited in them a seed. This (seed) became a golden egg, resplendent as the sun in which he himself was born as Brahma, the progenitor of all the world....That Lord having continued a year in the egg, divided it into two parts by his mere thought. With these two shells, he formed the heaven and the earth, and in the middle he placed the sky, the eight regions, and the eternal abode of the waters."*

Other writers on the subject of creation had their own theories, and in practically every Hindu sacred book will be found an account of creation substantially different from any other. And all these conflicting accounts are held to be equally sacred and true by a line of argument peculiar to the Hindus with which the reader will soon become familiar.

The Hindu conception of the universe is essentially cyclic; that is, they do not believe in an absolute beginning or end of the universe, but maintain that creation, existence and destruction are endless processes ever repeating. This does not preclude a belief in the creation or end of a particular universe. The present world of ours, for example, had a beginning and will have an end; but it is a mere link in the endless chain of universes that preceded it and is yet to succeed it. Our world was created by Brahma, and after a definite period will be destroyed and replaced by another world which will suffer a similar fate.

The Hindus have evolved an ingenious mathematical table for measuring this cyclic process. Their unit of time, in this respect, is the Kalpa or a Day of Brahma. The Kalpa is equivalent to 4,320,000,000 of our years and is divided into 1,000 Mahayugas or great ages of equal length. The Mahayuga is subdivided into four Yugas or ages, namely, the Kritayuga, the Thretayuga, the Dwaparayuga, and the Kaliyuga. The Kritayuga is the Golden Age of the Hindus, and they believe that in this age all men are equal and good, and evil is entirely absent from the world; the length of the Kritayuga is 1,728,000 years. In Thretayuga, the second age, evil appears for the first time; its length is 1,296,000 years. Though men of this age are not so happy as those of Kritayuga they are much happier and more religious than the men of Dwaparayuga or the third age in which good and evil, equally strong, struggle for supremacy. At the end of Dwaparayuga, which lasts 864,000 years, evil overcomes good and the world enters Kaliyuga, the fourth age of strife, sweat and toil. As the Kaliyuga progresses, evil gathers momentum till good is completely destroyed and the redemption of the world can only be brought about by its destruction and reconstruction. And for this purpose Vishnu, the second of the Hindu triad, will, the Hindus believe, incarnate himself as Kalki, the destroyer, and bring about the end of the world by a deluge or by fire. The Kaliyuga lasts 432,000 years. It is interesting to note that according to the Hindus we are now living in the sixth millennium of Kaliyuga, and there are as yet more than 425,000 years for the end of the world.

We have noticed elsewhere that the Kalpa is a Day of Brahma. This divinity is not immortal but is destined to die like all other beings, human and divine. The span of Brahma's life is one hundred years (computed at the rate of 4,320,000,000 of our years per Kalpa or Day of Brahma). On completion of his term of life, Brahma dies and the universe is engulfed in what is called Mahapralaya, the Greater Chaos, which destroys all gods, demons and humans. After one hundred years of Chaos, another Brahma is born, and the cycle is thus continued without end.

Mention must also be made of Pralaya, Chaos, which succeeds every Kalpa or Day of Brahma. This chaos and the attendant confusion are believed to be caused by the Night of Brahma when this god goes to sleep. The Night of Brahma, obviously, is of equal length as the Kalpa, but in the morning, when Brahma wakes up, order is again restored and life and light reappear.

The exact age of the reigning Brahma is known; he has just completed the 50th year of his life.

Like the Hebrews, the Hindus have a legend of the flood. To understand this, the reader must have

---

* *Sacred Books of the East*, Vol. XXV, edited by Max Muller.

some idea of another division of the Kalpa, known as Manwantara. The Kalpa is divided into 14 Manwantaras over each of which presides a Manu or world teacher. The Hindu legend of the flood narrates how the present Manu was saved by Vishnu in the form of a fish from the deluge that brought about the destruction of the world which immediately preceded ours. This is the story:

"There lived in ancient times a holy man
Called Manu, who, by penances and prayers,
Had won the favour of the Lord of Heaven.
One day they brought him water for ablution;
Then, as they washed his hands, a little fish
Appeared, and spoke in human accents thus:
'Take care of me, and I will be thy Saviour!'
'From what wilt thou preserve me?' Manu
                                              asked.
The fish replied: 'A flood will sweep away
All creatures; I will rescue thee from that.'
'But how shall I preserve thee?' Manu said.
The fish rejoined, 'so long as we are small,
We are in constant danger of destruction,
For fish eat fish; so keep me in a jar,
When I outgrow the jar, then dig a trench,
And place me there; when I outgrow the
                                          trench,
Then take me to the ocean—I shall then
Be out of reach of danger.' Having thus
Instructed Manu, straightway rapidly
The fish grew larger; then he spoke again:
'In such and such a year the flood will come;
Therefore construct a ship, and pay me
                                          homage.
When the flood rises, enter thou the ship,
And I will rescue thee.' So Manu did
As he was ordered, and preserved the fish,
Then carried it in safety to the ocean;
And in the very year the fish enjoined
He built a ship, and paid the fish respect
And there took refuge when the flood arose.
Soon near him swam the fish and to his horn
Manu made fast the cable of his vessel.
Thus drawn along the waters, Manu passed
Beyond the northern mountain. Then the fish
Addressing Manu, said, 'I have preserved thee,
Quickly attach the ship to yonder tree;
But lest the waters sink from under thee,
As fast as they subside, so fast shalt thou
Descend the mountain gently after them.'
Thus he descended from the northern mountain.
The flood had swept away all living creatures:
Manu alone was left."*

In another version of the myth it is said that Manu took with him the Seven Sages and a pair of every living creature, who re-peopled the world after the deluge.

PREHISTORY

The peoples now known as Hindus are not ethnologically homogeneous. Most of the Hindus have very little in common except the name. Even their name, 'Hindu', is of foreign origin. There is no common word of indigenous origin which is applicable to all the Hindus. The word 'Aryan' was applied to the three higher castes, but the fourth and the fifth castes, who form the majority of the Hindus, used to be known by their caste or sub-caste names.

The Hindus consist mainly of the aborigines of India and the various races that invaded and settled down in the country upto the time of the Muslim conquest. From time immemorial, India has been considered fair prize for the invader, and the races that burst into the country from the North-West were numerous. They invaded the country in different periods of its history, conquered the inhabitants and settled down, slowly absorbing their religion and culture. The Hindus and their religion are the results of these racial migrations and fusions.

Of all the races that conquered India, the Aryans are the most important. They have managed to dominate the cultural life of India from the time of their irruption into the country down to our own times. The Aryans, after their settling in the country, were, no doubt, conquered by more virile tribes from Central Asia; but the traditions and the culture of the latter were readily assimilated by the Aryans and they themselves thought it a privilege to be recognized as a unit of the Aryan social system. All the literature and social theories of the Hindus are so permeated with overt and insidious statements of Aryan superiority that even non-Aryan kings who managed to subdue the Aryans had to recognise the superiority of the conquered. Hindu literature, dominated by Aryan prejudices had, for a long time, misled even impartial historians, and till very recently it was generally believed that, prior to the Aryan conquest, India was wild country inhabited by savages and cannibals to whom the conquerors brought the blessings of civilisation. Ancient Indo-Aryan literature describes the peoples whom the Aryans conquered as demons, monsters and Sons of the Night.

Recent discoveries at Mohenjo-daro and elsewhere disprove this ancient assertion and indicate that the races whom the Aryans conquered were a civilised people, culturally far more advanced than the warlike Aryan nomads who invaded their country. Excavations at Mohenjo-daro unearthed a civilisation which flourished in the Indus Valley five thousand years ago. The inhabitants of Mohenjo-daro, from what we can make out from the ruins of their city, were a refined, artistic people who knew how to plan and build cities, palaces, and houses for the common folk, and who loved a peaceful life. "The town (of Mohenjo-daro) is well laid out. Its streets are at right angles, running due north and south and east and west. The main street which is 33 ft. wide has been traced for half a mile and is unpaved. The side roads are about half this width. The buildings are of burnt brick set in mud mortar. No stone is used and the absence of any kind of ornamentation is conspicuous. The windows and doors open upon the main street and it is probable that some were several

---

* Monier Williams, *Indian Wisdom*.

storeys high, with flat roofs. An unusual feature of the houses is the presence of bathrooms, and also of an elaborate drainage system, greatly in advance of anything known in later India. For this purpose, pottery drain pipes and receptacles were laid down, communicating with the street drain or gutter. No temple has been discovered, but a large public bath, 39 ft. by 23 ft., has been unearthed. This bath which was rendered water-tight, is provided with steps leading down to the water, a promenade, and compartments for the bathers. Ingenious arrangements for filling and emptying it are provided. Just to the south of the bathroom is a large building, over two hundred feet long and one hundred feet wide, which may have been the royal palace."*

Ornaments, toys, sculptures and beautiful works of art in bronze and clay have been discovered together with seals with inscriptions on them. Mohenjo-daro folk had a genius for works of clay, and earthen pots and jars with patterns of concentric circles in black, or ornamented with figures of trees, birds and animals, are found in large numbers. Though temples have not been discovered, there is sufficient proof to show that the people of Mohenjo-daro had a fairly well developed religion. The supreme spirit they worshipped was the Mother Goddess; "she is represented in numerous pottery figures and on seals and amulets." The worship of Shiva and the Lingam also appear to have been prevalent. These religious ideas, no doubt, influenced later Hinduism although the Brahmins with their notions of Aryan superiority never acknowledged the source.

All this may not sound very impressive when compared to modern achievements. But 5,000 years ago this was something really remarkable and it gives us a picture of India radically different from that painted by Indo-Aryans. Mohenjo-daro culture was widely distributed, at least from the Punjab right down to the Makran coast, if not further east. The culture is believed to have been Dravidian.

The rich cities of the Dravidians very naturally attracted the attention of the warlike Aryan hordes who successfully invaded the country, and either enslaved the native population or drove them towards the east and south-east. From the scanty records left by the Aryans themselves, it can be seen that the battles were bloody and fierce. But eventually the Dravidians were subdued and the Aryans occupied the country. After a time the conquered and the conquerors began to mix freely and to intermarry. This probably alarmed the leaders among the Aryans who had an exaggerated idea of their racial purity, and codes began to be laid down prohibiting inter-marriage and free social intercourse. Thus were laid the foundations of the caste system, the most rigorous social code in the world.

The Aryans were racial and not religious fanatics. They found no difficulty whatsoever in borrowing the gods of the conquered races and giving them niches in their pantheon. Nor were the gods of the conquered the only ones the Indo-Aryans admitted into their pantheon. In course of time the fate that befell the Dravidians befell the Aryans too, and they, in turn, were conquered by foreign races. The Indo-Aryans had to make room for these peoples in their social system, and for their gods in the pantheon. But social intercourse with the foreign races had to be prohibited in order to preserve the racial purity of the Aryans. Hence each community that was admitted into the all-embracing Hindu fold was organized into an independent social unit with a definite status and a code of its own, and all social intercourse between any two communities was prohibited. In religious matters, however, a more lenient attitude was adopted. People were allowed to worship any gods they pleased and hold any views they liked as long as these did not seriously challenge the fundamental principles of social organization.

These tendencies gave rise to the main distinguishing feature of Hinduism, i.e., social rigidity flourishing side by side with religious elasticity. Down to the present day, Hinduism permits its followers to worship any deities they like or no deity at all, but transgression of social codes in matters such as inter-dining or inter-marrying very often led to excommunication.

HISTORY

The Hindus have no proper history. Ancient Indians had distinguished themselves in many arts and sciences, and the works they have left us on philosophy, medicine, architecture, etc., compare favourably with those of any other ancient race. But no historical work of any merit is found in the voluminous literature of the Hindus. The real history of India begins only after Muslim conquest, and upto that period Indian history remains mostly a matter of conjecture. There are some accounts of India which have come down to us from foreigners who visited the country as travellers or invaded it, and these together with what can be gleaned from the literature and monuments of the ancients give us some inkling into the condition of the country and its people at certain periods. But we look in vain into the literature of the Hindus for a continuous history of India.

The first authentic account of India and its people comes from the Greeks. Alexander invaded the Punjab and the Indus Valley in the fourth century B.C. and his historians wrote an account of the people they saw in India. The original was lost, but copious extracts were preserved in the writings of later authors. After Alexander's conquests there was constant contact, for a long time, between the Greeks and Indians, and some of the Greek rulers of Alexander's empire, it would appear, entered into matrimonial relationship with Indian kings and sent envoys to them. One of these envoys, the celebrated Megasthenes, wrote an account of India. Megasthenes was the envoy of Seleucus Nicator, the Greek ruler of the North-West Frontier which Alexander had conquered, sent to his ally Chandragupta Maurya, the Hindu emperor of

---

* H. G. Rawlinson, *India*.

Magadha. Megasthenes lived in Pataliputra (modern Patna), the capital of Magadha, for a number of years and had plenty of opportunities of studying the people of the country. The picture he paints of India is a very pleasant one. The country was prosperous and the people were contented and happy. The land was well-irrigated, and famines were unknown. The country was traversed by numerous highways connecting all the great cities of the empire and trade flourished. There was an efficient postal system. Profiteering was not permitted and prices were controlled.

Pataliputra had a municipal government of its own administered by six boards, each consisting of five members. The first board dealt with trade; the second with foreigners coming into and going out of the city; and the third was concerned with registration of births and deaths; the remaining three were in charge of commerce.

"Megasthenes tells us that a noble simplicity was the predominant Indian characteristic.... 'No Indian has ever been convicted of lying.... In the whole of Chandragupta's camp of 400,000 men there was no conviction for theft exceeding 200 drahmae (£8/). They were not litigious'."

Whatever might have been the high sense of integrity or honesty of the people, their king, as we shall see presently, was far from being an example to his subjects.

Chandragupta Maurya was the first great emperor of India and we have accounts of him, left by Greek writers and by Indians, which show that he was a remarkable man. He seems to have been of low origin, but ambitious and unscrupulous. By intrigue he managed to usurp the throne of Magadha and extend the frontiers of the kingdom. In all his activities he was ably assisted by his Brahmin adviser Chanakya or Kautilya, the Indian Machiavelli. Kautilya's *Arthasastra* (manual of politics), written 23 centuries ago, reads strikingly modern. Treating the traditional Hindu theories of statecraft and diplomacy with contempt, Chanakya struck a line of his own. He held that deceit, harshness and violence were indispensable to a king, and that a kingdom could be properly ruled only through spies, exaction, and a powerful standing army.*

However much we may deplore the methods of Chanakya, Chandragupta appears to have flourished under his guidance. He managed first to foment rebellion in the Punjab, which was at that time under the Greeks, and take possession of it. He then successfully conspired against the king of Magadha and had him assassinated. He usurped the throne of Magadha and built a powerful and beautiful city called Pataliputra on the banks of the Son, which he made the capital of his vast kingdom. He organized a powerful army and defeated Seleucus Nicator, the Greek ruler of Western Asia, who tried to reconquer the Punjab from the Indian king. After his defeat the two kings seem to have lived on friendly terms.

Chandragupta loved the pleasures of the world. His palace was the wonder of all those who beheld it. "In the Indian royal palace," writes Megasthenes, "there are wonders with which neither Memnonian Susa in all its glory, nor the magnificence of Ecbatana can hope to vie." He had a well-stocked harem and an army of dancing girls, and the chief courtesan of the palace received almost the wages of a minister.

Having won his kingdom by intrigue, and maintaining it by violence, Chandragupta "took elaborate precautions against assassination. He never slept twice in the same bed, and all food and drink were carefully tested in order to guard against poison. No one could enter the palace precincts without a permit, and an army of spies and agents provocateurs was employed to watch what was happening in the city, and no methods were considered too unscrupulous for getting rid of enemies of the state. He was surrounded by a host of slave girls who cooked and served his food, tended to his wants, massaged his limbs and entertained him with dancing and music. A body-guard of foreign Amazons kept watch over the palace day and night. Chandragupta seldom went abroad except on festal occasions, when he rode in solemn procession through the streets in a litter on the back of an elephant."†

The country, under this oppressive rule, prospered! The people lived in peace with one another and the ever vigilant monarch allowed neither a neighbouring monarch nor an ambitious subject to disturb the peace of the land. He permitted no one except himself to oppress his people. The officers of the state were carefully watched by spies, and those who showed a tendency to amass wealth by accepting illegal gratification were dismissed and punished. Hence though the government was bureaucratic, the officials went in fear of the king and seldom dared to harass the people.

Chandragupta died in 298 B.C. It appears towards the end of his life he became a penitent and died a Jain monk in the famous monastery of Shravan Belgola in Mysore. According to another story he committed suicide.

Bindusara, his son, succeeded Chandragupta, but little is known of his long reign. Bindusara's son Asoka ascended the throne in 273 B.C., and this emperor is recognized by all as the greatest of ancient Indian monarchs.

Brought up in the tradition of Chanakya and Chandragupta, Asoka's first concern, on coming to power, was to extend the frontiers of his kingdom. He led an army against the kingdom of Kalinga, the modern Orissa, with no better excuse than the desire to annex it. The people of Kalinga resented this wanton invasion of their land and fought fiercely. In the end the brave Kalingans were defeated and put to the sword. The carnage was terrible and Asoka was profoundly moved by the bloodshed and misery caused to millions of people through his ambition and love for power. He turned away from

---

* A more detailed account of Chanakya and Chandragupta will be found in the author's work *The Story of the Cultural Empire of India*.
† H. G. Rawlinson, *India*.

the field of battle in disgust, determined no more to conquer kingdoms. The teachings of the Buddha profoundly affected the king, and becoming a convert to this faith, he devoted his whole energy to the spread of Buddhism and to teaching men how to tread the noble path of virtue.

Throughout his vast empire he caused stone pillars to be erected on which were engraved rules of conduct for his subjects. Some of these edicts are still extant and we know a good deal of the character of the monarch from these. "The Law, wherever pillars of stone or tables of stone exist, must be recorded so that it may long endure." "The Law as enjoined by Asoka was strictly practical and suited to the popular understandings. No mention is made of metaphysical subtleties. It consists of compassion, liberality, truth, purity, gentleness and saintliness of life, 'harkening to elders, reverence to elders, and seemly treatment of Brahmins and ascetics, of the poor and wretched yea, even of slaves and of servants'."

The emperor extended his kindness even to animals. He abolished the royal hunt and brought the slaughter of animals to a minimum. Hospitals were built in the kingdom not only for the sick among humans but even for animals and birds.

Chandragupta's elaborate spy system was converted by Asoka into a body of "Overseers of the Law" who had to report to him periodically on the progress of religion in their jurisdiction. Though a Buddhist, he established complete religious toleration in his kingdom. The harsh and oppressive laws of Chandragupta were abolished and force was treated as a necessary evil to be used only in case of extreme necessity. In his edicts he adjures his successors to bear in mind, "If ever they are tempted by the lust of empire, the worthlessness of conquest by force. 'The conquest of the Law,' he assures them, 'is alone a conquest full of delight'."

Asoka's attempts to lead men to the path of virtue were not confined to his own kingdom. He sent Buddhist missionaries to all the known parts of the world. Not only were great cultural centres like Alexandria, Asia Minor and Greece visited by these missions, but even the animistic and wild tribes of Central Asia were brought under the civilizing influence of Buddhism by the efforts of Asoka's missionaries.

The empire of Asoka extended from the Hindu Kush to the Bay of Bengal, from Kashmir to Mysore. The vast dominions were well governed and the example of the saintly emperor inspired the civil servants and the people. The great highways that traversed the length and breadth of the empire were safe for tradesmen and pilgrims, and the land was prosperous.

"Asoka has been compared at various times to Marcus Aurelius, Saint Paul and Constantine. But no Christian ruler has ever attempted to apply to the government of a great empire the principles of the Sermon on the Mount, or to announce, in a public edict addressed to his subjects, that 'although a man does him injury, His Majesty holds that it must be patiently borne, as far as it possibly can be borne.' Two hundred and fifty years before Christ, Asoka had the courage to express his horror and remorse at the results of successful campaign, and deliberately to renounce war as a means of policy, in spite of the fact that his dominions included the unsubdued tribes of the North-west Frontier, and was able in practice to put an end to cruelty to man and beast, and establish complete religious toleration throughout India. Asoka fulfilled Plato's ideal of the state in which 'kings are philosophers and philosophers kings'."*

Asoka died in 232 B.C. after a reign of over forty years. Towards the end of his life he joined a Buddhist monastery and lived the life of a recluse.

We know little of Asoka's successors. They were not equal to the task left to them by Asoka, and in the beginning of the 2nd century the Mauryans were overthrown by a Hindu chief who founded the short-lived Sunga dynasty and established Brahminism as the state religion of the empire.

The Mauryan empire disintegrated soon after Asoka's death, and India again fell into chaotic conditions in which every chieftain fought for dominion and supremacy over his neighbour. The ever vigilant tribes of Central Asia, finding their opportunity in the weakness of Indian rulers, made several inroads into the country. Kanishka, the chieftain of one of these tribes known as Kushans, established himself in the north-west of India, and from Peshawar extended his kingdom eastwards and towards Kashmir. Like Asoka, Kanishka too came under the influence of Buddhism and was converted by the celebrated Buddhist scholar Asvaghosha. Kanishka appears to have tried to emulate Asoka. He strenuously worked for the spread of the Buddhist faith. To reconcile the differences of the various sects that had by now sprung up in Buddhism he convened a council of the leaders of the different sects. The council met at Kundalavana Monastery in Kashmir and was attended by about 500 monks from different parts of the country. After six months of discussion they seemed to have come to some sort of an agreement.

Though a great patron of art, literature and religion, Kanishka was, after all, a newly converted barbarian from the north and lacked the poise of Asoka, born and brought up in the land of the Buddha. The Buddhism that emerged out of Kanishka's efforts was the Mahayana or Northern Church, "which differs as much from the primitive Buddhism of the Hinayana, or Little Vehicle of the South, as Medieval Catholicism does from the simple creed of the Christians of the first century."

Situated at the extreme north of India, Kanishka's capital Purushapura (Peshawar) was a meeting place of the civilisations of the east and west. Kanishka was a great builder and his capital was embellished by many magnificent buildings. Of these the wooden tower of Purushapura, over six hundred feet in height, erected to enshrine certain relics of the Buddha deserves particular mention. "It consisted of fourteen

* H. G. Rawlinson, *India*

storeys, and was crowned by an iron pinnacle, surmounted by a number of copper gilt umbrellas...Its sides were adorned with numerous images of the Buddha, and it was many times restored. It was still standing in the 6th century A.D. and foreign visitors to India regarded it as one of the wonders of the world." But because of the impermanence of the material used, the tower did not survive the ravages of time and has not come down to our own times.

The Kushans cultivated friendly relations with the Roman emperors to the mutual advantage of both, and a brisk trade flourished between the Kushan empire and the Asiatic provinces of the Roman empire, both by land and by sea. The overland trade route ran through Balkh, and the sea route started from Barygaza (Broach) on the mouth of the Narbada and ended in the Persian Gulf whence the merchandise went by land. This trade brought much prosperity to the Kushan Empire and its capital Purushapura was reckoned the wealthiest city in the East.

The exact date of Kanishka's death is not known, but he is believed to have died in the third quarter of the second century A.D. A legend says he was assassinated by his people because of his tyranny. According to one account, Kanishka "is greedy, cruel and unreasonable; his campaigns and continued conquests have wearied the mass of his servants. He knows not how to be content but wants to rule over the four quarters. The garrisons are stationed in distant frontiers, and our relatives are far from us. Such being the situation, we must agree among ourselves and get rid of him. After that we may be happy." Kanishka was a Buddhist, and this account of the great Kushan emperor was probably inspired by Brahmins.

After Kanishka's reign, India again relapsed into a period of disorder and strife. The beginning of the fourth century A.D. was, however, marked by the rise of the Guptas. The Guptas were orthodox Hindus. The Gupta empire reached the zenith of its glory in the reign of Chandragupta II, known in Indian legend as Vikramaditya. In the reign of this monarch, the Chinese traveller Fa Hian visited India on a pilgrimage to the holy places of Buddhism. Chandragupta had transferred his capital from Pataliputra to Ayoddhya, the city of Rama, but it appears he lived the better part of the year in Ujjain which was the centre of his activities as told in legends connected with his life.

Fa Hian tells us of the great car processions of Pataliputra, of hospitals founded by charitable persons throughout the country, and of physicians competent to deal with every kind of sickness. The caste system was in full swing and the low castes had to live outside the city walls. The people were intensely religious, whether Buddhists or Hindus, and temples and monasteries could be seen everywhere in India. There were great centres of learning, conducted mainly by Brahmins or Buddhist monks, to which students and scholars from the different parts of the country flocked.

After the death of Chandragupta II, the Central Asian hordes again invaded India. The White Huns made many inroads into India and Mihiragula, who established himself in Kashmir in the beginning of the 6th century A.D., is described by Buddhist writers as a ferocious iconoclast who destroyed monasteries and shrines and massacred the monks. One of his favourite pastimes was to watch the death agony of elephants hurled, at his command, from the precipices of Himalayan hills.

The Huns penetrated deep into India. They overran the Punjab, but were prevented from expanding eastward by a confederacy of Hindu princes who checked their advance. This, however, did not stop them from penetrating southwards as far as Gujarat and the sea coast. All these wild tribes settled down in India and were, in due time, absorbed in Hinduism; they too enriched its religion, legends and mythology.

The strife between the different warring elements in the country continued till the seventh century when the rise of Harsha of Kanauj again restored order and peace for some time. Harsha was a lad of sixteen when he ascended the throne. "He went from east to west, subduing all who were not obedient. During this time the elephants were not unharnessed nor the soldiers unhelmeted. After six years of incessant campaigning he was able to rule in peace for thirty years without striking a blow."

Harsha's empire stretched from the Vindhyas to the Himalayas, from the Bay of Bengal to the Indus. South of the Vindhyas the Chalukyas ruled, and Harsha's attempts to reduce them were not successful.

We know more about Harsha and his kingdom than any of his predecessors because of the visit, in his reign, of the Chinese scholar and pilgrim Hiuen Tsang. This celebrity was an enthusiastic admirer of Harsha and he has left us panegyrics of the emperor and his kingdom.

Hiuen Tsang's descriptions of the customs and manners of the people show how little the Hindus have changed during the last fourteen hundred years. He writes: "The Kshatriyas and Brahmins are cleanly and wholesome in their dress, and they live in a homely and frugal way. There are rich merchants who deal in gold trinkets and so on. They mostly go barefoot; few wear sandals. They stain their teeth red or black. They bind up their hair and pierce their ears. They are very particular in their personal cleanliness. All wash before eating; they never use food left over from a former meal. Wooden and stone vessels must be destroyed after use; metal ones must be well-polished and rubbed. After eating they cleanse their mouth with a willow stick, and wash their hands and mouths."

The land was prosperous and the people were contented and happy. Literature and art flourished in Harsha's reign. Harsha himself was a man of no mean literary talent and was the author of some works. The period was one of intense intellectual activity, and Harsha's religious toleration emboldened every thinker to propound his religious and philosophic theories fearlessly. Assemblies were often convened in which famous scholars discussed and argued abstruse subjects for days. These discussions were not always conducted in the spirit one expects of learned men. "On one occasion a professor of the

Lokatya sect, who were extreme materialists, wrote out forty theses and hung them at the gate of Nalanda college with the notice: 'If any one can refute these principles, I will give him my head as a proof of his victory.' Hiuen Tsang accepted the challenge and defeated his rival in a public disputation. He spared his head and made him his disciple."

Hiuen Tsang appears to have loved these discussions, and Harsha, as a mark of honour to the distinguished "Master of the Law from China," had a huge debating hall constructed, and invited all celebrated scholars of his kingdom to attend the discussion. During the debates feelings ran high and it was even feared that Hiuen Tsang's life was in danger, and Harsha had to declare that "if anyone should hurt or touch the pilgrim he should at once be beheaded, and whoever spoke against him should have his tongue cut out." This gave the pilgrim complete freedom to air his views, and we are told that Hiuen Tsang fought "the followers of error" for eighteen days at the end of which 'there was none to enter the discussion.

The favour Harsha showed the Buddhists brought upon him the ire of Brahmins who conspired to kill him. After many unsuccessful attempts the Brahmins fomented a rebellion, and Harsha was assassinated by his own troops.

Harsha was killed in A.D. 647. He was the last of the great Hindu emperors, and on his death India was again broken up into several petty kingdoms each warring against the other, and all living in fear of foreign invaders. We know little of this period of strife and turmoil, but when the curtain rings down again, we see the stage set for the Muslim invasion and the end of Hindu suzerainty in India. Before proceeding further with the history of North India, we may however, briefly survey the history of South India.

Though not possessing so eventful a history as that of North India, the Deccan and the extreme south were prominent in the ancient world. From the very dawn of history, Malabar then known as Chera, had trade relations with the great Mediterranean centres of civilisation. The Chera kingdom was ruled by a king whose titular name was Perumal. "The chief port was Muziris or Mushiri, the modern Cranganoor where there appears to have been a Roman colony and temple of Augustus." It was at this port that Apostle Thomas landed, preached the Gospel and founded the Church the members of which are even now known as St. Thomas Christians.*

The most important South Indian kingdom in the ancient world was the Pandyan. Megasthenes mentions this kingdom and says that the Pandyan king possessed a powerful army and great wealth derived from trade. The principal articles of commerce were pepper, ginger, cinnamon, rice, coral, pearls, ivory, apes and peacocks.

Madura was the capital of the Pandyans and this city was famed throughout the ancient world for its wealth and splendour. The Pandyans were on friendly terms with the Romans and the trade between the two countries cemented their friendship. The Pandyan king is recorded to have sent an embassy to congratulate Augustus Caesar on his accession to the throne. A large number of Roman coins were found in South India, showing that Roman currency was legal tender in the principal cities of the South. The Pandyan kings used to employ as bodyguards Roman mercenaries who are mentioned in Tamil literature as "dumb Mlecchas with their long coats and armours and their murderous souls, who might be seen acting as sentries at the palace gate."

To the north of the Pandyan and to the south of the Andhras who ruled in the Deccan was the ancient Chola kingdom. The Cholas were of later origin but overran the Pandyan kingdom, waged successful wars with the Pallavas and the Chalukyas who had risen in the East and the North, and by the end of the 10th century A.D. had gained complete mastery over South India. The Cholas were great builders and seamen. Their irrigation projects were on a stupendous scale and the whole country was well watered and cultivated. The Cholas had a powerful fleet and were the undisputed masters of the Bay of Bengal. Rajendra Chola Deva I (A.D. 1018-1035) even made a landing in Bengal and defeated the armies of Mahipala, the king of Bengal.

The Cholas waged incessant war with the Chalukyas who had risen in the Deccan. These wars had not reached the final stage when the Muslims from the North invaded South India and put an end to all Hindu ambition.

MUSLIM CONQUEST AND AFTER

At the time of the Muslim conquest, we find India divided into a number of kingdoms ruled by clans called Rajputs. The origin of the Rajputs is obscure. Though at present the Rajputs claim to be blue-blooded Hindus, the probability is they invaded India on the disruption of the empire of Harsha, took possession of North India and were absorbed into Hinduism.

The Rajput was brave to a fault and his loyalty has never been questioned. But few Rajput leaders could see beyond their clans, and no one appeared to have been inspired by the greater interests of the race or the country. The Rajput was never so happy as when fighting, and no excuse was too trivial to pick up a quarrel. "Too proud and indolent to undertake menial work, he spent his time quarrelling with his neighbour and raiding his territory. Haughty and punctilious, he seized upon the most trivial slight as an offence to be wiped out in blood; on one occasion, a sanguinary campaign was fought because a Raja when out hawking had picked up a partridge which had fallen over his neighbour's boundary." The Rajput considered war as an end in itself.

Although some Muslim generals had crossed into India before and subdued the Hindu Kingdoms in the Indus Valley and the North-West Frontier, the real invasion of India was started by Mahmud of Ghazni,

---

* Readers interested in the origin and growth of Christianity in India are referred to the author's work *Christians and Christianity in India and Pakistan.*

known to the Hindus as the Idol Breaker. Year after year this audacious invader descended on the rich plains of Hindustan and carried away to Ghazni enormous wealth in gold, silver, precious stones and slaves. Jaipal, the Rajput king of the Punjab, could not stop him. His son Anandpal made a fervent appeal to the other Rajput kings of India to realize the danger and come to his aid; and for once the Rajputs appreciated the need for unity and formed a confederacy to resist the invader. But the unwieldy and quarrelsome Rajput hosts were badly led and were no match for the disciplined armies of Ghazni.

Mahmud started on his expeditions in the month of October every year and went back to his northern home at the start of summer, laden with booty. He invaded India seventeen times and in his depredatory expeditions visited practically every city of northern India. Mahmud's most famous exploit was his raid on the temple of Somnath in Kathiawar. He destroyed the temple and carried away immense booty.

Mahmud had no territorial ambition and never cared to govern or annex the places he conquered. He was content with the booty he collected and left the Hindus to rule their impoverished kingdoms as best as they could. The fact that Mahmud with an army, much inferior in numbers to the hosts of the Rajputs, plundered India seventeen times without meeting any serious resistance throws a sad reflection on the lack of organisation and discipline of the Rajputs.

In A.D. 1030 Mahmud died and the Rajputs enjoyed half a century's respite during which time they recovered sufficiently from the shock to indulge in internecine wars. Prithwiraj Chauhan, the Rajah of Delhi, the most powerful of the Rajput kings, abducted the daughter of Jaichand of Kanauj from the wedding hall and this led to a war between the two Rajahs.

When the Rajputs were thus engaged in their interminable quarrels, Mohammed Ghori, who had overthrown the kingdom of Ghazni, invaded India. In his first attempt he was unsuccessful. But the next year he came again and defeated Prithwiraj who died on the battlefield. The Hindus died with their king or fled in panic and the carnage was terrible. When news of the defeat reached Delhi, the Rajput women, headed by the queen, committed mass suicide in the terrible rite called jauhar (mass suicide by fire). The Muslims entered Delhi and established themselves in the city. Unlike Ghazni, Ghori believed in the Muslims occupying and ruling India, and he left his general Kutub-ud-din Aibek in Delhi to continue the conquests and bring the whole of India under subjection. Mohammed Ghori fell by the assassin's dagger in A.D. 1206 but his Indian conquests were ably ruled by Kutub-ud-din who now assumed independent sovereignty with his capital at Delhi. Kutub-ud-din was the first Sultan of Delhi, and to commemorate his conquests, he built the Kutub Minar, still extant. "rightly considered by Fergusson to be unsurpassed by any building of its type in the world."

Kutub-ud-din brought the whole of North India under subjection, and the other Muslim dynasties that succeeded his, extended their conquests southwards. In fact, from the ascension of Kutub-ud-din to the throne of Delhi in the early part of the thirteenth century till the death of the Moghul emperor Aurangazeb in 1707, the Muslims were the undisputed masters of India. What Hindu princes remained in North India were vassals of the central Muslim power; but in the south some Hindu princes enjoyed a certain amount of independence, especially under weak Muslim rulers. It is, however, worthy of note that an independent Hindu Kingdom (Vijaynagar) flourished in the Deccan for about two centuries. This kingdom was overrun by Muslims in the 16th century A.D.

The death of Aurangazeb and the disorder that followed marked the rise of the Maharathas and the Sikhs. The religious policy of Aurangazeb caused much discontent among the Hindus, and Shivaji, the great Maharatha leader, carried on an incessant war with the Moguls till his death, and this was not a little responsible for the weakening and the break up of the Moghul empire. The Maharatha power grew with surprising rapidity and it appeared as though the Hindus had reconquered India and brought the Muslims under subjection. The Muslims, however, united themselves to check the power of the Maharathas. The confederacy was led by Ahmad Shah Durrani, the ruler of Afghanistan, who was alarmed by the rising power of the Maharathas whose activities had reached the Punjab as far as Lahore. The Muslims and the Hindus met on the historic battlefield of Panipat near Delhi, and the Maharathas were defeated (1761) and put to flight. Durrani did not stay in India, but returned to Kabul leaving India in the hands of weaklings, and thus paved the way for the British conquest of India.

The British who came to India as traders took advantage of the political confusion that followed the disruption of the Moghul Empire and by a steady policy of expansion gained complete supremacy over India and ruled the country from the nineteenth century till August 15th, 1947 when they relinquished control to Indians. Unlike the other conquerors who settled down in the country, the British were birds of passage who have left no lasting ethnic impression on the population of India, though the political institutions they have bequeathed are of an enduring nature.

THE MUSLIM AND BRITISH INFLUENCE ON THE HINDUS

We have seen that prior to the arrival of the Muslims all the peoples that invaded India and settled down in the country were absorbed into Hinduism. They received a definite status in Hindu society and their religious beliefs and traditions were incorporated in Hinduism. The main reasons for this were that the newcomers' religion was little better than primitive, that they had no dogmas, philosophical or theological systems, and no powerful sacerdotal classes to guard them. The more intelligent members of the community were probably conscious of the superiority of the Indo-Aryan religion and were anxious that their community should be accepted into the Hindu fold.

I

(Halebid Photo: India Pictorial Features)

1 GANESHA, THE MOST POPULAR DEITY OF THE HINDU PANTHEON. HE IS WORSHIPPED BEFORE EVERY UNDERTAKING TO REMOVE ALL OBSTACLES

2 SHIVA SYMBOLS AND IMAGES IN PROCESSION, KERALA
(Photo: S. S. Aiyar)

ANCIENT HINDU COINS
(Moor's *Hindu Pantheon*)

4 DETAILS FROM A CARVED BRACKET
(Journal of Indian Art and Industry)

5 THE FORT OF CHITOR, MEWAR, A RAJPUT STRONGHOLD OF HISTORIC IMPORTANCE
(Journal of Indian Art and Industry)

IV

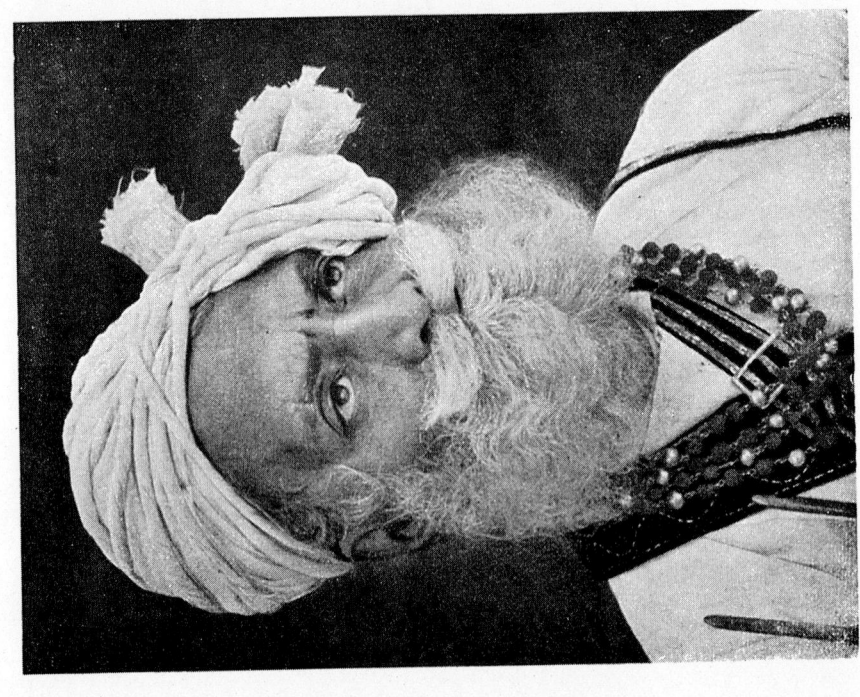

7 A RAJPUT NOBLEMAN
(Photo: A. L. Syed)

6 A KATHIAWAR SHEPHERD
(Photo: A. L. Syed)

The Muslim conquerors, on the other hand, had a traditional culture of their own and théy believed that the salvation of mankind could be achieved only through their religion. They hated idolatry, and considered it their duty to efface it from the world. They had definite dogmas on religion, and the slightest deviation from them, even in thought, was believed to lead to eternal damnation. While they held such strong views on religion, they had the most lenient social code in the world. They were free from many social prejudices and believed that all men were equal in the sight of God and social inequalities were man-made. Thus Islam is, in every respect, the antithesis of Hinduism with its social rigidity and leanings towards spiritual anarchy. It is obvious that these two religions could not absorb each other.

In their first onrush the Muslims were extremely violent towards the religion of the Hindus. They destroyed Hindu temples and idols, plundered and forcibly converted the Hindus and put to the sword those who would not accept Islam. This worked very well at the time of Mahmud of Ghazni, who did not trouble himself with the government of the Indian territories he conquered. But with the occupation of India by Muslims, they became responsible for the good government of the country and had to adopt a more conciliatory attitude towards Hinduism, the professed religion of the majority of their subjects.

The two religions influenced each other appreciably. The lower castes were attracted by the social status they stood to gain by conversion, and the proselytizing zeal of the Muslims made them embrace Islam in large numbers. The social democracy of the Muslims profoundly affected Hindu society and wherever Muslim influence has been predominant and prolonged, Hindu society does not show its most undesirable caste features. Idolatry among the Hindus is less prevalent in provinces which had Muslims for masters for a long time. The uncompromising monotheism and the simplicity of worship of Islam attracted many Hindu religious thinkers and these founded sects among the Hindus which were akin to Islam. One of the undesirable results of Muslim contact was, however, the adverse effect it had on the position of Hindu women in society. The status of Hindu women at the time of the Muslim conquest was anything but enviable; with the advent of the Muslims, the Hindus began to imitate the ways of the rulers and the Purdah became the fashion among the higher classes of Hindus.

The contact with the British had its own effect on Hinduism. Although the British did nothing actively to force their social or religious codes on the Hindus, the tendency of all subject races to imitate their rulers resulted in the introduction of many innovations among the Hindus. The position of women was definitely raised both among the Muslims and Hindus because of the freedom enjoyed by women among Westerners. The taboo prohibiting sea voyages, which contributed not a little to make the Hindus narrow-minded and conceited, was definitely broken under British rule, and many Hindus travelled abroad and were impressed by the achievements of the Western nations. They tried to teach their people that there is much good outside India which could be profitably adopted by the Hindus. The spread of English education was instrumental in bringing to the Hindus a political and social consciousness which eventually brought independence to the country.

Details of the social, religious and political reforms brought about by Muslim and British contact will be found in the following chapters.

CHAPTER II

THE CASTE SYSTEM

WHAT distinguishes Hindu society from others is its independent self-sufficient unit called caste, each with a definite unalterable social status deriving its sanction from religion. Birth alone decides a man's status and he cannot change it by effort. In every society, it is true, birth is the principal factor that decides a person's status, and inequalities are not only tolerated but maintained by law; but the essential difference between Hindu society and others is that while the others are inclined to consider inequalities as superfluous, orthodox Hindus believe that inequalities are based on immutable principles.

The word 'caste' is of Portuguese origin. Its Sanskrit equivalent is 'Jati' meaning race. The Hindu social structure is known as Varnashrama Dharma (social duties based on colour) in Sanskrit, and both these words indicate that caste originated from racial pride and colour prejudice. The Aryans were probably a fairer race than the then inhabitants of India and the caste system originated out of the anxiety of Indo-Aryans to preserve their racial purity. Whatever its origin, caste became the most jealously guarded institution among the Hindus and is, to this day, the dominant feature of their society. An orthodox Hindu shall not marry outside his caste; he shall not eat with any one not belonging to his caste; he shall not attend social functions of people outside his caste; and if he is excommunicated, he lives as an outcaste, no one of any caste daring to help him or mingle with him.

The main castes, as we have mentioned in the first chapter, are four: The Brahmin, the Kshatriya, the Vaisya and the Sudra. Each of these main divisions has numerous subdivisions, each an independent unit, and outside these are the Panchamas (the fifth caste) with their innumerable divisions of untouchables, unapproachables and unlookables. The vast majority of aborigines of India belongs to the fifth caste, and these together with the Sudras, form the bulk of the Hindu population.

BRAHMINS

By virtue of his supposed origin from the head of Brahma, the Creator, the Brahmin is considered the highest of the castes. Worship of and sacrifice to the gods formed an important duty among the Indo-Aryans from the earliest times. Material gains such as victory in war, plentiful crops, health and happiness, as well as spiritual bliss after death were believed to come from the pleasure of the gods who had to be kept in good humour by singing hymns of praise and by offering sacrifices. In course of time those who were engaged in these duties became an exclusive hierarchy, proud of their occupation and jealous of their knowledge. Gradually they began to instruct the public in theories of their divine office and origin. Not only were the ignorant masses made to accept their lofty pretensions, but even the proud Kshatriyas were made to bow down to them. The warrior caste, as we shall see presently, did not submit to the yoke meekly; there was in India, as in Europe, a war between priests and kings in which the latter lost. So great was the supremacy of the priests over kings in India that they had managed to amass most of the wealth of the country in their temples, and the king's treasury contained little in comparison with the riches of the temples. The fact that Mahmud of Ghazni in his raids on India mainly confined his activities to the temples and seldom troubled himself with palaces is proof of this.

The privileged position Brahmins occupied in Hindu society, and to a certain extent still occupy, can be understood from the following eulogy of the Brahmin found in the Code of Manu: "Him, the Being who exists of himself produced in the beginning from his own mouth, that having performed holy rites, he might present clarified butter to the gods, and cakes of rice to the progenitors of mankind, for the preservation of the world. What created being then, can surpass him with whose mouth the gods of the firmament continually feast on clarified butter and the manes of ancestors on hallowed cakes? The very birth of Brahmins is a constant incarnation of Dharma (god of religion); for the Brahmin is born to promote religion, and to procure ultimate happiness. When a Brahmin springs to light, he is born above the world, the chief of all creatures, assigned to guard the treasury of duties, religious and civil. Whatever exists in the universe, is all in effect, the wealth of the Brahmin, since the Brahmin is entitled to it all by his primogeniture and eminence of birth. The Brahmin eats but his own food, wears his own apparel, and bestows but his own in alms; through the benevolence of the Brahmin, indeed, other mortals, enjoy life."* In certain books the Brahmin is exalted even above the gods who are said to exist by his permission. Every member of a Brahmin's body is said to be a centre of pilgrimage. The holy Ganges is in the Brahmin's right ear; the sacred fire in his right hand; and all the holy places of the world on his right foot. The Brahmin's mouth is the mouth of the most exalted of the gods and anything put in it is sure to bring prosperity to the world; hence the need for feeding Brahmins by all those who desire happiness in this world and in the next. It is even said:

---

* *Sacred Books of the East*, Vol. XXV.

The whole world is under the power of the gods,
The gods are under power of the Mantras
The Mantras are under power of the Brahmin;
The Brahmin is therefore our God.

This exaltation of the Brahmin, it must be mentioned, has a background of social need. By creating a class of men devoted to the pursuit of knowledge and the study of the law, the ancient Hindus hoped to build their social structure on unshakable foundations. It was, however, necessary to free this class of men from the oppressive need for earning a living by their labour; hence a Brahmin was not permitted to engage himself in certain kinds of work. Mostly he was to live on gifts received from charitable persons of noble birth. In times of distress a Brahmin was allowed to do manual work, and in extreme need even "to steal grain from any one who is not a Brahmin." But a Brahmin is rarely reduced to this necessity; for the laws enjoining gift-giving to Brahmins are scrupulously respected by all classes of Hindus and this ensures plenty to the Brahmins. In all the various ceremonies a Hindu from his birth till death has to undergo and in funeral rites, Brahmins have to be fed and given presents. Princes and nobles used to spend millions of rupees on some of these occasions, and the poor peasant what he got by borrowing. Practically every law book dwells at length upon the benefits that accrue from giving presents to Brahmins: "Heinous sins are atoned for by giving them presents. If a man sells his cow, he will go to hell; if he gives her in donation to a Brahmin he will go to heaven. If on Ganga's (the river goddess Ganges) anniversary whole villages be given to Brahmins, the person presenting them will acquire all the merit which can be obtained; his body will be a million times more glorious than the sun; he will have a million virgins, many carriages, and palanquins with jewels; and he will live in heaven with his father as many years as there are particles in the land given to Brahmins. Land given to Brahmins secures heaven; a red cow, a safe passage across the boiling infernal river Vaitarani; a house, a heavenly palace; an umbrella, freedom from scorching heat; shoes, freedom from pain when walking; perfumes, freedom from offensive smells; feasting of Brahmins particularly at births, marriages and deaths, brings the highest merit. If a house be defiled by an unclean bird sitting down upon it, it becomes pure when presented to a Brahmin. A proper gift to a Brahmin on a death-bed will secure heaven to a malefactor. The Brahmins oblige the other castes, in fact, when they condescend to receive their presents. Money given to them should be dipped in water, lest the latent glory of their hands should burst forth and consume the donor."*

The person of the Brahmin is sacred and the murder of a Brahmin is the most heinous crime a mortal or god can commit. Assaulting a Brahmin is the second worst. Even a king has no right to inflict corporal punishment on a Brahmin. If a Sudra assaults a Brahmin, the culprit should be put to death; if he slanders a Brahmin, his tongue should be cut off; if a Brahmin assualts a Sudra the Brahmin is severely reprimanded for polluting himself by the touch of a low caste man.

Next in sanctity to the Brahmin's person comes his property. Stealing it is a crime almost as heinous as Brahminicide. The Brahmin's property is too sacred for the king to levy taxes on. The state cannot confiscate it. The property of a Brahmin dying intestate should be divided among other Brahmins.

The wrath of a Brahmin is said to be more dreadful than the wrath of gods. The curse of a Brahmin is believed to have deadly effect on the victims. Gods have been known to have withered away by a Brahmin's curse. Hence orthodox Hindus are very particular not to offend a Brahmin in any way, but accede to his most unreasonable demands.

The duties and responsibilities imposed on Brahmins by law are, it must be mentioned, in keeping with their high social position. Though no other castes can dictate rules of conduct for a Brahmin, he is enjoined to impose strict self-discipline on himself. His life is to be one of duty towards society, the gods and himself. He is to live a frugal and contented life, be hospitable and selfless. A Brahmin's life is to be divided into four Ashramas or orders, i.e., Brahmacharya, Grahastha, Vanaprastha and Sanyasa. In Brahmacharya, a Brahmin lives as a student in the house of his teacher studying the Vedas and the sacred law, and serving the teacher. The Brahmacharya begins soon after a boys' initiation to Brahminhood (investiture with the 'munja' or sacred thread) and lasts till he completes his studies which, in some cases, are prolonged upto the age of thirty. The Brahmachari shall "collect wood for the holy fire, beg food of his relations, sleep on a low bed, perform such offices as may please his preceptor, until his return to the house of his father." He should implicitly obey his preceptor whom he is commanded to worship as a god. The preceptor's wife should be treated as his own mother and his daughters, if any, as his own sisters. The Brahmachari should abstain from "honey, flesh, perfumes, garlands, vegetable juices, women, acidulated substances, the killing of animated beings, unguents for his limbs, black powder for his eyes, wearing sandals, using an umbrella, sensual desires, wrath, covetousness, dancing, singing, dice, disputes, detraction and falsehood." He is enjoined to sleep alone, and to perform the duty of a religious mendicant.

After his education the Brahmin, having paid his teacher's fee, returns to his father's house, marries and enters Grahasthashrama or the order of the householder. The girl he marries should be "a virgin of noble birth, good to look at, sweet of speech and soft to touch." The Grahastha should not, however, give himself over too much to her company; he should not eat with her, nor see her eating. He should not talk to her unnecessarily. Conjugal relations should be reduced to a minimum, the Grahastha always remember-

---

* J. Wilson, *Indian Caste.*

ing that the object of sexual intercourse is progeny and not pleasure.

The Grahastha should be regular in the performance of religious duties especially Shraddhas, ceremonies for departed ancestors. On these occasions he should treat Brahmins to a feast, but undesirables should not be invited. "Among the parties thus to be avoided are the attendants upon images, the sellers of flesh, the party supporting himself by traffic, a young brother married before the elder, a dancer, the husband of a Sudra, the pupil or preceptor of a Sudra, a seller of the moon-plant, a navigator of the ocean, an oilman, a maker of bows and arrows, a father instructed in the Veda by his son, a tamer of elephants, bulls, horses or camels, an astrologer, a keeper of birds, a breeder of sporting dogs, a shepherd, a keeper of buffaloes, the husband of a twice-married woman." During the course of the ceremony and feasting, the Grahastha has to maintain absolute composure of spirit, lest the rite be deranged and the manes suffer.

The Grahastha is not to accept presents from unworthy persons. Any one between a miserly king and a pimp is considered unworthy in this respect. He should be generous and benevolent, and free from arrogance, greed and pride. He should observe ceremonial purity and make atonement for defilements contracted. "He must suspend the reading of the Vedas during thunder, rain, earthquakes, and other atmospheric and terrene changes and movements. He must intermit the reading of the Veda for a day and night when a beast of labour, a frog, a cat, a dog, or a snake passes between him and his pupil." The Grahastha should not indulge in intoxicating drinks, and should avoid eating meat and causing injury to animals. Meat eating is not strictly prohibited for Brahmins in their law books but the generality of Brahmins at present look upon it as an unclean and sinful practice, and abstain from it.

When he has begotten sons and reared them to manhood, the Grahastha has paid his debt to society and his ancestors, and is free to look after his own salvation. For this purpose he leaves his house and property to the management of his son or sons and repairs to a forest to live a life of meditation and asceticism. This order is called Vanaprastha. The life of the Vanaprastha is one of strict discipline and austerity. He should not wear fine garments but should be content with a loin cloth of antelope hide or bark of a tree. Unlike the Grahastha who should be scrupulous in his personal cleanliness, the Vanaprastha neglects his health and is not to interest himself in beautifying his person. He suffers his hair, nails and beard to grow continously and seldom washes himself. He subsists by food obtained by begging and owns nothing but his begging bowl. His constant joy should be the reading and recitation of sacred texts, and meditating on the absolute. Self torture is also recommended as leading to perfection.

When the Vanaprastha has schooled himself long enough in austerity, self torture and meditation, he is qualified to enter the final stage of the drama. The fourth order of Sanyasa is one of complete indifference to the world and its affairs, and of freedom from all bondage. The Sanyasi is not grateful for favours shown, nor is he spiteful against offenders. The man who gives him food or gold, and the man who drives him out from his house are treated alike. He should not eat more than one meal a day. He must have no fixed abode but must wander from place to place, the earth being his house and the sky the roof. Rain, thunder and storm should not frighten him, nor should he run away from wild creatures. He tortures the body so that the union of his soul with the Absolute may be hastened. After having carried the mortal frame as long as it lasts, the Sanyasi, indifferent to the nature of his end, is finally absorbed into the Absolute and liberated from the tedious process of living and dying.

This ideal of life is, no doubt, grand. But alas, human nature has been found too weak for it. While most of the Brahmins forgot their duties and responsibilities, all have been most careful to jealously guard their privileges.

It is doubtful if at any time in the long and eventful history of the community the Brahmins have followed the ideal of the four orders as a general and practical principle. Hindu literature however is full of references to a glorious past in which Brahmins lived as they ought to, and in the **Mahabharata** and **Ramayana** there are beautiful passages describing the idyllic life of the Vanaprasthas who lived in large colonies in forests. But the Hindus always evince a tendency to exaggerate the greatness of their past, and how far these passages refer to facts cannot now be ascertained. Whatever might have been the achievements of the past, the present day Brahmins in India do not appear much enamoured of the "four orders," except in their literature and religious arguments. The Gurukula system of education in which the pupils live permanently with the teacher in the latter's house till the completion of their instruction, is followed by few at present; all Brahmin boys, on the other hand, are educated in modern schools run in Western style. Few Brahmins of respectable families are interested in Vanaprastha and Sanyasa, and most of them die as Grahasthas under the roofs of their own dwellings in the midst of their kith and kin. There are, however, large numbers of wandering mendicants and Sanyasis in India who profess to have forsaken the pleasures of the world for the sake of identifying themselves with the infinite; but a good many of them are disappointed men who on failing in life have taken to religion as a means of livelihood, and few of them have gone through Brahmacharya and Grahastha. There are, of course, exceptions to this, and once in a way one comes across a real Vanaprastha or Sanyasi who has seriously taken the injunctions of his religion to heart and tries to live up to the ideal.

We have described above the Brahmins as painted in the sacred literature of the Hindus especially in the law books. But centuries have elapsed since these books were written and the present day Brahmins are, in many respects different from their ancestors. With the advent of the Muslims and the British into India, many of the iniquitous laws which gave the Brahmin his extraordinarily privileged position have been repelled. But the Brahmins have remained from time immemorial the accredited leaders of Hindu society, and they still enjoy many of their traditional privileges by the common consent of Hindu society. Besides, they have long established economic and intellectual superiority over other castes, and this makes them even now the most powerful caste among the Hindus.

The taboo prohibiting working for a living is not now respected by the Brahmins. Because of their numerical unwieldiness and the reluctance shown by educated Hindus of other castes to support idling Brahmins, these have taken to all sorts of professions and to government service. They have still a prejudice against all work involving physical exertion and seldom engage themselves in agriculture, craftsmanship and in workshop duties. In law they have found a profession suited to their genius. Large number of Brahmins work in the secretarial, clerical and accounts branches of public service and of well-known firms. They have, in fact monopolized these branches of service. Brahmins have taken to trade and shop-keeping, and some have even recruited themselves in the army for active service.

Though they have thus far violated the codes of Hindu law-givers for promoting their material interests, they still jealously guard their social position and rigidly observe some of the ancient laws prohibiting social intercourse with other communities.

All Brahmins, it must be noted, are not of equal sanctity. There are various subdivisions among the Brahmins each with its own social code, traditions and legends to support its origin from some god or sage of the Hindu pantheon. The blue-blooded Brahmins trace their origin to one of the celebrated Saptarshis (seven sages) who are believed to be the priests of the gods. Each division of the better class of Brahmins profess themselves attached to one of the Vedas or parts thereof. This subdivision among the Brahmins probably originated from the systematization and elaboration of sacrifices, in which priests had to specialize themselves in particular branches of the rites. Those who were allotted the more important kind of offices were naturally treated with greater respect, and they and their progeny built up the well-known Gotras (clans) of Brahmins. Some Brahmins of our day, it is noteworthy, are not recognized as such by others and they are probably apostates or lower castes who arrogated to themselves the name and privileges of the higher caste.

It is quite impossible to state with anything like accuracy how many subdivisions of Brahmins exist at present. The labours of the late Rev. J. Wilson who did considerable research in the matter show that the Brahmins of India fall into two main divisions: The Dravida Brahmins who inhabit the country south of the Vindhyas, and the Gaudas of the country north of the Vindhyas. The Dravidas consist of: (1) Maharashtras, speaking the Mahrathi language, (2) the Andhras or Tailangas, the Telugu language, (3) the Dravidas, Tamil and its cognates, (4) the Karnatas, Canarese, and (5) the Gurjaras speaking Gujarati. The Gaudas are also divided into five, namely, (1) the Sarasvatas (hailing from the country watered by the Sarasvati), (2) Kanyakubjas (of Kanyakubja, modern Kanauj), (3) the Gaudas (of the country of the lower Ganges), (4) Utkalas (of Utkala or Orissa), and (5) the Maithilas (of the country of Mithila, an ancient Hindu kingdom of N. India). Each of these is again subdivided into numerous branches. According to Rev. Wilson the Maharashtra Brahmins consist of no less than 34 subdivisions, the Andhras sixteen, the Dravidas five, the Karnatas seventeen, and the Gurjaras, one hundred and sixty. Of the Gaudas, the Sarasvatas have more than four hundred subdivisions, the Kanyakubjas two hundred, the Gaudas seventeen, the Utkalas twenty-five and the Maithilas twenty. In addition, we have the Kashmir Brahmins with their numerous subdivisions, the Brahmins of Kerala Rajasthan, Nepal, and Madhya Pradesh and Bengal who do not fall into any of these divisions but stand alone. It is neither profitable nor possible to describe in detail each of these subdivisions. We would, however, make some mention of two peculiar divisions of these, who rank high among the Brahmins of India, namely, the Kulins of Bengal and the Nambudiri Brahmins of Kerala.

The Kulin Brahmins of Bengal claim themselves to be one of the purest of the caste. They are believed to have come from Kanauj at the request of Adishura, king of Bengal, in the ninth century A.D., and settled down in his kingdom. Originally only five families came; these increased and multiplied, and gradually tendencies set in which began to affect the purity and morals of the community. Bellala Sena, therefore, the then king of Bengal (eleventh century A.D.), made a rigorous selection and declared those in whom he found the nine noble qualities to be Kulins or high born. The nine noble qualities are: "Observance of Brahminical 'Achara' (duties), meekness, learning, good report, a disposition to visit holy places, devoutness, asceticism, liberality, and observance of marriage among equals."

The last named virtue seems to have disappeared among the Kulins, for they married below their social level for a consideration, and this led to one of the worst social abuses of Hinduism. The Kulins being blue-blooded, Brahmins of inferior purity vied with one another in giving their daughters in marriage to a Kulin. This gentleman, at least in theory, lowered his social position and that of his progeny by such a marriage, which he readily agreed to do when well paid. The Shrotriyas especially, who had only eight of the nine qualities believed to be possessed by Kulins, and were hence, lower in social scale than the Kulins, always tried to improve their position by giving their daughters in marriage to Kulins. At the same time, no woman being allowed by orthodox Hindu codes, to be given in marriage to a man of a caste lower than hers, all the Kulin women had to be married to Kulin husbands and not to any one else. This led to polygyny with a vengeance. The Kulins made a trade of marriage and were willing to marry any Brahmin woman of any subcaste on payment of a dowry. He married the lady, collected his dowry and went his way. The wife lived in her parents' house and the husband very rarely visited her, and in certain cases never. Some Kulins are known to have married about three hundred wives, and the marriage contracted in a single day by a needy Kulin Brahmin at times exceeded a score. Only one or two of these wives lived with the Kulin and the rest lived in their parents' houses. He visited them when he needed cash, which the father-in-law of every Kulin was expected to furnish him without asking. Those who had many wives and sufficient cash did not visit most of their wives even occasionally. The Kulins do not legally recognize children born to them by wives who do not reside with them but live in their parents' houses.

The bad results of the system are quite obvious. Marriage for the Kulins having lost its meaning, boys of sixteen or eighteen often got married to women older than themselves and old men of eighty to girls of fourteen and sixteen. A much married Kulin could not remember the number of his wives and, but for the record kept by a special class of Brahmins of Kulin genealogy, would never be able to ascertain it. Wives did not often know their husbands and husbands their wives. Children did not know their male parents and men their children. The neglected wives of the Kulin lived in utmost misery while their parents ruined themselves by providing their sons-in-law with dowry.

Education and enlightenment have improved matters. The inferior class of Brahmins do not, at present consider it a very great privilege to form connections with the Kulins, and are content to have husbands of equal rank for their daughters. Besides legislation in India since independence has prohibited polygamy and both Kulins and non-Kulins now practise monogamy.

The Nambudiris of Malabar belong to a different category. They are believed to have been brought from the north, out of the pure Aryan stock, by the warrior priest Parasurama who is said to have reclaimed the Malabar coast from the sea and presented it to them as an atonement for the sins he committed in destroying Kshatriyas. Whatever the origin of the myth, the Nambudiris divided among themselves the rich lands of the Malabar coast, and were the wealthiest landlords of the country. They had for a long time enjoyed the privilege of instructing the Rajahs of the Malabar states, and the coronation ceremonies of these Rajahs were not valid unless performed by one of these Brahmins. Their pretensions to purity were very lofty. The idea of ceremonial purity was so strong in them that if they happened to approach certain lower castes by sixty paces they had to wash. Some others were unlookables to the Nambudiris.

Because of this, a Nayar always walked ahead of a Nambudiri when this dignitary went about, shouting in a peculiar tone to all low castes to keep out of the way of the Nambudiri. More of this presently. The Nambudiris are strict vegetarians and are very kind to animals, birds and insects though so cruel to their low-born fellow beings.

The Nambudiris are polygynists. Only the eldest son of a Nambudiri was allowed to marry and bring his wives into his house. His younger brothers lived with him in the same house but had no right on marriage; they were however, allowed to form temporary connections with the Nayar women of Malabar, whom they consider to be Sudras. The Nayar woman had no legal status of a wife but lived in her own house and was visited at night by her lover. The children born of such unions lived with their mother and belonged to her caste and had no right to the name and property of their father. The matriachal social system obtaining among the Nayars eminently suited the convenience of the Nambudiris and made the institution, which looks ridiculous to Westerners, not only possible but even respectable.

The arrangement worked very well with the Nayars and the male members of the Nambudiri community who found, in the free and charming Nayar women, more congenial and interesting partners than the dull women of their own community who observed a sort of Purdah more strict than that of the medieval Muslims. But the real victims of the inequitable institution were the Nambudiri women. These were not allowed to marry men of any other caste and all the women of the community had to be shared by the eldest male members, which led to the evils of unlimited polygyny and trading in marriage. Every Nambudiri demanded exorbitant sums from his father-in-law for the trouble of marrying his daughter. A Nambudiri with few sisters and daughters was a lucky individual, growing rich by every marriage he contracted, while one with a dozen sisters and daughters almost ruined himself in the marriage market.

The custom that limits the legality of marriage to that of the eldest son was designed to prevent the disintegration of the wealth of the family through division among the various members. This has worked well, and to this day the Nambudiris are the richest landlords of Malabar.

The women of the Nambudiris were jealously guarded. They were not allowed to go out alone or to talk to any men except their husbands. A girl, once she attained puberty, was not allowed to speak even to her own father or brothers. As far as possible the Nambudiri women remained inside their houses and when necessity compelled them to move about they travelled in groups escorted by Nayar women. Each Nambudiri lady so moving about protected herself with a huge umbrella made of palm leaves which, when turned on the side, covered the whole person of the lady from head to the knee. The Nayar ladies who walked ahead warned all men who came in the opposite direction to keep away, and indulged in violent language if they showed the least hesitation to do so. The present writer had watched, from a safe distance, these processions of young Nambudiri ladies, naked except at the loins, dexterously tilting their umbrellas and turning their supple gold-laden necks to have a hasty glance at the wonderful world, and the still more wonderful men who watched them from a distance!

The Nambudiris are probably the most conservative of all the Brahmins of India. Extremely proud of their ancestry and wealth, they do not wish to learn anything from others nor to teach others anything. They look upon English education with extreme disfavour and imagine that there is nothing good in any language except Sanskrit. These tendencies have shut them out from the outer world, and in progress they lag behind most of the other Hindu communities of the country. The younger members of the community are, however, showing signs of rebellion and some have even gone over to communism.

We will conclude this survey of the Brahmins of India with a word about their present condition in India. The Brahmins are the most intelligent caste among the Hindus. They have a holy fear of personal uncleanliness and wash twice or three times a day. No Brahmin worth his name fails to bathe once a day, especially in the morning. Hence the community is probably the cleanest in the world. The men wear simple clean clothes while going about; inside the house they wear but a loin cloth. Drinking of spirituous liquors is taboo to Brahmins and those who violate it are negligibly few; hence the Brahmins are one of the most sober communities in the world. The majority of Brahmins are vegetarians, the Brahmins of Kashmir and certain minor subcastes of other provinces being the only exceptions.

Always the recipients of gifts, the Brahmins are seldom liberal with their cash. The Hindu law books even maintain that it is a sin to receive presents from a Brahmin, and as such no one expects charity from a Brahmin. Because of the tiresome taboos connected with eating and drinking and the elaborate religious instructions that regulate every detail of a Brahmin's life, it is impossible for any one to have free social contact with an orthodox Brahmin. A Christian or Muslim will never feel quite at ease in a Brahmin's presence; the Brahmins' predicament is as bad. The omission of some trival formality on the part of the visitor may raise eternal problems for the Brahmin; if, for instance, a person lifts or receives anything with his left hand, it may mean an omen portending evil to the Brahmin. If, while conversing, even a molecule of saliva were to drop anywhere on the Brahmin's person or clothes, it may mean so terrible a pollution as can be atoned for only through hell fire. If the visitor inadvertently looks in a certain direction, it may mean death to his host. With these and numerous other beliefs even now governing the life of orthodox Brahmins, it is conceivable why Europeans find it difficult to move freely with the better class of Indians.

THE KSHATRIYAS

The Kshatriya is believed to have sprung from Brahma's arms, and on him rests the burden of protecting the community from external aggression and internal trouble. The Kshatriyas are, by right of birth, kings and soldiers. The law books maintain that no one but a Kshatriya has the right to rule, and any land governed by men of inferior castes should be abandoned by the virtuous.

A king, some texts say, should be worshipped by his subjects as a god and implicit obedience to him is enjoined. The king should treat his subjects as his children, and their prosperity should be his all absorbing care. He should not levy oppressive taxes, but should always exert himself to maintain law in the kingdom by punishing criminals and eliminating unsocial elements. Above all he should see that Brahmins are well taken care of, and the lower castes do not in any way challenge the supremacy of the Brahmins. He should give freely to Brahmins, and gifts of lands should be recorded lest his successors should dispute the Brahmins' claims. His counsellors should be Brahmins of repute, well versed in the Vedas and the Dharma Sastra (law codes). The Kshatriyas should be ever willing to die for the protection of Brahmins and cows.

Courage and fearlessness are the essential qualities of the Kshatriya. Although, as a rule, no one can obtain liberation without passing through life as a Brahmin, a Kshatriya dying in the battlefield is believed to go straight to the heaven of Indra where the beautiful Apsaras (celestial dancing girls) of Indra's court vie with one another for the favour of his embraces.

Because of his warlike activities, the Kshatriya is exempt from many of the tiresome taboos that bind the Brahmin. The Kshatriya is allowed to keep himself and his troops in training by hunting. The Hindu kings have all along been great hunters, and many of their romantic amours are recorded to have taken place while out hunting in the forests. They are allowed to kill for pleasure and for food, and are, as a rule, meat eaters. They also drink spirituous liquor, although the law does not encourage this. They need not observe the four Ashramas of the Brahmins, but many Kshatriyas are said to have abandoned their kingdoms in their old age in favour of their sons and repaired to forests to live a life of quiet and contemplation. This may sound quite strange to Westerners, but the better class of Hindu princes have always shown a spirit of renunciation seldom met with among kings of other nations.

The sacred books of the Brahmins say that the Kshatriyas are an extinct race and they put this down as the main reason why the Muslims conquered India without much difficulty. If this is so, the Brahmins have themselves to thank for it; for they maintain that Parasurama, a Brahmin warrior, supposed to be an incarnation of Vishnu, the second of the Hindu triad, was the destroyer of the whole race of Kshatriyas. The legends say that the Kshatriyas became so powerful and arrogant that they began to persecute the Brahmins and treat them with contempt. To punish them, therefore, Vishnu himself incarnated as a Brahmin and brought about the destruction of the whole race. Parasurama, this incarnation of Vishnu, was the son of Jamadagni, a Brahmin sage, who lived in the forest with his wife and eight sons. Karthavirya, one of the most powerful kings of the time, while hunting in the forest, happened to visit the hermitage of Jamadagni. There was no one in the house except the sage's wife who entertained him in right royal fashion with the help of the boon-granting cow Kamadhenu that was capable of complying with any and every request of her owner. Karthavirya was much struck by the powers of the cow and wished to possess her; and his hostess not willing to part with the cow he drove her away by force. Sometime after this incident, Jamadagni and Parsurama returned to the hermitage and heard from the old lady all that had happened. Parsurama immediately followed Karthavirya and on the outskirts of the forest met him and his army, and defeated them. In the combat Karthavirya was killed.

News of Karthavirya's death reaching his kingdom, his sons set out with a powerful force for the hermitage of Jamadagni. They reached the hermitage at the time when Jamadagni alone was in the house. The feeble old man showed no fight and the sons of the king put him to the sword. Before they could escape, Parasurama came on the scene and killed every one of the king's sons. His wrath, however, did not stop here. So devoutly was he attached to his old father that he swore that he would avenge the dastardly murder by the annihilation of every male member of the Kshatriya race. The fiery Brahmin now applied himself to the study of the art of war and mastered the use of many secret weapons which made him invincible. The chief of his weapons was a magic axe which nothing could resist (Parasurama means Rama of the axe). Parasurama is fabled to have traversed the length and breadth of India and annihilated the Kshatriya race in twenty-one campaigns. Those who are known as Kshatriyas at present, the Brahmins say, are the progeny of Kshatriya women whom Brahmins married.

Whatever the mythological embellishments of the legend, there appears to be some truth in it which points to a conflict between the priests and the ruling classes in which the former won. We know that a similar conflict occurred in Europe in which the ruling classes won. The result has been disastrous for both countries. The desirable check priests and kings exercise on one another gone, Europe became excessively martial and India excessively spiritual.

Of all the communities now claiming to be Kshatriyas, the Rajputs deserve particular notice. They consider themselves blue-blooded Kshatriyas and trace their origin to the Lunar and Solar dynasties of the epics. Their ancestors were, they believe, born of the sun or the moon and hence they pride themselves to be the most ancient of royal clans. "But modern research seems to show that they are mainly the descendants of the Gurjara, Huna and other Central Asian tribes who found their way across the north-west frontier in the fifth and sixth centuries. These invaders carved out kingdoms for themselves and eventually settled down in the country, taking Hindu wives; the ruling classes had no difficulty in persuading obsequious Brahmins to admit them into the Hindu fold, and to provide them with genealogies going back to heroic times, very much as Virgil and Livy traced the ancestry of the founders of the Roman Empire back to the heroes of the Trojan War. Confirmation for the theory of the foreign origin of many of these clans is found in the Puranic legend of the creation of the Agnikula or Fire-born Rajputs. When Parasurama, at the behest of the Brahmins, destroyed the ancient Kshatriyas, the land was left masterless, whereupon the gods repaired to Mount Abu in Southern Rajputana, and there from the sacred fire pit produced the four fire-born clans — the Powar, the Parihar, the Chauhan and the Solanki. There is little doubt that here we have an allegorical account of the rite by which the foreign chieftains were initiated into Hinduism. It is interesting to note that the destruction of the original Kshatriya caste is admitted. Other Rajput clans, such as the Chandel, appear to have originated from indigenous tribes like the Gonds who rose to power and were similarly ennobled and admitted into the Hindu fold."* The Rajputs at present number about thirty-six clans, and their titular head is the Rana of Mewar of the Sisodia clan. This dignitary exercises royal and priestly functions "as the priest-king of the god Shiva."

Whatever their failings, it must be pointed out that from the time of the first Muslim conquest to the rise of the Maharathas, the Rajputs were the chief people who stood up to the Muslim invader and kept the flame of ancient Hindu chivalry burning in moments of darkness and despair. Rana Pratap who lived at the time of Akbar, the great Moghul emperor, is particularly worthy of mention in this connection. Because of Akbar's conciliatory policy towards the Hindus and his anxiety to fuse the Hindus and Muslims into one community which led to his marrying into many Rajput royal families, Pratap held Akbar to be an enemy of his race. The astute Akbar won the confidence of most of the Rajput princes who accepted positions of trust in the emperor's army and formed matrimonial connection with the imperial family; but Pratap would do neither and treated those princes as no better than the "Moghul barbarian" himself. Akbar was naturally offended by this attitude of Pratap and waged incessant war with him. Pratap was forced to abandon his kingdom and wander in the hills of Rajasthan with his wife and children and a few devoted followers, suffering many privations, including starvation and destitution. Even at this stage, Akbar sent him messengers asking him to surrender, and promising him honourable treatment and his kingdom. Pratap treated the offer with contempt and sent a reply saying that he would rather keep his independence in the jungle than rule a king-

---

* H. G. Rawlinson, *India*.

V

8   BEGGARS ON A TEMPLE STEP, BOMBAY
(Photo: Stanley Jepson)

9 A PARTY OF BRAHMINS GOING ON A BEGGING ROUND IN ACCORDANCE
WITH SOME SPECIAL VOW
(Photo: S. S. Aiyar)

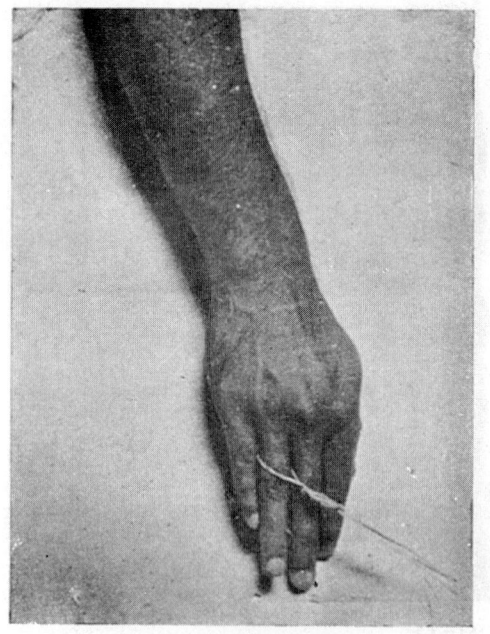

10 RING OF SACRED KUSA GRASS USED IN RELIGIOUS CEREMONIES
(India Pictorial Features)

11 A FESTIVAL IN HONOUR OF SURYA, THE SUN GOD
(India Pictorial Features)

12 A HINDU MENDICANT
(Rousslet's *India*)

13 A FOLK DANCE OF FISHER BOYS
(Photo: B. F. Ferreira)

VII

14 FEASTING BRAHMINS, A VERY MERITORIOUS ACT
(Photo: S. S. Aiyar)

15 DEMON: CEMENT
STATUE FROM MYSORE
(India Pictorial Features)

16 A TYPICAL VAISHNAVA BRAHMIN: ON HIS
LOIN CLOTH IS PRINTED THE NAME OF RAMA
(Photo: S. S. Aiyar)

VIII

17 IMAGE OF RAMANUJA, FOUNDER OF
VAISHNAVISM
From a Temple in Mysore
(Photo: India Pictorial Features)

18 THE CHILD KRISHNA, EIGHTH INCARNATION
OF VISHNU
(From Grierson's *Modern Vernacular Literature of Hindustan*)

IX

19 NANDILINGA

20 RAMA AND SITA, AFTER THE DESTRUCTION OF RAVANA

21 SURYA, THE SUN GOD
(Moor's *Hindu Pantheon*)

22 BHAIRAVA, A FORM OF SHIVA

X

23　SARASVATI, GODDESS OF MUSIC

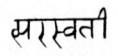

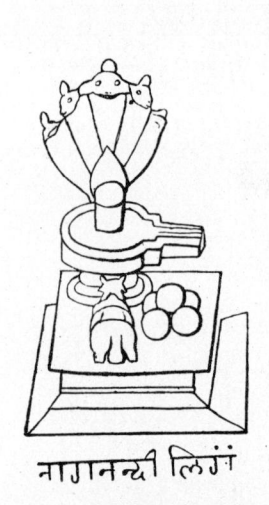

24　INDRA, GOD OF THE FIRMAMENT

25　SACRIFICIAL IMPLEMENT: THE LINGA

26　A SACRIFICIAL VASE OF COPPER

(Moor's *Hindu Pantheon*)

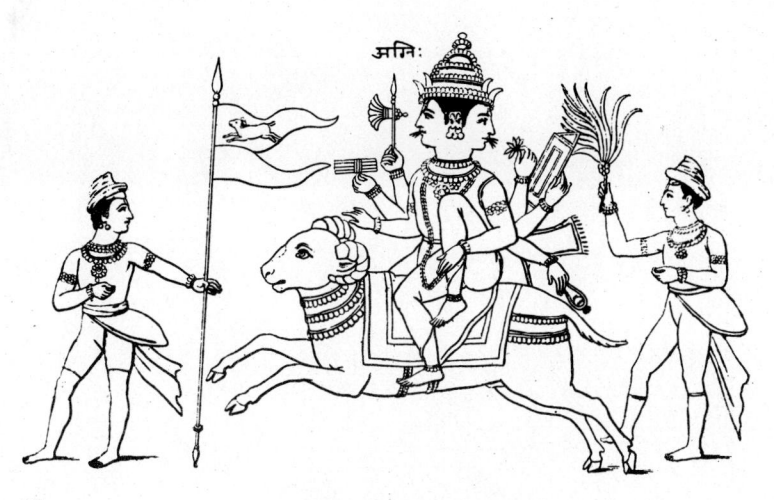

XI

27 AGNI, GOD OF FIRE

28 KAMALA, WIFE OF VISHNU 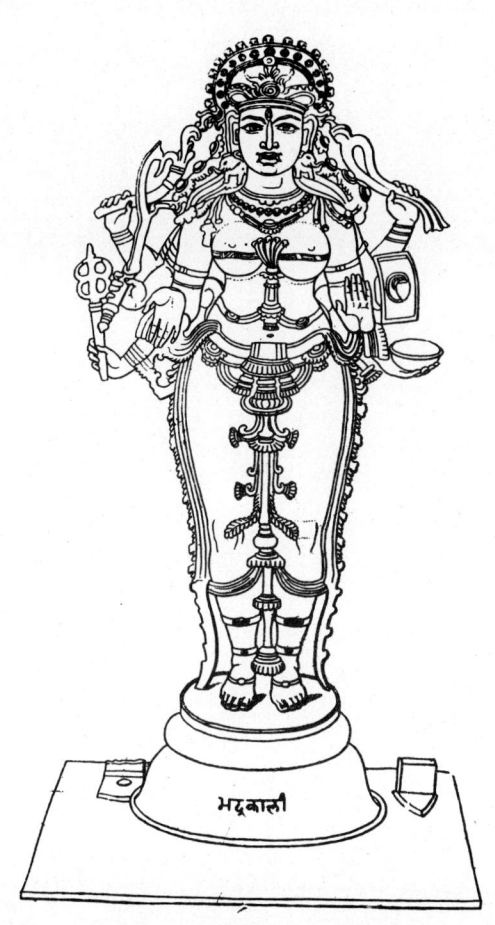   29 KALI, GODDESS OF TERROR   30 GOMATESVARA, A JAIN SAINT

(Moor's *Hindu Pantheon*)

XII

31 SHIVA AND HIS WIFE PARVATI

32 VISHNU WITH HIS WIVES LAKSHMI AND SATYABHAMA
(Moor's *Hindu Pantheon*)

dom under someone else. The generous Akbar, it is said, seeing the unbreakable spirit of the Rajput, gave secret instructions to his general who was hunting Pratap, to relax his efforts and let Pratap wander at will in the hills of Rajasthan. Hearing of this Pratap exclaimed that it was the most painful blow his enemy could deal him!

There are many other communities besides the Rajputs who claim to be Kshatriyas at present. The Amils of Sind, for instance, consider themselves to be Kshatriyas. Some of the ruling Hindu princes and chieftains have genealogies that trace their descent from blue-blooded Kshatriyas. Their claims do not appear to be based on truth. The fact that many of them have to undergo various ceremonies of an initiatory nature which alone entitle them to be considered as Kshatriyas is proof of this.

THE VAISYAS

The Vaisya emanated from Brahma's thighs and as such is inferior to the Brahmin and the Kshatriya. The Vaisya's duty is to increase the prosperity of the country. Agriculture, cattle-keeping and trade should be his special care. "With the prices of mercantile commodities he has to be acquainted, especially of gems, pearls, coral, iron, cloth, perfumes and liquids. He must be skilled in sowing seeds, in the qualities of land, in weights and measures, in the excellence and defects of articles of traffic, in the advantages and disadvantages of different districts, in the probable gain and loss on goods, in the breeding of cattle, in the wages of servants, in the various languages of men, in the best place for keeping cattle, and in all measures for effecting purchase and sale." Acquisition of wealth is commendable in a Vaisya and he is encouraged to make money by all legitimate means. Giving freely to Brahmins and feeding them, and contributing generously to the building of temples and shrines are recommended as the best means of spending money.

The Vaisyas are the lowest of the twice-born castes who alone are entitled to be known as Aryans. The distinctive sign of the three higher castes is the sacred thread they wear on their bodies diagonally. On attaining a certain age (the age differs for the three castes), a boy belonging to one of the Aryan castes is invested with the sacred thread, in a ceremony known as Upanayanam which admits him to the privileged Aryan fold and entitles him to be known as twice-born, the ceremony being considered as a sort of rebirth. The ceremony will be described later.

The Vaisyas like the Kshatriyas are an extinct race; so at least the Brahmins say. There are, however, many communities in India at present who claim to be Vaisyas, though the Brahmins are inclined to believe that they are either apostates from higher castes or Sudras who, by virtue of their wealth, style themselves as Vaisyas. Whatever their origin, some of the trading communities among the present day Hindus are extremely prosperous business men. The Vaisyas seem to have developed an aversion for agriculture which occupation is now mainly left to the Sudras. Of the various Vaisya communities of India, those of Marwar deserve particular attention. The enterprising traders who hail from this place can be found anywhere in India, and even outside, wherever money can be made.

The trading communities of northern India, most of whom hail from the west coast and from Sind, are commonly known as Banias, a corruption of the Sanskrit word 'Vanik' meaning a trader. From the very dawn of the history of the country, they seem to have monopolized the trade of the country and amassed large fortunes. The French traveller Tavernier who visited India at the time of Aurangazeb in the seventeenth century speaks of them as the Jews of India. A good many of them at present follow Jainism, a religion we shall deal with later on.

In southern India the Banias are not so powerful as in the north. Although they are found in large numbers in all the ports of the West and East Coast, the inland trade and usury business of South India are conducted by Chettiars who consider themselves Vaisyas. The members of this enterprising community of traders are found in Burma and Malaya where they have monopolized petty shop-keeping and money lending among the lower classes.

The Banias and Chettiars, like all mercantile communities, are very religious. They contribute generously to the building of temples and give freely to Brahmins, although lately the Chettiars have shown some inclination to join hands with the anti-Brahmin forces that are now collecting in South India. Hindu sacred books clearly mention that money making is an occupation with many spiritual pitfalls and a rich man can atone for sins committed in acquiring wealth only by giving freely to Brahmins and to religious institutions.

THE SUDRAS

Next to the Brahmins the Sudras are the most interesting community in India at present. They are more numerous than all the three Aryan communities put together and form the real bulwark of Hinduism.

Their status, according to the Hindu law books, is very low in the social scale. The laws and codes of the Hindus are meant for the three Aryan castes, and the Sudras in religious and social matters are to be guided by their own traditions and usages. The principal social duties of a Sudra is to serve the three higher castes, especially the Brahmins. "Servile attendance on Brahmins learned in the Veda, chiefly on such as keep house and are famed for virtue, is of itself the highest duty of a Sudra, and leads him to future beatitude. Pure, humbly serving the higher classes, sweet in speech, never arrogant, ever seeking refuge in Brahmins, he may attain the highest class (in another birth).*" The Sudra is not allowed to read the Vedas, the most sacred of Hindu religious books. If

* H. G. Rawlinson, *India*

a Sudra transgresses this law, his tongue is to be cut off. If he listens to the reading of the Veda, molten lead is to be poured into his ears. If he assaults a Brahmin, he is to be hanged. If a Brahmin kills a Sudra, the crime is equivalent to a Brahmin "killing a cat, an inchenumon, the bird Chasha, a frog, a dog, a lizard, an owl, or a crow."

The Sudra is not to interest himself in literacy. Orthodox religious rites are prohibited to him. Lest he should try to emulate his superiors the law lays down how he should conduct himself even in the minutest detail of daily life. "The stick with which a Brahmin rinses his teeth is to be twelve inches long, that of a Kshatriya is to be eleven, that of a Vaisya ten; and that of a Sudra nine. When a Brahmin, to remove a natural defilement, is to make five applications of clay, a Kshatriya is to make four, a Vaisya three; and a Sudra and a woman two."

The Sudras, it is worthy of note, have never remained content with the lot assigned to them by law. With the decay of the Kshatriyas and the Vaisyas, the Sudras appear to have seized the power that once belonged to these castes. Though prohibited by sacred law to serve Sudras, the Brahmins, when well paid, have always shown an accommodating spirit in this matter and Sudra adventurers who managed to usurp thrones or carve out kingdoms for themselves have never found learned Brahmins wanting to fill in posts of ministers and preceptors. Moreover, Brahmins well-versed in sacred lore and genealogies of kings have been able to trace the descent of the new hero to some celebrity of epic fame.

Many of the ancient dynasties of India were of low origin. The Maurya dynasty, founded by the celebrated Chandragupta, is a classic example. In later times, the rise of the Mahrathas brought into forefront the Sudras. Before the Peshwas, who were Brahmins, assumed the leadership of the Mahrathas, they were led and ruled by their own chieftains who belonged to their own caste. Of the Mahrathas Mountstuart Elphinstone wrote: "If they have none of the pride and dignity of the Rajputs, they have none of their indolence or want of wordly wisdom. A Rajput warrior so long as he does not dishonour his race, seems almost indifferent to the result of any contest he is engaged in. A Mahratha thinks of nothing but the result, and cares little for the means, if he can attain his object. For this purpose, he will strain his wits, renounce his pleasures, and hazard his person; but he has not the conception of sacrificing his life, or even his interest for a point of honour. The chiefs in those days were men of families who had for generations filled the old Hindu offices of heads of villages or functionaries of districts, and had often been employed as functionaries under the government of Ahmadnagar and Bijapur. They were all Sudras, of the same caste with their people, though some tried to raise their consequence by claiming an infusion of Rajput blood."

The Sudra princes and chieftains who attained eminence could not, for obvious reasons, be treated with contempt by the Brahmins under their pay. So most of the adverse laws concerning Sudras were never enforced, especially in case of the better class of Sudras who enjoyed almost all the privileges of an Aryan community. In spite of Manu, the Sudras read the scriptures and some of the greatest religious poets and reformers of India rose from this caste. The Brahmins, no doubt, made some feeble efforts to persecute them; but enjoying the patronage of the public and powerful chieftains of their own castes, they could not be smothered by the Brahmins.

In places where Sudras are powerful, it is not uncommon to see Brahmins serving them as cooks and domestic servants, thus reversing the injunctions of Manu!

Fortunately placed outside the pale of Aryan law, the Sudras are not plagued with the numerous taboos that hamper growth of individuality. They are allowed to eat anything except beef, and drink anything they like. They engage themselves in all kinds of trade, and form the bulk of every Hindu fighting force. The majority of the peasants, craftsmen, artisans and professional soldiers among the Hindus belong to this caste.

The Sudras are not "twice born," and do not wear the sacred thread. Among them there are innumerable sub-castes, each of which taking its name mainly from the traditional occupation it follows. There are thus, among the Sudras, sub-castes of 'carpenters', 'masons', 'weavers,' 'washermen,' 'ploughmen,' etc. Every village should have at least one family of every sub-caste of tradesmen to attend to its needs, as the castes are strictly prohibited from changing their occupation. If a family of carpenters were to perish in a village, and there is no family in the same village to replace them, no one else is allowed to work as carpenters, but the villagers have to import a family of carpenters from some other village to work for them. The profession of a man is inextricably connected with his social status and has a definite bearing on his practical religion. Each sub-caste of Sudras is an independent social unit, and interdining and intermarriage between any two is prohibited.

THE PANCHAMAS

The Panchamas (or the fifth) are the outcastes who are not considered good enough by the Aryan castes even to serve them. They are known in different parts of the country by different names. In the law books they are mainly referred to as Chandalas. The vast majority of the aborigines of India belong to the Panchamas, although certain hill tribes have a status higher than that of the majority of Panchamas. Progeny of mixed marriages and children born out of wedlock have also contributed to their increase, as Hinduism is particularly strict with its erring female members. According to Manu, children born to a Brahmin woman by a Sudra male are Chandalas, "the lowest of mortals." Progeny of unions between a man of one caste and a woman of a higher caste usually sink below the level of either, and are treated as outcastes from both the communities.

Whatever the origin of the Panchamas, they have all along been the victims of Hindu social tyranny. We have seen, that although the Sudras were allotted an unenviable position in society, they have all along enjoyed a better status; the same, unfortunately, is not true of the Panchamas. These were not allowed to enter villages and towns except to do scavenging work. Their touch was considered defiling even by Sudras.

Among the Panchamas too there are various sub-castes with varying social status. A mention of some of them and their relation to the higher castes would be interesting. In Malabar, the Hindus of which place have all along been living apart from the rest of India, and have, hence, been free from Muslim influence, society still shows many of the distinguishing features of the caste system, and the working of caste here is particularly worth noticing. Of the highest caste in Malabar are the Nambudiri Brahmins mentioned elsewhere; next in importance come the Pattar Brahmins, immigrants from Tamil districts; the Nayars from the bulk of the Hindu population of Malabar, and they are considered as de-casted Kshatriyas by themselves, and as pure Sudras by the Brahmins: the Thiyas may be said to be intermediary between Sudras and the Panchamas. Of the Panchamas, Pulayas, Cherumars and Parayas are the highest; these were once the slaves of the Nayars and the Syrian Christians who are found in large numbers in Malabar; but on the abolition of slavery they were treated as their servants. The lowest among the Panchamas are the Ulladahs living on the outskirts of the forests eking out a living by hunting lizards and digging for edible roots. There are numerous subdivisions among these castes, but it is not necessary to mention them all.

A brief description of the working of the caste system in Malabar will be interesting. The Nayar is an untouchable to the Nambudiri, but the latter can take to bed a Nayar woman in her own house, for which permissible defilement he purifies himself by a ceremonial wash in the morning, without which he is not allowed to enter his own house. Children born of such a union are Nayars and, as such untouchable to their male parent. A Nayar, in conversation with a Nambudiri is not allowed to refer to his house in more flattering terms than as 'my hovel' even if this be as good as a castle. A Nambudiri's residence, on the other hand, should always be mentioned as a palace. The Nambudiri should be addressed as a god, and the Nayar himself mentioned as a slave. The Nayar, while addressing a Nambudiri, should cover his mouth lest spittle that might spurt out should defile the Brahmin. On seeing a Nambudiri, a Nayar should remove his upper garment and tuck it under his arm and stand at a respectable distance. There are numerous other courtesies of a similar nature a Nayar is expected to perform; these are duly performed even now by Nayars who are dependent on the Nambudiris; but others, under the influence of modernism, are inclined to treat the Nambudiris with contempt.

The Thiyas are untouchable to the Nayars. To a Pattar Brahmin a Thiya is unapproachable by twenty paces and to a Nambudiri by twenty-five. The Pulayas, Cherumars and Parayas are untouchable to one another, each one claiming superiority over the others and indulging in a wash when touched and defiled. A member of any one of these communities is unapproachable to a Thiya by ten paces, to a Nayar by twenty, to a Pattar Brahmin by forty and to a Nambudiri by sixty. An Ulladah is "unlookable" to a Nambudiri and Pattar, and unapproachable to the others. Because of this, the Ulladahs seldom venture into a village, and when they do so utter mournful cries for others to take warning. The Nambudiris when moving about generally order a Nayar to go in front shouting at the top of his voice, 'Ha-Ha', as a warning to unapproachables to keep aloof. The unapproachables, when they are engaged in putting up fences or in other work which requires their continued presence in the village lanes, take care to put up, at the distance of about 60 paces on either side of them, a sign which usually consists of a couple of green branches kept down by a stone, as an indication of their presence to wayfarers. I have often seen in Malabar villages the Nayars accompanying highborn Nambudiris chasing poor Pulayas all over the village so that their masters might go about without defilement and detaining the work of putting up fences indefinitely. And I remember a case when a Pulaya who was engaged by a Syrian Christian farmer, was thus stopped from his work for several hours by Brahmins who were on that day busy going to attend some feast; the enraged Syrian resented this and it led to a free fight among the villagers.

Ingenious methods were invented to distinguish the unapproachables from others. During Fa Hian's visit he noticed that the unapproacables, on entering the city, had to go about striking a gong. Huien Tsang says that they were not allowed to use the public thoroughfares but to keep to a certain foot path allotted for their exclusive use. In the Punjab, the sweeper castes had to go about always holding a broom. In the reign of the Peshwas the Mahars had to drag a bush of leaves with them wherever they went. They were not allowed to enter the city of Poona after 3 P.M., as towards the evening they cast too long a shadow which falling on their superiors might defile them.

The Panchamas, as a rule, were not allowed to live in villages inhbited by the higher castes. They had to keep away from village wells and temples and certain main thoroughfares leading to the streets of the Brahmins. They were not allowed to build houses of stone or wood, but had to construct hovels of mud, reeds and straw. The entrance to their houses were to be low so that a Panchama could not enter his house without stooping. The idea was that as a Panchama grew older he should learn to stoop lower. Wearing of clean clothes was forbidden to the Panchama. He was not allowed to own land. This law alone ensured his observance of other laws, as by this he became completely dependent upon the higher castes.

In the case of the Panchamas, all the adverse laws were strictly enforced, and they had for long remained a degraded people with no self-respect, and absolutely no chance of improving their condition.

Condemned to slavery and misery, without even an opportunity for protest, their wretchedness had been complete. They ate beef and carrion. No law restrained them from eating the filthiest of things and drinking the foulest of waters. When they fell sick the doctors would not treat them. The community that had hospitals for animals and birds had no doctors to treat their low-born brethren. The death of a Panchama was considered of less importance than the death of a dog or a cat. For the offence of entering streets forbidden to them or approaching public wells inadvertently, Panchamas had been put to death by the higher castes. Mutilation and flogging were the punishments for the slightest offences.

GENERAL REMARKS ON 'CASTE'

The tendency of the caste system all along has been to divide the community into innumerable watertight compartments. This had rendered the Hindus incapable of thinking in terms of any interest larger than that of their sub-caste or the village. A man's occupation, his ambition, his social activities and even the details of his daily life were fixed at birth and he could seldom rise above his caste, try as much as he could.

Caste is believed to be predestined and immutable. Transmigration of souls being the principal dogma of popular Hinduism, birth in a particular caste is not considered an accident but the natural consequence of deeds done in a former life. Hence a man is not allowed to change his caste, but has to work out his destiny in the caste he is born in. Nor can non-Hindus, as a rule, be admitted into the Hindu fold. The theory is that a non-Hindu, by living well according to the dictates of his own religion, can, if he is lucky, be reborn in the Hindu fold in some low caste and from here, after successive rebirths, may finally get born as a Brahmin when he may aspire for union with the infinite. We have, however, seen that this rule had not been strictly adhered to and many races of non-Aryan origin have been admitted into the Hindu fold and some of the Sudras had even managed themselves to be recognized as Kshatriyas by persuasion and by threats.

Brahmins, however, form an exclusive hierarchy, and their caste is most jealously guarded; not even a Kshatriya can be admitted into this caste. The only instance of a non-Brahmin ever having become a Brahmin by achievement is that of King Vishwamitra. The story of this metamorphosis is worth telling as it shows at once the greatness of the Brahmin and the difficulty of attaining Brahminhood.

King Vishwamitra, the most powerful Kshatriya of his time, once went out hunting and strayed into the hermitage of Vasishta, a Brahmin of great repute. Vasishta entertained his royal guest on such a lavish scale that the king began to wonder how a hermit, living in a forest, could afford luxuries which, he, Vishwamitra, could not. The king made enquiries and came to know that the secret of Vasishta's wealth was in the wonder-working cow Kamadhenu of which Vasishta was then the possessor. King-like, Vishwamitra wished to have the cow and asked his host to sell her to him which Vasishta refused. Vishwamitra offered fabulous sums for the cow, and when every offer was refused made known that he was willing to part with half his kingdom if Vasishta would sell him the cow. Even this grand offer was refused, upon which Vishwamitra, getting annoyed and angry, called forth his army and tried to drive away the cow. Vasishta, by the help of the cow, produced greater armies and more powerful weapons than those of Vishwamitra and put the king and his men to flight.

Vishwamitra was overcome with shame, and started brooding over the impotence of kings before the might of Brahmins. He despised his own caste and status and wanted to become a Brahmin. Accordingly he gave up his kingdom and royal status and repaired to a forest where he began to practise austerities. Because of the extreme heat produced by the severity of his austerities, Brahma, the creator, could not sit on his throne and appeared before his devotee to enquire of him why he was thus torturing himself. But on learning from the king his intention of becoming a Brahmin the god expressed regret and told him that, creator as he was, he could not convert a Kshatriya into a Brahmin, and disappeared. But Vishwamitra would not be put off like that. He started practising the most painful austerities and made Brahma appear before him several times with no better results than the first one. This so disgusted Vishwamitra that, by the accumulated merit of his austerities, he began to create a world of his own to make Brahma and his creation look ridiculous. His success was striking, and Brahma had to beg of him to desist from creating. This divinity, however, presented him with a weapon with which, he assured Vishwamitra, he would be able to defeat Vasishta. Proud of this missile, Vishwamitra went to Vasishta and challenged him to single combat in which the king, to his utter dismay, was defeated and put to flight. The exasperated Kshatriya now started a course of austerities which immediately brought down Brahma from heaven, and this divinity was forced to convert him into a Brahmin.

Vishwamitra is now recognized by all the worlds as a Brahmin, but some of the proud Brahmin's of Indra's court hold the view that even Brahma cannot make a Brahmin of a Kshatriya, and are contemptuous of the Brahminical pretensions of Vishwamitra.

This myth will give the reader some idea of what the Brahmins think of themselves.

It must be mentioned that the Brahmins have not been able to enjoy their privileged position without a challenge. The iniquity of caste disturbed the peace of mind of some of the greatest spiritual leaders among the Hindus and they made efforts to abolish it. The greatest of these leaders was Gautama, the founder of Buddhism. Gautama belonged to the Kshatriya caste, and in the religion he preached the pride of birth was subordinated to individual morality. He gave caste an ethical interpretation and maintained that it was not birth that decided caste but achievement, i.e., any one who lived a noble life should be considered a Brahmin, and the one who was a good ruler a Kshatriya, a trader, a Vaisya and a man of mean and low habits a Sudra. Buddhism was a direct challenge to the pretensions of Brahmins and many of the kings of India, who were jealous of the power of Brahmins, patronised it. But later it lost its hold on the people, and Brahminism and caste again became supreme. Even in the heyday of Buddhism, caste was tolerated as a social necessity although its religious sanctions were getting undermined. After the decay of Buddhism in India, no one had been able to challenge caste successfully till our own times.

It need hardly be mentioned that caste is not all evil. No institution which has existed in a community for so long can be without some good, and caste is no exception to this rule. By defining every one's scope of activities in society, it eliminated the undesirable competitive spirit which is the curse of modern communities, and tended to cultivate a co-operative spirit between the several castes that inhabited a village or town. The caste, occupation and practical religion of a man were inseparably welded together and the workman or craftsman developed almost a spiritual interest in his work and not a purely commercial interest. By keeping the Brahmins free for religious and scholastic pursuits, caste ensured the cultivation of literary, aesthetic and scientific knowledge.

It is interesting to note that there is no mention of or sanction for caste in the Rig Veda, the most ancient and sacred book of the Hindus. Even in the great epic, Mahabharata, the repository of Hindu legend and tradition, caste does not show many of the undesirable features of later Hindu society. Vyasa, one of the greatest sages of Hinduism and the compiler of the Vedas, is mentioned as having been born of a Brahmin and a fisherwoman. Vidura, the greatest moralist of the Mahabharata who instructed kings in matters of virtue and morality, is mentioned as low born. Karna, one of the heroes of the Mahabharata, was born illegitimate and was brought up by a low-born charioteer.

It was later, especially at the time of the promulgation of the codes, that the institution of caste got ossified to the detriment of the free development of the community.

CASTE AT PRESENT

Much water has flowed down the Ganges since Manu wrote his code regulating the lives of Hindus. The Muslim invasion was a serious blow to caste. The large number of low caste Hindus who were converted to Islam and who, belonging to the ruling classes, claimed equality with the Brahmins, did much to bring down their pride. The advent of the British and the activities of Christian missionaries gave another impetus to the forces that were working against caste. The British government, it is true, did nothing directly to undermine the caste system; but the ideas they propagated through their educational system and their own social structure were powerful forces that aided the reform movements which started warring against caste.

Enlightened Hindus, educated in English schools and colleges, became conscious of the iniquities of the caste system and the degradation of their low-born brethren. Some of them, in the teeth of orthodox opposition, broke the taboo against sea voyages, travelled abroad and were struck by the social structure of the West. These individuals were persecuted on their return to their motherland, but their number and influence gradually increased and they became pioneers of reform movements. Indigenous reformers (Swami Dayanand for instance) also became conscious of the degradation of a large percentage of the community, and started religious movements which drew their inspiration from the 'casteless' Vedas and discarded later works which supported caste.

By far the greatest force that is working against caste at present is the political movement. The need for the uplift of the depressed classes, or Harijans as they were christened by Gandhiji, was strongly felt by the leaders of political thought who realized that a country, with a large percentage of its population sunk in misery and wretchedness and treated by their own countrymen as unapproachables, could neither fight for independence nor keep it, when won. Another factor that weighed with Hindu leaders was communalism. In the large number of converts to Islam and Christianity from the depressed classes, the upper class Hindus found a possible challenge to their numerical superiority, and vigorous measures were adopted to fight orthodoxy, and give the 'depressed classes' a better social status than they had hitherto enjoyed! 'The depressed classes' themselves became conscious of their rights, and in the absence of a Hindu power to enforce the ancient caste laws, organized themselves to gain their due share in the commonwealth. The British Government actively supported them, and they were, under able leadership, able to get many privileges and concessions from the government. With the coming of independence and the equality of rights guaranteed by the Indian Constitution, most of the iniquities of caste have been abolished by law.

As a result of all this, caste at present is in the melting-pot. The Harijans can now enter most of the temples of India if they care to and can walk along the highways as they please. The cosmopolitan population of the great cities of India are casteless in their out-door activities. Most of the hotels and common eating houses of the cities are open to all castes. Hindus of all castes may be seen eating in the tea shops and coffee clubs run by Muslims and Christians. When they go home, it is true, they come under the influence of their womenfolk who still have great respect for caste. A Brahmin who will unhesitatingly eat with a Christian in a hotel will refuse to eat with another Brahmin of a different denomination in his own house. Nor will an orthodox woman allow the scavenger to enter any place in the house except the lavatory.

In the villages things are still bad. Although the old order has changed appreciably, the Indian village moves so slowly that a great deal remains yet to be done. The age old economic dependence of the lower castes still persists in the village, and the higher castes, being naturally orthodox, are extremely reluctant to accord to their low born brethren anything approaching equality of status.

Pride of race and nobility of birth have still a fascination for the generality of Indians. They are more easily impressed by a vain nobleman than by a commoner of outstanding merit.

CHAPTER III

RELIGION

HINDUISM is not a religion established by a single person. It is a growth of ideas, rituals and beliefs so comprehensive as to include anything between atheism and pantheism. Having grown out of the practices and speculations of various communities that were admitted into the Hindu fold at different times, Hinduism, as it stands at present, has very few set dogmas. A formal recognition of the Vedas as revealed wisdom is all that is required for a Hindu to be known as such. But the latitude permitted in interpreting the Vedas is so wide that the atheistic Sankya philosophy of Kapila and the polytheism of the Puranas are both recognized as orthodox.

For a Hindu, religion is inseparable from what we call the accident of birth. A man born of Christian or Muslim parents may believe in all the gods of the Hindu pantheon and worship them thrice a day according to the prescribed rites, yet he has no right to be known as a Hindu. On the other hand a person born of Hindu parents may believe in the divinity of Christ and may offer prayers to all the saints of the Catholic calendar and yet remain a Hindu and be treated as such by his co-religionists if he would only tell the world that Roman Catholicism is not incompatible with the precepts of the Vedas. This is not merely a technical point. As a matter of fact there are many Hindus who pray sincerely at Christian shrines, who believe in the divinity of Christ and offer candles at the altars of the madonna. Hindus find no difficulty in recognizing divinity in any great person who has changed the course of history. Nay, they maintain that God incarnates Himself into human or other forms, whenever mankind goes astray to bring them back to the correct path, and it is no news to them to learn that Jesus Christ is an incarnation of God or Muhammad a messenger. They will only dispute the exclusiveness and finality of Christ and Muhammad.

The earliest form of worship, the nucleus from which the present day Hinduism has developed, is known as Vedic religion. It consisted mainly of worship of the powers of nature such as the storm (Maruts), fire (Agni), the dawn (Ushas), the sun and the moon. Rain, lightning, thunder and the terrors of the heavens implied the existence of a powerful being in the sky whose activities were believed to have caused these. This being was called Indra. In Indra, we have the nucleus of the idea which later developed into monotheism among some sects of the Hindus.

Vedic worship consisted mainly of singing hymns of praise to one or other of the deities, in offering oblations of Soma (a kind of liquor made of the Soma plant) to the gods (which, later, the offering priest drank) and in sacrificing animals. The caste system had not developed and there were no regular priests. In domestic worship, the head of the family, in all probability, officiated as priest and, in public gatherings, the military leader. Any way, ritual soon became an elaborate and complicated affair, and professional men had to devote themselves to religious duties and these men eventually developed into the priestly caste.

The following hymn will give the reader some idea of the nature of Vedic hymns. It is addressed to the god Indra.

> "For thee, O mighty, here is strong drink
> And potent unto victory, as thou
> Victorious Indra, hero, conqueror,
> Urgest to victory the chariots of men,
> Burn thou the lawless Dasyu as a flame,
> Who stolest from the sun his chariot wheel
> To quell the demon of destroying drought.

> "Mighty is thy rapture, thy might sublime,
> O slayer of foes, giver of bliss, winner of steed,
> O joy of ancient singers; as drink to thirsty men
> Send food to us who sing thy praises now,
> And lead us to water and safe bivouacs."*

Vedic Aryans loved a healthy life and strove after the pleasures of the world. The ascetic and pessimistic tendencies which later pervaded most of the Hindu forms of thought are conspicuously absent in the Rig Veda (the earliest of the Vedas). Rig Vedic Hindus loved the hunt, the fields, the Soma juice and manly sports. They prayed for long life and sturdy sons. They did not brood over death and after-life. We have very little to guide us, in the earlier hymns, as to what was the Vedic Aryan's conception of life after death. It appears they believed that the soul of the virtuous went to the heaven of Indra, the pleasures of which were not very different from those of this world; the wicked were annihilated at death. Some hymns indicate the grave as the final abode of the virtuous and the wicked. The following funeral hymn is worth noticing in this connection:

> From the dead hand I take the bow he wielded,
> To gain for us dominion, might and glory.
> Thou there, we here, rich in heroic offspring,
> Will vanquish all assaults of every foeman

> Approach the bosom of the earth, the mother,
> This earth, extending far and most propitious:

---
* Monier Williams, *Wisdom of the East.*

Young, soft as wool to bounteous givers,
May she
Preserve thee from the lap of dissolution.

Open wide, O earth, press not heavily on him,
Be easy of approach, hail him with kindly aid:
As with a robe the loving mother hideth
Her son, so shroud this man, O earth our
Mother.

The worship of the powers of nature did not satisfy the bolder spirits among the Indo-Aryans. In one of the later hymns, the poet raises, probably for the first time in the history of the Aryans, a question which upto this day remains unanswered. He visualizes an unknown power above all the gods of the Vedas and speculates about the origin and extent of that power. This is the hymn:

"Non-being then existed nor not being:
There was no air, nor sky that is beyond it.
What was concealed? Wherein? In whose
protection?
And was there deep unfathomable water?

Death then existed not, nor life immortal;
Of neither night nor day was any token.
By its inherent force the one breathed
windless:
No other thing than that beyond existed.

Darkness there was at first, by darkness
hidden;
Without distinctive marks, this all was water.
That which, becoming, by the void was
covered,
That one by force of heat came into being.

* * * * *

Who knows for certain? Who shall here
declare it?
Whence was it born, and whence came this
creation?
Then who can know from whence it has
risen?

None knoweth whence creation has arisen:
And whether he has or has not produced it;
He who surveys it in the highest heaven,
He only knows, or haply he may know not."*

This speculative spirit dominates the Upanishads, later treatises attached to the Vedas, from which the philosophic systems of the Hindus draw their inspiration.

As the Indo-Aryans absorbed into their religion the beliefs of other communities admitted into the Hindu fold, Vedic religion underwent a material change. While the Vedas were still regarded as the most ancient and sacred texts of the community, the gods and spirits of the Vedas were gradually replaced by deities and beliefs which originally had nothing to do with Vedic religion. The new gods were probably tutelary deities of powerful clans who were able to extend their dominion over the greater part of the country and whom the Brahmins did not dare to defy. Whatever the origin of the new gods, as India enters the historic period we find Vedic religion replaced by the current Puranic religion, and Vedic gods dominated by the widely worshipped Vishnu and Shiva, the great Puranic god. The copious Puranas together with the epics became the dearly loved religious literature of the community and the Vedas degenerated into mere objects of study for the scholar, the philosopher and the ritualist. The Vedas were, however, still revered as the most sacred and ancient texts, but Pundits found no difficulty in tracing a Vedic origin to the newly risen gods whose names are not found in the Vedas.

Puranic Hinduism i.e., the orthodox Hinduism of the present day, is divided into six sects. Before we deal with these sects it is necessary for the reader to have some idea of the principal deities of the Puranic pantheon, as sectarian worship mainly centres round them.

PRINCIPAL DEITIES OF THE PANTHEON

Strange as it may seem, the Hindus are monotheists as well as polytheists and pantheists. They believe in a Supreme Being, the Prime Cause of everything, a Being above gods and goddesses. This Being is eternal, without beginning or end, above time, space and causation. It is being without attributes. But as being without attributes cannot be conceived by the ordinary run of mankind, for their benefit Godhead is reduced to three main aspects: i.e., the creative, preservative and destructive. The personification of the creative aspect is known as Brahma, already mentioned in the first chapter as the creator of the universe; Vishnu is the preserver and Shiva the destroyer. These great deities constitute the Hindu trinity.

Brahma is represented as a four-headed deity, indicative of his intellect. He is the author of all creation and has for his wife Sarasvati, the goddess of all creative arts. Brahma is not now worshipped by the Hindus as a principal deity and there is not an important temple dedicated to him except one at Pushkar. It seems Brahma worship was once popular but was overthrown by the devotees of Shiva and Vishnu. At present he is worshipped as a subsidiary deity, and in some of the temples of Shiva and Vishnu there are niches allotted to minor images of Brahma.

Unlike Brahma, Vishnu the preserver is widely worshipped. He is represented as a deity of pleasant countenance with four arms, eternally sleeping on his couch the serpent Ananta (eternity). He is only disturbed in his slumbers by the supplications of other gods when his intervention is needed for the preservation of the universe when its existence is endangered by the activities of the powers of evil. Vishnu is believed to have assumed various forms to destroy evil and maintain the reign of virtue in the world. His principal incarnations are said to be ten. Of these, nine are already past and the tenth one is yet to come.

* Muir's translation.

The ten incarnations are known as Dasavatara and it is as one of these incarnations that he is generally worshipped. When not engaged in the combat against evil, Vishnu sleeps on his couch, with his wife Lakshmi dutifully sitting at his feet and pressing them. Lakshmi is the goddess of prosperity.

The ten incarnations of Vishnu are: Matsya (fish), Kurma (tortoise), Varaha (boar), Narasimha (man-lion), Vamana (dwarf), Parasurama, Dasaratharama, Krishna, the Buddha, and Kalki.

Vishnu incarnated himself as a fish to save the sage Manu when the world was engulfed in a deluge. The myth is mentioned in Chapter I.

The tortoise incarnation was necessitated by the helplessness of the gods who, while churning the milk ocean (the abode of Vishnu) for ambrosia, found the mountain Mandhara, which was used as a churning stick, sinking into the mud of the ocean. Vishnu as a tortoise supported the mountain on his back which enabled the gods to agitate the milk ocean properly and obtain its cream, the ambrosia.

As Varaha, Vishnu destroyed the demon Hiranyaksha who, out of sheer wickedness, had dragged the earth below the waters. Varaha dived into the primeval waters, killed Hiranyaksha with his powerful tusks and caused the earth to float.

The Narasimha (man-lion) form was assumed by Vishnu for the destruction of the demon Hiranyakasipu, a powerful devil who posed as God himself and prohibited the worship of Vishnu throughout the fourteen worlds. But Hiranyakasipu's son Prahlad was a persecuted devotee of Vishnu and this deity, to deliver the son from his father, assumed the form of Narasimha and killed Hiranyakasipu. The man-lion form was chosen as the demon had obtained a boon by which he could be destroyed by neither man nor beast.

As Vamana Vishnu reclaimed the celestial kingdom from the Asura king Bali who had conquered it and driven the gods out of their native soil. Bali was an upright and virtuous ruler and Vishnu, in this case, had recourse to stratagem and not to direct action. Vamana, dressed as a Brahmin, approached Bali for three paces of soil to squat and meditate. The unsuspecting king seeing the size of the dwarf readily agreed to accede to his request, when Vamana grew into such height that in three strides he measured all the dominions of Bali and then exiled Bali from his kingdom. The poor king, getting no asylum in heaven or earth, was driven to the nether regions.

When the Kshatriyas became overpowerful and started persecuting the Brahmins, Vishnu incarnated himself as a Brahmin (Parasurama) and destroyed the whole race of Kshatriyas in twenty-one campaigns. An account of this incarnation has been given in Chapter II.

The object of the Dasaratharama incarnation was the destruction of the demon king Ravana of Ceylon (Lanka) who waged war against gods and Aryans, and persecuted them in many ways. The story is beautifully told in the Hindu epic Ramayana, a work of which we shall take notice later.

Although the express object of Krishna Avatar was the destruction of the demons Kansa and Shishupala, the activities of Krishna are so varied that, in the present day worship of Krishna, the main object is often lost sight of. It is believed that Vishnu manifested himself more fully in Krishna Avatar than in any others. In Krishna we have the ideal child, the ideal lover, the ideal soldier, the ideal statesman and the ideal philosopher. He advocated a philosophy of action, and tried to work out his salvation living amidst men and women rather than in the lonesome forests of the Himalayas.

The Buddha, as is well-known, taught, according to Brahmins, heretical doctrines, and it may appear strange to the reader why he is considered by them an incarnation of their favourite deity. The Brahmins explain this by the argument that Vishnu as the Buddha taught heresy so that people might go astray which would give added chances to Brahmins to bring them back to Hinduism!

Kalki is the tenth incarnation, yet to come. As mentioned in the first chapter, the Hindus believe that in Kaliyuga (the present age of evil) men will degenerate to such an extent that even Vishnu will be unable to save them except by destroying them and building up a new world. For this purpose, it is fabled, Vishnu will appear in the world as Kalki riding on a charger, waving the sword of destruction in his right hand.

Lakshmi, the wife of Vishnu, and his charger Garuda (the man-bird) are also worshipped by the Hindus.

The third of the Hindu triad, Shiva the destroyer, is a deity as popular as his compeer Vishnu if not more. His manifestations are many, but incarnations few. Shiva is the mendicant of heaven, an eternal wanderer, delighting in the society of those ghosts, imps and devils who haunt cremation grounds and wild places. He has no palaces to live in, but dwells with his family on a hillock (Mount Kailas) in the Himalayas. Shiva is believed to have been condemned to this kind of existence by a curse of his compeer Brahma, one of whose heads he is said to have cut off in an argument about each other's supremacy.

Shiva, the god of destruction, is also the god of regeneration, and some of the sex cults of Hinduism are traced to the worship of Shiva. He is the god of ascetics, and of those who believe themselves to be above the moral codes of society. His charger, Nandi, the bull, is an object of worship among Hindus.

Shiva has a wife and two children. His wife, variously known as Parvati, Durga, Kali, Sakti, Devi, Uma, etc., is the most widely worshipped goddess of the Hindu pantheon and has an independent cult of her own. Of the two sons of Shiva, Ganesha, the elephant-headed deity of prudence is the elder, and Kartikeya, the war-god, the younger. Ganesha, as the remover of obstacles, is propitiated by every Hindu before the commencement of an undertaking, and is, hence, the most widely remembered deity of the pantheon. Yet his younger brother, comparatively little known, probably has as many temples dedicated exclusively to him as Ganesha. Kartikeya is generally known in South India as Subrahmanya.

Besides these principal deities, there are innumerable other gods in the Hindu pantheon. All the Vedic deities are there, though occupying a subordinate position. The number of deities in the Hindu pantheon is

XIII

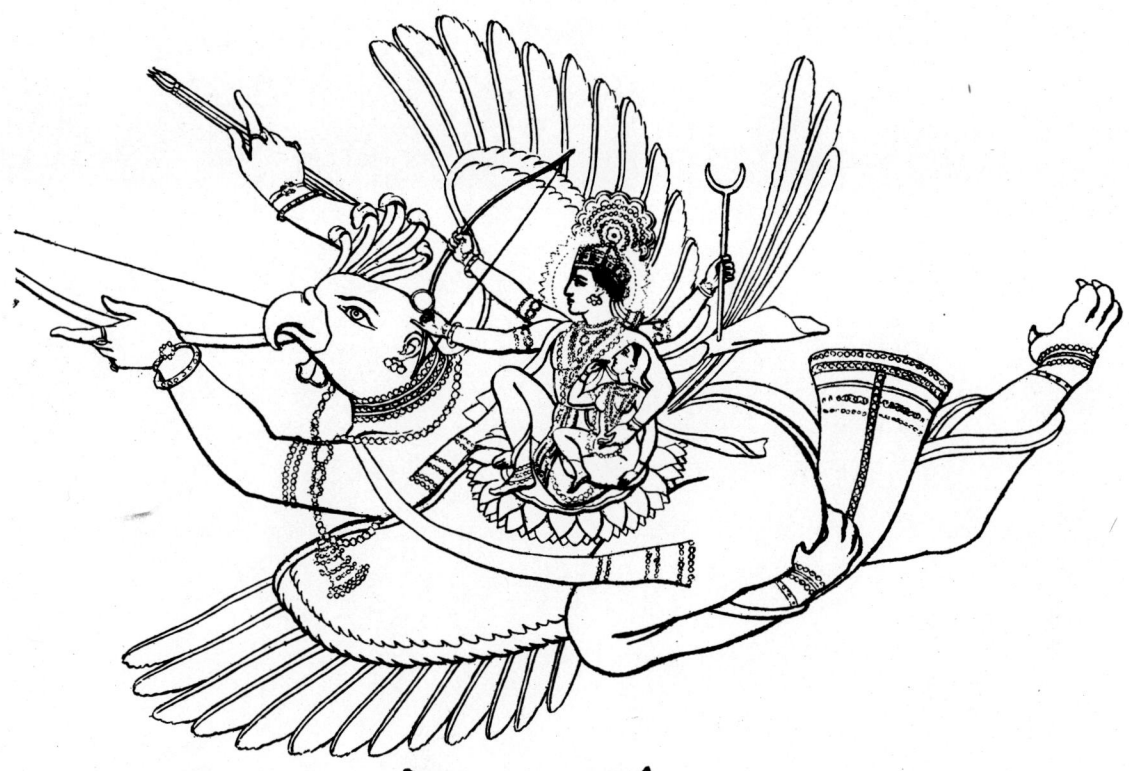

गरुडः   विष्णुः   लक्ष्मी

33 VISHNU WITH HIS WIFE RIDING ON THE MYTHICAL BIRD GARUDA
(Moor's *Hindu Pantheon*)

34 BIRTH OF BRAHMA FROM VISHNU'S NAVEL
(From a sculpture in a cave temple, Undavalle)

XIV

35 A SACRIFICIAL UTENSIL

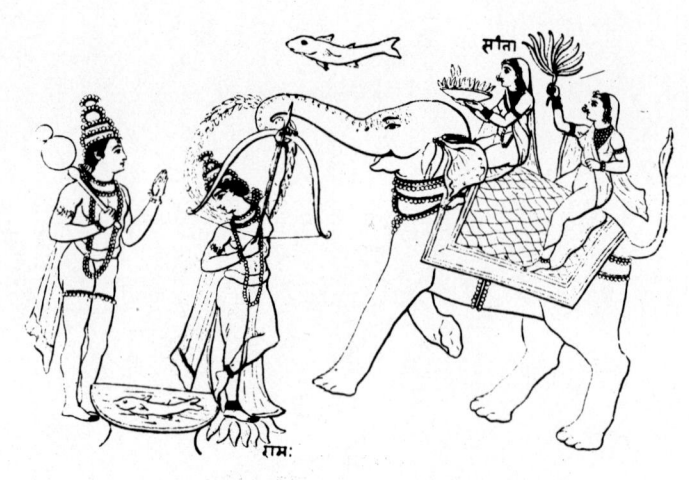

36 RAMA WINNING SITA IN AN ARCHERY CONTEST
(A SCENE FROM *RAMAYANA*)

37 A SACRIFICIAL IMPLEMENT

38 SHIVA, DESTROYER, OF THE HINDU TRIAD
(Moor's *Hindu Pantheon*)

XV

39 RADHA AND KRISHNA

40 MAHAKALI OR BHADRAKALI, THE GODDESS OF TERROR
(Moor's *Hindu Pantheon*)

XVI

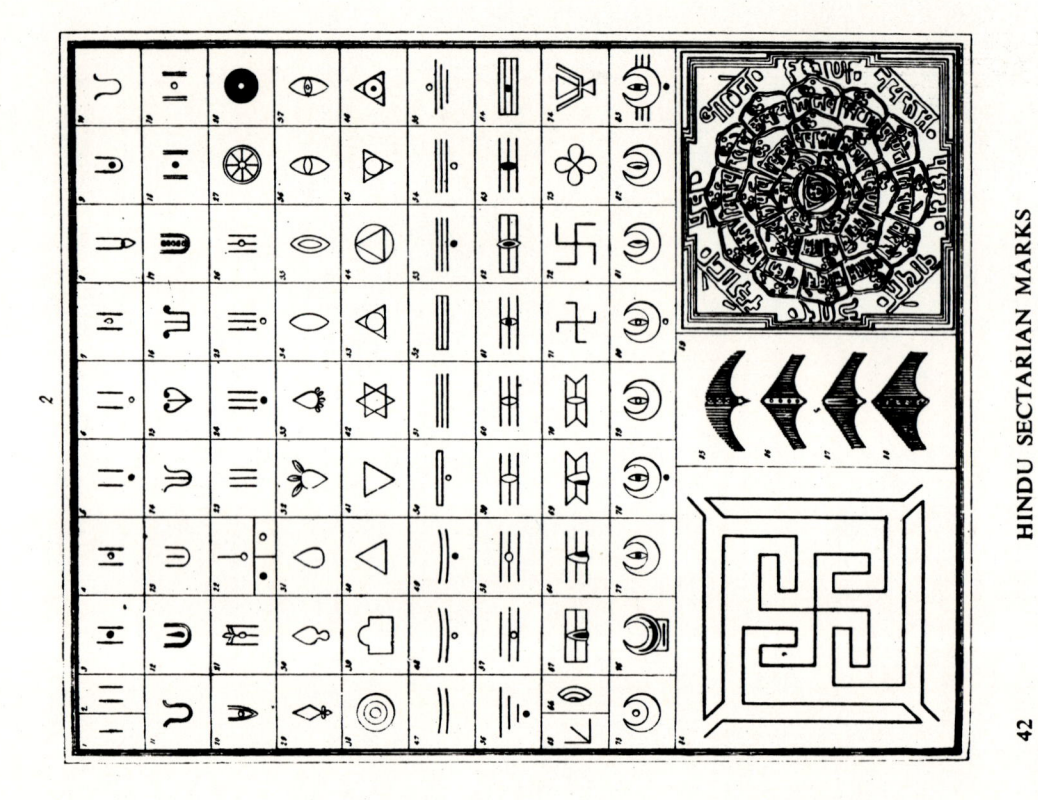

41 VIRABHADRA, A WARLIKE FORM OF SHIVA

42 HINDU SECTARIAN MARKS

(Moor's *Hindu Pantheon*)

XVII

43 VAISHNAVA SYMBOLS ON THE DOOR OF A TEMPLE
(India Pictorial Features)

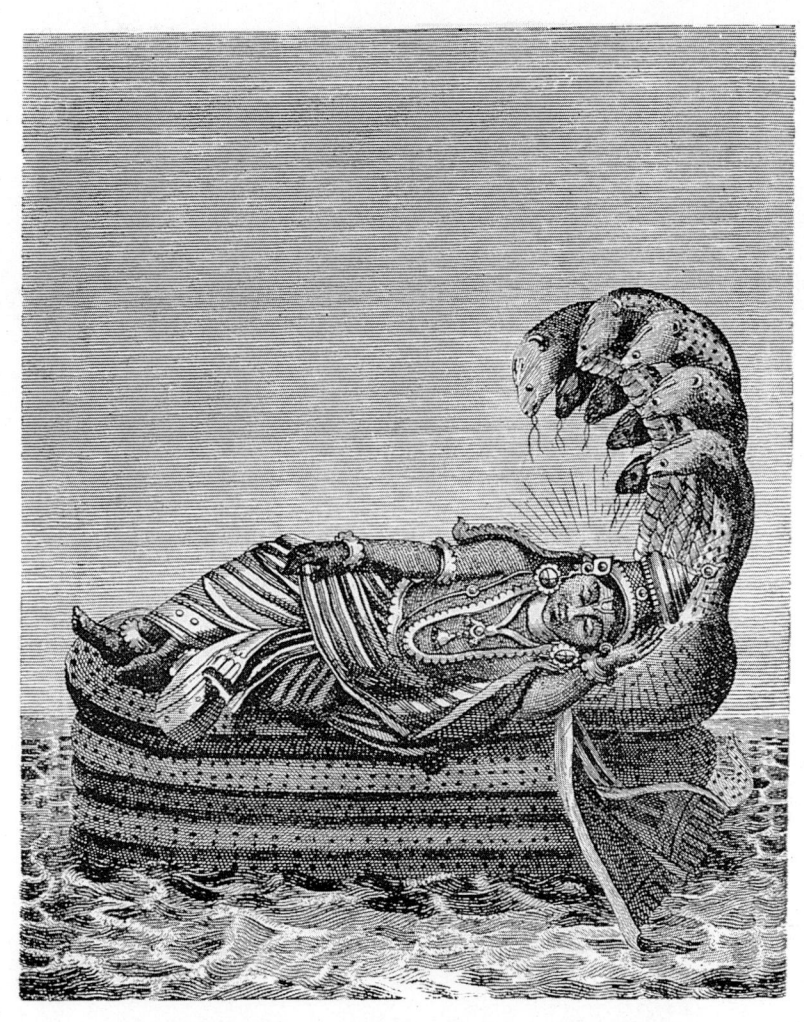

44 VISHNU SLEEPING ON HIS SERPENT COUCH ANANTA
(Moor's *Hindu Pantheon*)

XVIII

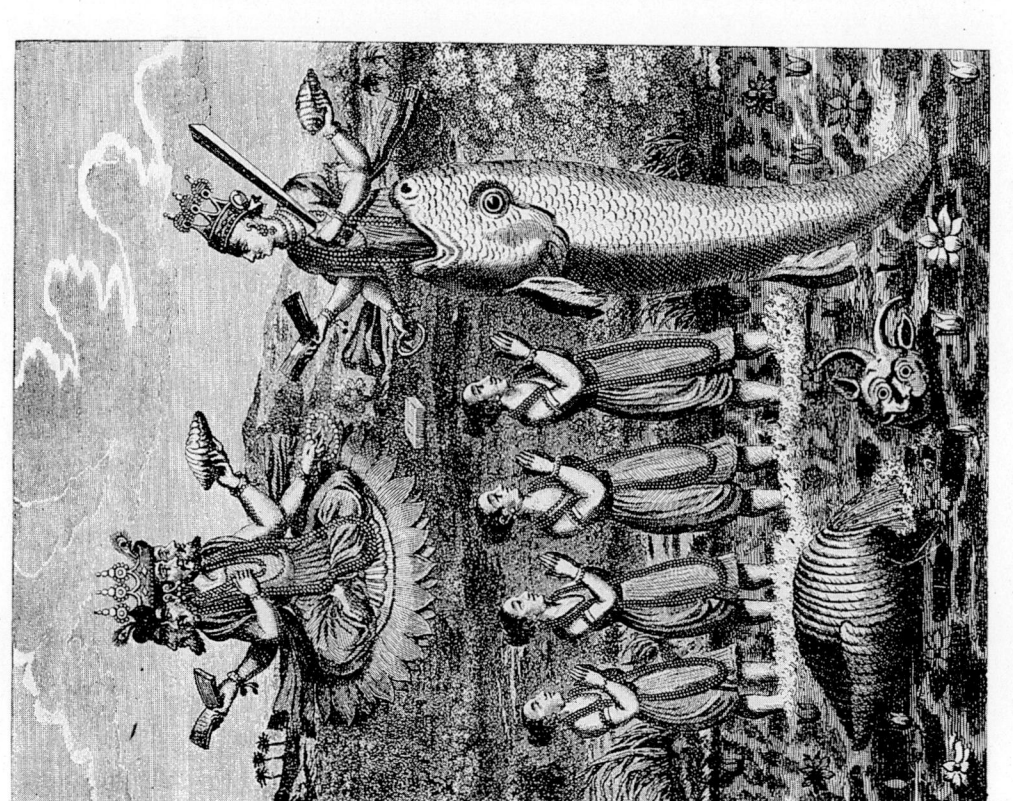

45 MATSYA (FISH) INCARNATION OF VISHNU   46 KURMA (TORTOISE), SECOND INCARNATION OF VISHNU
(Maurice's *Hindustan*)

XIX

47 VARAHA (BOAR), THIRD INCARNATION OF VISHNU    48 VAMANA (DWARF), FOURTH INCARNATION OF VISHNU

(Maurice's *Hindustan*)

XX

49 NARASIMHA, (MAN-LION) FIFTH INCARNATION OF VISHNU  50 PARASURAMA, SIXTH INCARNATION OF VISHNU

(Maurice's *Hindustan*)

computed to be thirty-three crores in addition to the great gods of the trinity. Hence it is quite impossible to describe all the deities in a work like this.*

ORTHODOX HINDU SECTS

There are six main sects among the Hindus. They are: (1) Vaishnavas, (2) Shaivas, (3) Saktas, (4) Ganapatyas, (5) Saurapathas, and (6) Smarthas.

VAISHNAVAS

Vaishnavas are those who worship Vishnu as the Supreme Deity. Vishnu is generally worshipped by them as in one of the Avatars. Lakshmi, the wife of Vishnu, Garuda, the charger of Vishnu, and Hanuman the monkey god, who is believed to have been of special help to Rama in his fight against Ravana, are also worshipped by the Vaishnavas. They daub their forehead with three perpendicular lines as their caste mark. The South Indian Hindus are particularly fond of parading sect, and paint their whole body with sect marks, and zealots can be seen with their foreheads, arms and bodies covered with the perpendicular marks of Vishnu or the horizontal marks of Shiva, all done in ashes or sandal paste. Farther north sect marks degenerate into a small circle on the forehead or a figure like a candle flame.

The Vaishnavas are most powerful in northern India and the west coast of the Bombay presidency. The worship of Vishnu leans more to the Bhakti cult (devotion) than to the Jnana cult (knowledge) which is a distinguishing feature of refined Shaivism. Vaishnavism, as a rule, is informed by a healthy respect for life, and no animal sacrifices mar the ritual connected with the worship of Vishnu. They believe in the sanctity and decency of life and hold doctrines opposed to the ascetic view.

There are various subsects among the Vaishnavas, and the more important ones may be mentioned. The Ramanuja sect was founded by Ramanuja, a Brahmin of South India, who defied the Absolute Monism of Sankaracharya and preached a philosophy of devotion to God. He rejected caste and maintained that a worshipper of Vishnu by virtue of his devotion, breaks the social bonds of caste and the god entertains no caste distinctions among his beloved devotees. Ramanuja's influence was confined mainly to South India and he died in the twelfth century A.D. But his disciple Ramananda improved upon Ramanuja's doctrines and carried his mission to the north. Both Ramanuja and Ramananda believed that Rama, the seventh incarnation of Vishnu, was the perfect ideal for devotion and worship. While Ramanuja attached great importance to religious practices and the prescriptions of legal purity and believed in the sanctity of the Sanskrit language, his fiery disciple proved a revolutionary who discarded Sanskrit, advocated the use of the dialects of the people for religious instruction, and took for his disciples "basket-makers, weavers, barbers, water-carriers, and curriers."

Another Vaishnava reformer who founded a sect was Madhavacharya, a Brahmin of Malabar coast, whose influence was confined to the extreme south. He taught the reality of individual souls and of the supreme soul, and that the two cannot merge. The teaching is similar to that of Christianity. Madhava was an observer of caste, but his doctrine of duality spread among the lower classes, and some of the Dasas, as the poets of the Madhava sect are known, are drawn from low castes.

In Bengal Chaitanya, a Brahmin of poor means who lived in the fourteenth century, was the prophet of Vaishnavism. He was an ardent advocate of the Bhakti cult (cult of devotion), and had Krishna, the eighth incarnation of Vishnu, as the object of adoration. His passionate devotion to Krishna very naturally led him to advocate the Radha-Krishna cult in which the relation between soul and god was symbolized by the love of the lady Radha for the youthful Krishna. The amours of the boy Krishna with the milkmaids of Gokul and his midnight dances with them in the arcadian fields of Vrindavan are the favourite themes of poets of Radha-Krishna.

Chaitanya's influence was not confined to Bengal. In the temple of Jagannath in Orissa where he resided for a good part of his life, many of the existing usages were originated by Chaitanya. Mathura, the birth place of Krishna and the home of the Radha-Krishna cult, also came under the influence of Chaitanya.

The sect of Maharajas founded by Vallabhacharya went a step further from the Radha-Krishna cult, and advocated the adoration of a person, called the Maharajah, as the living embodiment of Krishna himself. He used to impersonate Krishna very realistically, demanding of his female disciples the favours the Gopis were believed to have bestowed upon Krishna. The cult came up for severe criticism in the notorious Maharajah case of 1862 when the then Maharajah was accused, in the Bombay High Court, of gross profligacy.

Some improvement in the sect was effected by the reformer, Swami Narayana.

Although the extreme left wing of the Radha-Krishna cult is not always well spoken of, Vaishnavism as a whole is marked by much sincerity of faith and purity of worship.

SHAIVAS

Shaivism is much more ancient than Vaishnavism and is connected with the hey-day of Hindu glory. The Shaivas worship Shiva as the Supreme Being and maintain that the other deities of the pantheon, including Brahma and Vishnu, are subordinate to Shiva or merely a part of him. The better class of worshippers of Shiva are the followers of the pantheistic Advaita philosophy, and as such do not consider the moral law as absolute. They believe Jnana (knowledge), as a surer way of obtaining salvation than Bhakti (devotion), and maintain that the Jnani (one

---

* Readers desiring to know more of the gods and goddesses of the Hindu pantheon are requested to read the authors' book, *Epics, Myths and Legends of India*,

who knows) need not trouble himself with the moral law as true knowledge is in itself a guarantee against moral lapse. This philosophy has obvious dangers, and some Shaivas, before they become Jnani's, develop tendencies which ignore moral values.

The Bhakti cult is also advocated by some Shaivas. Tamil poets like Manikka Vasagar sang ecstatically of the loving god Shiva, and their influence on South Indian Shaivism is very marked. It was probably the success of the Bhakti cult of the Vaishnavas that prompted the Shaivas to adopt it in their sect.

The celebrated Advaitin (monist) Sankaracharya, though himself a Smartha, had Shaiva and Sakta leanings, and he was, in no little measure, responsible for the popularity of Shaivism. In his attempt to bring Shaivism to the masses and thus drive out Buddhism from India, Sankara accepted many of the fetishes of the aborigines as manifestations of Shiva, and his followers invented legends to support the theory. Himself a brilliant intellectual, Sankara in his crusade against Buddhists, pandered to popular ignorance, and encouraged idolatry to such an extent that on his deathbed he is said to have craved pardon of the Almighty for confining His Limitless Self to stone and mortar.

Shiva and his wife Parvati are usually worshipped together. Certain temples are exclusively dedicated to Shiva, but images of Parvati, Ganesha, Kartikeya, and Nandi, the bull, are installed on minor altars in the same temple and worshipped. Various manifestations of Shiva, such as Khandoba, Bhairava, Virabhadra, etc., forms the god is fabled to have assumed for the destruction of certain demons, are also worshipped.

The god of destruction, as mentioned elsewhere, is also the god of regeneration, and the most popular form of worship of Shiva is as the Lingam (the symbol of the male organ of regeneration). Phalli of stone are enshrined in temples and worshipped. There is, however, nothing in the shape of the Lingam to revolt the sentiments of the worshipper, and none but the 'initiated' will recognize in the Lingam the real object it represents. There are various legends which explain the origin of Lingam worship. One myth tells us that it was in this shape that Shiva appeared to Brahma and Vishnu when the three deities were born out of primal chaos; another that Shiva was too much attached to the company of his wife which caused some inconvenience to the sage Bhrigu who cursed the god to be worshipped as the organ of his lust; a third that the over-sexed god committed rape for which he was cursed to be known as the Lingam; and so on and so forth.

Whatever the legends, from passages in the Vedas it is clear that the worship is of un-Aryan origin. For the Vedas speak contemptuously of the people whose god is the Shishna (Lingam). Later, probably, these people became powerful enough to enforce on the Indo-Aryans a respect for their gods.

As among the Vaishnavas, there are different subsects among the Shaivas. The Tridandins (bearers of the triple batons) profess to exercise a threefold sovereignty, viz., over their words, thoughts and actions, and carry as a symbol of this sovereignty a stick with three knots. The Tridandins are again subdivided into ten and are, on account of this, also known as Dasanami (those with ten surnames). They trace their origin to Sankara. They are all ascetics and live in monasteries or wander about in gangs. Their headquarters are at Benares.

The Lingayats are Shaivas, so called because of their wearing about their persons small Lingams. The sect was founded by Basava, a Brahmin of Deccan, who carried on a regular crusade against Vaishnavas, Jains and the Buddhists. Because of his excesses he was persecuted. He committed suicide in order not to fall into the hands of his enemies. But the sect he founded flourished and has much influence in the Deccan and in the south. The ascetic order among the Lingayats are known as the Jangamas, 'the vagrants'. Basava was an abolisher of caste, but the laymen among the Lingayats observe caste as a social necessity.

The Sittar Shaivas of the south profess a pure monotheism and their religious literature is comparable to that of the Hebrews in its passionate belief in the unity of God and in its hatred of idolatry. The hymns of the Sittars are attributed to ancient sages like Agastya, the fabled civiliser of South India, but are in reality later works of Tamil sages. Because of their monotheistic leanings and repudiation of the doctrine of metermpsychosis and of idolatry, it is even believed that the sect was founded through Muslim and Christian influence. Though this possibility cannot be entirely ruled out, we must remember that Hinduism is sufficiently rich in material to produce a sect of passionate monotheists without outside influence.

It is in the country south of the Vindhyas that Shaivism has shown itself at its best. Its great exponents like Sankara and Basava were from the South as well as its great bards like Manikka Vasagar. In North India, Shaivism is in a state of decay and has been superseded by Vaishnavism. Even the great city of Benares, reputed to be Shiva's own city, is slowly but surely coming under the influence of Vaishnavism. For this the Shaivas of northern India are themselves responsible. By their over-insistence on asceticism and self-mortifications, practical Shaivism is losing its hold on the enlightened members of the Hindu community. Shaivism in North India is now tending to be identified with the various sects of ascetics who wander about the country. The practices of some of these emphasize the need for torturing the flesh to elevate the soul. The Bahikathas for instance tear their bodies with knives and daggers. The Kanphatas slit the ears of their novices as the initiation ceremony. The Aghoris feed on carrion and excreta, and because of their predilection for burial places are even suspected of worse things. The Kapalikas use a human skull for a drinking bowl. The Akasamukhins go about looking at the sky without turning their faces, and the Urdhavabahus keep their hands always lifted up. There are various other sects of these ascetics who select forms of self-torture which appeal to them most without referring to texts or traditions, while nameless sects of Shaivas organize themselves into gangs and terrorize the countryside in the name of Shiva.

It is, however, unfair to judge Shaivism by these misguided enthusiasts. We have seen that Shaivism has produced, especially in the south, great saints and sages who compare favourably with not only the great personalities of India but of the world. Yet, because of its extreme intellectualism, it appeals less to human nature than Vaishnavism which is more appealing to the religious yearnings of common men. Of the two, Shaivism is more ancient and the great early literary works of the Hindus, such as the works of Kalidasa and Somadeva were dedicated to Shiva and his consort, who together with their son Ganesha were invoked by every ancient Hindu poet. But in religious poetry the Shaivas have not produced any work comparable to the Ramayana of Tulasidas, the Gita Govinda of Jayadeva or the inimitable Bhagavat Gita, all Vaishnava works enjoying universal respect.

There is very little rivalry between Vaishnavas and Shaivas at present except in South India where ancient sectarian quarrels are at times pursued with vigour.

SAKTAS

Saktas are the worshippers of Sakti (literally, energy). They believe that Sakti is essentially feminine and she is personified as an Almighty Woman, identical with the Supreme Being. The goddess exalted to this position is Devi, wife of Shiva. Although the Hindu ideal of a wife is of absolute submission to her husband, Devi, in her capacity of Sakti, is the object of adoration by Shiva himself who is often depicted as worshipping and supplicating her.

Sakti has many aspects of which two are important: that of the Divine Mother in which capacity her worship is comparable to the madonna-worship of the Roman Catholics, and that of the goddess of terror. While worship at home is generally confined to the Mother aspect, public and secret worship of Sakti is usually devoted to the terror aspect with its undesirable practices and rituals. Public worship of the goddess is at times connected with the shedding of blood, and at her altars flows the blood of victims sacrificed to quench her insatiable thirst. Secret worship of Sakti is connected with 'mysteries' the nature of which we shall describe presently.

Sakti is generally worshipped as Durga, Kali or Bhavani, forms the goddess is believed to have assumed for the destruction of certain demons. Of these forms Kali is the most popular, and the most terrible; she has her shrines in every part of India. The appearance of images of Kali is suggestive of the nature of the goddess. Kali is black, her mouth red with blood; she has tusks for teeth, is insufficiently clad, wears a garland of skulls, and dances in mad frenzy on the prostrate body of her husband. She is the goddess of epidemics, cataclysms and of all natural phenomena that strike terror or destroy life on a large scale. At present only animals and birds, mainly goats and cocks, are sacrificed at her altars. But there is sufficient indication in Sakta texts to show that human sacrifices were once common. Even now it is possible that at some obscure and remote shrine, Kali secretly claims her human victims.

Bengal and Assam are the strongholds of Saktism, and at Kalighat (Calcutta) is the most famous shrine of Kali. The temple at Kalighat is not very impressive, but the number of victims sacrificed and the flow of blood are. Sakti is also widely worshipped as Durga, a manifestation of the goddess, less terrible than Kali. She too delights in blood, though not to the extent Kali does. As Bhavani, she was the tutelary deity of the thugs, the notorious bandits who once infested the country.

Strange as it may seem, many of the great saints and philosophers of India were Saktas. Sankara had Sakta leanings and had composed some hymns in praise of the goddess. The great Ramakrishna Paramahamsa, the Bengali saint who lived in the 19th century, was a professed worshipper of Sakti. He used to say that Godhead can be conceived in no better way than as the Mother. Ramakrishna's well-known disciple Vivekananda was no less enamoured of Sakti; he even advocated the assiduous worship of the terror aspect of the goddess, and maintained that the terrors of nature were as much part of Godhead as pleasant phenomena, and was contemptuous of the weaklings who were frightened of blood and skulls.

The Saktas are mainly divided into two sects: The Dakshinamargis or the right hand worshippers, and the Vamamargis or the left hand worshippers. The Dakshinamargis do openly what they profess and constitute the majority of the Saktas, whereas the Vamamargis are a secret sect whose mysteries consist of rituals the exact nature of which is not known to any one except themselves. The Vamamargis strive to obtain salvation by means of the five M's. These are Madya (liquor), Matsya (fish), Mansa (flesh), Mudra (corn) and Maithuna (sexual union). One of the sacred rites of the Vamamargis is called Chakrapuja. For this form of worship an equal number of men and women secretly collect together at midnight in an appointed place. They sit in a circle and partake of the first four M's after which the congregation give themselves over to sexual union. As no religious ceremony is completely free from restraints and formalities, the participants in the Chakrapuja have also certain rules to observe. The congregation should not partake of the M's as an indulgence but as a duty and a sacrament. As a rule, sexual union is permitted only between husband and wife. If, for any reason, a man in Chakrapuja desires to have sexual relation with a woman other than his wife, she has to undergo a Tantric form of temporary marriage.

In another form of worship of the Vamamargis, a naked woman is enthroned on an altar and the congregation worships her as the goddess, the leader of the congregation performing certain ceremonies which emphasize the omnipotence of sex.

It should not, however, be imagined that the Vamamargis are mere debauchees. They have an apparently sound philosophy which attributes to sex all active principles in nature, and these are said to be worthy of adoration. In fact, outside the sanctuaries of worship the morality of the Vamamargis is considered excellent. They take so much pride in their beliefs and practices that they style themselves as Viras (heroes) and others as Pasus (beasts). To their credit must also be mentioned that they observe no caste and are more chivalrous to women than the other sects; in fact they advocate widow marriage and, years before the advent of the British, actively worked for the abolition of Sati.

The sacred texts of the Vamamargis are the Tantras. These are guarded books but enough is known about them to make their main characteristics public. The Tantras are based on the Kaula Upanishad (attached to the Vedas and hence the Vamamargis are also called Kaulas. Though thus admitting the authority of the Vedas, the Kaulas maintain that the Vedas are obsolete works not good enough for the Kaliyuga for which are the Tantras are the only reliable guide. The Tantras give in detail instructions for the sacrifice of various animals, birds, and of humans and describe the pleasure the deity derives from each. The blood of a tiger satisfies the goddess for 100 years and that of a man for 1,000 years. When the goddess feels thirsty she will not hesitate to send into the world epidemics and cataclysms by which means she will forcibly claim victims; to avoid this the devotees are instructed to keep a constant flow of blood at her altars.

Secrecy of worship and doctrine is especially enjoined by the Tantras. The open forms of worship of other Hindus are compared to harlots who give themselves up to all, and the secret Tantric form to a lady of noble birth who gives herself only to her husband. The following passages from the Tantras show the importance the sect attaches to secrecy:

"One should guard the Kaula system from the Pasus (uninitiated; beasts) just as one guards money and grain and clothes from thieves.

"One should conceal the Kaula system like the water in a cocoanut; one should be a Kaula internally, a Shaiva externally and a Vaishnava while talking at public meetings."

This duplicity is successfully practised by the Kaulas and it is impossible to ascertain their real strength.

Sakti, like Vishnu and Shiva, has more than a thousand names. Her manifestations are also many. There are eight Divine Mothers who are in some accounts said to be manifestations of Sakti, in others as subordinate to her. Like many other Hindu conceptions, this idea is also given to confusion; for some texts mention seven Divine Mothers, some nine, some sixteen and some fifty-two. The wives of most of the gods of the Hindu pantheon are also considered manifestations or forms of Sakti and are worshipped by Saktas.

GANAPATYAS

The Ganapatyas are those who worship Ganesha as the Supreme Being. Ganesha is the god of sagacity and prudence. He is a pot-bellied, elephant-headed deity with short legs and a small body, very jovial, always fond of a good feed and never liking any kind of physical exertion.

The Ganapatyas are few in number, and there is very little that is peculiar to them.

SAURAPATHAS

The Saurapathas are still less important. Solar cults were once popular in India, but at present those who worship the sun as the Supreme Being are few. He is, however, worshipped as a minor deity by all Hindus and the Sandhyas (morning and evening prayers of the Hindus) are addressed to him. The celebrated 'Gayatri,' believed to possess miraculous powers, is a solar incantation. The text of the Gayatri is: "This new and excellent praise of thee, O splendid playful sun is offered by us to thee. Be gratified by this my speech; approach this craving mind as a fond man seeks a woman. May that sun (Pushan) who contemplates, and looks into, all worlds be our protector. Let us meditate on the adorable light of the Divine Ruler. May it guide our intellects. Desirous of food, we solicit the gift of the splendid sun (Savitri) with oblations and praise." This incantation was revealed to the sage Vishwamitra, and by its power this sage is said to have created a world of his own. The Gayatri is repeated by all sects, but it is a secret prayer which is not to be uttered in other people's hearing. The proper way of repeating it is by one's selecting a lonely place or a room, sitting crosslegged with the eyes closed, and keeping count of the number of times repeated by means of a rosary held under cover of a cloth.

SMARTHAS

The Smarthas are broad-minded sectarians who believe in all the deities and worship whichever they like. They are more numerous than the Ganapatyas and the Saurapathas, but their influence as a sect is not very considerable.

WORSHIP AT HOME AND IN THE TEMPLE

For purposes of worship the Hindu has three principal deities. The first is the Gramadevata (the god of the village or town), the next the Kuladevata (the tutelary deity of his family) and the third, Ishtadevata (personal deity). Of these the first two are fixed for him by birth, and the third he selects for himself from the many deities of the pantheon. Thus a man may have Kali for his Gramadevata, Ganesha for his Kuladevata and the bull Nandi for his Ishtadevata. In rare cases all the three may resolve into one by coincidence.

Worship of the Gramadevata is generally performed in the temple of the village or the town in which the person resides. The pious Hindu goes daily to the temple, after his morning bath, where he adores the deity by muttering prayers or offering flowers or fruits. Once or twice a year a festival is held in honour of the Gramadevata in which all the villagers take part. There are the usual pageants and processions, dances, music and all the noise and hubbub common to a religious festival. The grandeur of the festival depends on the ability of the villagers to spend and the wealth of the temple trustees, some small villages not being able to pay for the services of one elephant, some towns taking out processions of silver cars attended by fifty or sixty elephants complete with gold and silver trappings.

Every Hindu family of consequence especially in villages has a shrine in the compound dedicated to the

Kuladevata. Here the deity is daily worshipped by the members of the family. Those who can afford to pay a priest, maintain a Brahmin priest for the daily services of the god. City dwellers of poor means who, for obvious reasons, cannot construct a shrine for their tutelary deities, keep them locked up in boxes and take them out when they are to be worshipped. Some have niches in their rooms for the Kuladevata.

The worship of the Ishtadevata is an entirely personal affair. The Ishtadevata is almost always worshipped in private. Heads of well-to-do families manage to install an image of their Ishtadevatas in private rooms the keys of which they always keep to themselves. Others who cannot afford this, wear an image of the Ishtadevata about their persons or keep a miniature idol of the Devata in a metal box which they are careful to have about them wherever they go.

In addition to the three mentioned above, an orthodox Hindu is expected to worship many other deities. It is good to worship Durga during Durga Puja, Ganesha on Ganesha Chaturthi, Krishna on Janmashtami, Lakshmi on Divali, Shiva on Shivarati, and so on. The cow is sacred to all sects and may be worshipped daily, and the manes of departed ancestors yearly. A pious Brahmin should not fail to perform the Sandhyas, morning and evening prayers, said by the side of a tank or river, the principal deity of worship being the sun.

The Hindus attach great importance to forms, incantations and rituals, and a mispronounced word or an act of omission is feared to lead the worshipper to perdition instead of to salvation. Hence ceremonial worship is an elaborate but precise affair. Those who are not well instructed in the ritual always requisition the help of a priest when performing an important Puja, though minor acts of worship are performed by householders conversant with the details of the rites. Professional priests minister to the needs of the idols of the temples and the worship consists mainly of bathing, clothing, feeding the idols and singing and dancing to them. The idols are believed to have needs like men and women, and to suffer like humans when maltreated. The famous idol of Jagannath at Puri, for instance, catches a cold every time it is washed ceremoniously in public, and remains in the sick chamber for fourteen days after the bath.

Householders engage priests, on payment of fees, to perform ceremonial worship in their houses as thanksgiving for favours received from the gods. These ceremonies vary in details, the image of the particular god whom the worshipper wishes to honour being given prominent place in the worship. To give the reader some idea of the nature of these ceremonies, I describe below the Panchayatana ceremony in which the five great sectarian gods are worshipped together, one of them being given the important place. In this ceremony, instead of images, five stones representing the five deities are used. The Salagrama (black stone) represents Vishnu; a white stone represents Shiva; a red stone Ganesha; a stone of vague combination of hues Sakti; and a crystal Sun. The five stones are arranged on a circular metal disc, the stone representing the deity to whom the worshipper wishes to pay special homage being given the central position. Within reach of the worshipper are kept a water vessel called Abhisheka-patra, a conch shell and a small handbell, all objects used for worship and at the same time worthy of worship. A plate containing Tulsi leaves (sacred to Vishnu), Bilva leaves (sacred to Shiva), perfumes, flowers and fruits is also placed on the right side of the officiating priest.

Before commencement of the regular ceremony, the worshipper performs the preliminary rite of Achman, common to all Hindu forms of ceremonial worship. This consists of sipping and swallowing water two or three times during which the twenty-four names of Vishnu are repeated. The worshipper is now clean for the ceremony. He pays homage to the water vessel, to the conch and to the bell; the bell is thus addressed: "O bell, make a sound for the approach of the gods, and for the departure of the demons. Homage to the goddess Ghanta (bell). I offer perfumes, grains of rice, and flowers, in token of rendering all due homage to the bell."*

The regular ceremony now begins. It has sixteen stages: (1) Avahana (invocation); (2) Asana (offering of a seat for the gods to sit down); (3) Padya (offering of water for washing the feet); (4) Arghya (offering of rice, etc.); (5) Achamaniya (offering of water for sipping); (6) Snana (offering of milk and honey for the gods to bathe in); (7) Vastra (offering of clothes represented by Tulsi leaves); (8) Upavastra (offering of upper garments and ornaments, represented by more Tulsi leaves); (9) Gandha or Chandana, (offering of perfumes and sandal paste); (10) Pushpa (offering of flowers); (11) Dhupa (offering of incense); (12) Dipa (illumination); (13) Nivedya, (offering of food); (14) Pradikshana (reverential circumambulation); (15) Mantrapushpa (offering flowers with recitation of texts); and (16) Namaskara (final adoration).

During each act, the worshipper repeats one of the sixteen verses of the Purusha hymn of the Rig Veda. The ceremony is concluded by the following prayer: "Veneration to the Infinite and Eternal Male (Purusha) who has thousands of names, thousands of forms, thousands of feet, thousands of eyes, thousands of heads, thousands of thighs, thousands of arms, and who lives for ten million ages.

"O great god, pardon my want of knowledge of the right way of worshipping thee. Sin, misery and poverty are removed; happiness and purity are obtained by thy presence. O great god: I commit thousands of faults every day and night; forgive me as I am thy servant. There is no other protection but from thee; thou only art my refuge; guard me therefore, and defend me by thy mercy; pardon my mistakes and defects in syllables, words, and measures; O mighty lord, be propitiated. I offer flowers with prayers. Let the five gods, of whom great Vishnu is the first† be pleased with the worship I have made. Let all this

---
* M. Williams, *Religious Thought and Life of the Hindus.*
† If the worshipper wishes to give the place of honour to other gods, one of these is addressed as the first.

be offered to the Supreme Being. I offer thee with my mouth, O Vishnu, the sacred salutation Vashat. Be pleased, O Sipivishta, with my oblations; let my songs of praise exalt thee; protect us ever with thy blessings."*

This is the form of Puja performed generally in the Mahratha country. The ceremony performed elsewhere differs very little from this except in the substitution of the appropriate image or images for the five stones.

For a pious Hindu, every day has some religious significance and the whole day and night can be turned into a round of religious duties. The number of deities to be worshipped are numerous; every day is under the influence of some planet which may be propitiated and the reading of sacred texts is always recommended. Great value is attached to the mechanical repetition of the names of Vishnu or Shiva, or of the mystic monosyllable AUM, representing the deity. In the evenings, children are made to repeat aloud the names of Rama, Hari (Vishnu), Hara (Shiva) or Govinda (Krishna), and a Hindu village at sunset resounds with Nama-japa (repetition of names). Elderly people repeat them in a lower tone, usually keeping count by means of rosaries. But they read the sacred texts aloud.

RELIGIOUS INSTRUCTION

It may appear strange how a religion with no central organisation manages to keep its members instructed in its main principles and doctrines. The fact is, tradition and usage have evolved an efficient system of religious instruction among the Hindus from which the followers of other religions have much to learn. A young average Hindu boy of any of the three higher castes, even if he is illiterate, will be found to know more about his religion than an 'educated' Christian boy of Europe knows of Christianity. The main reason for this is that religion for the Hindu is so wedded to daily life that the two are inseparable. The literature, entertainments, music, folklore and even street songs of the Hindus are permeated with religious ideas and the child learns with his mother-tongue the names of his gods and the stories of their doings. Hindu sacred literature is so rich in material that for stories interesting to children (such as Jack the Giant Killer or Alice in Wonderland, so dear to the children of the West) Hindu parents need not go out of their sacred texts. The heroic doings of the Pandava princes, of Rama and Lakshmana, and the follies and wickedness of their enemies are all of absorbing interest to children and the Hindu child is never tired of hearing from his parents or nurses the stories of the heroes of his religion; his Western brother, on the other hand, gets bored with his Sunday classes.

For adults religious instruction is no less interesting. The temple, as a rule, is not only the centre of religious life, but also of the social life of the community. Very often, drama, pantomime dances, etc., are organized, the subjects of which are invariably drawn from some incidents in the epics. Occasionally, a Pundit well versed in the epics and the Puranas is invited by some rich individual for the purposes of Katha (story telling). The Katha is one of the most pleasant methods of religious instruction. It is generally held in summer, on a moonlight night, in an open ground. The whole village or town flock to the place, all the audience, men and women, squatting on the ground. The Pundit, an expert in the line, reads some interesting incident from the epics or the Puranas in a sweet and melodious tone and explains the subject with appropriate gestures and interesting adornment of language. The atmosphere is so well suited to the occasion that a good Pundit seldom finds any difficulty in carrying the audience with him, making them sigh, weep or laugh, or in working up their emotions to a pitch of religious frenzy.

It should not, however, be imagined that Hinduism is a religion utterly without any organisation. The temples which are still very wealthy afford a sanctuary for those who devote themselves to religious study and practices. There are certain well-known centres of learning such as Benares in the North and Sringeri in the South where learned men meet and discuss points of law and doctrine. Every scholar, philosopher and reformer who wishes to make his ideas widely known, takes pains to visit these centres, especially Benares where he gets ample opportunities of discussing religion with the best brains among the Hindus.

Among the Hindus there are a good many professional philosophers and scholars, who make it their duty to visit places of learning and pilgrimage. These men easily spread all over India the doctrines preached at one place, and are links that connect the different centres of learning. As the supreme head of orthodox Hinduism there is a Sankaracharya (an office called after the great philosopher of that name) who may be consulted on points of law and doctrine, and whose decision in disputes, though not necessarily infallible, is accepted as the last word on the subject. Originally the see was established in Benares, but now other places have Sankaracharyas.

ANIMISM, SERPENT AND TREE WORSHIP, ANCESTOR WORSHIP, ETC.

Animism probably originated among the aborigines of India and was later incorporated by the Aryans into their religious system. In the earlier Vedas we find no trace of the Aryans having been animists. But the Puranic Pantheon has many animals in it, and Puranic literature advocates and encourages animism. The epics Ramayana and Mahabharata are particularly rich in animal, bird and reptile gods.

Of all the animals, the cow is the most sacred to the Hindu. In fact the cow is believed to be a personification of all the gods of the pantheon and of the centres of pilgrimage. Everything that comes out of the cow is sacred, including dung and urine. A dose of the mixture consisting of milk, curds, ghee (clarified butter), cowdung and urine is considered extremely purifying to the soul and to the body, and

---

* M. Williams, *Religious Thought and Life of the Hindus.*

the Hindus who act up to it are many. Cowdung cakes dried in the sun are used as firewood by the Hindus. In the streets of Hindu cities, pious men and women of the lower classes may be seen following cows, catching the urine of the cow in the cupped palm of their hands and sipping it. No pious Hindu will pass a cow without touching it with his hand and raising the hand so touched to his head, as an act of homage. Feeding the cow is of very great merit. Hence, in the early morning cows may be seen led into city streets by women who carry bundles of grass with them for the benefit of citizens who may buy the grass and give it to the cows. The cow and the grass belong to the same person who makes a living by the piety of the citizens, and manages to feed the cow free of charge.

The cow is held in great honour in heaven, and the highest heaven of Vishnu 'Goloka' is named after her. The cow and the Brahmin were created by Brahma on the same day, and are equally sacred. Hence the killing of a cow is a sin as heinous as Brahminicide. The cow is sacred to all sects and to the four castes, and beef-eating to the Hindu is something more horrible than cannibalism. This is one of the reasons why free social intercourse between Hindus and Europeans or Muslims is so difficult. Some of the Panchamas, however, eat beef, mainly carrion. Killing of cows in Indian states ruled by Hindu Rajas was strictly prohibited.

With all the sanctity of the cow, her mouth is unclean. This was caused by her telling a lie. It appears that the gods Brahma and Shiva had an argument between them and the cow was called as a witness of certain imaginary happenings which Brahma wished to prove. In cross examination by Shiva the cow was found telling deliberate lies, and Shiva cursed her mouth to become foul, while allowing her general sanctity and purity to remain.

The cow is particularly sacred to Vaishnavas because of the boyhood days of Krishna when he lived as a cowherd. The most beautiful idylls of the Hindus are of the lives of Krishna and his brother Balarama when they lived among the cowherds of Gokula tending their cattle and courting the milkmaids.

Shiva has the bull Nandi for his charger and hence the bull is also sacred to the Hindus.

Next in importance to the cow come the serpents. The worship of these dreaded reptiles is common to all Hindus, but South India and Bengal are the strongholds of serpent worship. In practically every important household in Kerala there is a serpent shrine where these reptiles live in numbers and are fed by the householder with milk and fruits. The most celebrated shrine is that of Meccad, a wealthy Nambudiri household in Malabar, where the present writer had seen venomous cobras playing with the children of the household. Cobras are easily tamed and it is very seldom that they hurt those who feed them.

The Hindus have a voluminous serpent lore. The king of the serpent gods is Ananta, the thousand-headed hydra, who forms a couch for Vishnu. Shiva adorns his person with a number of serpents; his sacred thread is a serpent, his girdle another and his hair is tied into a knot by means of a third. He has serpents for bangles and anklets. The majority of the great serpents of Hindu lore are not, however, found in the worlds above, but in Patala, the nether world. Serpents are fabled to possess the richest precious stones in all the worlds, and Bhogavati, the capital of the serpent kingdom, is said to be built mainly of precious stones, and is, hence, the richest city in the fourteen worlds.

In Bengal, Manasa is worshipped as the goddess of serpents. A legend says that a wealthy merchant named Chandsadagar objected to her worship and that, in a feud that lasted several years between the goddess and the merchant the latter was defeated and made to worship her. This is an indication that serpent worship was not recognized as an orthodox form in Bengal without a struggle. At present, however, Manasa is as popular as any other deity and Nagapanchami, a feast held in honour of serpents, is celebrated in Bengal with more pomp than in other parts of India.

The worship of Hanuman, the monkey god, is popular among Vaishnavas. Hanuman was the chief monkey who helped Rama to regain Sita from the demon Ravana, and his loyalty to his master has become a byword among the Hindus. In pictures and statues of Sita and Rama, Hanuman is invariably represented as sitting dutifully at their feet, ready to perform his master's command. Some temples are exclusively dedicated to him. Because of his heroism and marvellous deeds in the battle of Lanka, Hanuman is considered the personification of physical strength, and Hindus, desirous of developing their muscles, usually worship Hanuman. In memory of the tribe of monkeys who helped Rama in the war with Ravana, all monkeys are held sacred by the Hindus.

Garuda, a mythical combination of eagle and man, is fabled to be the charger of Vishnu, and hence kites and eagles are considered worthy of adoration. The peacock is the charger of the goddess Sarasvati, the goose of Brahma, the rat of Ganesha, the lion of Durga, the buffalo of Yama, the elephant of Indra, and hence all these creatures are sacred to the Hindu and Advaita, the pantheistic philosophy of the Hinus justifies the worship of anything.

Of trees, the Banyan and the Pipal (Indian fig tree) are sacred to Vishnu and the Bila to Shiva. Of plants, the most sacred is the Tulsi, believed to be an incarnation of the wife of Vishnu, and every pious Vaishnava takes care to plant and water a Tulsi plant in his compound. The daily circumambulation of the plant is a meritorious act of worship and its leaves are believed to be capable of purifynig the soul and the body. The plant being an incarnation of Lakshmi, its marriage is performed every year with an idol of Vishnu. More popular is the marriage of the Tulsi plant with the Salagrama, the sacred ammonite found on the bed of the Ghantaki and believed to be Vishnu himself.

Plant worship is traced to the Vedas. The Soma plant, which yielded an intoxicating juice, was an important deity of the Vedic pantheon, and many hymns of the Rig Veda are addressed to the plant and its juice. The identity of this plant is lost and the present day Hindus have no idea what actually this celebrated plant was.

Of grass, the Durva (Agrostis liearis) and the Kusa (Poa cynosuroides) are sacred, and used in ceremonial and worship.

The Hindus also worship the spirit of their departed ancestors and the Shraddhas, annual rites performed in honour of the manes, form an important part of Hindu rituals.

WORSHIP OF EVIL SPIRITS

The deities above referred to are worshipped mainly by the three higher castes and the better class of Sudras. But the Panchamas and a good many Sudras worship aboriginal fetishes many of which cannot be found in the regular religious literature of the Hindus. Some of their objects of worship are incorporated in Hinduism as manifestation of some recognized deity of the Hindu pantheon, and local legends have been invented to lend support to these myths; but the majority of the fetishes of the aborigines form a class by themselves and have little to do with the Hindu pantheon except probably as forming part of the copious demonology of the Hindus. In the Ramayana, the powers of evil are mainly mentioned as Rakshasas and Asuras who delight in the destruction of humans and drinking of their blood. The chief of the Rakshasas was Ravana, the ten-headed emperor of Lanka, a mighty demon who commanded legions of spirits of all descriptions and enslaved the gods themselves. Ravana's relatives and generals, and his sister, Surpanakha, a mighty monstress of huge proportions, devastated the forests of South India, striking terror into the hearts of men and animals, and the chief concern of Rama, the incarnation of Vishnu, was to rid the world of these monsters. In the Mahabharata they are mentioned as less powerful, but their depredations were serious enough to draw the attention of the five princes, the heroes of this epic. These demons were not averse to have sexual relations with humans. Ravana's sister fell madly in love with Rama and his brother Lakshmana, and Ravana abducted Sita, Rama's wife. Bhima, one of the Pandava princes, married a demoness named Hidimbi and a mighty son was born of the union. Some of these demons are said to have attained invincible power by religious austerities and by boons granted by the gods themselves.

A different class of imps are the army of uncouth and devilish spirits that follow Shiva in his midnight wanderings in cremation grounds and wild places. This god often delights in horrible dances with these goblins and in his wrathful moods lets them loose on his enemies. Many Asuras and Rakshasas and even gods who were rash enough to offend the god of destruction, have suffered many things at their hands. These devils and the Rakshasas are described as powerful beings varying in form and shape. Some are dark, others fair and luminous; some are uncouth and deformed, others very beautiful; some are of huge build looking like hills from a distance, others as small as one's thumb, some have mouths like caves, others teeth like tusks; some malevolent, others beneficent.

It is not, however, demons of the above category that are most dreaded by the generality of Hindus, but spirits of departed men and women who for some reason or other, are feared to be wandering in the world haunting the living. Monier Williams classifies them into three: Bhuta, Preta, and Pisacha. "A Bhuta, they say, is a spirit emanating from a man who had died a violent death either by accident, suicide or capital punishment, and has not had proper funeral ceremonies performed afterwards.

"A Preta is the spirit of a deformed or crippled person, or of one defective in some limb or organ, or of a child that dies prematurely, owing to the omission of ceremonies during the formation of the embryo. It is not necessarily wicked or malicious towards living men.

"A Pisacha is a demon created by a man's vices. It is the ghost of a liar, drunkard, adulterer or criminal of any kind, or of one who has died insane."*

This classification is not, however, very rigid, and the name of one kind of evil spirit is freely used for another. In each district and province of India there are devils of indigenous origin with definite characteristics. Among the common folk of Malabar, for instance, women who die in their pregnancy are feared to assume an uncouth shape called Potti and trouble children, while a lordly devil called Thendan walks about the village lanes with a cudgel in his hand laying low any man who happens to come in his way.

Places where men have suffered violent deaths are dreaded and avoided by the Hindus. Evil spirits are believed to be oversexed and young women and men are feared to receive special attention, the former from male spirits and the latter from females. Hence Hindu mothers take care to adorn their marriageable daughters and sons with lockets and charms. There are peculiar ways by which demons get into human bodies. A yawn may give a chance to a spirit to enter the person by the mouth, and a sneeze through the nose. The sexual orifices are also used as entrances. In fact all the Navadvaras (the nine orifices of the body) are means by which these spirits may enter the body and possess a person and every Hindu who fears demons takes care to keep them constantly clean. The Yakshas and Yakshis, a kind of imps created as such by Brahma, are believed to be capable of assuming human forms and having relations with men and women in a more direct way.

I have mentioned only a few of the evil spirits of Hindu demonology. The Gonds, the Bhils and other well-known hill tribes of India have, for instance, tribal deities which have no place in the regular Hindu pantheon. The worship of an imp named Kuttichathan is very common among the lower orders in Malabar and even among the Nayars, and of a hill godling named Shashtav among the hill tribes of Travancore and Cochin. Shashtav is recognized as a

---

* *Religious Thought and Life in India.*

51 RAMA, THE SEVENTH INCARNATION OF VISHNU, DESTROYING HIS ENEMY RAVANA

52 KRISHNA, EIGHTH INCARNATION OF VISHNU

(Maurice's *Hindustan*)

XXII

54 KALKI, TENTH INCARNATION OF VISHNU, YET TO COME

53 BUDDHA, NINTH INCARNATION OF VISHNU

(Maurice's *Hindustan*)

XXIII

WORSHIPPING THE BANYAN TREE
(Forbe's *Oriental Memoirs*)

XXIV

56 PAINTINGS ON TEMPLE WALLS, MADURAI
(Photo: R. Purniah)

57 GANGOTRI, THE SACRED SOURCE OF THE GANGES
(White's *Views of the Himalaya Mountains*)

XXV

58 IMAGE OF BALKRISHNA (THE BABY KRISHNA)
(India Pictorial Features)

59 SERPENT SYMBOLS UNDER A SACRED TREE, TRIVANDRUM
(Photo: S. S. Aiyar)

XXVI

60 DHANURASANA: A YOGIC POSTURE
(India Pictorial Features)

61 PADMASANA: A YOGIC POSTURE
(India Pictorial Features)

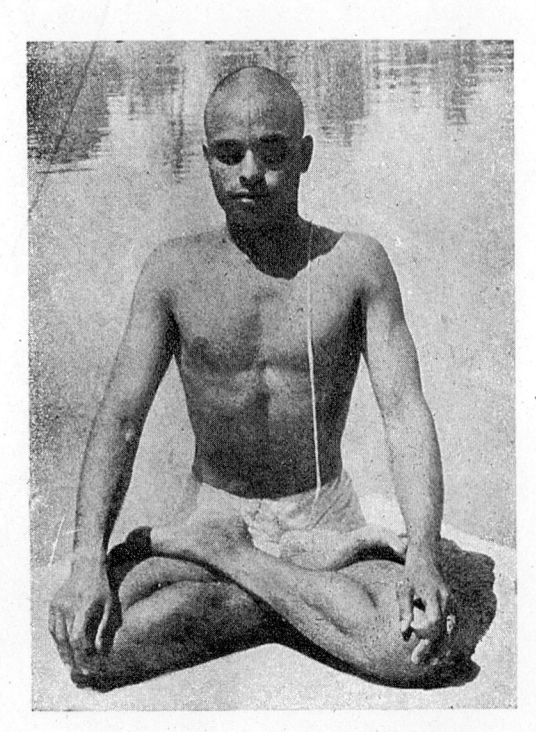

62 PADMASANA: A YOGIC POSTURE
(India Pictorial Features)

XXVII

63 SARVANGASANA:
A YOGIC POSTURE
(India Pictorial Features)

64 BHAGIRATHASANA
A YOGIC POSTURE
(India Pictorial Features)

65 YOUNG GIRL STUDYING A YOGIC POSE
(India Pictorial Features)

XXVIII

66 MAYURASANA: A YOGIC POSTURE
(India Pictorial Features)

67 GOMUKHASANA, A YOGIC POSTURE
(India Pictorial Features)

68 VRISCHIKASANA: A YOGIC POSTURE
(India Pictorial Features)

manifestation of Shiva but Kuttichathan is an independent devil.

The religion of the lower orders is mainly inspired by fear. Sickness, death, bad crops, floods whirlwinds, in fact all phenomena adverse to men are supposed to be caused by evil spirits. Possession by these is commonly believed in and diseases such as epilepsy, madness, etc., are solely attributed to the activities of evil spirits. Hence a Hindu villager, when any one in the family falls sick, first consults the village medicine man, astrologer or necromancer, and only when these fail to cure or kill the patient does he seek the aid of a medical practitioner. Similarly, when a villager wishes to harm his neighbour, he generally consults a necromancer who, on payment of certain fees, undertakes to let loose some devil on the adversary.

The favourite form of public worship among the very lowest is in organizing a drinking party in which the person who performs the priestly office works himself up into a pitch of frenzy under the influence of liquor and the mad beating of drums. He poses himself as possessed of the spirit of the tribe and orders certain things for the supposed benefit of the tribe. Some rebellious individuals, however, take the liberty of questioning the wisdom of the oracle and the congregation usually disperse after a free fight. The Sudras and the better classes of Panchamas are less boisterous and disorderly in their public worship. Although much argument and at times violence take place when they meet for religious or social functions, very often their religious rites terminate peacefully. The lower classes always prefer the night for public worship, and the singing, dancing, the beating of drums that begin at sunset do not cease till sunrise.

PILGRIMAGES

For the Hindus, visiting of holy places is an act of great religious merit. Throughout India there are centres of pilgrimage, some of them very holy, others less so.

The most sacred city of the Hindus is Benares, on the bank of the Ganges, called Kasi (the resplendent). The antiquity of the city dates back to the palmy days of Shaivism; for it is a city sacred to Shiva who is believed to have made it his permanent abode. When Shaivism reached the zenith of its glory, the city became the leading centre of Hindu culture and learning, a position it has retained to the present day. With the rise of other sects Benares lost none of its sanctity or fame; on the other hand, these sects tried to emulate the Shaivas in their attachment to the city by building temples in it sacred to their gods and founding centres of learning to diffuse a knowledge of their beliefs.

A Christian can have no idea of the feelings of a Hindu pilgrim on beholding Benares. Every inch of ground, the grass that grows in the city, the pebbles and dust of the roads, the wells and tanks, and above all the waters of the Ganges that flow past it, are so sacred as to remove all sins and traces of sins from a Hindu. Every pious Hindu wishes to die in Benares, especially in the magic circle called Panchakosi, a radius of about ten miles from the centre of the city. Even the most abandoned criminal of any caste or creed is said to go straight to heaven if he happens to die in this hallowed spot. Hindus, in their old age, flock to Benares from all over India for the pleasure of dying in the holy city. Every orthodox Hindu of every sect considers it his duty to visit Benares as many times as he can, and wash in the Ganges near the city. Hence the number of pilgrims that come into and go out of the city forms a floating population as big as the permanent population of the city.

The number of temples in Benares is computed to be over two thousand, and idols half a million. Most of the temples are dedicated to Shiva and the members of his family; Vaishnava temples are also becoming numerous. In addition to these temples, there are countless minor shrines each with its own legends of sanctity.

Though temples are numerous in Benares, there is none to match the majestic temples of South India in size or in architectural beauty. The early Muslims had been particularly harsh on Benares. Though they succeeded in destroying the structures in stone and mortar, and left in the city no temple of antiquity, they could not conquer the spirit of Hinduism that centres round the holy city. The chief of the existing temples in Benares is the 'golden temple' dedicated to Shiva. A place most sacred to the Shaiva is the Jnana-vapi, the well of knowledge, in which Shiva is believed to have taken refuge when the temples were destroyed. Pilgrims flock round the well and throw flowers into it which, decaying, cause the water to emit a foul stench. But its sanctity loses nothing by this, and a Brahmin is permanently employed in drawing the water of the well and distributing it to the pilgrims, who store it in bottles and take to their distant homes. The Manikarnika well (the jewel of the ear) not far off, is still more sacred. It is so called because the ear-ring of Shiva is once believed to have fallen into it. A bath in the waters of the Manikarnika is supposed to clean body and soul.

Benares typically represents Hinduism in all phases. Alongside centres of culture, in which abstract forms of thought are almost scientifically analysed, there exist gross superstitions and fetishes. The eagerness of the pilgrims to court death in this city, its vast burning Ghats clouded with smoke, the stench of burning bodies and eternal round of funeral ceremonies makes it appear one of the saddest cities in the world.

Benares is the seat of the modern Hindu University founded by Mrs. Besant to diffuse Hindu knowledge and ideals.

Though not enjoying the fame of Benares, Mathura is an important city sacred to the Vaishnavas. This city on the Jumna is honoured as the birth place of Krishna. The river and the fields on its banks are believed to have been scenes of his activities when he tended the cattle of the cowherds of Gokula. Vrindavan, the groves where he danced with the Gopis (milkmaids) on moonlight nights of the beautiful Indian spring, the Kadamba forests where, wounded by the arrows of Kama, he sent messages of burning love to his beloved Radha and while waiting for her arrival, whiled away his grief by playing love tunes on his flute, are pointed out to the pilgrim by the priests of Mathura. On Janmashtami and Holi festivals, pilgrims from all parts of India flock to Mathura, and festivals and religious dances in honour of Krishna are organized. The pious maintain that pilgrims with sufficient spiritual vision can even now see, during the Holi festival of spring, visions of Krishna dancing with the Gopis in the fields of Vrindavan on clear moonlight nights, and listen to the music of his distant flute!

Mathura and its atmosphere are in direct contrast to Benares. Mathura represents the religion of the living, while Benares emphasizes the permanence of death.

Dwarka, in Kathiawar, is another important shrine sacred to the Vaishnavas. It was the capital of Krishna's kingdom. The original Dwarka is believed to have been lost in the ocean on the death of Krishna. The present centre of pilgrimage is said to be very near the site of the original city.

The temple of Jagannath in Orissa is a celebrated shrine which attracts pilgrims from all over India. The temple, a vast meandering structure built on the seashore, overlooks the Bay of Bengal and during the feast of Jagannath, the whole area is a sea of humanity. In medieval times the influx of pilgrims to this shrine was so great that, prior to the occupation of the province by the British, no organisation could cope with the large mass of humanity that floated towards the shrine, and thousands of pilgrims used to perish on the way and at Jagannath for want of food and shelter and through overcrowding. But this had no deterrent effect on the pilgrims; because it was considered a blessing to die within sight of Jagannath and pilgrims often courted death by throwing themselves in front of Jagannath's car when the image was taken in procession.

Jagannath is considered a manifestation of Krishna and the idol is somewhat peculiar. Together with Jagannath, the idols of Balarama, Krishna's elder brother, and of Subhadra, his sister, are worshipped. During the feast of Jagannath, caste is temporarily dispensed with, and all pilgrims from the highest Brahmin to the lowest pariah have to partake of food cooked by low caste men at the shrine. Nor are people allowed to fast at the temple of Jagannath.

Orissa was a stronghold of Buddhism and the temple of Jagannath is believed to be a Buddhist shrine converted into a Hindu temple when that religion lost its hold on India. There are many practices at the temple and legends connected with the image that lend support to this view.

Rameshwaram, at the extreme south of India, is a centre of pilgrimage sacred to the Shaiva and Vaishnava alike. It is at this point that Rama is believed to have launched his epic attack on Lanka, the island of Ceylon. After the conquest of Lanka he is believed to have landed at Rameshwaram with his wife Sita. The magnificent temple at Rameshwaram is dedicated to Shiva, and Sita herself is fabled to have made the Lingam it enshrines. A legend says that Rama, to purify himself of the sin committed in slaughtering the soldiers of Ravana, wished to worship a Lingam. For this purpose he sent the monkey god Hanuman to Benares to bring a Lingam from this city. But the emissary was delayed on the journey and, Rama being in a hurry, Sita made for him, out of the sand of the seashore, a Lingam which the hero consecrated and worshipped.

Of all pilgrimages, the double one of visiting Benares first and washing in the Ganges, and then proceeding by foot to Rameshwaram and bathing in the sea at this sacred spot is considered the most meritorious. The distance from Benares to Rameshwaram is about twelve hundred miles and there is a regular flow of pilgrims from Benares to Rameshwaram. Travelling by train or by any other conveyance decreases the virtue of the pilgrimage and the more devout of the pilgrims cover the distance on foot.

Gaya on the Ganges, once a stronghold of Buddhism, is at present a centre of pilgrimage for the Hindus. Ceremonies connected with death are considered of particular merit when performed at Gaya and it is mainly for this purpose that Hindus visit the city at present.

The river Ganges from its very source is a holy stream and its waters are said to be capable of washing away all sins. Even bones and ashes of dead persons, when thrown into the river, are capable of sending straight to heaven the persons whose remains they are. One of the Puranas says that the bone of a dead dog which a crow, while carrying across the river, happened to drop in the water caused the dog to be transported to heaven as a resplendent god. When fables like these are current among the people and are believed in as revealed truth, the anxiety of every devoted son to throw the ashes of his parents into the river can very well be imagined. The priests at Gaya and Benares thrive mainly on the fees collected from pilgrims who bring the bones of their parents to be thrown into the river, for which certain preliminary ceremonies are essential.

The Ramayana gives a vivid description of the origin and sanctity of the river. Formerly, so says the Ramayana, the river flowed only in heaven. A famous king, Sagara, who happened to lose his sixty thousand sons in the nether regions through the ire of a sage named Kapila, wished to bring down the river from heaven to the nether regions through the medium of the earth as the waters of the Ganges alone (so goes the story), could revive his dead sons. Sagara could not succeed in the attempt, nor could his surviving son Anusuman; it was given to Bhagiratha, grandson of Anusuman, to achieve the object. After many labours Bhagiratha succeeded in bringing the heavenly Ganges to earth, himself riding on a quick-footed steed leading the great river to its destination. It is at the island of Sagar, at the mouth of the river, that the Ganges is believed to enter the nether regions. Hence this island is a centre of pilgrimage and the sage Kapila is worshipped here.

All points of the Ganges are not equally sacred. We have mentioned Benares, Gaya and Sagar where the waters of the river are considered especially sanctified. The confluence of the Ganges and the

Jumna at Prayag, is an important centre of pilgrimage, and the Kumbhamela held once in twelve years on the bed of the river is attended by thousands of pilgrims from all over India. Haridwar, where the river leaves the hills and enters the plains of Hindustan, is also an important centre of pilgrimage; the natural scenery here is exceptionally beautiful and many of the wandering pilgrims of India make this place their summer headquarters.

All waters in the world are mystically traced to the Ganges, the supposed mother of all Indian streams. Many orthodox Hindus would drink no water except that of the Ganges. Those who happen to live far away from the river, get the water by a regular supply service.

Hinduism caters to all tastes. Those pilgrims who wish to contemplate the greatness of God in quiet places, far from the madding crowd, can do so in certain centres of pilgrimage established for the purpose. Badrinath and Kedarnath in the heart of the Himalayas are two such centres, which only dauntless spirits dared to visit. The journey was fraught with many risks as the pilgrims had to pass through wild forests, ravines, and snow covered peaks. The cave of Amarnath, about forty miles away from Srinagar in Kashmir, up in the Himalayas, is another lonely place of Hindu pilgrimage.

In addition to these centres of all India fame and interest, there are holy places and temples which have but a provincial importance. The temple of Meenakshi (wife of Shiva) in Madura is visited by pilgrims from all over South India. The temples of Chidambaram and Tanjore are of peculiar interest to Shaivas of the South, and those of Conjeevaram and Srirangam to Vaishnavas. The river Kaveri is considered very sacred by South Indian Hindus and there are holy places on its banks visited by pilgrims from all over South India. Pandharpur is an important Vaishnava shrine among Mahrathas, and the presiding deity Vithoba is believed to be a manifestation of Vishnu. Khandoba of Jejury, on the other hand, is a manifestation of Shiva and is the tutelary deity of the Mahrathas. Nasik on the Godavary holds the same place among the Mahrathas as Gaya among North Indian Hindus, as a centre of funeral rites.

THE DOCTRINE OF METEMPSYCHOSIS

The object of all worship and pilgrimage is salvation. But the Hindu idea of salvation is different from that of the Christian. The Hindus call ultimate salvation Mukti or liberation. Birth in any form whatever is considered by certain Hindu philosophers as undesirable, and every one is exhorted to achieve by means of religion, liberation from the tiresome cycle of births the soul is ordinarily subjected to. The notions of the nature of liberated soul vary; but the need for getting rid of births is recognized by almost all.

The Hindus do not believe that one life is all that is allotted to an individual in this world. On the death of a person, the soul leaves the body and, after some time, takes birth in another form according to the actions of the person. For instance, an adulterous woman may get reborn as a jackal, and a fornicator as a donkey. A pious person, on the other hand, may be reborn as a king. The codes give detailed accounts of all sins and their effects in rebirth; some of these are so elaborate and minute that by looking at a man a really learned person can say exactly what sin he had committed in the previous birth. Only the most holy persons get Mukti on their death, and the vast majority of living beings are reborn to reap the fruits of their actions. It is not however necessary for a person to be reborn in this world. He may take birth in any of the fourteen worlds even as a god, a demon or a Naga. The gods too, as we have mentioned in the first chapter, have their allotted span of life and strive after Mukti; so do the demons. Birth and death are usually referred to by the Hindus as the soul's changing of garments.

The dogma of transmigration, now generally believed in by Hindus, has no Vedic background. The Vedic idea of after-life was of a place of bliss for the virtuous and annihilation for the wicked. When the doctrine of transmigration began to gain ground among the Hindus, the learned found much difficulty in reconciling the Vedic conception with the new theory. A compromise was, however, effected by which a soul, on its departure from the body was made to appear before Yama, the god of death, where it was judged and, after a brief period of stay in heaven or hell, was left to be reborn.

As the belief stands at present, the departed soul appears in Yamapuri, the court of Yama, where Chitragupta, the record keeper of Yama, reads out an account of all the deeds the person had done in his life. The soul is given a chance to explain its misconduct and, on hearing this, the god of death pronounces judgment. If the soul is condemned, Yama's minions take him for torture into one of the several hells maintained for the purpose. The Hindu hell is not a place of endless suffering. It is something of a purgatory and the soul, after its allotted term of punishment, is taken to one of the heavens for enjoying the reward of good deeds done during its life on earth. Nor is the bliss of heaven endless, for the soul, after its term in heaven, gets reborn in one of the worlds to continue its long and weary pilgrimage towards Mukti.

The practical effect of the doctrine of metempsychosis is that the belief has made the Hindus fatalists. All one's troubles, even preventible ones, are attributed to the actions done in a previous life from the result of which there is no escape; because of this attitude towards life, the Hindus have developed a philosophy of patience towards suffering, and some of them would rather put up with any kind of trouble than exert themselves to overcome it. Another result of belief in transmigration is the somewhat callous attitude towards human misery. The misery of man is traced to his own misdeeds in a previous existence and hence he deserves neither sympathy nor pity. If anybody does him anything by way of charity or help, it is because of his intention of improving his own chances in the next life and not because of his sound human sympathies. The attitude of the Hindu towards misery is that of the ancient Jew who asked Christ pointing a blind man to him, "who sinned, Lord, this man or his father?"; nay the Hindu's attitude is worse, for he does not blame the father even, but the man alone. And no one would dare answer, "neither this man nor his father."

The dread of killing animals, insects, and of cutting down trees, obtaining among certain Sections of Hindus, is traceable to the doctrine of metempsychosis. No one is sure of the bugs on one's bed or the shrubs in one's garden. The man who inadvertently steps over a worm may be stamping to death his own father, who knows?

In marked contrast to the fatalistic and animistic doctrine of transmigration, there are certain schools of thought which teach a noble philosophy of action and duty as the means to salvation. These are also popular among the Hindus and will be dealt with later.

CHAPTER IV

PHILOSOPHY

THE Hindus have no theology; they only have mythology and philosophy. Mythology is the religion of the masses, and philosophy of the intellectuals; the two, however, are so blended that it is difficult to say where the one begins and the other ends. No branch of thought has so much claimed the attention of Hindu thinkers as philosophy and speculation on the hereafter. The Vedic Aryans were sacrificers and hymns singers; but sacrifices and hymns did not satisfy bold spirits who wished to know the true nature of soul and body, and exerted themselves to solve the profound mystery of life and death. The results of these enquiries are embodied in the Upanishads, mystical doctrines attached to the Vedas. Most of the orthodox systems of Hindu philosophy trace their origin to the Upanishads; but before dealing with the orthodox systems, I would like to give the reader some idea of the heterodox philosophy of the materialists of India who once flourished in the country and argued with the most bigoted Brahmin, but later lost their power. They are now mentioned in Hindu scriptures as a contemptible sect of hedonists.

THE MATERIALISTS

We know of the materialists of India mainly from the writings of their enemies. Their own works were probably destroyed by the orthodox school, and what we have now is a caricature of them by their opponents. This, however, does give us some idea, though inadequate, of what the materialists professed and practised.

The materialists were known as Charvakas (sweet tongued). They rejected the authority of the Veda and the existence of the soul. The only heaven was the pleasure of this world, and hell, bodily and mental pain. Death was considered a necessary evil, but pleasures of life were not to be shunned on that account. "Nobody casts away the grain because of the husk." Unlike the Buddhists they believed in the permanence of pleasure and the transience of pain.

The Charvaka's contempt for the Veda was profound. He maintained that the Vedas were the vapouring of fools or rascals. Their hatred of animal sacrifice was also marked. Since sacrifices were believed to give salvation to the sacrificer and the sacrificed, the ardent advocate of sacrifice was asked to sacrifice his own father. Their writings show that the Charvakas had a predilection for Ghee (clarified butter) and a horror of meat eating. In their days the Brahmins were probably meat eaters and the innovators vegetarians.

The Charvakas were contemptuous of asceticism, and the various doings of the ascetics who tortured the flesh to elevate the soul. The rich were exhorted not to waste their money on pilgrimages, feeding the Brahmins, or building temples, but to enjoy themselves. The poor were asked to borrow money from their wealthier neighbours and eat exquisite viands and butter while yet there was time. 'For after death no one comes back to this world.'

The Charvakas rejected two (Dharma or duty, and Moksha or salvation) of the four objects of life believed in by the orthodox schools, and accepted the other two, namely Artha or wealth, and Kama or pleasure.

The opposition of the Brahmins to such a philosophy was naturally very strong and they managed to smother it. The philosophy has ceased to exist in India as a system, and it has no professed followers at present among the Hindus. Yet from the writings left to us, it is clear that the Charvakas were once popular in the country and their system enjoyed considerable reputation among the intellectuals. A work of no mean merit is ascribed to Brahaspati who is recognized as the ablest exponent of the system. A commentary on Brahaspati's work is also mentioned, but both works were lost or destroyed.

The Charvakas' rejection of Moksha is but natural; but how he could reject Dharma is not easily understood. For without some sense of duty, it is clear no organized society is possible.

THE ORTHODOX SYSTEMS

All the orthodox systems of Hindu philosophy formally recognise the authority and revealed nature of the Vedas. These systems are six, namely: Nyaya, Vaiseshika, Sankhya, Yoga, Purva Mimamsa and Uttara Mimamsa.

All the orthodox systems not only strive to arrive at truth by certain processes of reasoning but also teach the method by which Moksha or salvation can be obtained. Hence these are essentially religious in character. In India, philosophy, as it stands at present, is indistinguishable from religion, and to the Hindu a philosophy that has no religious background is meaningless. Religion and philosophy are so inseparable that every Hindu philosopher has also been a pious Hindu. Sankara, for instance, who is considered the greatest intellectual India has ever produced, was an ardent devotee of Durga, and his hymns in praise of her are as well-known as his masterly exposition of Vedanta. Every recognised philosopher has a position in Hinduism similar to that of St. Augustine or Thomas Aquinas in the Catholic Church.

The original exposition of each system of Hindu philosophy is embodied in Sutras or metrical aphorism, a literary form dear to the Hindu. The Sutras are usually traced to some sage of antiquity, but the systematisation of the philosophy they taught was done by commentators who lived at a much later period than the author of the Sutras. In India philosophical systems are not taught or propounded by a single individual but have grown out of teachers and disciples working at it for generations.

NYAYA-VAISESHIKA

The Nyaya system is traced to a sage named Gautama whose "Nyaya Sutras" are the original work on the subject. It is probable that the Nyaya school of thought is much more ancient than Gautama who embodied them in the Sutras. Gautama's date is not ascertained with precision. The earliest commentary on the Sutras is by Vatsyayana who is believed to have lived in the fourth century A.D. The most outstanding commentary on the Nyaya Sutras, is the 'Tatva Chintamani' of Gangesa, a Bengali philosopher who flourished in the twelfth century A.D. This work is accepted as the final authority on the Nyaya system.

The 'Vaiseshika Sutra' is ascribed to the sage Kanada, and the earliest commentary on it is the 'Bhasya' of Prasastapada, belonging to the fifth century A.D. The most authoritative works on Vaiseshika are, however, the 'Kiranavali' of Udayana, and 'Kandali' of Sridhara. Both these writers were contemporaries and lived in the tenth century of the Christian era.

Because of their close resemblance, the Nyaya and the Vaiseshika are generally treated as a single system known as Nyaya-Vaiseshika. Both teach the reality of various objects of knowledge which are classified under several heads. Of these the most important is called Dravya, substance, subdivided into nine, namely, earth, water, fire, air, ether, time, space, self and mind. The Dravyas form the frame-work of the universe; these together with six other categories of the system (namely, Guna or quality; Karma or action; Samanya or universals; Visesha or individuality; Samavaya or necessary relation; and Abhava or Negation) explain, according to the Nyaya-Vaiseshika, the whole universe. The laborious literature that enunciates the doctrine need not here be described in detail; suffice it to say that by the relationship of the various categories (with their numerous subdivisions) the whole universe is explained to exist.

The Sutras make no mention of God or a Universal Soul, but the commentators do. These classify God under 'self' (Atman) of the Dravya category and as such the God of Nyaya-Vaiseshika is essentially an unimportant factor; yet some of the commentators attribute to him the whole work of creation and destruction and postulate him as the First Clause. But it is difficult to reconcile this conception of God with the spirit of the system. The philosophers of the Nyaya-Vaiseshika school maintain that the existence of God can be proved by inference without the aid of revelation, and this attitude is in keeping with the teaching of the system with its emphasis on reasoning. It is also difficult to ascertain whether the God of Nyaya-Vaiseshika commentators is personal or impersonal. According to some authorities, he has volition and is hence personal, while others described God as mere existence without attributes or activity.

The goal of life, according to the system, is Mukti, or release. It does not preach the annihilation of soul or even its merging into the Infinite; for the Nyaya-Vaiseshika teaches the reality of individual souls. What it preaches is the release of the "self" from its bondage to life. The self or soul in its independent state is free from pleasure and pain; and since the school teaches the predominance of pain over pleasure, and the inseparableness of pain from life, release from life is considered a desirable object.

A person's attachment to life is attributed to a wrong conception of self obtaining among the generality of mankind. Self in its true nature is without a sense of pain or pleasure, but self wedded to life begets Moha or delusion which mistakes pain and pleasure as real and as belonging to self. In avoiding pain and seeking pleasure, a living being is really pursuing the path of pain, for no pleasure is possible without a predominant amount of pain.

The right path to Mukti, then, is in the right knowledge of the true nature of the Atman or soul. A mere intellectual conviction of the nature of the Atman is not enough. A person, by meditation and self-discipline prepares the ground for the intuitive perception of the real nature of Atman, and the truth should not only be conceived by the intellect but must be experienced, which alone will lead to Mukti. "The way of securing the saving knowledge is as follows:— (1) Formal study of philosophy which is to be carried on under a competent teacher who can properly instruct us; (2) reflection upon what has been thus learnt with a view to get conviction for oneself about it. These two stages secure mediate knowledge or knowledge by description as we might say. Then follows; (3) meditation upon the true nature of self. It leads to direct experience of the truth which will banish ignorance at once. A person who has such experience, it is supposed, will reach the final goal of life (apavarga) as soon as he is dissociated from the physical body at death."*

The Nyaya-Vaiseshika has lost its importance as a living force. A study of the system, especially of Nyaya, is, however, indispensable to the student of Indian logic and philosophy, for Nyaya literature is distinguished by its profound interest in correct reasoning. It has, in fact, come to be looked upon as a system of logic rather than of philosophy.

SANKHYA

The Sankhya is considered the most ancient system of Indian philosophy. Though formally recognizing the authority of the Vedas and of the Upanishads, the philosophy is believed to have developed before the Upanishads and independently of them. This however is a controversial point and we need not here dwell upon it.

The system is traced to Kapila, a sage of antiquity, but the existing Sankhya Sutra attributed to Kapila is a recent compilation not more than six centuries old. The earliest work on the system is the Sankhyakarika of Isvarakrishna, who lived near about the fifth century A.D. It is a small work of seventy stanzas, but gives a lucid exposition of the theoretical teaching of the system. It is a literary work of a high order and is described as "the pearl of the whole scholastic literature of India". It has been commented upon by various writers, some its advocates and

---

* Hiriyanna, *Outlines of Indian Philosophy*.

others opponents. The burden of the latter is to show that it has no Vedic authority and hence should not be considered as orthodox. But as the exponents of the system formally recognize the infallibility of the Vedas and claim to base their arguments on Vedic texts, the efforts of its adversaries to reject it as heterodox have been of no avail.

According to the Sankhya, the universe can be resolved into two, i.e., Purushas and Prakriti. Purushas may be translated as souls, each with its own individuality and reality. The Purushas are inactive, above any kind of experience of pain, pleasure or desire. But the Purushas do not remain in their natural state because of their contact with Prakriti. Prakriti is dynamic and in its wide scope includes the whole perceptible universe not excepting time, space and causation. Prakriti has three main Gunas or qualities i.e., Satva, Tamas and Rajas. Satva represents refinement, Tamas grossness or coarseness, and Rajas activity. Each of these Gunas has numerous subdivisions and it is in the combination of these in various proportions that differences in the universe result.

A living being is said to consist of three components: The Purusha or soul, a subtle body, and a gross body. At death only the gross body is cast off. The subtle body is imperceptible to the naked eye and is composed of eleven organs of sense, together with Buddhi (intellect), Ahamkara (egoism) and the five elements. The subtle body is called Lingasarira; it is a storehouse of the man's Karma (the result of actions). It clings to the Purusha causing changes, till the Purusha is finally liberated from its tyranny and gains its independence and sentience.

It is noteworthy that the Sankhya is silent about the universal soul or God, and hence is considered an atheistic system. It explains the universe without the aid of a creator or a Primary Cause. Individual souls and Prakriti are eternal reals, indestructible, unchangeable in essence. The cause of union between the two, which is responsible for the phenomenal world, though not explained satisfactorily, is said to be inherent in Prakriti, and does not depend upon an outside agency.

Though godless, the Sankhya believes in the doctrine of Karma and of transmigration of souls. It is not Purusha, or soul proper which transmigrates; for the soul, even when wedded to Prakriti, is above all experience. What actually undergoes transmigration is the Lingasarira or subtle body which is a sort of permanent annex to the Purusha and clings to it till the Purusha is completely liberated. For Sankhya, like some of the other orthodox systems, believes that life is essentially sorrowful and liberation of the soul from its bondage to Prakriti is the goal of every thinking man.

The Sankhya system is believed to have profoundly influenced Mahavira and the Buddha. Neither Jainism nor Buddhism postulates God but both teach the finality of the law of Karma. Some Buddhist philosophers, however, improved upon the Purusha theory, for according to them the liberated Purusha does not remain an entity but passes into non-entity.

While preaching the need for liberation, the Sankhya does not teach the method by which it can be effected. This was probably due to the fact that Yoga, the sister system, was mainly concerned with the method of liberation and flourished side by side with the Sankhya when this system became a popular philosophy. The Sankhya has now lost its ancient hold on the peoples of India, and has passed into a system of philosophy, of interest only to the professional philosopher and the scholar.

YOGA

The Yoga is attributed to Patanjali. His Yoga Sutras (fifth century A.D.) is still the final authority on the subject and is more reliable than most of the commentaries. Vyasa (6th century A.D.) is believed to be the earliest commentator on the Yoga Sutras and his commentary has two excellent glosses, one by Vachaspati and the other by Vijnanabhiksu, two famous philosophers of a later date. King Bhoja who lived in the eleventh century A.D. also wrote a commentary on Yoga.

Unlike the Sankhya, which is mainly theoretical, the Yoga is thoroughly practical. The system is not so much concerned with the nature of the soul as how to liberate it from its bondage to matter.

The Yoga, by implication, accepts the pessimistic view of life common to all orthodox forms of Indian thought, and teaches, by a system of mind and body training, how to obtain release from the cycle of births and deaths. The two necessary conditions that lead to this goal are Vairagya (detachment from worldly affairs) and Yoga (meditation). Vairagya arises out of a conviction of the evil that is life, and a realisation of its ills. Meditation should be on ultimate truth. As all forms of Indian thought (except the Charvaka doctrine, of course) lead to pessimism, and the Indian philosopher's notion of truth is very elastic, the Yoga system is found acceptable to all sects and castes, and even to the followers of heterodox schools such as Jainism and Buddhism.

The Yoga system of training is intellectual as well as moral. The virtues that the trainee is to cultivate are ten: (1) non-injury (Ahimsa), (2) truth speaking (Satya), (3) abstinence from stealing or misappropriation of other people's property (Asteya), (4) celibacy (Brahmacharya), (5) disowning of possessions (Aparigraha), (6) purity (Sucha), (7) contentment (Santosha), (8) fortitude (Tapasa), (9) study (Svadhyaya), and (10) devotion to gods (Isvara-pranidhana).

After the student has trained himself sufficiently long in the practice of these virtues, he enters the training of Yoga proper. This training has two stages and the first comprises Asana (postures), Pranayama (control of breath) and Pratyahara (withdrawal of senses from their objects); and the second Dharana, Dhyana and Samadhi, different forms of concentration. Of these Samadhi is the highest stage of Yoga which has two sub-stages called Samprajnata Samadhi and Asamprajnata Samadhi, the latter being the highest and most desirable state. In this state, the mind is so controlled that the Yogi loses all consciousness of the outside world and of self, and passes into the realm of mysticism. In the lower Samadhi, the Yogi is not past the stage of experience, and hence is in a stage of ecstasy, all sources of distraction having been eradicated and the satva quality shining forth. A person who has attained Samprajnata Samadhi is still of this world, although well nigh passing it; but he who has attained Asamprajnata Samadhi dissolves at death into the natural elements, and his Purusha is liberated having developed permanent immunity from the attack of Prakriti.

The training of Yoga is an elaborate process and the trainee has to spend a good part of the day in practising the various postures, (some of them contorting the body and extremely difficult to practise), in controlling the breath in prescribed ways and in concentrating the mind on God or nothing. But the result achieved through the training is remarkable, and the system is unique. Apart from its spiritual value, for which alone the system was originated, the Yoga is a sound system of training the mind and body. Hence its basic principles are acceptable even to those who believe in no god, in no Purusha and in no liberation.

The occult powers the Yogi claims to possess are tremendous. He can make himself invisible at will, can suspend himself in mid air, can dart through space with the speed of light and can perform many other miracles besides. Although these appear exaggerated claims, there is no doubt that the Yogi possesses remarkable control over the central nervous system, over his mind and body, and is able to perform actions which are not easily explained. It is a common practice among Yogis to cleanse their stomach by bringing the intestines out and washing them. There are reliable eye-witnesses who have seen Yogis raising themselves two or three feet above ground and remaining suspended in air for quite a few minutes. I have seen minor Yogis, who perform for the public, stopping their heart beat for quite a minute (there were Allopathic doctors present who witnessed and examined the performer's heart at the time) or burying themselves under three feet of earth and coming out alive after two hours. There is the historic case of a Yogi who, in the time of the Sikh monarch Ranjit Singh, and under his able supervision, remained buried alive for 45 days !*

Yoga, as it stands at present, is much rationalised. Although its spiritual side is often overlooked, its material and psychological side appeal to all; Hindus and even non-Hindus assiduously practise it for getting mastery over the mind and body, very much in the same way as Pelmanism is practised in the West. Every important city or town in India has a Yogic culture centre where able Yogis impart instruction to students in Yoga. These are modernised Yogis. Those who follow the ancient school attach themselves to teachers in some holy city such as Benares or Haridwar and practise the system purely for the purpose of liberation. They are interested only in individual liberation and do not care to perform in public or parade their powers. The originators of the system expressly mention that Yoga is meant for such alone, and should not be disclosed to those who wish to obtain occult powers or material gain.

PURVA MIMAMSA

The word "Mimamsa" means investigation and "Purva" means the earlier. The philosophy is so called because it professes to investigate the truth embodied in the Brahmanas (ritualistic precepts attached to the Vedas) which precede the Upanishads (mystical doctrines); the Uttara (later) Mimamsa, is solely based on the Upanishads, and it is to distinguish it from the latter that Purva Mimamsa is so named.

The original work enunciating the doctrine is the Mimamsa Sutra of Jaimini, believed to be a compilation of the third century A.D. It contains about 2,600 stanzas and is the biggest of the philosophic Sutras; it is not, however, more elevating on that account. For a good part of it is unintelligible even to the most erudite Sanskrit scholar who looks up the commentaries to get some meaning out of them. The earliest commentary is of Sabarasvamin who wrote in the fifth century A.D. Many other commentaries, and commentaries on commentaries appeared later and the Purva Mimamsa, as it stands at present, has lost its originality and has become a confused mass of ideas borrowed from other systems.

The burden of the Purva Mimamsa is to establish the revealed nature of the Vedas by reasoning, and to show that the Brahmanas (those portions of the Vedas dealing with rituals and ceremonials) are more important than the rest. The Mimamsa, by implication, believes that revelation can be proved by reasoning and need not be blindly accepted as a dogma.

Avoiding theories, the original Mimamsakas believed in rituals and activity rather than in intellectualism, and in keeping with this belief they laid undue emphasis on Dharma (social and religious duty) and even rejected Moksha (liberation). The other systems with their ultimate object centred on individual liberation cannot be said to be completely free from desire and selfishness for to strive after liberation is the result of a selfish desire to be free. The Mimamsakas, on the other hand, reject even this desire as a hindrance to a full life and maintain that doing one's religious and social duty is in itself the end of life.

This dry philosophy of the earlier Mimamsakas was, however, superseded by the doctrines of later commentators who introduced God and Mukti into the system. While the earlier school insisted on Dharma, the doing of some positive good as the goal of life the advocates of Mukti taught release or escape of the soul from its environments by what is called Jnana-Karma (enlightened activity).

The Purva Mimamsa developed and flourished at a time when Vedic sacrifices and rituals were the main religious activities of the Hindus. With the rise of Puranic Hinduism and the worship of Shiva, Vishnu and Sakti, Vedic rituals, based on the Brahmanas, fell into disuse and Purva Mimamsa lost its importance.

In its conception of God, soul and matter, Purva

---

* The late Dr. V. G. Rele, an Allopathic doctor of standing, gave a scientific explanation of the wonderful powers of the Yogis. He attributes them to the Yogi's control of the vagus nerve and of the sympathetic nervous system. Readers interested in the subject will do well to read his *The Mysterious Kundalini* (Taraporevala).

XXIX

69 AT A JAIN SANCTUARY
(National News Photo Service)

70 AT THE FEET OF GOMATESVARA
STATUE

71 A JAIN PILGRIM WITH OFFERING
OF MILK AND COCOANUTS FOR
GOMATESVARA

(India Pictorial Features)

XXX

72 A PROCESSION OF JAIN WOMEN
(Photo: Stanley Jepson)

73 IMAGE OF A GODDESS IN THE SANCTUM
OF A JAIN TEMPLE
(India Pictorial Features)

XXXI

74 JAIN TEMPLE, CALCUTTA
(India Pictorial Features)

75 IMAGES OF THIRTHANKARAS IN THE FAMOUS
JAIN TEMPLE AT SHRAVAN BELGOLA, MYSORE
(India Pictorial Features)

XXXII

76   A JAIN THIRTHANKARA
(Journal of Indian Art and Industry)

XXXIII

77 CEREMONIAL SEA BATH, BOMBAY
(Photo: B. F. Ferreira)

78 A RELIGIOUS PROCESSION, MADRAS
(Photo: S. S. Aiyar)

XXXIV

HINDU AND JAIN MENDICANTS
(From Forbe's *Oriental Memoirs*)

XXXV

A HINDU MARRIAGE PROCESSION
(From dressed models: *Journal of Indian Art and Industry*)

XXXVI

SATI, A THING OF THE PAST

(From a painting by Solvyns)

Mimamsa is not fundamentally different from the Nyaya-Vaiseshika and Sankhya, from which it has borrowed freely. At present it shares the same fate as the Nyaya-Vaiseshika and the Sankhya systems, as of being interest only to the scholar, the student and the pedant.

UTTARA MIMAMSA

Uttara Mimamsa is based on the teaching of the Upanishads, which being found at the end of the Vedas, the philosophy is also called Vedanta or the end of the Vedas. This is the predominant school of Hindu philosophy at present. It is so popular that the word "Vedanta" is used as a synonym for all higher forms of thought or speech. One who brags on spiritual matters is also dubbed a Vedantin.

The original work on this system is the Vedanta Sutras of Badarayana belonging to the fourth century A.D. While Badarayana is believed to be the originator of the philosophy, the compilation of the Sutras or rather their arrangement is attributed to Vyasa, the mythical compiler of the Vedas and the reputed author of the Mahabharata and the Puranas. This was, no doubt, inspired by a desire on the part of Vedantins to trace their system to the unquestionable authority of Vyasa.

Commentaries on the Vedanta Sutras are many and there are a dozen schools of philosophy which go by the name of Vedanta. But all these pale into insignificance before the celebrated commentary of Sankara (eighth century A.D.) advocating Advaita or Absolute Monism. Next in importance to Advaita comes the Vishishta Advaita (qualified monism) of Ramanuja. The former explains the philosophic view and the latter the theistic view of Vedanta. The other schools of Vedanta are unimportant, of interest only to the scholar.

ADVAITA

In opposition to the Sankhya system which denies the existence of God, the Advaita maintains that there exists nothing but God. Yet strictly speaking, God cannot be said to exist; for all existence, according to Advaita, is conditioned by space, time or causation, and God is above all these. Nor should the God of Advaita be confused with the Almighty of the theists. The highest form of divine conception in Advaita is Nirguna Brahmam, or Reality without Attributes. Brahmam alone is real, and all the rest is nought.

If there is nothing but Brahmam the question very naturally arises how we can account for the bewildering multiplicity of objects we find in the universe. The Advaitin denies this diversity, and maintains that it is an illusion (Maya) created by Avidya or ignorance. The whole of the phenomenal world, the seven worlds above and the seven below, all the creatures in the world, the gods above and the demons below, even Saguna Brahma (the personal God of the theists) are, the bold Advaitin maintains, unreal and a figment of your imagination. Beyond all this, is the Real. This Real which appears so distant is not actually so; for it is in you; nay, it is Yourself (That Thwam Asi).

The doctrine which appears so perplexing will be found less so on analysis. No thinking person can deny that a sort of unreality pervades the whole universe. You and I will sure be as nought in a little while; so will be the millions of creatures that go about the world as if they were immortals. All our forefathers have passed into oblivion and but for the works in stone or palm leaves they have left they would be to us absolutely non-existent. Hence the Advaitin stoutly maintains that "It is all a magic shadow show."

As regards the contention that "You Yourself are That" the assertion is rather difficult to prove by reasoning, but can be experienced. The Vedantin recognizes the validity of intuition and revelation and maintains that all cannot be known by pure reasoning. Anyhow, it cannot be denied that persons who are sufficiently detached from the affairs of this world, do feel, in some of their quietest moods, an essential unity between them and the universe. and this is a glimpse of the Real that is in you and me.

If the phenomenal world is unreal, life naturally becomes meaningless, and all our ideas of morality, duty and virtue tumble to the ground. The Advaitin is not perturbed by this, but he maintains that as long as a person is caught in Maya and remains in it he has to observe rules of conduct as a part of the game of illusion. For, those who value the superficialities of life, must, of necessity, value Maya. Those who are above Maya are above morality.

It should not, however, be imagined that Maya is mere illusion. It has a sort of ephemeral reality of its own. The relation between Maya and reality can best be described in the following manner:

Suppose a man had a dream that a white elephant was chasing him, and he screamed in his sleep. Was the white elephant real? You cannot say it was nothing, because in relation to the dreamer it had a definite existence in time, and did make him scream; yet you cannot say that it was a real white elephant. The dreamer is the real, and the white elephant is Maya. Apart from the Real, Maya has no existence. Maya is, in fact, a projection of the real, though not the Real. The waves of the ocean are not essentially different from the ocean, yet the waves are not the ocean.

The object of life, according to the Advaitin, is not release but realisation. This is in keeping with the spirit of the philosophy; for you being fundamentally one with the Real, it is meaningless to talk of liberation from the Real. The object of life, then, is to dispel the ignorance which prevents you from realizing your true nature. The one who has "realized oneself" is not, however, fundamentally different from the ignorant one. This enigma is explaind by a simile. A prince, brought up as a hunter, imagines himself to be a hunter till one day he comes to know his true origin. This knowledge, however, does not change the man; for even when he was imagining himself a hunter, the man was really a prince. Similarly, every man is truly Real itself, but its realization means a fuller life. It is the story of the dreamer, again, who has woken up from his dream.

The path to realization lies through Jnana or knowledge. The training has two stages; the preliminary stage consisting of a studied cultivation of an attitude of detachment from worldly affairs, and the other Vedanta training proper. This consists of Srvana, Manana and Nididhyasana. Srvana means the study of the Upanishads with the aid of a Guru who has "realized himself". When the disciple has learnt all that the Guru can teach him, he enters the Manana stage when he should think for himself independent of a teacher, on the meaning of the doctrines taught in the Upanishads. After having thus attained the intellectual conviction necessary for realizing himself, the trainee enters the last stage of Nididhyasana, wherein by constant meditation of the truth that he is one with the Infinite, he ultimately becomes the Real. A man in this stage is a Jivan Mukta; though living in this world, he is completely detached from it and is not of it. He lives not for himself but for others. Thus, the philosophy, though appearing to aim at inaction, is not in practice so; for all great Advaitins like Sankara and Vivekananda were noted for their exuberant energy and untiring activity.

From the foregoing, it is plain that the Advaitin lays greater emphasis on knowledge than on devotion, or ethics. For ordinary morality, the Advaitin has but contempt, though he recognizes its utility for people who cannot do without it. Swami Vivekananda's Song of the Sannyasin abundantly illustrates this point. The poem summarizes the attitude of the Realized One towards life, and incidentally gives an insight into the whole philosophy of Advaita; so, I quote it in full:

Wake up the note! the song that had its birth
Far off, where worldly taint could never reach;
In mountain caves, and glades of forest deep,
Whose calm no sigh for lust or wealth or fame
Could ever dare to break; where rolled the stream
Of knowledge, truth, and bliss that follows both.
Sing high that note, Sannyasin bold! Say—
    'Om Tat Sat, Om!'

Strike off thy fetters! Bonds that bind thee down,
Of shining gold, or darker, baser ore;
Love, hate—good, bad—and all the dual throng.
Know slave is slave, caressed or whipped, not free;
For fetters though of gold, are not less strong to bind;
Then off with them, Sannyasin bold! Say—

Let darkness go; the will-o'-the-wisp that leads
With blinking light to pile more gloom on gloom.
This thirst for life, for ever quench; it drags
From birth to death, and death to birth, the soul.
He conquers all who conquers self. Know this
And never yield, Sannyasin bold! Say—

"Who sows must reap," they say, "and cause must bring
The sure effect; good, good; bad, bad; and none

Escape the law. But whoso wears a form
Must wear the chain." Too true; but far beyond
Both name and form is Atman, ever free.
Know thou art That, Sannyasin bold! Say—

They know not truth, who dream such vacant dreams
As father, mother, children, wife and friend.
The sexless Self! Whose father He? Whose child?
Whose friend? Whose foe is He who is but One?
The Self is all in all, none else exists;
And thou art That, Sannyasin bold! Say—

There is but One — The Free — The Knower —Self!
Without a name, without a form or stain.
In Him is Maya, dreaming all this dream.
The Witness, He appears as nature, soul.
Know thou art That, Sannyasin bold! Say—

Where seekest thou? That freedom, friend, this world
Nor that can give. In books and temples vain
Thy search. Thine only is the hand that holds
The rope that drags thee on. Then cease lament,
Let go thy hold, Sannyasin bold! Say—

Say 'peace to all: From me no danger be
To aught that lives; In those that dwell on high,
In those that lowly creep, I am the Self in all!
All life both here and there, do I renounce,
All heavens, and earths and hells, all hopes and fears.'
Thus cut thy bonds, Sannyasin bold! Say—

Heed then no more how body lives or goes,
Its task is done. Let Karma float it down;
Let one put garlands on, another kick
This frame; say naught. No praise or blame can be
Where praiser, praised, and blamer, blamed are —one,
Thus be thou calm, Sannyasin bold! Say—

Truth never comes where lust and fame and greed
Of gain reside. No man who thinks of woman
As his wife can ever perfect be;
Nor he who owns the least of things, nor he
Whom anger chains, can ever pass thro' Maya's gates.
So, give these up, Sannyasin bold! Say—

Have thou no home. What home can hold thee, friend?
The sky thy roof; the grass thy bed; and food,
What chance may bring, well cooked or ill, judge no.
No food or drink can taint that noble Self
Which knows itself. Like rolling river free
Thou ever be, Sannyasin bold! Say—

Few only know the truth. The rest will hate
And laugh at thee, great one; but pay not heed.
Go thou, the free, from place to place, and help

Them out of darkness, Maya's veil. Without
The fear of pain or search for pleasure, go
Beyond them both, Sannyasin bold! Say—
Thus day by day, till Karma's power's spent
Release the soul for ever. No more is birth,
Nor I, nor thou, nor God, nor man. The 'I'
Has All become, the All is 'I' and Bliss.
Know thou art that, Sannyasin bold! Say—*

It is clear from the Song of Sannyasin that the Advaitin, though contemptuous of ordinary morality —the dual throng—believes in a higher morality. "To realise one's identity with Maya and the Real is to accept both the Supreme commandments of Christ at once; that of loving God, and of loving one's neighbour as oneself. The one who has realized oneself is perfect.

Advaita, in practice, does not always lead to perfection. Many of those who have not "realized themselves" claim to be above the moral law, and some of the vast army of maniacs of whom we had occasion to speak in the previous chapter take refuge in Advaita.

The greatness of Advaita lies in its opposition to the pessimistic views held by Buddhism and the other schools of orthodox Hindu thought. For the Advaitin, life has to be lived down, the object of life being not release but realisation. But the extreme intellectualism and boldness of the philosophy have been found too elevating for the generality of mankind. For while every Hindu will quietly submit to the genius of Sankara or Vivekananda and easily admit that all is in reality One, he finds it difficult to "realize himself" as such; nay he is frightened to say "Ahm Brahmam Asmi" (I myself am God). Hence, the Advaita, though extremely popular in India, especially among Shaivas, is treated by the generality of Hindus as impracticable of realisation by them in the present life. They believe that only certain individuals who have the accumulated advantage of past Karma behind them can "realize themselves"; the rest of the Hindus are content to live according to the common ideas of morality, worship and rituals, leaving the Jnana method of "realization to a future life."

VISHISHTA ADVAITA

Vishishta Advaita or qualified monism, is, more or less, a revolt against the unmoral intellectualism of Advaita. The exponents of the philosophy trace it to the Upanishads, and the Vedanta Sutra is, as in the case of Advaita, the authority for Vishishta Advaita too. Yet outside influences are clearly traceable in its teachings. From the resemblance of the philosophy to the theistic conceptions of Christians and Muslims, some writers have traced it to these foreign influences. The fact that Ramanuja, the earliest exponent of the system, hails form the South where Christianity had established itself from the very start of the Christian era lends considerable support to this view. In the absence of positive proof, this will however remain a controversial point.†

Ramanuja, like Sankara, was a South Indian. He lived in the eleventh century, and his Sribhasya, a commentary on the Vedanta Sutras, and Vedartha Samgraha, an independent exposition of the system, form the chief works on Vishishta Advaita.

According to Ramanuja, there are three reals: God, soul and matter. These are not however independent reals but interdependent. The soul is the controlling factor of the body or matter and God controls both. Without God neither soul nor matter has any existence except as a conception. The three are in fact inseparable and form a complex whole and hence Vishishta Advaita is neither dualism nor pluralism but monism with a qualification.

The object of life, according to Vishishta Advaita is not realisation, but deliverance. The liberated soul does not lose its individuality but finds God and is released from the cycle of births and deaths. To attain this state, Karmayoga (right activity) and Jnanayoga (knowledge) form the preliminary discipline. But it is not enough to act and to know. To find God one should seek him as a fond child seeks his mother or as a fond lover seeks his lady. Hence Bhakti (loving devotion) is essential for salvation. For "God is conceived as completely personal. He is looked upon as having pity for erring man and as actuated by a desire to show mercy to him. Benevolence, indeed, is one of his essential features."‡

The Vishishtadvaitin believes in something greater than Bhakti. For the highest activity, the highest knowledge, the highest devotion is Parapatti, complete self-surrender to God. A person who surrenders his body, mind and soul to God with absolute faith in Him is freed, through divine grace, from all the bonds of Karma. In this highest expression of devotion, there is no place for caste, creed or colour. Even the most abandoned pariah may be saved through divine grace if he has the faith and will to surrender himself completely to God.

The reason why Vishishta Advaita is traced to Christian sources is now plain. The doctrine has a close resemblance to Christian theology, and its belief in divine grace is characteristically Christian.

Here then is a doctrine comprehensible and acceptable to the generality of mankind. The appeal of a personal God to whom man can pray, do homage and ask for forgiveness is universal, and Vishishta Advaita rapidly spread throughout India. The deity of the Hindu pantheon elevated to the position of Isvara, God, by Ramanuja and his followers was Vishnu. The loving and amiable nature of this deity was probably responsible for the preference; further, Advaita being the pet doctrine of Shaivas, and Vaishnavism not having assumed an all-India importance, Ramanuja and his followers thought it wise to establish an essential difference between their philosophy

---

* Advaita Ashram's *Selections from Swami Vivekananda's Works.*
† The subject has been discussed in greater detail in the author's book *Christians & Christianity in India and Pakistan.*
‡ M. Hiriyanna. *Outlines of Indian Philosophy.*

and the Advaita of Sankara by giving greater importance to Vishnu than to Shiva.

The message of Ramanuja was carried all over India by a host of Vaishnavas such as Ramananda, Chaitanya, Thukaram, Tulasidas, Mira Bai and many others. The extraordinary appeal of the doctrine did not fail to attract the attention of Shaivas, and efforts were made, especially in South India, to exalt Shiva to the position of a God of Mercy and Grace. But the attempt was only partially successful, and Shiva remains to this day the lean, irascible god of ascetics.

THE BHAGAVAD GITA

The Bhagavad Gita (the song celestial) can be said to be the cream of Hindu philosophy. It is a poem of about 700 verses found in the Mahabharata, put in the form of a dialogue between two principal characters of that epic. The poem so brims with the spirit of Hinduism that every school of philosophy and every sect believe that it teaches their particular doctrines. The Advaitin, the Vishishtadvaitin, the Yogin, the Sannyasin, the soldier, the saint and even the common rogue will quote the Gita as his authority; so thoroughly does the work represent the Hindu view of life. The poem, though so popular now, was little heard of till Sankara wrote his commentary on it. This has led some writers to conclude that it is an interpolation by Sankara. Though the evidence for this view is not strong, its possibility cannot be entirely ruled out; for the philosophy of the Gita is worthy of the genius of Sankara and is in keeping with the line of thought that characterises his works.

The object of the Gita is to elucidate a highly complex moral situation, and incidentally it briefly surveys the whole field of philosophic thought. Arjuna, one of the heroes of the Mahabharata, stands in the battlefield, bow in hand, awaiting the signal for action. He sees arrayed against him the armies of his cousins led by generals, some of whom are his near relatives, and most of whom held in great reverence by him. (The Mahabharata, as we shall see later, was a war between cousins). On his side are his own brothers and relatives and their armies. Suddenly the hero becomes troubled by fears and despondency. Of what use, he asks himself, is a kingdom to him if it be won at the cost of so many lives? Besides, would he be justified in killing those men, many of them his seniors in age and enjoying the reputation of being venerable, for any gain whatever? Would he not be committing a foolish sin in becoming a party to this senseless blood bath? Arjuna is overcome by these thoughts and the bow drops from his hand. Now Krishna, his charioteer, comes to his aid and infuses courage into him by revealing the Gita.

First and foremost, the Gita teaches a philosophy of action. The correct type of action which ennobles a man is duty done with no thought of personal gain. The soldier's duty in the battlefield is to fight his foes, and not to question the wisdom of war. When killing becomes a duty, kill with a vengeance. For only the ignorant have an exaggerated notion of the sin of killing. All creatures that are born are destined to die, and a soldier's pity or cowardice is not going to save mankind from death. Besides for the higher thinker, death is non-existent. For reality is indestructible, is above all sense of pain and pleasure. Even in the change of form we call death, it is destiny or God that destroys; the apparent slayer of a person is only an instrument in the hands of God. Says Krishna, in his character of God:

> "Death am I, and my present task
> Destruction. View in me
> The active slayer of these men;
> For though you fail and flee,
> These captains of the hostile hosts
> Shall die, shall cease to be.
> They are already slain by me;
> Be thou the instrument."

The Gita upholds the doctrine of Bhakti to a personal God. The dogma of incarnation is also taught. For Krishna says that whenever Dharma fails and Adharma (evil) begins to predominate the world, God incarnates Himself for the destruction of Adharma. The Gita breathes the spirit of universal toleration, and reiterates the orthodox view that every form of religious worship, even if it is apparently crude, is in effect a stepping stone towards a higher form, and hence should be respected. "Whoever with true devotion worships any deity, in him I deepen that devotion; and through it he fulfils his desire." "Those who devotedly worship other gods, they also worship me though only imperfectly." The different forms of worship are compared to different roads that lead to the same destination, some long, some short and some round about.

It is difficult to say whether realisation or liberation is the gist of the teaching of the Gita. Nor is the true nature of the liberated soul explained. But these questions appear pointless when discussing the philosophy of the Gita. For, the Gita is eminently concerned with life in this world. The burden of the Gita is to teach the social nature of man and to show that it is not in lonely forests that a man should seek salvation but in the midst of life. To live in this world, to do the duty allotted to one by birth and special circumstances without fear of consequences or love of gain, without the bonds of love or hatred marring one's vision, is the object of life; a man in this state is a Jivan Mukta and it is its own reward.

CHAPTER V

BUDDHISM, JAINISM, SIKHISM, BRAHMO SAMAJ AND ARYA SAMAJ

IN the foregoing two chapters we have discussed the religion and philosophy of the orthodox Hindu sects. But Hinduism has never been a static religion and from time immemorial reformers have revolted against practices and beliefs which they thought harmful or erroneous, and side by side with orthodoxy have been flourishing reform movements some of which rejected the Vedas; others passed it by, and still others violently attacked the orthodox sects on the ground that they had no Vedic sanction. All these movements have, however, retained the spirit of Hinduism and in this chapter we shall describe the important few of these revolts.

BUDDHISM

The earliest and probably the greatest revolt against orthodox Brahminism took place under Siddhartha, called the Buddha, founder of Buddhism. Siddhartha was born of a royal clan and he was heir to the kingdom of Kapilavasthu. His father, Suddhodana, wished his son to become a great monarch. Legends say that the astrologers who cast the child's horoscope predicted a brilliant future for Siddhartha either as a spiritual leader or as a conquering hero; in the former case he was to be guided by four signs, i.e., old age, sickness, death and renunciation. Suddhodana wanted his son to become a great conqueror and hence took precautions against his son coming across any of these signs. So that his son might not even have an idea of the "four signs", Suddhodana had three castles built for his son's residence where "every delight abounded, and sorrow and death might not even be mentioned." But life in the palace bored the prince. One day the prince went out for a drive, and in spite of Suddhodana's strict instructions to keep all sick and deformed people away from the prince's path, Siddhartha came across a sick man leaning on a stick. The sight profoundly upset him and he learnt from his charioteer all about sickness. The next day he met an old man, on the third a dead body and on the fourth a recluse. The Buddhist scriptures say that the gods had assumed these forms for detracting the prince from the wordly life Suddhodana had planned for him.

Mythological embellishments apart, from the very boyhood Siddhartha had shown apathy towards the pleasures of the world and his sensitive nature led him to brood over the tragedy of pain connected with all life he had seen around him. A story typical of the boy is narrated in the Buddhist scriptures. One day some swans were flying over the city towards their Himalayan homes and one of them, wounded by an arrow shot by Devadatta, a cousin of Siddhartha, fell in the park where this prince was loitering. The prince immediately took the swan, dressed its wounds and nursed it. The swan recovered but Devadatta claimed the bird for himself as he had shot it; Siddhartha refused to surrender the swan and maintained that Devadatta's cruelty in shooting a harmless bird did not establish his claim over it. Devadatta appealed to a Court of Elders who upheld Siddhartha's claim on the principle that the live bird belonged to the one who nursed it back to life and not to the one who had wounded it.

Seeing the religious bent of the boy's mind, which was unbecoming of a Kshatriya, Suddhodana got his son married to Yasodhara, daughter of Dandapani, a noble of his kingdom. But marriage did not solve life's problem for Siddhartha. The company of his wife and the pleasures of the palace only added to his troubles. Shortly a son was born to him and when the great news was brought to the prince he could only mutter to himself: "Alas! one more fetter to be broken!" Life in the palace became so intolerable to Siddhartha that he decided to run away from home and live the life of a recluse. Accordingly one dark night when his wife and child were sleeping, the prince with the help of his charioteer Channa, quietly left his palace for the spiritual freedom of the wilderness. The story of his departure is narrated with much pathos and tenderness. His baby son Rahula was sleeping by the side of Yasodhara, and the prince, after stepping out of the room, came back to impress a last kiss on the beloved child. But Yasodhara was sleeping with her hand on the child and afraid to disturb her, Siddhartha left the room without kissing the child.

After leaving the palace Siddhartha attached himself to several teachers, one after another, but in his attempt to find a solution to the mystery of life none was helpful. At last he decided to tread the path alone, and disappeared in the wild forests of the Himalayas. For seven years did he wander in the Himalayas practising Yoga, concentration and asceticism, all recognised methods of salvation of the Hindus. But none of these brought him near the goal he was seeking. If anything, he felt he was going away from the goal. Giving up asceticism, Siddhartha took food, but formed a determination that led him to enlightenment. He proceeded to a Bo-tree and sat under it in meditation, bent upon discovering the truth about life or perishing in the attempt. After many temptations and direct attacks by the powers of evil, the Buddhist scriptures say, enlightenment one day suddenly dawned upon him and Siddhartha became the Buddha (enlightened).

The solution of the mystery of life brought him doubts as to its appeal to the generality of mankind. The Blessed One thought thus: "I have penetrated this doctrine which is profound, difficult to perceive and to understand, which brings quietude of heart, which is exalted, which is unattainable by reasoning, abstruse, intelligible only to the wise. These people, on the other hand, are given to desire, intent upon desire, delighting in desire. To these people, therefore, the law of causalty and the chain of causation will be a matter difficult to understand; most difficult to understand will also be the extinction of all Samskars, the getting rid of all the substrata of existence, the destruction of desire, the absence of passion. quietude of heart, Nirvana. Now if I proclaim the doctrine, and other men are not able to understand my preaching, there would result but weariness and annoyance to me."*

After much doubting, the Buddha decided to preach the doctrine to his fellowmen. The unexpected success of his first sermon which converted two casual visitors encouraged him, and very soon the number of his followers and disciples increased. His fame spread throughout the kingdom and all kinds of people, from great philosophers and princes to common peasants, flocked to him to learn and to discuss. The glamour of a prince who became a recluse was irresistible to men; besides, the personality of the Buddha, his gentility and "sweet reasonableness" added immensely to the popularity of the new religion.

The Buddha's religion is founded on what is called the four Sublime Verities of the faith. The first of the Verities is that pain predominates life; the second that desire is the cause of pain; the third that pain can be ended in Nirvana, annihilation of individuality; and the fourth is the path that leads to Nirvana. The immediate object of life is to get rid of desire and when this is accomplished, Nirvana is near; for a man who has conquered all desire destroys himself completely at death and is not born again. But no one attains this stage in one life; thousands of lives in various forms are necessary before a man is perfected and is fit for Nirvana. In Buddhism there is no easy way to Nirvana; there is no place for divine grace or mercy that transforms the sinner into a saint in the twinkling of an eye. Every deed of man has its inevitable effect and the inexorable Law of Karma (cause and effect) is blind, pitiless and impersonal. The man who does evil begets evil and he lives through countless lives of sorrow before he is purified. The Buddha himself, it is said, lived for more than 500 births after he became Bodhisatva (Buddha-elect) his lives prior to attaining this exalted stage being countless!

Buddhism has been rightly described as morality without God. The eightfold path of Buddhism that leads to Nirvana is a code of morality, not the commandment of God, but a law in itself which governs the world. The Buddhist conception of universe is the antithesis of the un-moral pantheism of the Advaitin. The Buddha, however, had profound compassion for the weakness of men and the acceptance of the eightfold path† was enforced on the monastic orders only; for common men the middle path which preached the common virtues of charity and a moral life was taught.

Buddhism, then, is not fundamentally different from orthodox Hinduism. It just emphasises the pessimism common to most Hindu forms of thought, and the liberation or Mukti of the Hindus is indistinguishable from the Nirvana of the Buddhist. Nor is religion without God new to Hinduism; for the Sankhya system, from which the Buddha appears to have borrowed much, postulates a universe without God and yet is intensely religious, claiming to draw its inspiration from the Vedas. The doctrine of metempsychosis is common to both Hinduism and Buddhism, though the latter gives the Law of Karma a peculiarly exalted position in its philosophic conception.

What made the new faith antagonistic to Hinduism was not so much its doctrines as the way of life it preached. At the time of the Buddha, Hinduism had lost all its spontaneity and degenerated into a routine of rituals and sacrifices based on the Brahmanas of the Vedas. It was the letter of the text that mattered, and religion had become a question of correct gestures, correct grammar, correct pronunciation and correct accents. It was the correct chanting of texts and the correct method of performing ceremonies that led to salvation. The Purva Mimamsa which supports this method of salvation seems to have been the prevailing philosophy of the time. As only Brahmins could read the Vedas, no one had any hope of salvation except through the intervention of Brahmins, and these claimed privileges which placed them even above the gods. The common man had no way of salvation except by paying the Brahmins and making them perform the prescribed ceremonies.

It was this monopoly of religion by Brahmins that the Buddha attacked. By rejecting the Vedas he rejected all rituals based on these books, and he told the people that ' he who paid the priest would be wasting his money as every one's salvation depended solely upon oneself". He also denounced the religious sanctions of caste and maintained that the pariah stood as good a chance of attaining Nirvana as a Brahmin. He gave a new interpretation to caste; for caste, according to the Buddha was a matter of worth and not of birth. "Birth cannot make a Brahmin any more than a non-Brahmin. It is by work and merit, by his wisdom, piety and self-sacrifice that one becomes a Brahmin."

The Buddha discarded Sanskrit, the favourite medium of religious instruction among the Brahmins, and addressed his message direct to the common people in their own dialect. He preached to all castes and took as his disciples men of all trades and of all social positions, and Buddhism soon began to be known as a religion of the people. The royal clans were also drawn towards the new religion for two reasons: firstly the founder was a man of their own caste, and secondly, they were jealous of the power of the Brahmins and were only too glad to patro-

---

* H. S. Gour, *The Spirit of Buddhism*.

† The Eightfold Path : (1) Right Understanding; (2) Right Mindedness; (3) Right Speech; (4) Right Action; (5) Right Living; (6) Right Effort; (7) Right Attentiveness; and (8) Right Concentration.

nize a religion which appealed to the people and shook the very foundations of Brahminism. The Buddha himself converted many kings, and on his death several monarchs claimed the relics of the Blessed One.

Buddhism reached the zenith of its glory under the able leadership and patronage of Asoka. Soon after his conversion to Buddhism (see chapter I), the emperor set himself out to spread the new faith. Short of persecution, he did everything in his power to make known the teachings of Buddhism, not only in India but even in countries far removed from his kingdom. Throughout the length and breadth of India he had stone pillars erected on which were engraved the moral commandments of Buddhism. There was a regular department of the State which ensured that the Law was given the widest publicity in the country, and inspectors had to report the progress of religion in every district under their charge. Colleges and monasteries were founded for the diffusion of knowledge. Missionaries trained in these institutions were despatched to Ceylon, Burma and even to distant Syria, Greece and Alexandria for the propagation of the new faith. The mission to Ceylon was headed by Mahendra, the emperor's son (brother according to other accounts) and its success was immediate. Rival schools of thought having begun to trouble the religion the Buddha founded, Asoka called a synod of monks in which the canons of the Buddhist law were established. This synod, no doubt guided by the emperor's own predilections, favoured the original puritanical ideal.

The next great king to interest himself in Buddhism was Kanishka, the Kushan Emperor. With his capital at Purushapura (Peshawar) this emperor, like Asoka, sent out missionaries for preaching Buddhism, and it was under his leadership that Buddhism started its long and successful pilgrimage towards Central Asia and distant China. The Kushans came from a colder climate and had warmer blood in their veins and they actively supported the Mahayana form of Buddhism against the older Hinayana or puritanic form. Kanishka, too, had to convene a synod of monks to settle the differences between various schools of thought that had sprung up in the country. The synod took place in Kashmir, and the resolutions passed were inscribed on copper plates and buried in a monastery "still awaiting discovery by the fortunate archaeologist."

Under the liberal patronage of kings and nobles, art and architecture flourished among the Buddhists. New trends of thought that set aside the original puritanism of the founder actively aided the growth of literature and art. The meek and lowly Sakyamuni (the Sage of the Sakyas) was deified and worshipped. The Hindu pantheon was borrowed in its entirety and improved upon, but the gods were given a place subordinate to the Buddha. Relics of the Buddha were enshrined in Stupas and other structures and assiduously worshipped. Images of the Buddha were carved out of stone and were installed in shrines with figures of the mighty gods of the Hindu pantheon depicted as bodyguards or door keepers. A copious religious literature sprang up, centered on the personality of the Buddha, and this depicted him as a miracle worker. The truth about his birth, life and death was lost in a mass of fable, romance and legend.

These tendencies, though helpful for the growth of fine arts and literature, were harmful for the progress of religion and eventually led to the decay and downfall of Buddhism in India. Royal patronage too had its disadvantages. Flourishing on the endowments of kings and growing extremely rich, the monasteries attracted a large number of ease loving monks who loved to lead an idle life of corruption at the expense of the people. Secret cults, worship of goddesses, midnight orgies, in fact all the vices the founder of the religion detested began to gnaw into the vitals of monastic life, and some of the monasteries degenerated into dens of debauchery. Devoid of the correcting hand of an Asoka or Kanishka, the yellow-robed monks tyrannised the people and became a burden to the country. The monastic orders which the Buddha founded thus developed into a parasitic community more obnoxious than the Brahmins against whose tyranny the Buddha had revolted.

In this decay of Buddhism, Hinduism found its opportunity for revival, and a vigorous attempt was made by the Brahmins to drive away Buddhism from India. The success of this attempt was comlete and final. Buddhistic monasteries and shrines were either destroyed or appropriated by the Hindus, and in place of the images and relics of the Buddha the great gods of the Hindu pantheon were installed. Just as Buddhism, in its rise, borrowed many of the gods and beliefs of orthodox Hinduism, the Hindu revivalists in their turn incorporated into Hinduism some of the beliefs, practices and gods of the Buddhists. The Hindu revival was led by the philosopher Sankara and by the time he died Hinduism was strongly re-established as the religion of the people and of the kings of India. The end of Buddhism appears to have been hastened by violence and the onslaught of Islam.

At present there are few Buddhists in India except in the hill countries that border on the Himalayas. In the plains of India including the birth place of the Buddha and the place where he received enlightenment, the religion he taught has disappeared. Yet it must be mentioned that Buddhism at present claims more followers than any other religion in the world. The vast population of China, Tibet, Japan, Korea, some parts of Central Asia, Burma and Ceylon profess the Buddhist faith. Buddhism, in these places, was necessarily influenced by the beliefs and practices of the people, and Buddhistic mythology and literature were coloured by their age-old traditions. As this book deals only with the peoples of India, it is, however, outside its scope to dwell upon the different forms of Buddhism that exist in the other countries.

JAINISM

Vardhamana, called Mahavira (the great hero), the founder of Jainism, was a prince of the royal Jnatri clan of Vedeha (modern Bihar), who, like the

Buddha, gave up a crown for the staff of the mendicant. He lived in the sixth century B.C. and was an elder contemporary of the Buddha. In East India there was, it appears, a general tendency of revolt against Brahminism at the time, and the religion Vardhamana founded was marked by this spirit. Though Siddhartha and Mahavira were contemporaries, the religions they founded grew up independently of each other, and the antagonism against Brahminism, common to both systems, appears to have been a coincidence.

The word 'Jaina' is derived from 'Jina' (the conqueror) by which name Mahavira is also known. The Jains, however, do not consider Mahavira as the sole founder of their religion. They trace their system to twenty-four Thirthankaras (ford-finders) of whom Mahavira is believed to be the last. The Thirthankara who immediately preceded Mahavira is said to be Parsva whose tradition the former is believed to have kept up. Of the other twenty-two Thirthankaras we know little except that they were big made and lived long. Thirthankara Rishabha, for instance, lived for 8,400,000 years and was 500 poles in height. The last two Thirthankaras were of ordinary size; Parsva lived for 100 years and Mahavira for 72. The former according to Jains, lived 250 years before Mahavira but the chronology of the Jains is not very trustworthy and it is probable that Mahavira was a disciple of Parsva.*

Vardhamana abandoned his crown when he was thirty years of age. For twelve years he lived the life of an ascetic and at the end of this period, while squatting in the open "with joined hands, exposing himself to the heat of the sun with the knees high and head low, in deep meditation, in the midst of abstract meditation, he reached Nirvana† the complete and full, the unobstructed, unimpeded, infinite and supreme, best knowledge and intuition, called Kevala total. When the Venerable One had become an Arhat and Jina he was a Kevalin, omniscient and comprehending all objects. He knew all conditions of the world, of gods, men and demons; whence they come, where they go, whether they are born as men or animals, or become gods or hell-beings; their food, drink, doings, desires, open and secret deeds, their conversation and gossip, and the thoughts of their minds; he saw and knew all conditions in the whole world of living beings."

After attaining this knowledge he lived thirty years in the world teaching humanity. It does not appear that Mahavira taught his doctrines to the masses as the Buddha did; his religion did not reach the people. But it gained considerable influence with kings and some intellectuals and it soon spread towards the west and south of India. Chandragupta Maurya, the grandfather of Asoka, as mentioned in the first chapter, is said to have become a convert to Jainism in his old age and lived in the Jain monastery of Shravan Belgola in Mysore.

In the first century of the Christian era a great schism split Jainism into two sects—the Digambaras and the Swetambaras. The difference between the two sects is not great, but the feeling is. The Swetambaras, who derive their authority for the practice from Parsva, maintain that wearing of white clothes is not an impediment to the higher life; hence their name Swetambaras (white robed). The Digambaras (sky-clad), on the other hand, reject all clothing as harmful to a spiritual life, and believe that the sky is the only clothing permissible for those who wish to obtain Nirvana. The Swetambaras, again, believe in sex equality whereas the Digambaras hold the view that women cannot attain Nirvana. The ascetics and holy men of the Digambara sect practise what they profess, and when they move about from place to place a cordon of lay Jains surround them lest the sight of the great man on the way to Nirvana offend the public. They exclude women from their monastic orders, whereas the Swetambaras have nunneries for women who choose the higher life.

The philosophy and doctrines of the Jains are not fundamentally different from those of the Buddhists or the Hindus. The Jains have produced few great thinkers whose works can compare favourably with those of the well-known Hindu and Buddhistic philosophers. Jain works which lay claim to philosophical speculation are marked by dogmatism and flair for figures and exactness. The metaphysics of the Jains is similar to the Sankhya system of Hindu philosophy. Jainism postulates matter and souls (Jivas) as real. The Jiva of the Jains is active and not completely passive as the Purusha of the Sankhya. The Jiva, like the Purusha, has a subtle body consisting of various fine particles and the elevation of the soul and its final release consists in dropping these particles by austerities which, more or less, enables the Jiva to float upwards to Nirvana. The Jains have an elaborate literature which tells us the exact number of these particles and their subdivisions, but it is likely to bore the reader rather than interest him in the subject.

Though the Jains do not believe in a God as the First Cause, they have a pantheon of gods who are lower beings than the Thirthankaras. These gods are themselves engaged in working out their own Nirvana, and as such do not help or hinder humans from working out theirs. Even the Thirthankaras are helpless in this matter. All the same, worship of Thirthankaras and of the gods is recommended because of the inherent power of all forms of true worship to elevate the soul of the worshipper. It is like giving alms with no intention of alleviating the suffering of the beggar, but on the principle that giving away in charity is good for the giver.

According to Jain theories, men are, in some respects, more favoured than gods; for no god can attain Nirvana without being born as man. Only by the practice of the discipline taught by the Thirthankaras is Nirvana possible, and man alone can practise them. Gods are calculated to undergo

---

* For Jain mythology the reader is referred to the author's work *Epics. Myths and Legends of India* (Taraporevala).

† Not the final Nirvana which is attained only at death, but Emancipation in Life, the state of the Jivan Mukta mentioned on page 44.

XXXVII

82 COLLECTION OF BRASSES (ICONS, SACRIFICIAL VESSELS AND DOMESTIC
UTENSILS) FROM CENTRAL INDIA
(Journal of Indian Art and Industry)

XXXVIII

CARVED SANDALWOOD BOX FROM MYSORE
(*Journal of Indian Art and Industry*)

XXXIX

IVORY CARVING REPRESENTING DURGA KILLING MAHISHASURA
(India Museum, S. Kensington, *Journal of Indian Art and Industry*)

XL

85 **BRACELETS OF CARVED BEADS**
(Journal of Indian Art and Industry)

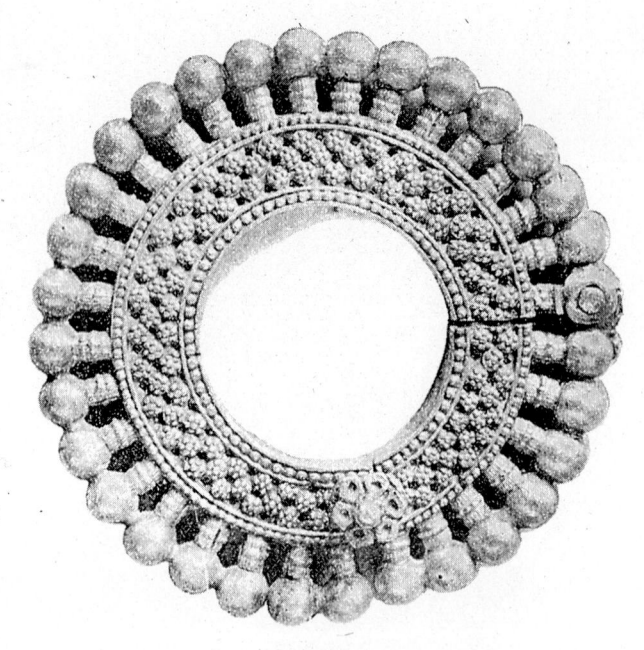

86 **ANKLET**
(Journal of Indian Art and Industry)

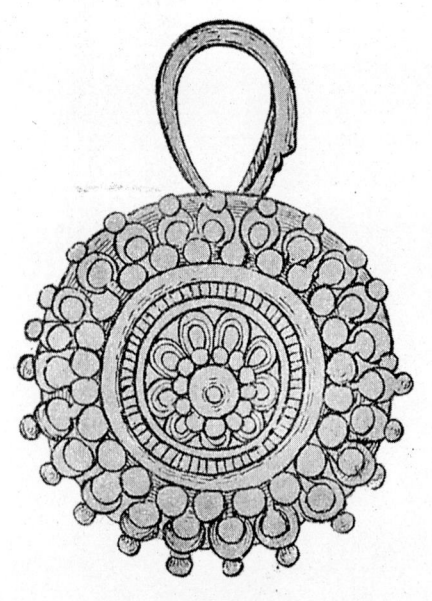

87 **TOE RING**
(Journal of Indian Art and Industry)

88 **MEDALLION WITH HANUMAN, THE APE GOD**
Moor's *Hindu Pantheon*

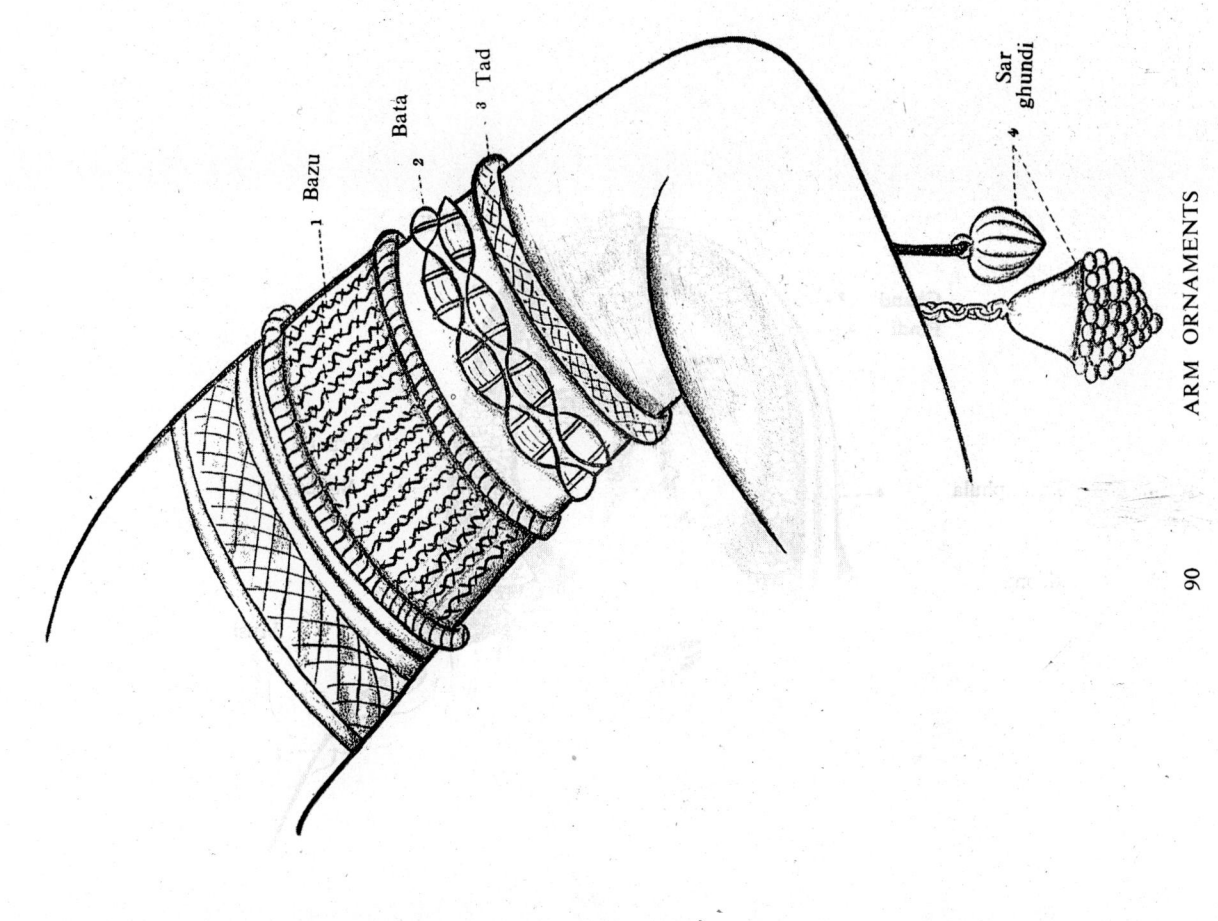

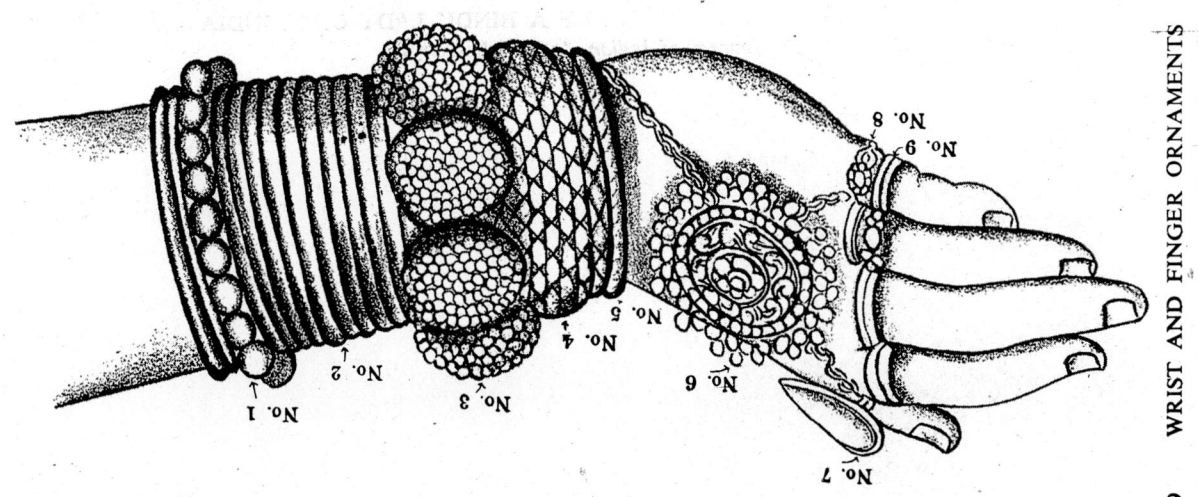

XLI

ARM ORNAMENTS

1 Bazu
2 Bata
3 Tad
4 Sar ghundi

(Journal of Indian Art and Industry)

WRIST AND FINGER ORNAMENTS

No. 1
No. 2
No. 3
No. 4
No. 5
No. 6
No. 7
No. 8
No. 9

XLII

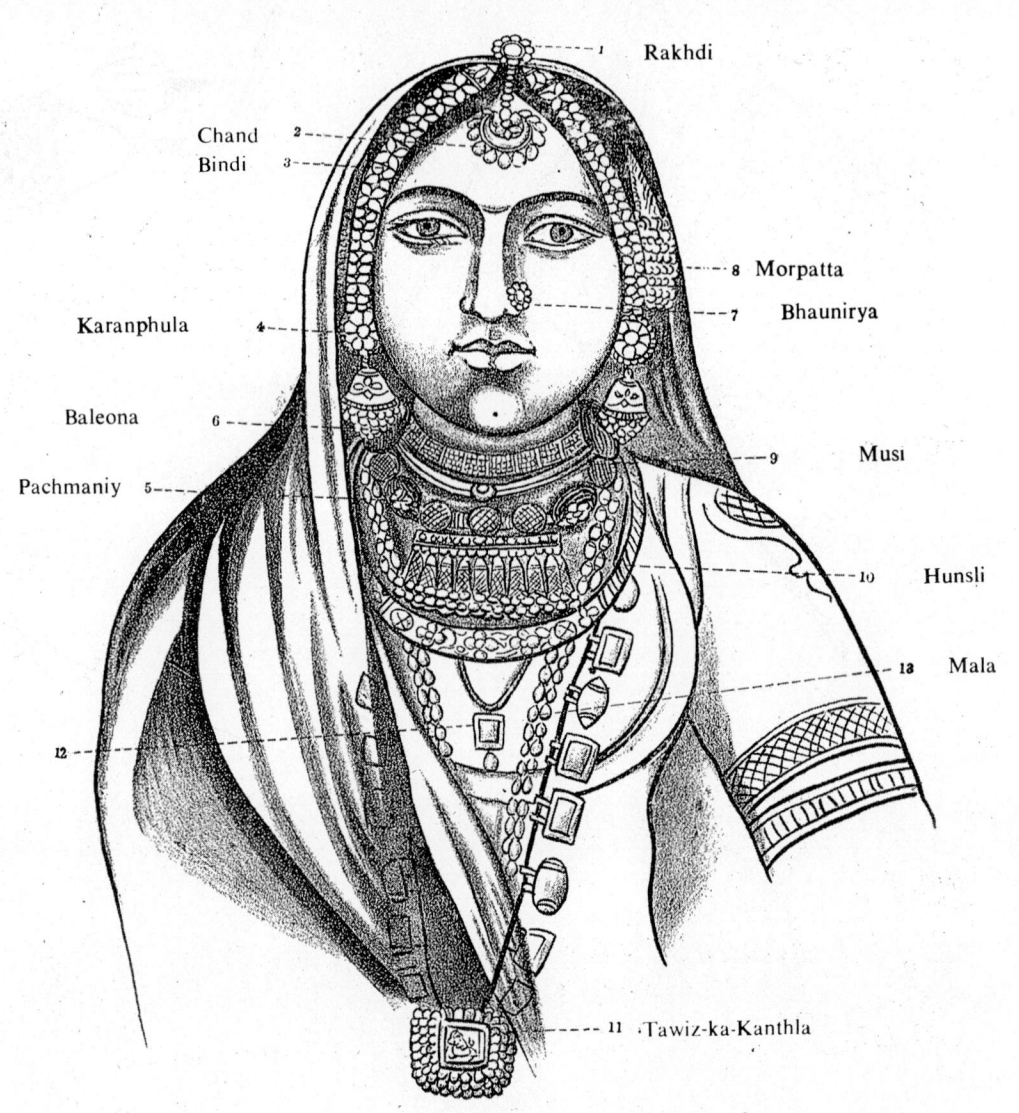

91 HEAD AND NECK ORNAMENTS OF A HINDU LADY OF N. INDIA
(Journal of Indian Art and Industry)

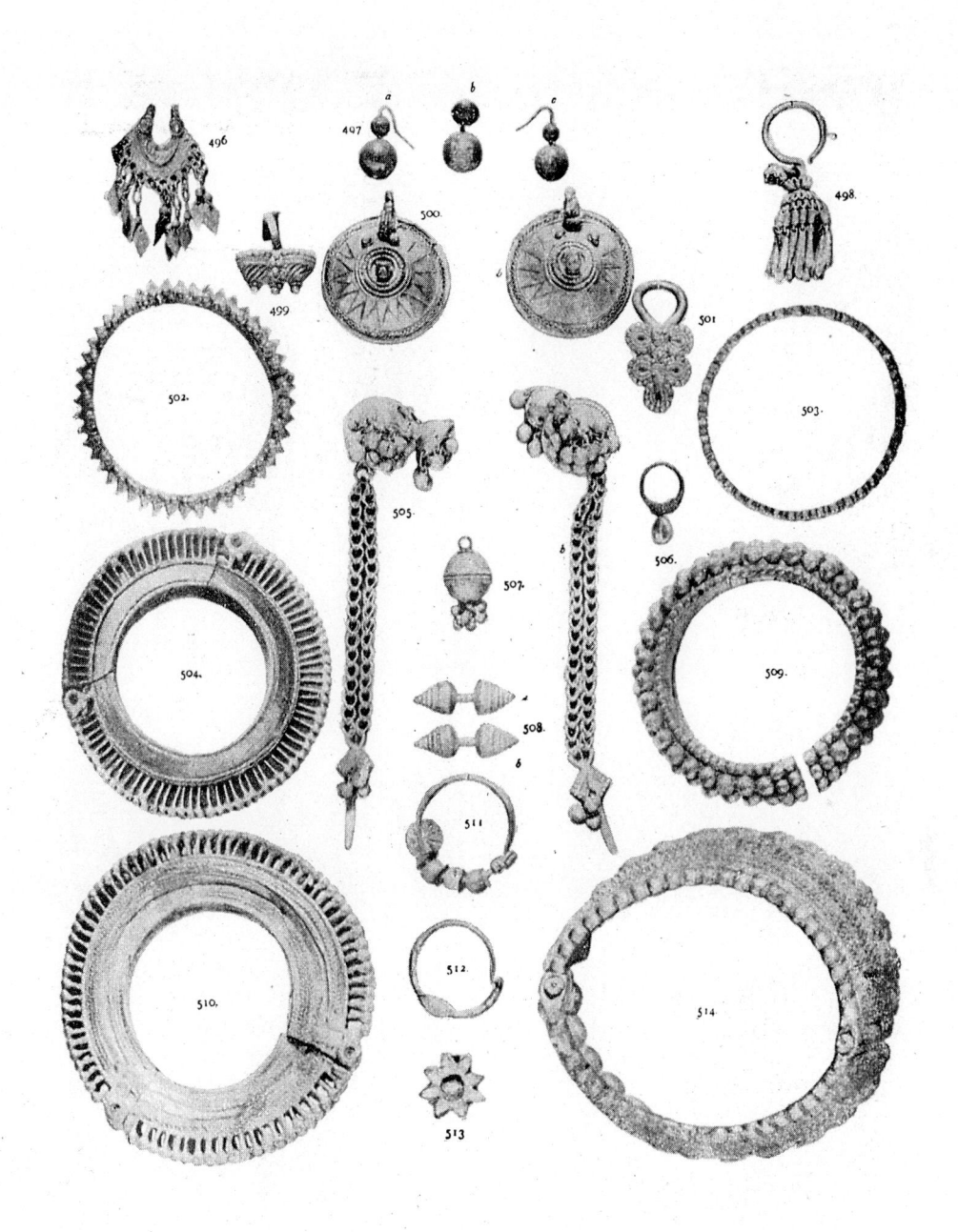

XLIII

PEASANT ORNAMENTS
(Journal of Indian Art and Industry)

XLIV

93 EAR-RING

94 ARMLET

95 A RAJPUT CROWN

96 HEAD ORNAMENT

(Journal of Indian Art and Industry)

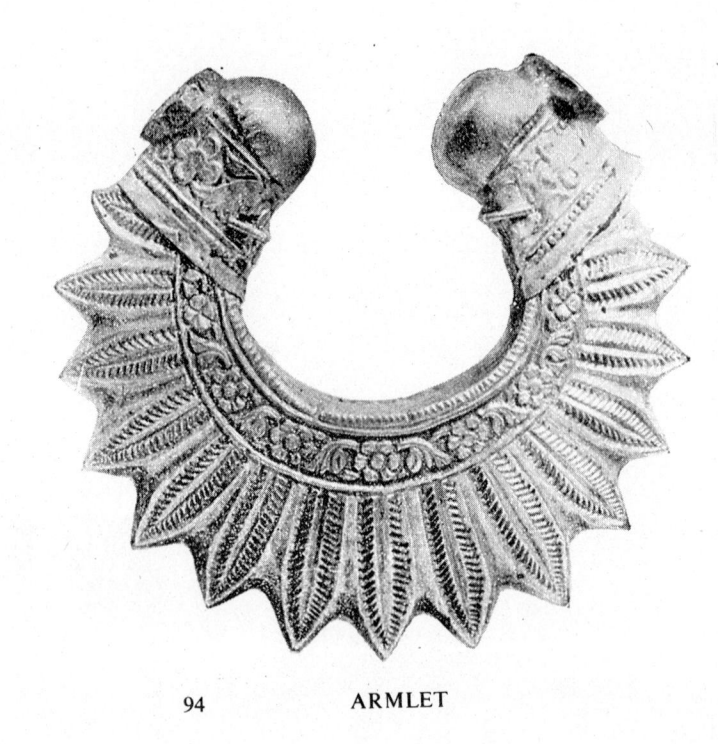

exactly 400,000 rebirths in the celestial plane while beings on earth are reborn 1,000,000 times; of the latter not more than eight births can be in human form. Women, according to the Digambaras, have to be reborn as men before they can attain Nirvana.

The Jain view of life is even more pessimistic than that of Buddhism, and its discipline is ascetic and rigorous. The monks and nuns have to take the five vows of the order and strictly observe them. The five vows are: (1) Abstention from taking life, (2) Abstention from falsehood, (3) Abstention from stealing, (4) Abstention from sexual intercourse, and (5) Abstention from worldly possessions. Jain monks who take these vows are known as Nirgranthas (freed from fetters). For the laity the discipline is less strict. They too have to take their vows but with certain reservations. Sexual intercourse is permitted to the laity within lawful limits and acquisition of wealth to a certain extent.

The Jains are probably the only people in the world who take the law prohibiting killing quite seriously. Jain monks will not eat after nightfall lest inadvertently insects get into the meal and get killed while eating. They will not drink water without straining it several times. While moving about they take care to cover their mouths with a piece of cloth suspended from the upper lip so that insects flying against their faces may not be trapped in their mouths. Even the eating of certain vegetable supposed to be 'alive' is prohibited. Nor is this virtue practised on the negative side only; active support to living beings, especially to cattle and insects, is given by Jains. Dropping grain near ant hills for ants to eat is a common sight on the roads and lanes where Jains live. Mosquitos, bugs and other bloodsucking insects are also considered worthy of attention. Wealthy Jains pay able bodied men, who can spare some blood, to sleep on their bug-ridden cots till the bugs are well gorged when the employee is sent away and the master goes to bed!

The main reason why the Digambara monks insist on nudity is that wearing of clothes attaches a person to his garments, and Nirvana is impossible as long as this attachment to worldly possession lasts. No wonder that so exacting a religion permits religious suicide. Indiscriminate suicide is not, however, allowed. Only those who, by following the vows strictly, have qualified themselves for Nirvana on death are permitted to put an end to their existence in this way. A minimum period of twelve years' mortification of flesh is necessary for suicide. The end is to be effected not by violence but by starvation and exposure. The Thirthankara Parsva and the celebrated Jain scholar Hemachandra are said to have adopted this method of attaining Nirvana.

Because of its extreme ascetic tendencies and its uncompromising attitude towards killing, Jainism has never been a popular religion. Yet many kings were converted to Jainism and under their patronage the religion that Mahavira founded in Bihar spread to other parts of the country. Jainism appealed mainly to the upper castes, especially to Vaisyas and Kshatriyas. The interest of the latter in Jainism was mainly inspired by political reasons and their jealousy of Brahmin supremacy; the fact that Mahavira and his predecessor Parsva were of royal blood might also have contributed towards the Kshatriyas actively supporting Jainism.

At the time of the Hindu revival which drove Buddhism out of India, Jainism too became a target of attack. But because of its limited power, the Hindus did not consider it a force strong enough to be a serious menace, and hence Jainism was allowed to exist as a minor heterodox sect and did not suffer the fate of its sister religion in India. One of the Jain innovations adopted at the time of the Hindu revival was the requisitioning of the services of Brahmins for the performance of ceremonial worship in Jain households and temples. The Brahmins perform Pujas in the same way as described in the previous chapter, the only difference being that instead of an image of some Hindu god the prayers are addressed to an image of one of the Thirthankaras. As the Brahmins are paid for these services and as the Jains are well known for their commercial acumen it is no wonder that Brahminism permitted Jainism to live side by side with it.

The Jains in India at present do not number more than two millions; but their influence in the country is quite considerable. The reason for this is that the Jains constitute one of the wealthiest communities in India. Their dread of physical injury to living beings has closed for them most of the occupations other communities engage themselves in. Agriculture for instance, involves ploughing which necessarily destroys earthworms, and large scale industry involves the use of machinery, which while working destroys insects and germs. So the conscientious Jain prefers trade as a profession. Nor does he indulge in indiscriminate purchase and sale of articles. A Jain for instance, would not engage himself in the fish trade. The commodities which appeal most to the Jains are gold, silver and precious stones. High finance also interests them.

Although Mahavira was a destroyer of caste, the present-day Jains, especially the Swetambaras, observe caste. Most of them belong to the Vaisya caste and intermarry with the Hindus of this caste. The Jains, for all practical purposes, are tending to become a Hindu sect.

SIKHISM

While both Buddhism and Jainism were inspired by religious and social ideas that grew out of an entirely Hindu background, Sikhism is a comparatively recent development which has much to do with Islamic ideals. The conquest of India by Muslims brought Hinduism into close contact with Islam, and the simplicity of Muslim worship and its theology began to attract many enlightened Hindus. The incessant quarrels between Hindus and Muslims which at times resulted in bloodshed also made intelligent men recognize the need for an understanding between the followers of the two religions. The astute Akbar as we have mentioned in an earlier chapter realized the political advantage of a union between Hinduism and Islam, and wished to found a national Indian religion with himself as the prophet of the new faith. He failed in his attempt. Guru Nanak who approached the problem from a purely religious angle succeeded in founding Sikhism.

Nanak was born at Talvandi, near Lahore, in A.D. 1469. He belonged to the Khatri caste of the Punjab, well known for their fine physique and martial spirit. The boy Nanak was of a religious turn of mind. He neglected his secular duties and kept company with holy men, spending most of his time in discussing and brooding over subjects which had no bearing on farming or trade and the villagers pronounced him mad. At last the call came, and Nanak left his home and wandered all over India in the manner of Hindu saints. Religious music profoundly moved him, and he himself was the composer of many hymns. In the course of his wanderings he was accompanied by Mardana, a Muslim musician who played on the Rebek for Nanak.

This was the time when the great saint Kabir was wandering from Bukhara to Kalighat preaching his revolutionary ideals, and Nanak came under his influence. A few words about Kabir will not be out of place here. Kabir was a remarkable man and both Hindus and Muslims, to this day, claim him as their own. The Hindus say that Kabir was really a Hindu brought up by a family of Muslim weavers, whereas the Muslims say that he was born a Muslim. Whatever his origin, at an early age he showed great interest in religion and became a disciple of the Vaishnava saint Ramananda who was a follower of Ramanuja, the founder of the Vishishta Advaita philosophy and of the Bhakti cult. Ramananda was persecuted in South India for his extreme views on caste and migrated to Benares. Here he preached the Bhakti cult, and "among his twelve disciples were a Rajput, a currier, a barber and a Mussalman weaver named Kabir."

Kabir excelled the master himself. He was blessed with a keen wit and in his 'sayings' and songs poured ridicule on all formalists. All ceremonials and formal worship, those endless repetition of sacred texts and words, circumambulations round idols and the numerous prayers addressed to gods as a matter of form were, according to Kabir, mere waste of time and energy. "The beads are wood; the gods are stone; Ganges and Jumna are water; Rama and Krishna are dead and gone, and the Vedas are empty words." The ascetic with his matted locks and unkempt beard struck him as resembling a goat. The shaven priest with his long face and lengthy religious discourses was a babbler who did not understand what he was teaching others. Those who wished to worship God were asked to flee from the temple and mosque, and seek Him in the fields, in the weaver's shop and the happy home. Only fools would try to find God in stones and structures. "God is One, whether we worship Him as Allah or as Rama. The Hindu worships Him on the eleventh day; the Muhammaden fasts at Ramzan; but God made all the days and all the months. The Hindu God lives at Benares: the Muhammaden God at Mecca; but He who made the world lives not in a city made by hands. There is One Father of Hindu and Mussalman, One God in all matter: He is the Lord of all the earth, my Guardian, and my Priest." Again,

"Oh Servant, where dost thou seek Me? Lo, I am beside thee.
I am neither in temple or in mosque: I am neither in Kaaba or Kailas*
Neither am in rites and ceremonies, nor in Yoga or renunciation.
If thou art a true seeker, thou shalt at once seek Me:
Thou shalt meet Me in a moment of time.
Kabir says: 'O Sadhu! God is the breath of all breath.' "†

Such revolutionary teachings, a saintly life and a ready wit made Kabir the most popular figure of his time. But, for obvious reasons, organized society could not tolerate him for long. He was persecuted by the ruling classes and exiled from Benares. He wandered all over India with a band of followers. Wherever he preached the people applauded him. Even in distant Afghanistan, which place he visited, Kabir became the pet of the people. This great wandering saint of India died in 1518, and on his death both the Muslims and the Hindus claimed the body, the former to bury it according to Muslim rites and the latter to burn it. A legend says that while the disciples were thus violently disputing for the possession of the dead body, a celestial voice was heard commanding them to remove the wrapper of the coffin and look inside. On this being done, no corpse was found but the coffin contained only a heap of fresh flowers. Even this miracle could not settle the dispute. It is said the heap of flowers were equally divided among the Hindus and Muslims. the former taking away their share for burning and the latter for burying.

Although Kabir founded no organized sect, he is considered by Indians as one of the greatest saints India has ever produced and his followers, known as Kabirpanthis, number more than a million souls.

The life and teachings of Kabir profoundly influenced Nanak. After some years of wanderings, the call came to Nanak to teach and he preached before Jain and Hindu temples and Muslim mosques and collected a number of Sikhs or disciples. Religion he thought, was a bond to unite men, but in practice he found it setting men against men. The antagonism between Hinduism and Islam he particularly regretted and his lifelong attempt was to weld them into one. That he actually succeeded only in founding a new religion, is unfortunately true; but Nanak was the first Indian saint who devoted his life to this cause. One of the familiar sayings of Nanak is: "There is

* Kailas is the abode of Shiva.
† Quoted from Rawlinson's *India*.

no Hindu and no Mussalman." Nanak rejected caste and the racial pride of the Hindus. "God has said", says Nanak, "that man shall be saved by his works alone. God will not ask a man his tribe or sect, but what he has done."

Like Kabir, Nanak vigorously attacked all formalism. He told the Muslims:

"Make love thy mosque; sincerity thy prayer-carpet; justice thy Koran;
Modesty thy circumcision; courtesy thy Kaaba; truth thy Guru; charity thy creed and prayer;
The will of God thy rosary, and God will preserve thine honour, O Nanak."

Nanak's definition of caste is this:

"Evil-mindedness is the low-caste woman; cruelty is the butcher's wife; a slanderous heart the sweeper-woman; wrath the pariah woman.
What availeth it to have drawn lines round thy cooking place, when these four sit ever with thee?
Make truth, self-restraint and good acts thy lines, and the utterance of the Name thine ablutions.
Nanak, in the next world, he is best who walketh not in the way of sin."*

Nanak is believed to have performed the Haj (pilgrimage to Mecca) like a good Muslim, but he got into trouble with the keepers of the Kaaba. The story goes that he went to sleep in the holy city with his feet towards the sacred stone. He was censored for this disrespect towards the Kaaba and was taken before the authorities. Nanak maintained the omnipresence of the Kaaba and asked them to drag his feet to a direction where the Kaaba was not.

Shortly before his death, Nanak appointed one of his disciples as the Guru or pontiff of his followers who was to be their spiritual head and guide. This institution of Gurus is a distinguishing feature of Sikkhism. The Sikhs recognize ten such Gurus and pay extraordinary reverence to them. The institution was abolished by Guru Gobind Singh, the tenth Guru, who substituted the Granth or Bible for a Guru.

Sikkhism was a peaceful religion under the first four Gurus and was pervaded by the spirit of Kabir and Nanak. The fourth Guru Ramdas lived in the time of Akbar and received from that generous monarch the grant of a piece of land at Amritsar (pool of immortality), so called because of a tank supposed to possess healing properties. The shrine that Ramdas built on the bank of this tank was rebuilt into the Golden Temple by the Sikh monarch Ranjit Singh and is at present the most sacred stronghold of Sikkhism. It was in the time of the fifth Guru, Arjun, that the Sikhs, for the first time, began to show political ambition. Arjun was drawn to the side of Khusru, Jehangir's son, who rebelled against his father, and when the revolt was suppressed Jehangir imposed a heavy fine on the whole community of Sikhs. Arjun refused to pay the fine and was tortured to death.

The martyrdom of Arjun made the Sikhs realize the need for a military organisation for their self-preservation and for promoting their political interests. During the peaceful reign of Shah Jehan, the Sikhs, however, did not fall foul of the Moghul power, but Aurangzeb saw in them an obstacle to his scheme for converting all India to Islam. The emperor summoned to Delhi Tej Bahadur, the ninth Guru; and during his stay at Delhi the venerable pontiff was charged with "presuming to gaze from the roof of his abode upon the apartments of the ladies of the royal harem," and put to death. Before his departure to Delhi Tej Bahadur had taken the precaution of investing his son Gobind with his sword. On hearing of the massacre of his father, Gobind swore undying vengeance on the Moghuls. Militarist ideals, originated by the sixth Guru Hargobind, Arjun's son, were perfected by Gobind. Gobind instituted the Baptism of the Sword, and every Sikh, on his initiation, had to drink water stirred by a dagger and partake of cakes made of consecrated flour. After this ceremony, a Sikh was to be known as the Khalsa or elect and adopt the affix Singh or lion to his name. The Khalsa was to be distinguished by the five K's, Kes (uncut hair), Kaccha (short drawers), Kankan (comb), Kirpan (a dagger), and Kangha (a steel bangle). The use of tobacco and wine was prohibited to the Khalsa. Valour and physical virility became the essential qualities of the Khalsa and everything else was made subordinate to them. To infuse the proper martial spirit in his followers, Gobind Singh introduced the worship of Durga, the war goddess of the Hindu pantheon, among the Sikhs.

Gobind Singh abolished the institution of Gurus. He was the tenth and the last Guru and the Khalsa, after him, was to be guided by the Granth or the Bible. The Granth is, more or less, a revised edition by him of the Adi Granth (the original Granth) compiled by Guru Arjun from the inspired sayings of Kabir, Nanak and other saints.

Gobind Singh was murdered by a Pathan, but the spirit he infused thrived among the Sikhs. War became the joy of the Sikhs and the more bigoted among them styled themselves as the Akalis or deathless. The Akali was contemptuous of death and was feared even by the Sikhs themselves. The sword was accepted as the last word in every dispute. This religious militarism eminently suited the genius of the hardy races of the Punjab to whom war, from the very beginning of Indian history, was a natural state of human relationship. Every Sikh had to discard caste, and the sacred thread had to be cut on undergoing the Baptism of the Sword. This made the higher castes fight shy of joining Sikhism; but it attracted a large number of lower classes from the peasantry who proved to be the bulwark and mainstay of Sikhism.

Thus the quietist religion preached by the meek Nanak was turned into one of the most powerful forces of aggression by Gobind Singh. Soon after Gobind Singh's death, the Moghul empire col-

* Quoted from Rawlinson's *India*.

lapsed and the Sikhs became the terror of the Punjab. The Afghan prince Ahmad Shah Durrani, who invaded India at this time, destroyed the temple at Amritsar and temporarily broke the Sikh power. But when Durrani went back to Afghanistan, the Sikhs appeared in the Punjab again; but these Sikhs had forgotten the teachings of Kabir, Nanak and even of Gobind Singh and had degenerated into disorganized gangs of bandits who robbed, looted and terrorized the peaceful population. The decay of the central power and the state of anarchy the country had fallen into at that time, suited the ambitions of these Sikhs, and they took a terrible toll of the Muslim population of the Punjab for the sins of the Moghuls and of Ahmad Shah Durrani. At this time, there arose a great leader among the Sikhs. He was Ranjit Singh, "short, deformed and blind in one eye, illiterate, but a born leader of men." He organized the Sikhs into a powerful fighting force and soon became the master of the Punjab. He extended his influence into Kashmir and Afghanistan, and the Mirs of Sind lived in fear of him. He had his army trained by famous French generals, and some of his most trusted generals were Europeans.

The Sikhs reached the zenith of their political power under Ranjit Singh. He rebuilt the Golden Temple at Amritsar, and had his capital in the ancient city of Lahore. The British and the Sikhs under Ranjit had a profound respect for each other's power and had managed to get on without a conflict. But Ranjit Singh passed away in 1839, and the leadership of the community fell into less able hands. Internal dissensions and intrigues started, and in their folly the Sikhs discarded the wary policy of Ranjit Singh and declared war on the British. A fierce and bloody conflict ensued which ended the suzerainty of the Sikhs in the Punjab. In the battle of Sabraon, fought on the 21st February 1849, the Sikhs were finally defeated and the Punjab passed into British hands.

The Sikhs at present number about five million souls, and the Punjab is still the noted stronghold of Sikhism. It is worthy of note that even so recent a religion as Sikhism has produced sects which differ from one another. We have already mentioned the Akalis, the extreme militarists among the Sikhs. The Nanak-panthis or Sahidharis (easy-going) do not believe in all the teachings of Gobind Singh, but follow the peaceful religion of Nanak. They do not wear their hair long and are not distinguishable from other Hindus. The Keshdhari Sikhs, on the other hand, believe in all the five K's and are distinguished by their uncut hair. The prohibition regarding smoking is observed by most of the Sikhs, especially the Keshdharis, but there are few Sikhs who abjure intoxicants.

Nanak, the founder of Sikhism, was a breaker of systems and forms, and hence it is difficult to say what exactly are the doctrines and dogmas of Sikhism. Nanak accepted the Hindu doctrine of metempsychosis, but rejected caste, polytheism and the authority of the Vedas. The theism of Nanak was a combination of Islam and the Vishishta Advaita doctrine of Ramanuja. Idolatry was prohibited, but the extraordinary position given to the Granth or the Bible by Guru Gobind Singh who installed it as his successor had made his followers pay exceptional reverence to it. In every Sikh temple a Granth is placed on an altar and devotees offer flowers to it. A person stands behind the sacred book and fans it with a yak tail fan day and night. When the Granth is taken out, it is accompanied by a procession and much music. Some of the Sikh temples began to adopt Hindu practices and installed idols in them, but the Akali revival that started early in the 19th century, made vigorous efforts to combat all tendencies that were at work to degenerate Sikhism into a Hindu sect.

Because of the long persecution of the Sikhs by the Moghuls, in social matters the Sikhs lean more towards the Hindus than to the Muslims. Though intermarriages between Sikhs and Hindus are rare, the Sikhs freely dine with non-vegetarian Hindus. The Sikhs burn their dead like the Hindus. The custom of burning widows was prevalent among the Sikhs, though prohibited by the Gurus, and four queens, we are told, died with Ranjit Singh. The cruel practice was stopped all over India by William Bentinck in 1829. The Sikhs consider killing of cows a sacrilege and abstain from beef.

Guru Nanak and, later, Gobind Singh freed the Sikhs from many of the tiresome restrictions imposed by caste rules on eating, drinking and social intercourse. Asceticism was condemned and every Sikh had to bear in mind Kabir's saying that "a hungry man is not in the proper mood to worship the Almighty." So every true worshipper of God should first work for a living, and religion was not to be made an excuse for indolence or laziness. Exceptions were permitted in cases of certain individuals who were allowed to leave their profession for a higher calling. As a rule, every man is to stick to his trade and his sword, and realize that work itself is worship.

This manly philosophy, and its practice have made the Sikhs one of the most enterprising communities of India. Nor have they lost any of their martial spirit. War is still the delight of the Sikh, and in valour and physique the Sikhs are second to none among the several races of India.

BRAHMO SAMAJ

While Sikhism was the result of contact between Hinduism and Islam, the Brahmo Samaj was inspired by Christianity and the civilisation of Europe. The founder of Brahmo Samaj was Raja Ram Mohan Roy, a Bengali Brahmin, who is known as the "Father of Modern India." Most of the reform movements that have revolutionized Hindu society can be traced to this great son of India. He was himself the victim of social evils, and throughout his life he worked indefatigably for the social and religious upliftment of his community. In his childhood he was married to two wives, and all his life he fought against the evil of child marriage. He saw his own sister mounting the funeral pyre of her husband, and it was through the agitation started by him that Lord William Bentinck abolished by law the institution of Sati. The idolatry, caste tyranny and animal sacrifices of Hinduism filled him with disgust. He was much attracted by Christianity and was a constant friend of the European missionaries of Bengal. A study of the Vedas and the Upanishads made him realize that idolatry, caste and other well-known features of Hindu society had no foundation in the Vedas and were accretions of a later age.

Ram Mohan Roy was deeply imbued with the culture of the West and East, and was a scholar as well as a reformer. He was a nationalist but had profound contempt for narrow-minded nationalism. In his days, the controversy regarding the adoption of English education in India reached a heated pitch, all orthodox Hindus and Muslims and even some Englishmen opposing it. The following extract from a letter Ram Mohan Roy wrote to Lord Amherst expresses his views on the subject: "If it had been intended to keep the British nation in ignorance of real knowledge, the Baconian philosophy would not have been allowed to displace the system of the Schoolmen, which was best calculated to perpetuate ignorance. In the same manner, the Sanskrit system of education would be the best calculated to perpetuate ignorance if such had been the policy of the British legislature. But as the improvement of the native population is the object of the Government, it will consequently promote a more liberal and enlightened policy of instruction." Raja Ram Mohan Roy was the first high caste Hindu to defy the taboo prohibiting sea voyages, and visit England.

In 1828, this versatile genius founded the Brahmo Samaj, "a Church open to all sorts and conditions of men for the 'worship and adoration of the Eternal, Unsearchable and Immortal Being, who is the Author and Preserver of the Universe'." The Islamic attitude towards idolatry was adopted by the Samaj, and any kind of images at places of worship was considered an offence. All great religious leaders like the Buddha, Jesus and Muhammad were to be venerated and Hinduism was to be interpreted in the spirit of the Vedas and the Upanishads. In the congregation of the Brahmo Samaj, "no sermon, preaching discourse, prayer or hymn be delivered, made or used but such as have a tendency to the promotion of the contemplation of the Author and Preserver of the Universe, to the promotion of charity, morality, piety, benevolence, virtue, and the strengthening of the bonds of union between men of all religious persuasions and creeds."

Such a teaching, it can be easily seen, lacks the dogmatism of a popular religion, and the Brahmo Samaj could not reach the peoples of India. But it appealed to all enlightened members of the Hindu community, and in Bengal, in spite of the antagonism and petty persecutions by the orthodox, all great leaders in the political, social and religious field were inspired by the spirit of the Brahmo Samaj. Ram Mohan Roy died in England in 1833, and on his death the affairs of the Brahmo Samaj fell in a bad way, due to lack of funds and proper leadership. In 1842, the Bengali saint Devendra Nath Tagore joined the Samaj and assumed its leadership. During his time an effort was made by some of the leading members of the Samaj to establish the new religion on a purely Hindu basis and to accept the Vedas as infallible. Opposition to this was very strong and the arguments between the parties began to affect the unity of the Samaj. On an effort being made to reconcile this quarrel, it was found that neither the adherents nor the opponents of the Vedas had an adequate knowledge of these ancient texts. Devendra Nath Tagore, therefore, immediately sent the most noisy of the disputants to Benares to study and scrutinize the Vedas. These men were so lost in the wranglings of the learned pundits of Benares, and they took so long to study Vedas that most of them died before coming to a definite agreement on the subject.

The third great figure of the Brahmo Samaj was Keshub Chandra Sen, also a Bengali. Even in the time of Devendra Nath Tagore, Keshub showed an independent and original spirit but the personality of the great saint restrained him from independent action. On Tagore's death Keshub Chandra Sen became the leader of the Brahmos. He was an impetuous genius, impatient of the slow progress of the Samaj. He wished to organize a universal religion, known as the New Dispensation Samaj, with himself as the prophet of the new faith. He had a remarkable personality and a convincing voice, but failed to convert all the members of the Samaj to his way of thinking. Those who adhered to the old school, then came to be known as the Adi Samaj or original Samaj. Keshub was a man of energy and drive and in his time, the Samaj became widely known all over India. But his overbearing attitude and claims of prophetship created many dissenters, and these founded the Saddharana Samaj of extreme views. Keshub died without being able to achieve anything like unity in the Samaj.

An offshoot of the Brahmo Samaj was the Prarthana Samaj (society of prayer) of Bombay. Keshub was the inspirer of this theistic movement and its most distinguished leaders were Mahadev Gobind Ranade and Ramakrishna Bhandarkar.

The Brahmo Samaj may be said to have paved the way for the success of the theosophical movement started by Dr. Annie Besant. The theosophists accept all religions as true, believe in the message of all the prophets that have lived in the world irrespective of caste, creed and colour, and celebrate their birthdays. The attempt of the theosophists, generally speaking, is to blend the religious conceptions of the East and the West. It must, however, be mentioned that the title of world Messiahship theosophy wished to confer on J. Krishnamurti, a Madrassi gentleman adopted in his childhood by Dr. Besant for the purpose, was rejected by him on his coming of age. He bluntly declared that he was no Messiah, but an ordinary human being possessing normal human faculties and nothing more.

The greatness of the Brahmo Samaj is not in its religious leadership but in its pioneering spirit in social reforms. Through the efforts of its members, the Brahmo Samaj has been able to give expression to those forces which abolished Sati, prohibited child marriage and other social evils, and brought home to the Hindus a sense of the shortcomings of their institutions. In the religious sphere it could only provide a sanctuary to those enlightened Hindus who hated the superstitions of their countrymen yet wished to be known as Hindus. Hence the Brahmo Samaj has at present more leaders than followers, and its influence on the popular religion of the Hindus is not very considerable.

THE ARYA SAMAJ

The Brahmo Samaj, we have noticed, was inspired by the culture and religion of Europe and its founder made no secret of his admiration for the social and religious institutions of the West. The Arya Samaj, on the other hand, was of purely Indian origin, and was marked by a vigorous antagonism to Christianity and Islam.

The founder of the Arya Samaj was Swami Dayanand Sarasvati, a Kathiawar Brahmin who was born in 1824. In his boyhood, Dayanand was of a religious turn of mind and a story is told how he decided to give up idolatry. On the night of the Feast of Shiva, the boy was keeping vigil near the idol. The rest of the devotees had fallen asleep. Suddenly the boy saw a mouse playing on the head of the idol, and this very naturally raised in his mind doubts as to the propriety of worshipping as god an image which could not protect itself from a mouse! Soon after this, he left his home and, in the manner of the great Hindu Sannyasins, wandered for many years in North India. He tried some of the conventional Hindu methods of salvation like Yoga and asceticism but found no solace in them. In 1860 he accepted a blind old Brahmin of Benares as his Guru. This Brahmin dispelled his doubts and fears, and infused a dynamic spirit in Dayanand which was responsible for his further activities.

Dayanand preached a militant cult. He deprecated the weakness of the Hindus and put it down to what he contemptuously called "Puranic religion." Real Hinduism was that of the Vedas, monotheism with no idolatry, caste and animal sacrifices to corrupt it. Idols, caste, animism, etc., drew their sanction from the Puranas which, according to Dayanand, were to be treated as fairy tales. The Mahabharata and the Ramayana were literary treasures and nothing more. He vigorously condemned idolatry and his horror of it is comparable to that of the Hebrews and the Muslims. Animal sacrifices, long pilgrimages and ablutions were rejected by Dayanand as not only worthless but positively harmful.

His rejection of the Puranas and other holy texts of orthodox Hinduism made him extraordinarily loyal to the Vedas. He put the Vedas down as eternal and infallible, and they were to be interpreted as he had done in his work Satyarthaprakash. His interpretations of these texts were at times fantastic. Not only all spiritual knowledge but all secular knowledge too, he told his followers, emanated from the Vedas. All the inventions of modern science such as steam engines, aeroplanes and poison gas originated, it appears, from the Vedas. Many more wonderful discoveries await the patient student of Vedic literature. The Arya Samajists believe that if a person could only understand the symbolism of the Vedas and apply it for purposes of aggression he could rule the world.

The movement Dayanand founded is marked by an intense patriotism of the militant type. India, the Arya Samajists believe, is the mother of all culture, spiritual and material. Mankind originated from somewhere in northern India. Sanskrit is the mother of all languages of the world. Ancient Hindus had subdued the whole world, and had discovered America long before Columbus did. Europe received her culture and scientific progress through prehistoric Hindu invaders who had conquered that continent and initiated them into the mysteries of the Vedas.

It can be easily understood how such a religious movement found ardent adherents all over India. Dayanand preached at a time when the feelings against the British were running high in India, and nationalism found an ardent ally in the Samaj. The Samaj took upon itself the task of combating the proselytizing activities of the Christian missionaries and of the Muslims. They started the "Suddhi" movement by which Hindus who had been converted into Christianity or Islam could be taken back into the Hindu fold. According to orthodox Hindu usages, as is well-known, no apostate could be accepted again as a Hindu. The activities of the Suddhi zealots often brought them into direct conflict with the Muslims, and on many occasions there were riots and bloodshed on that account; for the Arya Samajists, if it comes to that, are always ready to appeal to the Lathi to settle a religious dispute.

Swami Dayanand was not a philosopher or a scholar, but essentially a man of action, hence the Samaj he founded lacks the philosophic background, so dear to the Hindu. If the times he lived in were a little more unsettled, and if the hand of the British had been less strong, he would probably have carved out a kingdom for himself and spread his doctrines by means of the sword. When his adversaries indulged in sarcasm or used violent language in the many religious disputes he had with the Sanatanists or the orthodox sects, the Swami was found quite ready to use his stick against them. On several occasions his enemies tried to kill him by poisoning.

The Arya Samajists are theists. They believe in the reality of God, soul and matter. Thus the philosophy of the Arya Samaj is nearer to the Vishishta Advaita philosophy than to any other school of Hindu thought; but unlike the Vishishta Advaitin, the Arya Samajist accepts the reality, and independence of all the three. The Law of Karma and the transmigration of souls are accepted in their entirety, and this has made the God of the Arya Samajists a much weaker personage than the God of the Christians and the Muslims. Protection of cows is enjoined on all Arya Samajists, and cow killing and beef eating are condemned as heinous sins.

The word Arya is used by the Arya Samajists in an ethical sense, and is interpreted to mean "the noble." Samaj means society and thus Arya Samaj is "the society of the noble" who follow the religion of the Vedas. Caste, likewise is given an ethical and occupational interpretation, as was given to it by the Buddha. Anyone, at least in theory, can be accepted as an Arya Samajist by means of the purification ceremony called Suddhi, and there have been a few cases of Europeans who were admitted into the Hindu fold by the Aryas.

The militant spirit of the Arya Samaj appealed to the people of the Punjab and it was here that the Samaj put forth its full vigour. The rising wave of nationalism that swept the country at the time gave it a tremendous impetus and for some time it looked as if the new movement was going to revolutionize Hinduism throughout India. But after some time, the power of the Samaj weakened. Dissensions arose, mainly on educational issues. One section of the Aryas advocated the ancient system of Hindu education, while the others maintained that to go back to this system would be suicidal for the political and social progress of the community. There was a prolonged controversy on the subject and at last the Samaj was divided into two, the advocates of modern education styling themselves as the 'College Section' and the others as the 'Gurukula Section.' The most important educational institution of the College Section was the Dayanand Anglo-Vedic College at Lahore where students received instruction in the principles of the Arya Samaj, and were equipped with the knowledge necessary to combat the religious activities of Christians and Muslims towards whom the Aryas always assume a polemic attitude. The Gurukula Section have their principal institution at Haridwar where boys are trained in the manner suggested in the Hindu codes.

An incident is worth noticing which shows the spirit of the Aryas and their uncompromising attitude towards the idolatry of the orthodox schools. A few years back, a prominent Arya Samajist leader was addressing a crowded gathering of all sections of Hindus, and he dwelt at some length on the evils of idolatry. A Sanatanist who was in the meeting immediately got up and asked the speaker if he thought a photograph or a painting no more deserving of respect than the paper on which it appeared. On being replied in the affirmative, the Sanatanist produced a photograph of Swami Dayanand and asked the speaker to stamp it under his feet if the photograph made no difference to the paper. In his zeal for the abolition of idolatry the speaker did as he was asked and was nearly excommunicated from the Arya Samaj.

The worship of the Arya Samajists is simple. They do not construct huge temples, but generally set apart a hall in the Samaj premises for purposes of worship. Worship consists of recitation of passages and hymns from Vedic texts, accompanied by a ceremony called Homa. The Homa is performed by burning clarified butter in a pit of fire constructed in the centre of the hall, and the worshippers usually squat round the fire. If asked why clarified butter is burnt away like this, the Arya Samajist will invariably reply that it has very little religious meaning and is done mainly for purifying the air. Swami Dayanand had also discovered some relation between rain and clarified butter, and in times of drought the Homa, when performed in various places with the burning of butter in large quantities, is believed to produce rain scientifically. The Samajists always maintain that their beliefs and practices are based on sound scientific principles.

On the social side the Arya Samaj has brought about many reforms. Child marriages are prohibited among the Aryas. They encourage widow marriages, but at present only virgin widows (i.e. girls married before puberty and widowed before living with their husbands) can find husbands. The Aryas run a number of rescue homes for women who have been seduced and abandoned, and who have absolutely no place in orthodox Hindu society. The educational activities of the Samaj especially of the College Section, is also considerable. With all this, it must be said that the strength and membership of the Samaj are on the decline.

CHAPTER VI

SOCIAL LIFE

THOUGH the pantheistic philosophy of the Hindus is the negation of individualistic conceptions, the Hindu, for all practical purposes, is essentially an individualist. He is never so happy as when alone. The structure of Hindu society, based on caste, is mainly responsible for this tendency. The caste system is designed to divide society and not to unite. Each caste, as we have noticed, has numerous sub-castes each prohibited from interdining and intermarrying with the other. Again, there are various taboos restricting a person from eating even with a man of his own caste, and rules regarding ceremonial purity has also to be observed. All these restrictions on free social intercourse make the Hindu seek solitude as the best method of ensuring religious and social purity. But no community can last long without some sort of social cohesion and the Hindus are no exception to this rule. They too have various social activities which make communal life possible, but a sort of philosophic detachment is discernible in a Hindu of the better class even when he is in the midst of social activities.

Every Hindu sub-caste inhabiting a village or town has a Panchayat of its own. The Panchayat is an ancient Hindu institution consisting of a certain number of persons with definite powers to decide disputes in their jurisdiction. The word Panchayat means an assembly of five, but this number is not always strictly adhered to. There are no hard and fast rules which qualify a person for the membership of the Panchayat. In certain cases members are nominated by some higher authority, in others they are elected, and in still others membership of the Panchayat goes by heredity. In spite of this vagueness in the matter of filling the post, it has worked very well for ages and is still working.

The caste Panchayat has the right of fining, inflicting other punishments, and of excommunicating members of the caste. Excommunication is a terrible thing for a Hindu. All important social and religious activities of a Hindu being confined to his own sub-caste, an excommunicated Hindu cannot have his sons or daughters married, nor can he get a dead body cremated according to the dictates of his religion. A Hindu of the higher caste, when excommunicated, will not be accepted even among the lowest caste. So terrible is the punishment of excommunication that no Hindu of any caste is even permitted to give a glass of water to a member of the family of the excommunicated person. The only course open to him is to embrace Christianity or Islam. For obvious reasons, the punishment of excommunication is more severe when applied in the villages than in towns.

A person can be excommunicated only for certain offences. These may appear to be no offence at all to a European, but the Hindus have different notions. Cow killing, beef eating and interdining with a person of a lower caste may constitute an offence among the higher classes, which may lead to excommunication. Sea voyages are also offences of this category. Nor is it necessary that the offence should be voluntary. If a person, without knowing, eats food offered or cooked by a person of a lower caste, the former can be excommunicated. Purity of women among Brahmins is a constant source of worry to the male members and an erring lady may bring the punishment of excommunication on all the members of the family.

It is noteworthy that the rules regarding excommunication are not applied with the same rigidity in all cases. The Panchayat is, after all, composed of human beings and these are not always perfect or above corruption. The offences have to be proved by reliable witnesses and in cases which have not led to public scandals, the offender is invariably given the benefit of the doubt and let off with a small fine. Even in wellknown and proved cases, purificatory ceremonies are substituted for outright excommunication and the offender is made to give feasts to Brahmins and spend lavishly on them. The Abbe Dubois mentions an interesting case in which eleven persons were accused by one person of having broken caste rules which called for excommunication. It seems all the twelve of them were going on a journey, but due to war conditions the village they passed through was deserted. The travellers were hungry and started searching for food. They happened to find some grain in a potter's house which they cooked in the vessel the potter used for cooking. Only eleven ate the defiled food and the twelfth Brahmin preferred to starve rather than break the rules of his caste. On the party reaching their native village, all the eleven Brahmins were accused, by the twelfth, of having broken the rules of their caste. Among the accused, there were, however, men of influence and they so twisted the case that all of them were honourably acquitted and the plaintiff was punished for slander and malicious accusations!

In addition to the caste Panchayat, every village has a major Panchayat that looks after the general welfare of the village community and decides disputes between different castes and communities. This Panchayat is a political body, and in the ancient days used to be final authority on all disputes affecting the inhabitants of the village, and its members were men of influence. The British recognized the soundness and the utility of this institution and reorganized the village Panchayat system all over India on the elective principle.

THE TEMPLE AS CENTRE OF SOCIAL LIFE

To the Hindu, the temple is not only a place of

XLV

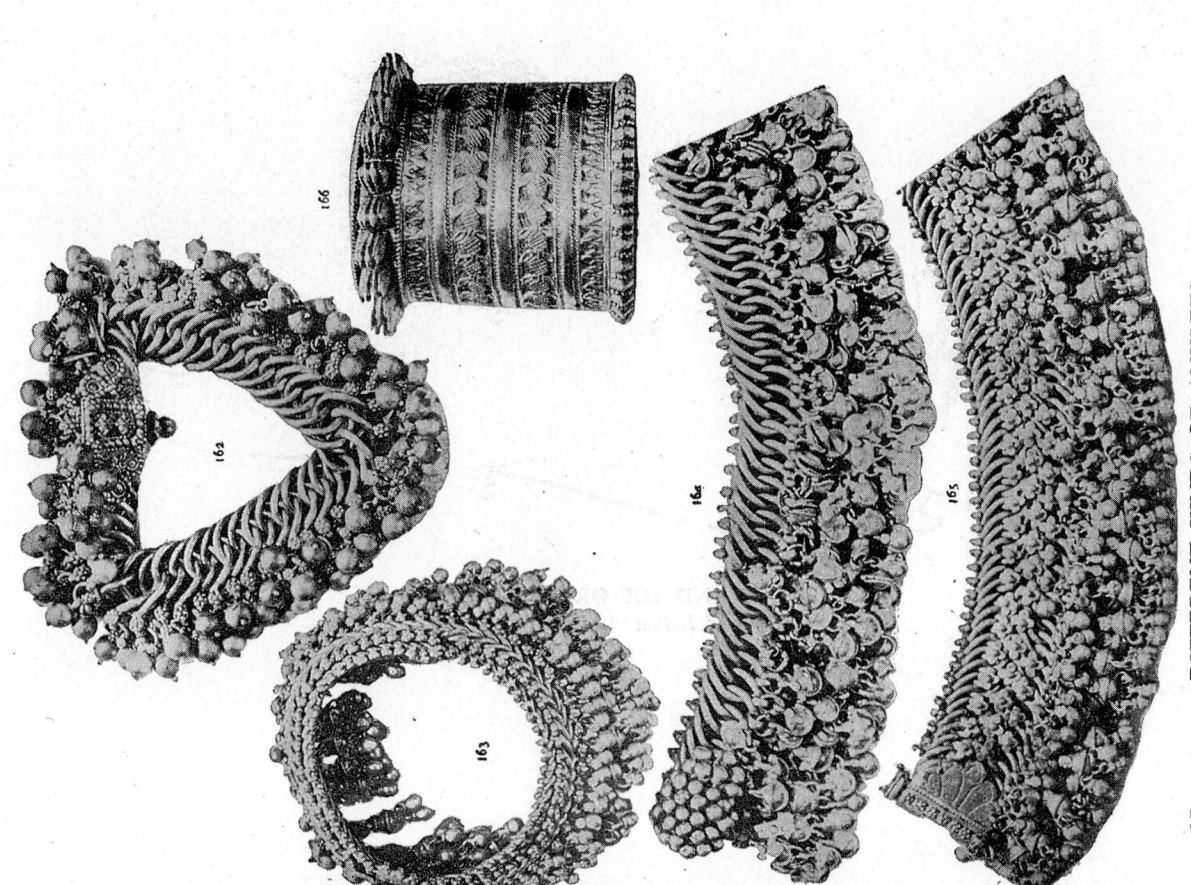

98 HAIR PENDENT

97 DIFFERENT KINDS OF ANKLETS
(Journal of Indian Art and Industry)

XLVI

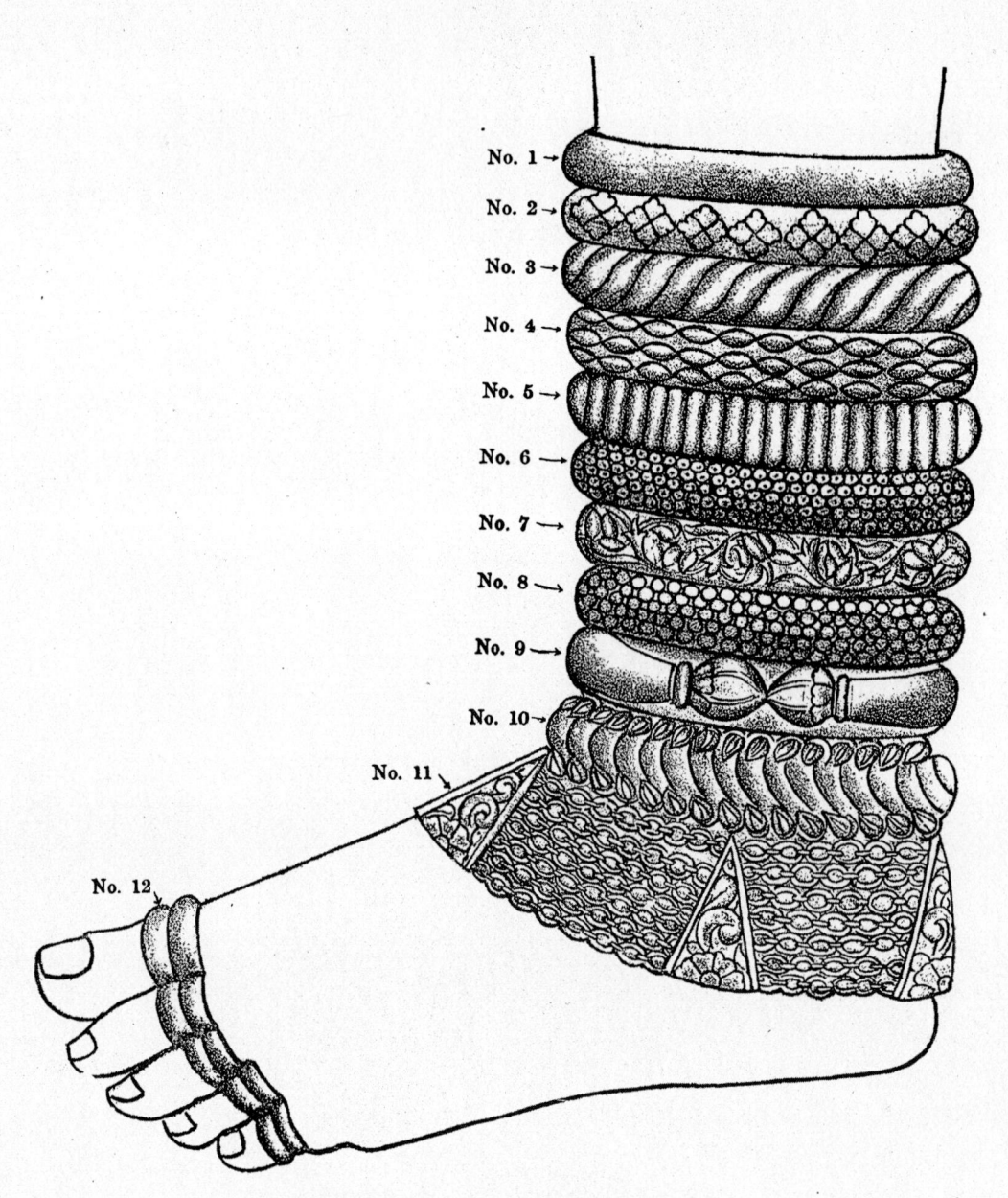

No. 1 →
No. 2 →
No. 3 →
No. 4 →
No. 5 →
No. 6 →
No. 7 →
No. 8 →
No. 9 →
No. 10 →
No. 11 ↘
No. 12 ↘

FOOT AND TOE ORNAMENTS
(Journal of Indian Art and Industry)

XLVII

100   SARANGI INDIAN FIDDLE

101   THE SARBATI, AN INDIAN MUSICAL INSTRUMENT
(Journal of Indian Art and Industry)

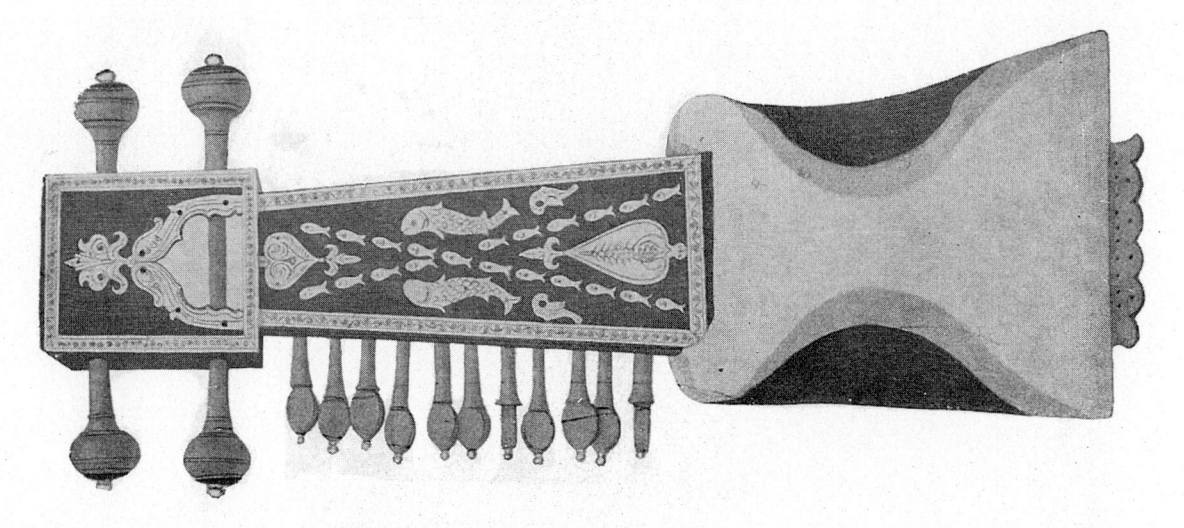

XLVIII

102 PLAYING ON JALA TARANG

103 A SITAR PLAYER

104 A SARANGI PLAYER

(From *Paintings* by Solvyns)

XLIX

105 ABHISARIKA, A NAYIKA OR HEROINE OF THE
SENSUOUS TYPE
(*Journal of Indian Art and Industry*)

106 PICTORIAL REPRESENTATION OF VASANT
RAGINI, A FEMALE MUSICAL MODE
(Rajput School: *Prince of Wales Museum, Bombay*)

107 TANSEN, THE FAMOUS MUSICIAN OF
AKBAR'S COURT
(From an Old Mogul painting)

108 PICTORIAL REPRESENTATION OF THE MALE MUSICAL MODE MEGHA RAGA
(Rajput School: *Prince of Wales Museum, Bombay*)

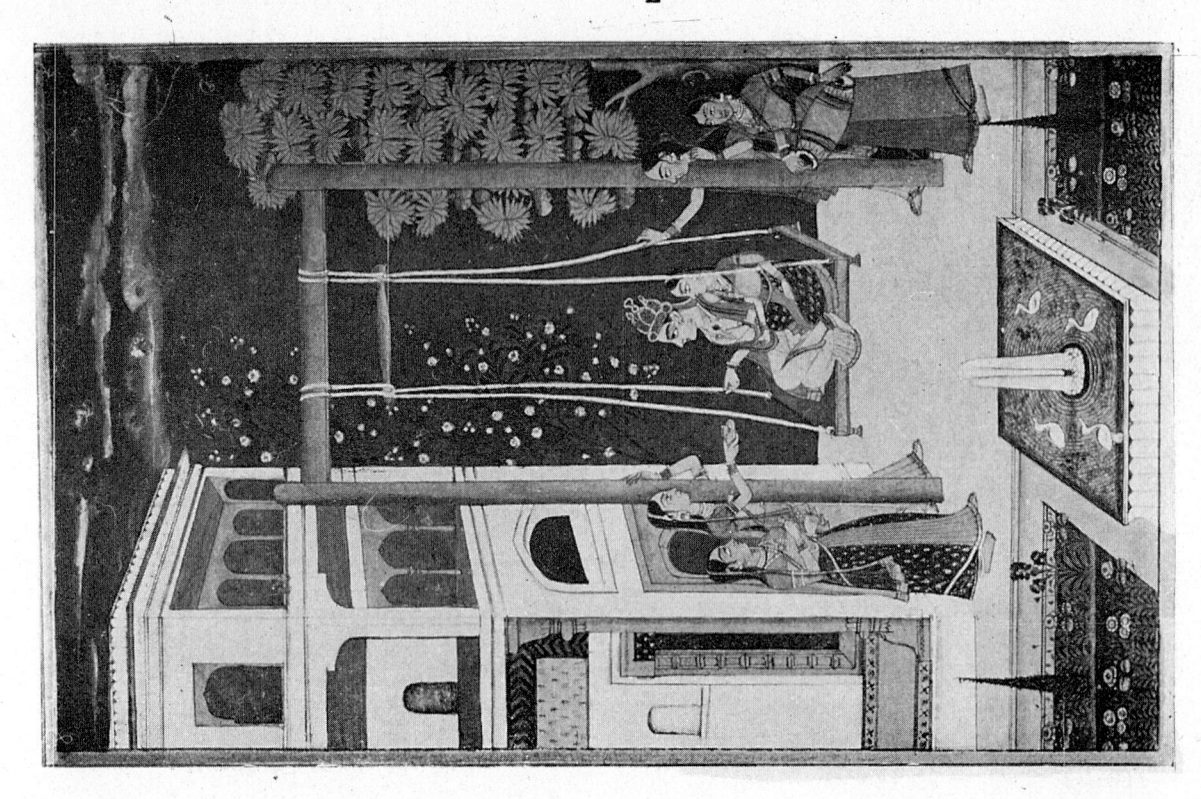

109 PICTORIAL REPRESENTATION OF HINDOLA RAGA, A MALE MUSICAL MODE
(Rajput School: *Prince of Wales Museum, Bombay*)

L

110 THE VILLAGE TRUMPETER
(Photo: S. S. Aiyar)

111 VILLAGE MUSICAL INSTRUMENTS: TRUMPETS
(India Pictorial Features)

112 A RAJPUT MUSICIAN
(Photo: A. L. Syed)

LII

113 THE TABLA PLAYER
(Painting by Solvyns)

114 DANCERS
(Kondane Cave, Bombay)

worship but the centre of social life. In fact, it is quite impossible among the Hindus to distinguish between social and religious institutions. The higher castes, especially in the village, have very little social life except in the temple. The temple tank is the public bath of the Hindu, and is a centre of immense activity because of the religious need for bathing in the morning and evening, and for performing ablutions. The foot of the inevitable Banyan tree that stands at the gateway of every important Hindu temple is the resort of all gossip mongers, and even the elders of the village who wish to hear the news of the day repair to this rendezvous of public gossip, and air their opinions on politics and philosophy. Young men on the look out for brides often loiter about the gates and compound of the temple, keeping a watchful eye on the figure and poise of the pious young ladies who throng to the temple in the mornings and evenings with offerings of flowers, scents and grain for the gods.

Public entertainments are usually held in the temple or in a place near about. As we have already mentioned, the public entertainments of the Hindus are religious in character, and their dances, pantomimes and plays always take place in the premises of the temple, and are attended by almost all the men and women of the locality. Every temple celebrates at least one major feast of the tutelary deity in a year, in which not only the village in which the temple is situated but even neighbouring villages and men and women from distant places take part. During such feasts every villager expects one or two guests from some other village, and hence every one takes care to see that there is nothing wanting in the house. New clothes are bought, rare and tasty sweetmeats are prepared, provisions are stored up for a number of days, and the whole village assumes an atmosphere of plenty. During the feast of a Hindu god, nobody seems to be in want except the beggars in rags who flock to the shrine in great numbers.

The principal feast of the tutelary god of a temple, whether in a town or in a village, usually lasts for a week. The festivities begin at least three days in advance of the actual date of the feast and ends three days after it. The pipe, the conch and the drum announce the beginning of the feast, and the music continues at regular intervals till the end of the festivities. Hawkers and petty traders, indispensable to feasts in an oriental place of worship, bring their wares and exhibit them for sale in the lanes and roads leading to the temple. This place is the Paradise of women and children, and from the date of their arrival till their departure, the hawkers are busy bargaining, disputing and shouting. The womenfolk of the village, as a rule, get very few chances of visiting cities and their market places, and hence the principal feast of the village god is also a season of shopping for them. They wait for a year patiently, laying up what they can save for this eventful day. The things they buy are of no consequence to the city dweller. They consist mainly of village luxuries such as combs, washing soap, toys, cowrie shells, glass bangles, etc. But these petty articles and the buying once in a year give the village dames more exciting entertainment than what the daily shopping gives the modern ladies in the cities.

For the three days prior to the actual date of the feast, there is nothing very important about the place, except the general atmosphere of liveliness in the temple and its compounds. Men are busy making various kinds of arrangements for the main items of the feast, women come in and go out of the temple ostensibly for purposes of worship, but in reality with a view to shopping, and children loiter about the musicians. Idlers sit under the Banyan tree discussing the relative merit of the elephants requisitioned for the occasion. If any of these animals has already arrived, they collect round it and watch, worrying the Mahout for its history and achievements.

Apart from the feasting of Brahmins, and the ceremonies connected with worshipping the idol, the main item of the festivity is the procession. It is here that the wealth of the temple and the village is displayed. The greatness or otherwise of the procession is decided by the number and noise of the drums and trumpets, and of the elephants that lead it. The elephants occupy the most important position, and the greater their number the better the procession. They are generally requisitioned from other temples or from well-to-do gentlemen who possess them. The elephants are gaily caparisoned and are given the leading role in the procession. In some processions about fifty of them may be seen, in others one or none at all. All depends upon the ability of the temple authorities to pay for their services and on the importance of the festival. At times, when there are too many feasts all at once in various temples, the prices of elephants go up, and not more than a couple of them can be hired for some temples even if these are rich enough to pay for a hundred elephants in normal times. The role of elephants in temple processions is more valued in South India than in the North.

The idol is carried either on elephant back or in a chariot. Music and dancing precede it and ministering priests fan it with peacock feathers or yak tail fans. For the pleasure of certain idols which delight in bad language, a paid expert in vulgar eloquence stands in front of them, when these are taken out, singing lewd songs and making indecent gestures. The motley crowd of men, women and children bring up the rear of the procession. The procession generally makes a round of the temple and winds through all the principal streets of the locality. In some cases the idol is taken to a small shrine at some water front, from where, after a bath and some rest, it is taken back to its main abode. At times, one of the elephants gets rowdy and the resultant confusion leads to many deaths.

On the night preceding the main feast the whole locality is illuminated by wicks dipped in oil. Fireworks are let off for the entertainment of the public. In certain temples, the idol is taken out in procession at night, and torches, as a rule, provide illumination on these occasions. In cities and towns, motor cars and gas lights are beginning to mar the grandeur of ancient pageantry.

SOCIAL CALLS

Social calls among the Hindus lack the intimacy and pleasantness of such functions in the West. For one thing, the number of people a respectable Hindu gentlemen can mix freely with are very few; for another, men never converse or move freely with women of even their own household. It is not considered proper for a man to eat or talk with one's own wife in the presence of other people, and it is nothing short of scandalous for women of a household to appear before male guests and converse with familiarity. As such, social calls among the Hindus are generally a matter of embarrassment rather than of pleasure. I must, however, make it plain that this applies only to orthodox families and not to the modern imitators of Western manners whose percentage of the Hindu population is at present negligible.

Again, leisured classes are very few among the Hindus, especially in the villages, and the women have always some household duties or religious ceremonies to perform. Men too have their daily work in the fields or in the shops, and the routine of domestic worship has to be gone through. Hence social visits have not, among the Hindus, developed into a social art. Men, however, visit other households very often on matters of business, and when these are not of a pressing nature indulge in petty talk, partake of refreshments and play indoor games with the hosts. Women occasionally get a holiday, when they visit other households. On these rare occasions, however, it is made a wholetime job and they spend hours in gossip. Women usually take their children with them and the occasion is made use of to adorn the children with all their ornaments and display the wealth of the parents of the children.

Sickness, petty ceremonies, etc., are made good excuses of by women for visiting neighbours and relatives. Men folk as a rule discourage women from leaving their households for any purpose whatever, least of all for making idle social calls, which they consider a waste of time and energy. But if some member of a family falls ill, or some ceremony is near at hand, which requires the assistance of a number of women for the preparation of the large quantities of sweetmeats which are indispensable for all Hindu domestic ceremonies, permission is readily granted to women to visit the sick person or the family needing their assistance, and the women take full advantage of the opportunity.

When men and women together visit a household, the men are conducted to the Mardana or men's apartments, and the women to the Zenana or women's apartments. Children are privileged to enter both and they often perform the office of messengers between the Mardana and the Zenana. During social calls, if the guests are allowed to interdine with the hosts, light refreshments are served. These vary according to localities, but nowhere in India will respectable Hindus think of entertaining their guests with liquor. Drinking is universally considered by Hindus as a bad habit, and even those who indulge in it will seldom drink in their own houses when guests or women folk are about. Sweetmeats, milk, coffee and tea are usually served. In Malabar the juice of the tender cocoanut is a favourite beverage during the hot season. After partaking of the refreshments, and gossiping for sometime, the guests, the male party usually, show signs of restlessness indicating that the time to part is come. This the host invariably considers an insult, and he pretends that he was all along under the impression that the guests had come to stay for the night. He may even make a show of passing orders to the servants to make arrangements for their meals and accommodation for the night. The guests, equally hypocritical, say that they had come with the intention of staying for a number of days, but pressure of business makes it imperative for them to return immediately. After a good deal of arguments, pleadings and pressing, the host is silenced and he 'resigns himself to his fate.' Upon this a message is sent to the ladies' apartment that the menfolk are ready to depart. On this all the ladies of the household pretend surprise and the scene in the Mardana is enacted in the Zenana with all the subtlety women are capable of. At last the women too take leave and join the men who are already at the gate. On the departure of the party, the women partially come out of the house and look mournfully at them through windows and doors left ajar, and the departing women look back in recognition. The men walk ahead and it is improper for them to look back.

As far as women are concerned, the privilege of making social calls is confined to elderly ladies and children. Girls of marriageable age and young ladies newly married are at times allowed to accompany the elderly women, but widows never.

The generality of Hindus consider social calls a nuisance, and the most respectable person is he who never visits another man's house without sufficient reason.

FEASTING

The Hindus lead a frugal life, but every year a well-to-do Hindu gentleman has to provide a number of feasts to Brahmins, his neighbours, relatives and dependents. As we shall see later, there are numerous ceremonies a member of a respectable Hindu household has to perform from his birth till his death, and each ceremony is attended by a feast; some of these are minor feasts confined to near relatives and a couple of Brahmins, others extending to the whole population of the village and costing large sums. Because of the joint family system, a well-to-do Hindu household consists of a large number of members and at short intervals there are ceremonies to be performed. The wealth of the Hindus is generally spent on these ceremonies and the attendant feasts, and many well-to-do families ruin themselves on this account.

The most important social function among the Hindus is the marriage feast. To get a boy or girl married is not an easy thing among the Hindus. Marriages are arranged by parents, and there is always the question of dowry to be settled. Several proposals are considered, the relatives and parents of the prospective brides and bridegrooms visit one another, and middlemen are busy for months before a marriage proposal is finally accepted. Then takes place the engagement ceremony which will be described later.

The marriage feast proper extends to several days. A few days prior to the date of the marriage ceremony, the relatives start coming and near by houses are requisitioned for their accommodation. Musicians appear on the day preceding the actual date of marriage and play at regular intervals. The well-to-do usually engage, in addition, a party of dancing girls and professional players. Those who cannot afford to engage a party, engage at least one dancing girl who sings and dances for the entertainment of the guests.

The wedding ceremony and the feast, as a rule, take place in the house of the bride. Adorning the bride for the marriage ceremony is one of the main items of the marriage festivities and this is the exclusive privilege of the ladies. The greater the number of ornaments a bride wears, the better is she admired, and hence, in addition to the ornaments expressly made for her, necklaces, bangles, anklets and rings are borrowed from neighbours and relatives, and the bride is covered from head to foot in precious metals and stones, and wrapped up in a costly Sari. The Sari is scarcely visible for the ornaments. As if this is not enough, flowers and garlands of flowers are hung on the hair, head and neck. A Hindu bride dressed for the marriage ceremony looks more like a heap of flowers, ornaments and silk than a human being.

The bridegroom and his party are expected to arrive a few hours before the fixed time of the marriage ceremony. It is customary for some members of the bride's household to go, accompanied by musicians, to a place about a mile or so distant from the bride's house and welcome the bridegroom's party. The bridegroom in the Punjab and certain other parts of North India comes on horseback, as gorgeously adorned as the bride. Among the martial classes he wears a sword or a dagger. In South India the bridegroom is usually carried in a palanquin. Those who prefer modern methods of transport bring the bridegroom in a motor car gaily decorated for the occasion. After the meeting and the usual exchange of courtesies both the parties join together and go to the bride's house, the musicians rending the welkin with their loud and wild notes.

At the entrance of the Pandal (a porch constructed for the occasion) the bride is led to the bridegroom by the ladies of the house, the crowd of spectators watching and comparing notes. The meeting is a tremendous moment and the musicians are expected to do their loudest. After the meeting, the bride and the bridegroom are conducted to their previously arranged seats where, in front of fire, the priest performs the marriage ceremony (for details of the marriage ceremony please see chapter IX). After the marriage ceremony the bride is conducted to the ladies' apartments and the bridegroom to the men's quarters. After some time they are taken in procession, accompanied by musicians and the guests.

The main feast consists of but one meal, but it is a sumptuous one. Providing plates for the guests is one of the problems which is difficult to solve, and in the countryside plates are borrowed freely from neighbours and returned after the occasion. In South India, Hindus generally serve their meals on plantain leaves and for them there is no problem of the plates. Among the better class of Hindus, the meal is purely vegetarian. The South Indians excel their northern brethren in the culinary art, and the number of dishes a South Indian feast provides and the amount eaten by Brahmins in the South must be seen to be believed. In the North the dishes are comparatively plain and unleaven bread and cakes of wheat form the principal item of food, whereas in the South, the Maharashtra countries and Bengal rice is the staple diet.

During the whole day of the marriage feast, musicians perform almost continuously and the dancing girls at intervals. Betel nuts are available in plenty and the guests sit in companies of five or six with a plate of betel leaves and areca nuts between them and spittoons in the centre. They talk, chew and spit continuously. Rose water is sprinkled on the guests at regular intervals. Trays containing glasses of cool drinks are passed occasionally through the rows of guests for the benefit of those who are thirsty. When the time for the principal meal comes, the spittoons and plates of betel nuts are removed and the Pandal is converted into a dining hall.

After the principal meal and the chewing of betel nuts, casual guests take leave of the host. The bridegroom and his party, near relatives and close friends remain. During the night of the wedding day, the party of dancers perform some play from the epics, and prizes are distributed by the bridegroom to the best players. At times the bridegroom's party also brings with them performers and dancers and in this case, both the parties perform, and there is keen competition between the two. From the time of the marriage till his departure, the bridegroom moves intimately with the members of the bride's household who take many liberties with him. His mother-in-law and sisters-in-law tease him and the bride, and many jokes are cut at the expense of the newly-weds. The bridegroom has to give presents to his sisters-in-law, and they have to sing songs in praise of him. Among some communities, insolent songs are sung and mock fights are staged, shoes and other missiles being thrown at the bridegroom for luck. On one occasion, I remember, this innocent insolence led to a court case and the bride's party was fined.

The rejoicings of these days are shadowed by the sadness of the parting of the bride from her people. For, on the third day the bride is taken away by the bridegroom to his village and the occasion is one given to expressions of heart-burning. The bride finds it extremely difficult to tear herself away for good from the home of her childhood, from her mother, brothers and sisters, and they too shed tears on the departure of the darling of the house. The pathos is heightened by the fact that the girl is just past childhood, her sex interests are not fully developed, and she clings to the joys of her home and her people. The guests and the Brahmins usually console the weeping bride and she is led away by the bridegroom's party.

After the departure of the bride and the bridegroom the musicians are paid off, and the relatives depart one by one. The Pandal is pulled down and the household gradually settles down to routine work.

In cities and towns, the middle classes, for obvious reasons, cannot afford to perform marriage ceremonies in this fashion. But here every community has a public hall of its own and the hall is rented for the occasion. The guests come an hour or so before the marriage ceremony, witness the ceremony, partake of the wedding feast, join the procession and depart before nightfall.

The expenses connected with a marriage feast varies according to the status of the household, but every Hindu is expected to spend more than what he can afford. Any show of parsimony in the matter of providing feasts is resented by the Hindus and cases have occurred in which guests depart at the time of marriage ceremony because of some fancied grievance in the matter of providing certain amenities to them. Such behaviour of the guests brings lifelong disgrace upon the host, if not excommunication, and every Hindu who values his good name will rather mortgage his property than appear stingy or parsimonious in the matter of providing feasts.

Among the lower classes of Sudras and the Panchamas, feasts are occasions for quarrels and free fights. Every guest who is invited to such feasts comes with an exaggerated opinion of himself and of his clan. The Hindus are extremely sensitive on these occasions and the slightest inattention is construed as an insult and made much of. I remember an instance when, during a feast, provided by a member of the carpenter caste to a number of men of his own caste, an old carpenter created such a scene that he broke up the feast. The guests were seated on the floor on a mat in two rows and the meal was served. As soon as they started eating, an old carpenter appeared, God knows from where, and asked the guests if they were so lost to all sense of decency as to eat in the house of a pariah who did not know how to respect his elders. The eating immediately stopped and the old man went on abusing not only the host but his fore-fathers. The host appeared on the scene, but all his pleadings and promises of atonement could not pacify the old man. It seems the ancient was a member of the village community of carpenters but had migrated long ago to a neighbouring village, and the host had forgotten to invite him to the feast. He had some distant relatives among the guests who were present and he called upon them, on the strength of the ties of blood, to leave the feast and return to their homes; which they were in honour bound to do, and really did. Upon this all remaining guests, except very ardent friends and close relatives of the host, left the unfinished meal and walked away.

This is an extreme instance, but the lower classes of Hindus generally delight in creating scenes during feasts. A feast is considered the proper time and place for airing grievances, fancied or real, not only against the host but his relatives too. Most of these scenes die down after the host makes his apologies or some mediators settle the dispute, and every man partakes of the sumptuous meal provided and goes home happy, to boast to the womenfolk of his bravado in the feast. But every dog has his day, and an insulted host in his turn becomes a guest and he pays off old scores with interest. Among the Panchamas, the exhilarating juice of the palm is freely served and the guests, under its influence, become quarrelsome and rowdy; the feasts of the Panchamas, like their religious congregations, almost always end up in free fights.

GAMES AND AMUSEMENTS

The Hindus are a serious people and sports and games are not so popular among them as in the West. Children and young men are privileged to play. Elderly people seldom play outdoor games but those who are willing to be amused watch games.

The ball, as among all people, is a favourite instrument of pleasure among the Hindus too. But the games they play with the ball have very few rules and are vague and indescribable. Before the advent of the British, the ball used to be made of leaves of trees or coir rolled round and well tied by strings or twine. This is still the practice in villages, where they play an Indian game very much like cricket. The use of one's foot for driving a ball was never favoured in India, but the methods of the West are now being copied and even in villages men can be found playing football using indigenous balls of the old type because of the poverty of the villagers which would not permit them to buy footballs. In cities and towns, cricket, football, tennis and badminton have become the favourite games of Indians as well as of Europeans, and the old fashioned Indian ball is never seen. With the arrival of the rubber ball, girls have invented an indoor game with it. They strike it repeatedly to the ground with just the force necessary to make it rebound to the correct height; after thus striking it to the ground a number of times, say one hundred, the player has to turn round and strike it several times, say ten. Of two persons the one who can do the feat for the greater number of times without missing the ball is the winner.

Among the martial classes there are many manly games intended to build up good physique and endurance, and even elderly people take a keen interest in them. The Mahrathas have a peculiar system of boxing (called Nakho-ka-kushti) in which they use steel claws. Wrestling is popular all over India but nowhere in the country is it so widely practised as in the Punjab. Here every village and town have Akkhadas (training ground for wrestlers) and every boy is trained to wrestle. Matches and tournaments are organized and the winners receive prizes. In the South and the Malabar coast wrestling is not so much in vogue as a sort of boxing. Indian boxers use not the closed fist but the open palm. During the Onam festival in Malabar, every village organizes boxing tournaments and village dignitaries attend them and distribute prizes. The dexterity of the Malabar boxers and the agility with which they fight must be seen to be believed. Some of them fight so desperately that they bleed profusely but will not give in. There is a system of self-defence in Malabar known as the Kalari system, but it is now rarely practised.

The Hindus are adepts in the use of the stick as a weapon of offence and defence. A well-trained man can wheel a stick so effectively that a dozen unarmed people are helpless against him. Display of fighting with sticks is as popular in India as wrestling and boxing.

The higher classes among the martial people, like the Rajahs and Zamindars, hunt for pleasure. Their hunting expeditions are elaborate affairs involving the use of elephants, trained panthers and an army of men who serve as beaters. The villagers often hunt for meat, and their stories of dangers braved and game lost are no less exciting than those told by the Rajahs and the modern Europeans, who come to hunt in India. The use of game birds like hawks for hunting is still in vogue, and the rich have hounds, cheetahs and panthers trained for hunting.

Bull fighting is common in villages during times of public festivities. Cock fighting and quail fighting entertain visitors to every Indian fair. The Punjabi and Sindhi peasants often organize camel races. Feelings of owners at times run high in these competitive activities and it is not rare that owners kill the beasts or birds that lose. Betting is not uncommon on these occasions, nor free fights. Jugglers, rope dancers, snake charmers and performing animals can be seen in the streets of all Indian cities.

The Brahmins as a rule do not participate in outdoor games. The favourite game of the higher classes of Brahmins is chess. They are more given to the cultivation of those arts that delight the intellect than develop the muscles. They love to organize dramas and dances. The Indian theatre, unfortunately, has not progressed since the time of Kalidasa. The themes of plays are generally religious, or exploits of legendary heroes. The dance that appeal to the intellectual Brahmin is the classical one connected with worship and ritual and not the popular one. The Nambudiri Brahmins of Malabar have evolved a remarkable pantomime dance called Kathakali which has now become popular all over India. In the Andhra countries wandering players perform a kind of shadow play illustrating scenes from the Ramayana and the Mahabharata. On a screen is projected shadows of figures thrown by a lamp kept hidden from the public. By a clever manipulation of the figures the shadows are made to move and give the effect of a moving picture.

Music is universally appreciated by the Hindus and it forms part of all their rituals and ceremonials. Though the higher classes are connoisseurs of music and dancing, it is considered derogatory to the dignity of the respectable to dance or to sing. As far as women are concerned, the word dancer or singer used to be a synonym for prostitute and hence the mixed dances which are so popular in all social circles in the West have not been copied by Indians. The better class of Indians love to see other people dance but are reluctant to dance themselves.

Playing at cards is a favourite pastime among all classes of Indians, from the beggars in the street to the princes in the palace. Gambling games played with cards are also popular.

The cinema has revolutionized the whole field of entertainment in India as in other countries. Every Indian city and town has many picture houses and all school boys and girls know the names of the principal film actors and actresses of the West and of India. Men and women who have English education and who wish to appear fashionable generally frequent English picture houses and profess contempt for Indian pictures. The low standard of the Indian screen is probably responsible for this. The generality of Indians, however, patronize Indian picture houses. The 'talkies' are now produced in all important Indian languages and the people of every province can listen to their favourite stars speaking their own mother tongue.

Indian producers usually cater for the craze of the Indian public for religious themes, and a good percentage of Indian pictures adopt stories from the epics for the screen. Incidents from the Ramayana and the Mahabharata have a perennial appeal for the Hindus. Next to religious themes come old fashioned love stories with their heroes, heroines and the inevitable villains. The Indian public have a keen sense of the proper. Love making is permitted on the screen, but nudity and kissing not. Flirting is permissible and loved, and such scenes are allowed to linger for a very long time. A good deal of music and dancing is indispensable to an Indian picture, whatever its theme, and their introduction in unsuitable places often mars the proportion of the story, when this has any. As a rule, these long winded stories begin and end nowhere and the Indian public is usualy critical only about music, dancing and the love-scenes.

The traditional stigma attached to all kinds of professional performers applies to the world of pictures too. It was very difficult, say two decades ago, to get educated women of the better classes to act, and the generality of Indian actresses came from classes with whom respectable men would not care to associate openly. This was a serious handicap to all those who wished to raise the standard of Indian pictures, and the status of the actors and actresses. Some bold spirits have, however, broken away from tradition and the Indian screen can now boast of a few cultured young ladies of the higher classes. They are the pioneers who are likely to give the Indian film world the respectability it rightly deserves.

The cinema is confined to the city and the town and rarely reaches the village. Except when some strolling company takes to the village an old film, the village is oblivious to this modern form of entertainment.

STATUS OF WOMEN IN HINDU SOCIETY

The story of Hindu women is a tragedy of gradual suppression. The earliest accounts of Hindu society show the position of women as one of superiority over men, and this indicates a matriarchal society in which women were the owners of wealth and the sole guardians of their children. This matriarchal system still prevails among the Nayars of Malabar and certain other Hindu communities which are not ruled by the code of Manu. The Mahabharata clearly states that there was a time in Hindu society when "women were not subordinate to men, but went about freely as they liked." From this time onwards a gradual subjection of women started which culminated in the complete slavery of women to men and in Sati, the burning of widows on the funeral pile of their husbands. This custom was restricted to the three higher castes, and to the better class of some Sudra sub-castes.

The position of women, according to the Hindu law books, is one of pitiable and complete dependence upon men. Manu, the most respected of Hindu law givers, lays down that a woman, from her cradle to the grave is to be dependent upon a male; in childhood on her father, in youth on her husband and in old age on her son; for "a woman is never fit for independence." Child marriages are insisted on by the codes. The proper age for the marriage of a Hindu girl is said to be between eight and ten; it is essential that a girl should be married before she matured. The law givers imprecate terrible curses on parents in whose houses unmarried daughters attain the age of puberty. This early marriage is designed to keep women out of mischief. Marriage is a sacrament among the higher castes and it establishes the complete right of man over his wife. Apart from the husband, the wife has no individuality; she cannot perform any important ceremony alone, she cannot possess property and must submit to the will of her husband in all matters. Nay a wife has no god apart from her husband. Whether a drunkard, leper, sadist or wife beater, a husband Manu says, is to be worshipped as God himself.

No laws of the Hindus were enforced with so much vigour as those affecting women. Child marriages, once enforced, became the fashion among the respectable Hindus and they even improved upon the codes. The earlier a girl got married, the better it was considered for all concerned, and the marriage of babies became a common affair. Instances are on record in which pregnant mothers were married to one another in the hope that one of the embryos would be male and the other female, the ceremony being considered not valid if it turned out otherwise. In almost all these cases the married girl lived with her parents till she attained puberty when she was sent to her husband for conjugal rights. Some law givers and commentators are, however, of opinion that it is good that a girl lives with her husband even before reaching puberty, because girls of even a tender age, they say, are apt to do improper things. These views found favour among some Hindus and they allowed conjugal rights to husbands before the girl reached puberty, with what results can very well be imagined.

The worst tragedy of child marriage was widowhood of girls in childhood. Orthodox Hindus do not allow widow marriage, and the child widows grew up to be a burden to themselves and to others. Widowers were, however, allowed to remarry and it often happened that a man of forty or fifty married a girl of eight or ten. Child marriage is prohibited by the Sarda Act, but is valid when performed, and the only thing the Government can do is to punish the parents and participants in the marriage ceremony. Such offences are rarely brought to the notice of the authorities and when they are, the punishment is in the form of a fine. Well-to-do Hindus of the orthodox classes prefer to pay this fine rather than break the laws of ancient sages and incur sin; and the Sarda Act, though certainly salutary, has not been adequate enough to stop child marriage completely.

The role of Hindu women in orthodox society is one of subordination to men. They are not allowed to move or speak freely with men. A woman shall not sit in presence of a man of her age and social position, but must always stand. She shall not look him in the face, but must turn her face away from him even when necessity demands that she speaks to him. This applies to conversation between husband and wife also, especially in presence of others. While walking, a woman must walk behind her husband at a respectable distance. Modern means of transport like trains, and tram cars have compartments or seats set apart for women as a concession to this ancient Indian prejudice. In provinces where Muslim influence has been considerable the higher classes of Hindu women observe Purdah. They seldom move out of the Zenana; when necessity demands their moving about, they take care to cover their faces with the end of their Saris. The Hindu ladies do not wear a veil proper like the Muslims, but make use of their Saris to serve as a veil in case of necessity. In social functions and feasts, men are served first and women afterwards.

The lot of the Hindu widow is even now a miserable one among orthodox Hindus. Although Sati has been abolished by law and no Hindu lady is now permitted to be burnt alive with her husband, the widow is the object of much persecution and humiliation. It is generally believed among the Hindus that widowhood is the result of sins committed in a previous life; as such a widow is looked upon as the cause of the death of her husband, and his mother and sisters among whom she lives treat her with cruelty and contempt. It is customary among villagers, even in these days to have the widow, on the death of her husband, to be dragged by barber women to some waterside and, after the bath, to be dragged back to her home where she is starved, abused and even beaten, at least for a week after her husband's death. The head of a widow is shaved and she is not allowed to wear bright garments or ornaments. She is not permitted to eat wholesome food. Her clothing should be white or black. She cannot attend social functions. In a marriage feast she is dreaded as an ill-omen portending evil to the bride and death to the bridegroom. Widow remarriage not being permitted among the orthodox classes, a widow's troubles end only with her death.*

HINDU WOMEN AND BEAUTY CULTURE

Hindu women, like their sisters all over the

---

* Those who wish to know more about the status of Hindu women in society are requested to read the author's book *Women and Marriage in India* (Allen and Unwin).

world, wish to appear attractive to men. But social codes have restricted the cultivation of beauty among the orthodox and certain traditions and usages have even perverted their notions of beauty. Hindus, as we have seen, prohibit free social intercourse between the sexes, and respectable women are considered those who hide away from men. Women are allowed to appreciate good looks and good taste only among themselves. The generality of women being unable to correctly judge beauty among themselves, what is more valued among them is the financial position of the husband and not the personal charms of the wife. Hence it is the cost of the ornaments and clothes a lady wears that is more interesting in the society of women than her good looks. Most of the Hindu women love to load themselves with silver and gold ornaments from head to foot, not to enhance their good looks but to cow down other women by a show of their husband's wealth. No Hindu lady of the orthodox classes worries how a Sari is worn, as long as it is costly.

Things change very slowly in India and fashion is no exception to this rule; hence a Hindu lady can wear a Sari till it becomes unserviceable through use. Indian husbands are luckier in this respect than Europeans for whose wives fashions change every season.

Hindu notions of beauty is in keeping with their social life. They do not want a lady to be active and flit about like a fawn, but to shuffle about like a swan. They do not care much for a slim body but delight in hips like an elephant's. They value long, black glossy hair reaching up to the ankles when left loose, and have a horror of red or golden hair. As regards eyes, it is the shape more than the colour that counts. Blue eyes, so dear to the European, is detested by the Indian who calls them "cat's eyes." According to Indian standards the eyes should be of the shape of a fish, and the eye brows arched like a bow with long lashes to match as arrows. Thus the eye of a lady should be Cupid's bow complete with arrows.

Though women of the respectable classes have neglected beauty culture, the courtesans in India from very early times have been most careful in studying and cultivating those arts that enhance beauty and please men.*

Music was once an accomplishment for ladies of the higher classes, but in the middle ages singing was considered disreputable among the orthodox. The reason for this was that music became the profession of courtesans and dancers. The medieval prejudice is now overcome and the better classes of Hindus teach their daughters music although they do not allow them to sing in public.

Because of early marriage and poverty, Indian women age soon. Upper class women are overfed and become flabby and sickly through sedentary habits. The women of the lower classes, on the other hand, are under-nourished and over-worked and are never attractive except in their youth. There is, however, the class of courtesans in India whose only occupation is to please and captivate men. We will have occasion to speak of these professional women and their art of seduction in another chapter.

It must be mentioned that the observations made above hold good only in the case of the orthodox classes. Contact with the West has brought about considerable changes in the social status of women in cities and towns. Here Hindu girls get educated in the numerous schools and colleges run by the Government or public institutions and these ladies have broken away from ancient traditions. Hence a visitor to a fairly big Indian city will often meet Hindu women frequenting places of entertainments, clubs and fashionable social functions and moving on terms of equality with men. Some ultra-modern Hindu ladies may be found even dancing with other women's husbands in Western fashion, though the Hindus who have got over the prejudice on this subject are extremely few. These modern ladies are the pioneers of a movement which may change Hindu society appreciably, given time. But it is wrong to judge the social status of Indian women by these few emancipated daughters of Mother India. They do not form even a thousandth of the total population of Hindu women.

---

* The beauty culture of women and the art of the courtesan have been dealt with in detail in the author's work *Kama Kalpa: Hindu Ritual of Love*.

CHAPTER VII

DOMESTIC LIFE

THE Englishman's conception of the happy home with the father, mother and the children collected round the fireside, and the contented cat purring on the hearthrug is foreign to India. A Hindu gentleman's household is a miniature state of fifty to hundred men and women ruled by a dictator who is the oldest male member of the family. All the decorum and formalities of a court are maintained in the family, in its own way. The head of the family is inaccessible to the younger members of the household, and the children go in fear of him. He eats alone and lives in a room all by himself, and his sons, and younger brothers speak to him only on business matters. Any show of familiarity is resented, and liberty taken punished. The younger brothers, however, who are about the same age as himself move with more freedom.

A young Hindu, on his marriage, does not set up house for himself, but brings his wife to his father's house or, properly speaking, to the joint family where his elder brothers, uncles and father live with their wives and children. The bride lives in the women's apartments with her sisters-in-law under the vigilance of her mother-in-law. The husband and wife meet only at night. Men and women live apart in a Hindu household, and it is bad taste for a man to visit the Zenana and for a woman to visit the Mardana. Conversation between a young man and his wife during daytime in presence of other members of the family is prohibited in orthodox households and the Cerberus-eyed mother-in-law sees to it that her daughters-in-law observe this ancient rule of propriety.

As regards property, a sort of communism prevails in the joint family. Every member of the household, whatever his calling or occupation, is required to hand over his income to the head of the family and it goes into the common pool. Each member is entitled to receive food and clothing and what pocket money the head of the family is pleased to give him. Expenses connected with the education of children, marriages, etc., are met from the common fund.

It can be seen that the system has advantages as well as disadvantages. Of the former, may be mentioned the economic security assured to all members of the family. A Hindu has always a home to look forward to in his old age and is never completely destitute. Hindus who go out of their villages for service or business earn very little, especially at the start, and cannot afford to maintain a family; in such cases a Hindu safely leaves his wife and children in the joint family, sending the head of the family what he can conveniently spare. It is the economic structure of the joint family that makes the Hindus marry young, regardless of the question whether or not they are able to support wives and children.

The disadvantages of the system are more numerous than the advantages. In the days gone by when every caste had its traditional occupation, all the male members of the joint family had to engage themselves in the ancestral trades, usually agriculture or shop-keeping, but now conditions have changed. The Hindu youth with a university degree or with a Matriculation certificate thinks it below his dignity to engage himself in agriculture, the occupation of the generality of Hindus. All work involving physical exertion being considered, by the better class of Hindus, as derogatory to the dignity of man, educated young Hindus seek service in some Government department or in some firm, and move into the city. Secretarial jobs, they love most. And once a young modern Hindu gets a living wage in the city, he tries to find excuses for not sending any money home but to save something for himself. He assumes the attitude that since he is entitled to a share in the common property, his wife and children, if he has any, are entitled to free lodging and boarding in the joint family. This gives cause for complaint from his brothers who may be engaged in agriculture in their native village. In such cases, usually an amicable settlement is arranged, but the modern tendency is rather to quarrel, which often leads to litigation and the division of property.

The ties of blood are stronger among the Hindus than among Europeans. A destitute member brings disgrace on the whole family, and every respectable Hindu householder is careful to see that the idlers and loafers of the family and their wives and children are as well-fed and well-clothed as the earning members. This, in away, has encouraged sloth among the irresponsible.

The worst feature of the joint family is its domestic structure. The disadvantage of a large number of men and women living together in one house is obvious enough. This handicap to domestic felicity in joint families is aggravated by various other causes. The head of the family is often an old fashioned individual who draws his inspiration from Manu and other ancient authorities. He is a stout defender of ancient customs and usages, and views with distrust the ways of the moderns and is always on the look-out for weeding out Western influences from his family. He upholds the rules of caste, insists that the younger members of the household should wear their clothes as he had done in his younger days and should dress their hair in the traditional manner. The last mentioned item may appear trivial to Westerners, but in India the manner in which one dresses one's hair has something to do with eternal verities. The hair of a man has a deep religious significance and often a man's caste is known by the way he dresses his hair. But not to digress, the head of the family is a pillar of orthodoxy, suspicious of the activities of the younger members of the family. Almost always he is a miser.

The young men of the family, on the other hand, get English education, read fashion journals, see pictures, visit cities and feel enamoured of the freedom

LIII

115 KATHAKALI DANCERS
(Photo: Stanley Jepson)

116 FOLK DANCE DURING HOLI
(Photo: B. F. Ferreira)

LIV

117   A TEMPLE PROCESSION, MUSIC LEADING
            (Photo: S. S. Aiyar)

LV

118 GROUP WORSHIP OF THE SEA

119 A VOW OF SILENCE
ENFORCED BY A MOUTH LOCK
(India Pictorial Features)

120 GIRL IN NEEM
LEAVES
(India Pictorial Features)

LVI

121   SCULPTURES OF DEITIES, HALEBID
         (Photo: S. S. Aiyar)

LVII

122 INDRA, GOD OF THE FIRMAMENT
(Somnathpur, Photo: India Pictorial Features)

123 GANESHA
(British Museum: *Journal of Indian Art and Industry*)

124 STATUE OF EMPEROR CHANDRAGUPTA MAURYA
(Birla Mandir, Photo: India Pictorial Features)

LVIII

125 SCULPTURE OF A ROYAL GROUP, MAMALLAPURAM
(Photo: S. S. Aiyar)

126 FALL OF THE GANGES, MAMALLAPURAM
(Journal of Indian Art and Industry)

LIX

127   VISHNU AS THE SUN GOD    128   SURYA, THE SUN GOD, WITH ATTENDANTS

(Journal of Indian Art and Industry)

LX

129 A HINDU SHRINE, KULU

130 A HINDU TEMPLE, CHAMPA STATE

(*Journal of Indian Art and Industry*)

of the young men and women of the cities. They are zealous advocates of reforms in their own houses. They think it preposterous that they cannot talk to their wives and sisters in their own houses when the young men of the cities are allowed to talk to other peoples' wives and sisters on the highway and even take them to pictures. They resent the stingy habits of the head of the family and think it a sin to lock up money in a box when the warm blood of youth craves for the pleasures of the world. This antagonism between the young and the old in the joint families of villages often results in open rebellion of the young against the authority of the head of the family.

LIFE IN THE JOINT FAMILY

The construction of a Hindu gentleman's house (especially in the village) is in keeping with the social and domestic notions of the Hindus. In front of the house there is usually a spacious courtyard where untouchables and other low-born visitors may stand and speak to the male members of the family who occupy the verandah of the house for the purpose. At the foot of the verandah there is a low platform for the accommodation of "touchable" visitors of low social status who cannot be admitted into the verandah which is open only to men of equal status. These may sit with the male members of the family on terms of equality and transact business, the visitor and the host usually squatting on the same mat, when they are of equal age, and chewing betel leaves. A door leads from the verandah into the house proper. The entrance usually is into a hall which opens into an inner courtyard on the sides of which are built the rooms in which the members of the family live. The male members occupy the more spacious and airy rooms and the hall nearest to the front verandah, and the ladies occupy the darker and smaller rooms away from the verandah and near the kitchen. Only very intimate male relatives are allowed to cross the verandah into the house proper.

The Hindus are very particular about keeping up social decorum, and the height of the seat one occupies is in direct ratio to the social position of the occupant. A man of a lower caste cannot sit in the presence of a man of a higher caste. Men of the same caste, but having different social positions on account of difference in wealth or due to some prejudice, may sit in one another's presence, but the lesser man must be careful to occupy a lower seat than his superior. If seats of the correct height are not available, the lesser man must stand. Social position being equal, age decides seniority. A person cannot sit on terms of equality with his elder brother, father, uncle or any relative older than himself, but must stand in a respectable manner while talking to him. If the conversation is likely to last he is permitted to occupy a seat lower than the one on which his senior is seated. A woman shall not sit in the presence of an adult male of the same social position even if he is younger than she. In the case of old ladies an exception is made of this rule.

The head of the family may usually be seen sitting or reclining on the wooden bench which is permanently fixed at one end of the front verandah. A carpet or mat is used if the bench is not quite clean, otherwise none. Within reach of him is the metal box of betel nuts and leaves, and a hand fan. During the day he has some visitor or other with whom to transact business, and has scarcely any time to idle or even to rest. The other male members of the house go out on business and are scarcely seen in the house during daytime. In villages it is as disreputable for men to sit at home as for women to lead an outdoor life. An exception is made in the case of the head of the family who, because of his age and venerability, is not expected to move out of the house very often. Grown up students and young men in government service who have come home for holidays take care to escape from the house to the freedom of the village coffee house or the foot of the Banyan tree by the temple for gossip and for playing at cards or chess. In the house, the head of the family will permit no laxity of domestic discipline and his presence in the verandah or near about is enough to make all the young men of the house speak in hushed tones and walk on their toes.

In the evening all the men return to the house after the daily work. Among the orthodox they will not enter the house without bathing. In less exacting families, when the pollution contracted during the course of conducting the daily business is not very great, it is enough if the man, on his return, washes his feet and hands before entering the house. Sandals made of leather are unclean to the Hindu and a person is not allowed to enter his house with the sandals on; hence a Hindu leaves his sandals in a corner of the outer verandah and enters his house barefoot. On his coming home in the evening, a working member is served light refreshments in one of the inner rooms, after partaking of which and taking some rest he renders an account of the day's work to the head of the family. Once this is done, the night is his. He eats his meal, usually alone, and repairs to his room where his wife joins him for conjugal rights. Married male members have a room each, but children and unmarried boys sleep in the outer hall during the hot weather and in crowded rooms in winter.

The women of the house live under the tyranny of the mother-in-law. This personage is the terror of all the young ladies, and her genius for ill-treatment has become proverbial in India. Too old and dry to have any interest in matters relating to sex, she insists that every daughter-in-law of hers be as virtuous as herself. It is her duty to see that every young lady of the household drudges from sunrise to sunset; that no young girl speaks to any male member of the household, not even to her husband during daytime; and that no young lady has any time for keeping herself clean and attractive. If a young daughter-in-law puts on a presentable appearance the old woman calls her a prostitute: if she is slovenly, she calls her mother names for not knowing how to bring up presentable children. Any slackness or oversight in the matter of domestic drudgery is pointed out by the mother-in-law as a reflection on her daughter-in-law's breeding.

Hindu customs demand that a married girl who returns to her husband after visiting her father's house should bring back with her certain things, mainly eatables, as presents to the husband and her people. The mother-in-law minutely checks up these presents and compares them with what is received from her other daughters-in-law. As it is impossible for every daughter-in-law to bring the same kind and amount of presents, the mother-in-law has always someone to abuse for bringing a lesser amount of things than the other. By showing marked partiality to those daughters-in-law who bring more presents to the family, she drops broad hints direct and indirect to others of the need for pressing their parents for better and more costly presents.

When the old lady's own married daughters come to her house for a few days' stay, she sees to it that they do not work, but that the daughters-in-law work for them. These daughters of hers are often pointed out to the daughters-in-law as models of good behaviour and hard work. The only comfort the daughters-in-law can derive from the situation is from the thought that when they, in their turn, go to their fathers' houses they can likewise make their sisters-in-law slog for them. If one of the sons of the mother-in-law dies, the persecution of the widow becomes the special care of the old woman.

The mothers-in-law all over India have established a notoriety for petty tyranny and wickedness. And since women in respectable Hindu households are never allowed an out-door life, and to complain against the mother-in-law is considered an offence against good breeding, young married ladies of an orthodox Hindu household lead a wretched life. The only escape they can have from this misery is on occasions when they are allowed to visit their parents and stay with them for a few days.

The domestic life of the Hindus is very economic. They eat two principal meals, one before noon and the other towards the evening or at night. Among the rice eating Hindus of the South and of Bengal, the meal consists of boiled rice, a soup made of pulses and a vegetable dish. The Punjabis and the people of the Gangetic plain eat wheat and their meal consists of unleavened bread and dal. Only the better classes can afford to use ghee (clarified butter) and curds with their meals. Among non-vegetarians, meat and fish are delicacies which are served only twice or thrice a week. On Ekadasi days, the eleventh day of the lunar month, every orthodox Hindu fasts, taking only light food consisting of fruits. On holidays and occasions of festival, a sumptuous feast is served to all.

Like social status, the need for nourishment goes by age in India. The daily meal of the head of the family consists of two or three special dishes which are made for him. Hard working male members, next in seniority, are served a part of these delicacies when there is something to spare. Women and children suffer most and are served as little as possible. The mother-in-law is entitled to special consideration, but the other women of the house are expected to live on next to nothing and work very hard on an empty stomach. Thus those who require the least nourishment obtain most. In addition to the principal meals, coffee or tea is served early morning and in the afternoon, especially in South India. In the north, coffee and tea have not yet become fashionable, but butter milk and certain other old fashioned beverages made at home by womenfolk are preferred.

Orthodox Hindus of the village seldom smoke cigarettes or cigars. Their substitute for smoking is chewing pan made of betel leaves, areca nuts and lime which colours the saliva a deep red; for women chewing is the equivalent of applying lip-stick. Some people use tobacco also with the betel leaf. The habit of chewing pan gives the teeth of the Hindus a repugnant colour. In North India, smoking the hookah is very common. The hookah or hubble bubble is an elaborate mechanism consisting of an earthen jar with one opening on the top and another on the side. The jar is filled with water up to the hole on the side, and a hollow reed is let in through the opening on top right into the water and held tight by means of cotton packing at the mouth of the jar which is made air tight. To the top end of the hollow reed is fixed a small earthen cup with holes at the bottom to let in air. The cup is filled with scented tobacco which is lit at the time of smoking. Smoking is done through a tube, about a yard long, fixed to the opening of the jar at the side. While smoking, the hookah emits a sound like the snoring of a deep throated man, hence its European name "hubble bubble." The richer classes use metal jars and cups, the very wealthy making them of gold and silver. Like drinking, the hookah gives little pleasure when enjoyed alone. Hence, the favourite method of smoking the hookah is for a few men to sit in a circle and pass the tube from mouth to mouth. The villagers of the Punjab and Uttar Pradesh are very fond of their hookahs and carry them wherever they go.

The hookah appears to have been invented and perfected by the Muslims, and borrowed from them by the Hindus. Its use, like the Purdah, is confined to those Hindus who have come under the influence of the Muslims. The better classes of Hindus in South India and in the Mahratha countries consider it a defilement to pass anything from lip to lip and have a horror of their hookah-smoking brethren of the north.

The Hindus do not use much furniture in their houses. Chairs are seldom seen in a Hindu household. They love to squat on the floor, and feel uncomfortable when sitting with their legs dangling down. Hence a Hindu gentleman, when offered a chair, pulls his legs up and squats on the seat, thus defeating the very purpose for which a chair is made. He is, however, careful to remove his sandals, if he wears them, before squatting. The favourite method of sitting is to squat on a carpet or mat on the floor, the knees bent inwards with the right foot resting on the left thigh and the right thigh on the left foot, somewhat in the posture of the meditating Buddha. The wealthy and the ease-loving recline on soft cushions or pillows. Most of the members of a Hindu household sleep on mats on the floor, but the head of the family and the mother-in-law may have cots for their use.

Orthodox Hindus have a keener sense of cleanliness than of aesthetics. Hence the house of a Hindu gentleman is kept scrupulously clean with the courtyards and verandahs kept swept and tidy. But there will be few curtains or other decorations in a Hindu house, which are so dear to the European. Curtains, the Hindus consider a waste of cloth. Extremely frugal, they have always an eye for the useful rather than the beautiful. On festive occasions, however, the Hindus take some pains to make the house look attractive. The ladies paint the floor at the entrance to the house with rice flour. There is a religious background to this art and the figures used are mystic symbols intended to ward off evil spirits.

HOW THE HEAD OF THE FAMILY AND HIS WIFE SPEND THE DAY IN A VILLAGE HOUSEHOLD

The head of the family, being very old, sleeps little and wakes up before daybreak. Before getting up from his bed he repeats the praises of his favourite god, very often in a loud tone, which serves the purpose of an alarm clock to the other members of the family. When he finds that daylight is sufficient for him to walk about without running into something or falling down the verandah, he stops his morning prayers and gets up from his bed. A good omen is an important thing for the success of the day, and he looks at his gold ring or on a precious stone. Then he goes to the cattle shed, touches his cow and raises the hand so touched to his head as an act of adoration. If he has contracted any defilement at night, he dares not touch the cow but worships her from a safe distance. On getting up, the ultra conscientious may bow down to the earth and beg the goddess of earth pardon for the sin of treading upon her. After the routine prayers, he repairs to the tank in the compound, if it has one, or to the common village tank or to the riverside, if this is nearby, for his morning ablutions. Cleaning the teeth is an important ceremonial with the Hindu, and he takes about an hour in doing it. He uses a green stick as a brush, and when the brushing is over splits the stick into two and uses it as a tongue cleaner. In South India charcoal and salt are used as tooth powder and the right index-finger as the brush. The deep guttural sounds a Hindu makes while cleaning his teeth are likely to be mistaken by a foreigner for death cries. These are made to get everything unclean out of the mouth and the thorax.

After cleaning the teeth and other washings necessary for purifying oneself from the impurities contracted while attending the calls of nature, the Hindu takes his morning bath. Usually he gets into the water with the loin cloth he wears. Soap is seldom used in villages, but the head and the body are rubbed with certain herbs which serve as soap. The morning bath coincides with the rising of the sun, and during the process of bathing, the sun is worshipped and water sprinkled around and many incantations repeated. Those who are initiated in the Gayatri repeat this text. After the bath he comes back to the house and changes his loin cloth for a fresh one. If he is very religious he immediately goes to the family shrine which, in certain households, is in the compound and in others inside the house in a separate and very dark room. After the worship of the deity he eats his breakfast which is served to him by a servant, his wife or some elderly lady of the house. Before cleaning his teeth and washing, no orthodox Hindu will eat anything. Brahmins are very particular on this point and other respectable classes follow their lead.

After breakfast he confers with the other male members of the family who have to go out on business or on work connected with farming. Some of these men have to go very early and in such cases they take care to consult him on all important matters the previous evening. By the time the head of the family finishes his breakfast, servants and visitors begin to come to him for orders or for consultation on matters connected with the daily work. He is thus busy till about noon when he eats his first meal. After the meal, if there is no pressure of business he sleeps for an hour or two. On getting up he washes his face and rinses his mouth with water. He chews the pan and takes his place on the bench in the outer verandah, where he is ready to receive visitors. If no visitors turn up, he broods on eternal verities or goes about the house finding fault with every one and scolding those who come in his way. To scold without cause is considered good for the maintenance of domestic discipline in India.

In the evening he again goes to the tank and bathes. The setting sun is now worshipped. After the bath he comes back to the house and on the sun going down he repeats his evening prayers. The male members who had gone out for their daily work begin to return home one by one and the head of the family learns from them what they had all done and what remains to be done for the next day. Then he eats his supper and goes to bed. If he does not feel sleepy, he repeats the name of his favourite deity, and this induces sleep.

The head of the family is a serious man and never goes out to other peoples' houses without sufficient reason, and takes particular care not to be seen anywhere like coffee houses, the foot of the village Banyan tree and such other places where frivolous young men collect to gossip. He certainly attends the meetings of the village Panchayat or some such conference of elders in which matters of weight are discussed, but rigidly keeps himself aloof from the young and the jovial.

The mother-in-law, like her husband, is old and sleeps little. She too gets up early in the morning and begins her prayers in the Zenana. She is more religious than her husband, and hence uptil daybreak she goes on repeating all the names of all the gods she can remember. The old lady and her husband, by means of their religious exercises, wake up all the members of the family. The women repair to the kitchen and get on with the cooking. The servants are woken up and ordered out on their respective duties. By the time the mother-in-law gets up from her bed all the women of the house are at their posts and the cooking has started.

On getting up, the old lady bows to the earth, worships the cow and gets on to the business of cleaning her teeth if she has any! After seeing that her husband has finished his ablutions, she repairs to the tank in the compound to start hers. Women generally do not go out of their compounds to the village tank or the riverside for their morning bath. If there is no tank attached to the house, they bathe in water drawn from the well. After the bath, the mother-in-law worships at the family shrine, comes to the kitchen and starts her daily duties by scolding her daughters-in-law. She watches their cooking and washing, and sees that the coffee and tea for the early risers are ready on time, and the head of the family has no complaints in the matter. She never eats or drinks before her husband does.

The mother-in-law generally eats alone. There is usually some old servant woman hanging about her who conveys to her all the shortcomings of the daughters-in-law and the latest village gossip. The only entertainment the mother-in-law permits herself is gossiping with this woman, between the meals, and in the evenings. This woman usually knows all the young men and women of the village and even of other villages, and if there is a marriageable young man or lady in the house, the topic is usually the prospect of a suitable match for the young person. Because of her old age, the mother-in-law has certain privileges denied to younger women. She is allowed to go at will into the Mardana and may even appear on the front verandah when visitors are about. In every house there is a window opening out to the verandah from one of the rooms adjacent to the entrance hall and the mother-in-law is privileged to come to this room and listen, through the window, to the conversation going on in the verandah. Her curiosity is very strong and as soon as a visitor arrives, she is at the strategic post, studying the visitor and promptly ordering refreshments when the visitor can be offered any. When a serious marriage proposal is discussed between men, her presence at the window is imperative and she even helps the men with her advice tendered through the medium of the window.

At night, the mother-in-law does not occupy the room of her husband. Age is too strong for cupid, and the old lady occupies a separate room of her own in the Zenana. Not blessed with sound sleep, she needs the assistance of a servant girl to press her limbs and body and lull her to sleep; even then she sleeps but little and often gets up in the middle of the night to see that all the doors are properly bolted.

CHILDREN IN JOINT FAMILIES

The size of the Hindu joint family prevents the numerous children from getting much individual attention. When compared to Europeans, the Hindus neglect their children. Early marriage leads to early breeding and a Hindu woman before she passes the age of thirty-five is the mother of about a dozen children. Pregnant women are not taken proper care of. Instead of proper medical supervision and dieting the expectant mother is subjected to certain superstitious humbug and to a diet prescribed by the village barber's wife who is the final authority on all such matters as far as the villagers are concerned. For confinement, the smallest, darkest and dirtiest room of the house is allotted. The barber's wife with her crude instruments acts as the midwife and the surgeon. Under these conditions it is not surprising that a good many Hindu babies are still born. Fifty per cent of the rest die in their infancy. But those who survive are numerous enough to make a joint family look like a small school.

Hindu children, till they are grown up enough to join the infant class, are usually let to run naked about the house. They wander about the compound of the house at will, play in the dust, pick up and eat what they can get under the mango tree, and contract various diseases inevitable for such a life. When they fall ill, astrologers and necromancers are consulted as the general belief is that evil spirits cause diseases in children. When these men fail to kill or cure the child, the village Ayurvedic doctor is consulted and bitter drugs are forced down the throat of the poor child. The Hindus pay handsomely to the doctors, the astrologers and the medicine men. Very often the trouble and expenses involved in curing a child of its many maladies is more than what would cost to engage a servant to look after the child. A healthy attractive child is a rare thing in a big Hindu household.

Babies are breast fed, and the Hindus hate the idea of feeding them from a bottle. The baby is usually suckled for twelve to eighteen months when the mother expects another baby. Because of the large number of children a woman bears, and because of the inherent difficulty in giving much individual attention to children in a joint family, the bringing up of children among the generality of Hindus is anything but satisfactory.

Children are taught to fear their elders rather than to love them. Children may not speak or move freely with the adult male members of the family. The venerable head of the family is pointed out to them as a person very severe on children. They dare not speak aloud when he is in the house and the mention of his name is enough to frighten naughty children. Towards their mothers and other female members of the house they develop an attitude of contempt born of familiarity and over attachment. Some Hindus even encourage their little sons to be disobedient to women as an exercise in developing their manliness. Such children are contemptuous of their mothers and aunts whom they learn to abuse.

Children are sent to school at the age of five to seven. Before the advent of the Western system of education the village school was merely the verandah of some house of few members. Slates were not used, but each boy or girl had a small bag of fine sand, and the alphabet was learnt by writing in the sand with the index finger. Boys and girls used to squat on small mats in a row in the verandah and, spreading the sand before them, used to write in it, under the supervision of the school master who was the terror of the children. This ancient method of primary education is still followed in certain remote parts of the country where there are no Government schools.

In no other part of the world is the maxim "spare the rod and spoil the child" so seriously taken to heart as in Indian villages. The Indian equivalent of the proverb is "knowledge must be grown in tears." Discipline at home and in the school is mercilessly maintained by means of the rod. Old fashioned school masters, in addition to the rod, used to indulge in rubbing the skin of the child with poisonous herbs resulting in swelling of the skin and excruciating pain. Parents never objected to such punishments but rather encouraged them. The school masters of the present modern primary schools of the villages are, in many respects, better than their predecessors, but flogging and merciless caning still form part of discipline in village schools. The male members of the family are no less strict in keeping discipline at home and are in many ways worse than the school masters. Under this double tyranny of the home and the school, the number of Hindu children who run away from their homes is considerable. A runaway child brings disgrace on the whole family, and a good deal of money is spent and time wasted in bringing the prodigal back.

THE TIES OF BLOOD

Among respectable middle class families, affection between near relatives is very marked. An earning individual will not allow his destitute or never-do-well brother to seek the protection of others; he would rather starve himself to feed his brother to avoid bringing disgrace upon the good name of the family. A father in his old age, when infirmity prevents his being of use to the family, is always respected by his sons and taken very good care of. The sons, as a rule, would do everything in their power to see that the old man complains of nothing. The curse of an old father is considered deadly among the Hindus; so is the slanderous tongue of the watchful neighbour. Hence it would be a bold Hindu indeed who would dare to neglect his father in his old age.

Family life, like many other social institutions, is considered a duty among the Hindus rather than a pleasure. A respectable Hindu virtually works and lives for his family. When working away from his native village, a dutiful Hindu lives a very frugal life, denying himself many of the pleasures of the place he lives in so that he may send money to his people at home.

But alas! human nature is proving too weak for the joint family. Modern conditions are disrupting ancient loyalties, and contact with other nations have filled the minds of the younger generation with novel ideas of domestic life. They are out to wreck the ancient institution, and old Hindus wail over the degeneration of modern youth and the disintegration of family life. Newly married sons often try, overtly or openly, to set up their own homes and ask for the division of property. Daughters-in-law now begin to show a spirit of independence which was unheard of two decades ago. Worse than this, they set up their husbands against their parents and brothers, and sow dissension among men of the same blood. Every mother shows favouritism towards her own children, and the interference of the mother-in-law only worsens matters. All told, the evils of Kaliyuga are manifesting themselves with particular force in the joint family and the tendency at present is to divide the family property and establish separate households when the membership of the family becomes inconveniently large.

DOMESTIC LIFE IN THE CITIES

The vast majority of the Hindus live in villages. The Hindu population of the great modern cities of India consists mainly of immigrants from villages who come to the cities for the purpose of making a living or amassing a fortune. Ancient Indian cities, however, have an indigenous population of their own, and in such cities there are well established joint families, the members of which can trace their origin to the mythical hero who built the city or some blood thirsty invader who conquered it. Apart from a few such families, the Hindus living in the modern cities of India consider the village as their real home and the city as a place of sojourn.

The middle class population of the cities consist mainly of people from the joint families of the village. What usually happens is this: A young member of the village joint family finds the atmosphere too hot for him or the ancestral occupation too prosaic for his ambitions, and he moves to the city to carve out a fortune or career for himself. Indian youths with English education detest agriculture, the pet occupation of the middle classes of the village, and invariably migrate to the city in search of secretarial jobs. The work that appeals most to the 'educated' Hindu youth is quill-driving. He is ready to work as a clerk or typist on half the wages of some technical job involving manual work he is qualified to get.

Clerks are miserably paid in India but the Hindu clerk can live on practically nothing. He may be a married man, but his wife gets free lodging and boarding in the joint family, and in India there is no need for a married man to support his wife if he is not willing to do so. What the Hindu clerk in the city usually does is to live with a dozen other men like himself, in a small rented house, spend as little of his wages as possible, and save the rest or send it home to the head of the joint family. When he has saved enough or has been fortunate enough to get a job carrying with it a decent remuneration, he brings his wife and children to the city. Here he takes a flat or house on rent, preferably in a locality where men of his caste and social position reside.

The city dwelling Hindu is a freer social individual than the villager. Few Hindus will care to bring their parents to the cities, even if they are willing to come, and hence there is no mother-in-law to stand between a man and his wife in the city. Ladies have considerable amount of freedom, and when the husbands are away at work, they often visit one another's houses for gossip, and even play indoor games. Very few women, however, do their own marketing and the men have to get up very early and go to the market to buy meat, vegetables and provisions for the day. The farther a Hindu couple are away from their native village, the more freedom they enjoy. Where they are not intimately known, people can afford to break the conventions of their caste without social stricture, and the sinful pleasures of petty offences against social codes are ardently courted by young ladies. Forbidden to talk to one another in their own houses while living in the joint family, a young Hindu couple who have migrated into the city may be seen walking abreast along the king's highway laughing and flirting. A young lady with some English education may even dare to enjoy the excitement of shaking hands with her husband's friend when he is introduced to her. But woe betide the couple who is unlucky enough to be seen doing such things by people known to them in the village! If such things get known to the head of the family or some elderly member of the household, the culprits may be made to suffer everything short of actual excommunication.

Those Hindus who have had the benefit of high education and are lucky enough to get four figure salaries are privileged to break all social conventions and live a life more free than that of the European who is believed by the generality of Indians to have no social and moral bonds. Such Hindus build and furnish their houses like Europeans; they eat beef and pork with knives and forks; they dress like Europeans, and drink like Europeans; they and their womenfolk go about like Europeans and may even dance like Americans; and they speak English with bad accents to be mistaken for Englishmen or Americans. These ladies and gentlemen form but an insignificant percentage of the population of the Hindus living in a city, but they set up the fashion for the city dwelling Hindus.

Even in the cities, free social intercourse between the sexes is prohibited among the lower middle classes. A Hindu living with his wife will not allow a stranger or a casual acquaintance to enter his flat especially if this is a small one. Such visitors, as a rule, wait outside and business is transacted at the door. Friends or relatives may obtain entrance into the house when the male member is in, but the lady of the house may not join them. Among the orthodox, the lady shuts herself up in the kitchen and if a guest has to be served tea or coffee, the servant, if any, or a child is made to serve him. If there are no servants or children, the host himself serves, but his wife is forbidden by social codes to serve a male guest. On the other hand, if the visitor happens to be a lady, the male member takes care to leave the flat and the women have a free run of the place. When a lady wishes to visit her neighbour, she is taken up to the door of the flat by her husband from where he goes back, accompanied by the host, if he is in. The two outcastes return after an hour or so when the lady guest comes out of the house, and the host gets in.

An orthodox Hindu lady of the middle class will not let an adult male into her house in the absence of her husband. This rule has few exceptions. Even intimate friends of the husband cannot enter the house in his absence. When a visitor knocks at the door and if the male member of the house is not in, the lady opens a lattice or peeps through the key hole to ascertain who the visitor is. If he happens to be a stranger, she goes back without saying a word from which the visitor is to surmise that the male member is not in and he may go away without waiting. If the visitor is well known to the lady, she takes the trouble of opening the door and telling him that her husband is away; on which he apologizes for the intrusion and goes away. If the visitor is a lady she is let in with alacrity and gossip starts.

Almost all Hindus live below the standard expected of men of their means. They have an eye for hoarding rather than for spending. The Hindus have an exaggerated idea of the fickleness of fortune and the helplessness of old age and save up most of their income for the rainy day.

In the cities too, the Hindus seldom use curtains for their doors and windows, and their flats have very little furniture. The space at the entrance to a flat occupied by a Hindu is invariably used for hanging rags and wet clothes for drying. This violence to aesthetics is emphasized by using the front balcony, the pride of every flat, as the dumping place for undesirable and useless articles. Middle class Hindu quarters in a city have usually a meaner appearance than those of Parsis or Christians of the same class; but inside the house, the Hindus are much cleaner than both.

CHAPTER VIII

CUSTOMS, MANNERS, COSTUMES, POPULAR SUPERSTITIONS, ETC.

MOST of the customs, manners and superstitions of the Hindus have a religious background. Caste and its various codes are the mainstay of their social life.

METHODS OF GREETING

The method of greeting depends upon the social status of the persons meeting. When a man of very low position meets a person of very high rank, the former is expected to fall flat to the ground with his hands folded in front. This custom of greeting is still in vogue in South India. Subjects who came with petitions to Zamindars and petty chieftains of the South were expected to greet their Highnesses in this manner. In Malabar such petitioners were not to wear upper garments, but appeared in loin cloths. The speech of the petitioner always was in terms of the meanest expressions when referring to himself and in the highest when referring to his patron. High officials of the state were allowed a little more freedom when visiting a Maharajah; they could come within a reasonable distance of His Highness, fold their hands at the chest and bow down to the ground. These methods of greeting were enforced only on the subjects of the Maharajah. Others, for obvious reasons, were allowed to greet His Highness in any respectable manner prevalent among themselves. The Maharajahs, however, are now an extinct race.

A son greets his father usually by bowing down and touching his feet, and raising the hand to his head. A young lady may also greet her parents in this way. The same method is adopted by young men greeting their mothers, pupils their teachers, and laymen greeting venerable religious heads. Before the man touches the feet, the person greeted usually raises the supplicant by the hand, pretending that he is not so great a personage as to be greeted in this fashion.

Among equals, the usual method of greeting in North India or rather Hindustan proper is to repeat the name of Rama twice thus: Ram, Ram. While uttering these words, the right hand is brought to the chest twice and the head slightly bowed. Among the Arya Samajists the method of greeting is to fold the palms in front of the chest and say "Namaste" meaning "greeting to you". When done by ladies, this method of greeting looks much more graceful than the Western method of shaking hands, and it is becoming increasingly popular all over India. Among the better classes of people, educated in Western style, wishing in English fashion and shaking hands are becoming common. But occasionally one comes across a highly educated Hindu lady who shows horror of touching the hand of a male. The present writer once found himself in an embarrassing situation while taking farewell of a cultured Hindu lady about to proceed to Europe for higher studies in medicine. After spending a day together in boating, picnicking and in entertaining conversation, the lady dined with the author and his wife in their house, and while parting the author cordially extended his hand to the lady and was pained to find no response! This is, however, a rare instance and Hindu ladies with modern education usually shake hands with men to whom they are introduced. Any way, my own experience shows that one can never know enough of Hindu prejudices, and it is safer not to extend one's hand to a Hindu lady till one is sure of one's ground.

RULES OF ETIQUETTE BETWEEN THE SEXES

Social freedom between the sexes being prohibited, a stranger is not allowed to speak to a lady he is not well acquainted with. Similarly it is considered immodest on the part of a woman to approach or speak to a stranger on any matter whatsoever. The only exception to this rule is when the lady is in peril of her life and the help of a man is needed to save her. It will be considered an insolence on the part of a stranger to help a lady out of a vehicle or a boat; and the lady and her husband, if he is with her, will resent it. On the part of a friend such an act will be considered officious. An orthodox Hindu lady, offered a seat in a bus by a stranger, may frown upon him instead of thanking him. A wayfarer asking his way of a Hindu lady in a street may receive a rude answer or no answer at all.

Among the conventional it is considered immodest for a lady to walk abreast of a man even if he is her husband or brother. For a young lady to take the hand of a man who is not her husband is very objectionable. A couple to be seen walking hand in hand is scandalous, and among the very orthodox may lead to anything short of excommunication. Bold, emancipated ladies may dare to indulge in dancing with their husbands. But for a Hindu lady to dance with any one who is not her husband is considered improper. Because of these conventions which still rule Hindu society, the orthodox Hindu has a low opinion of the morals of Europeans, and they jealously guard their young sons and daughters against the "corruption" of the West.

The Hindus are chivalrous, and when women are in danger or their honour threatened, they will not hesitate to risk their lives to save the womenfolk. But in daily life and social relations, the subordinate position of women is maintained. Men are given precedence and places of honour in all walks of life. If a man and a woman go shopping it is the woman who is expected to carry the parcel. It is improper for a woman to sit in a bus, while her husband is standing. A woman may eat only after her husband is fed. Cash is always kept with men and for all domestic expenses and for shopping, the womenfolk are to go daily to their husbands and get the money necessary for the day. A man who allows his wife to get the upper hand in any of these things is considered henpecked by the orthodox.

In the villages, one often comes across a man of the middle class walking along the highway unencumbered by anything but an umbrella or a walking stick while his wife struggles along at a respectable distance behind him with a child sitting astride her right hip, a load on her head, the hot Indian sun beating mercilessly on her. If, on the other hand, the man were to carry the baby and the load, and his wife to walk about protected by the shade of the umbrella, the party would be the laughing stock of every passerby and children may throw stones at them. In orthodox Hindu households young ladies are not allowed to open their mouths in presence of elderly male members of the house, and the mother-in-law or some other elderly lady alone may speak on their behalf to the head of the family.

It is an offence against good manners for a man to address a woman by her name. Nor may a woman address a man by name. This code of etiquette is more rigidly observed among husbands and wives than among others. A woman always refers to her husband as "the child's father" or by some other euphemistic term. The husband, likewise, refers to his wife as "so-and-so's mother". Europeans may wonder how in a family a man and a woman are able to pull on without addressing each other by name. But there are children handy who may be made to call their mothers or fathers. It is true that at times difficult situations arise when a man has to call his wife direct; in such cases he calls her as one would call a stranger whose name he does not know, by making a noise. The Hindus have superstitions connected with names and ladies are very careful not to give out theirs; besides the obvious familiarity a name inspires, a man who knows a lady's name is believed to possess power over her. Hence a stranger is never allowed to know the secret of a lady's name and he who asks for it is suspected to possess evil designs.

On a woman getting married, she does not change her name for her husband's as the Europeans do. Very few Hindus have surnames and even those who have, do not attach much importance to them. A Hindu is generally known by his personal name, his father's name, his caste and the name of the village he lives in. Surnames being insignificant, a married woman retains her own name and in documents her personal name appears as the wife of such-and-such a person.

Speaking of names, it is customary to add to the names of the Hindus the affix Ji as a mark of respect. Thus Gandhi in polite speech becomes Gandhiji. The word Ji is more respectful than Mr. and is often used in conversation while assenting or dissenting from the views of others. Thus when a person wishes to show his approval of another's opinion he says, "Ah-Ji" meaning Yes Sir; to show disapproval he says, "Nahin-Ji" meaning No Sir. The affix Urlu is used by the Telugus in place of Ji. In the Punjab the prefix Lala is favoured (*i.e.*, Lala Lajpatrai); and in Sind, Diwan (as Diwan Jhamatmal Advani, Jhamatmal being the personal name and Advani, name of the subcaste). In Bengal, Babu takes the place of Mister and this is the epithet used by supercilious Europeans for all Indians, especially those who do clerical and secretarial jobs. In North India the word Babu is understood by all, but in the South it is neither understood nor appreciated. Kuppuswami Mudaliar or Ramaswami Aiyar may not appreciate being called Babu Kuppuswami or Babu Ramaswami and may even express his resentment when he is in a position to do so. In polite correspondence and in invitation cards South Indians and the Mahrathas often use the classic Sanskrit prefix Shriman for men and Shrimati for women. This is, however, used all over India by Hindus who show a predilection for Sanskrit and is now enforced by the Government of India; the prefix Mr. is now replaced by Shri: in all official correspondence. Among the Mahrathas of Maharashtra State it is fashionable for a person to be known by the name of the town or village from which he hails. A person from Mangalore will be known as Mangaloreker, one from Khar as Kharker. This stands in place of the surname of the Europeans, the personal name, father's name and the subcaste name (when one wishes to include this also), being indicated by the initial letters that precede, much in the manner of Europeans.

MEN'S DRESS

The generality of Hindus practise admirable economy in the matter of wearing clothes. In South India throughout the year and in the North during the hot season, men in their houses wear loin cloths and leave the upper part of the body and the head bare. Those young men who consider the loin cloth too scanty for modern ideas of modesty wear the Dhoti at home, which, as a rule, is used only out of doors. The Dhoti is a single piece of white cloth, about five yards long and three to four feet broad. It is passed round the waist upto half its length and the other half is drawn between the legs and tucked at the waist behind. The aristocrats in Bengal wear unusually long Dhotis which leave, when worn, about a yard of cloth in front which is passed over the upper part of the body and thrown over the shoulders somewhat like the toga of the Roman aristocrats. While walking about, the Bengali holds this portion of the Dhoti in his hands. Inside the house all Hindus walk about barefoot, sandals made of leather being considered unclean.

The generality of Hindus in South India wear only Dhotis and go barefoot and bareheaded, the upper part of the body uncovered. The better classes, especially on ceremonial occasions, wear long coats and turbans. In Malabar, however, aristocracy is

LXI

131 THOUSAND PILLARED HALL IN CHIDAMBARAM TEMPLE
(Photo: S. S. Aiyar)

132 MAIN ENTRANCE, KESAVA TEMPLE, BELUR
(Photo: S. S. Aiyar)

LXII

133   ORNAMENTAL ARCHITRAVE FROM A HINDU TEMPLE

134   CARVINGS IN A JAIN TEMPLE
(*Journal of Indian Art and Industry*)

LXIII

135 BIRLA MANDIR: A MODERN HINDU TEMPLE
(India Pictorial Features)

136 TEMPLE OF MAHADEVA (SHIVA), KHAJURAHO
(Rousslet's *India*)

137 DWARKA TEMPLE
(Photo: N. J. Oralwalla)

138 ENTRANCE TO A SHIVA TEMPLE: THE BULL ON TOP IS NANDI, SHIVA'S CHARGER
(India Pictorial Features)

LXIV

139 HALABID TEMPLE
(Photo: S. S. Aiyar)

140 CARVING ON WALL OF BELUR TEMPLE
(Photo: S. S. Aiyar)

measured in proportion to the amount of bareness of the body, and the less a Hindu is covered the more aristocratic is he considered. Some of the Nambudiri Brahmins wear just a narrow piece of cloth in front when inside the houses, and a loin cloth when going out of doors. The Malabar Brahmin usually protects himself with an umbrella made of the leaves of the talipot palm. In North India, except in Bengal, the Hindus wear head-dresses. These vary in shape and size according to the caste and social position of the wearer. The middle classes wear oval shaped caps. The turban is the favourite head-dress of the Sikhs and the Rajputs. All turbans are not however alike. The turban of the Madrassi aristocrat is a neat affair in white with a bright band winding up the sides to the crest, symmetrical in shape. When worn, it leaves the ears free and becomes the head very well. The turban worn by the lower classes in Bombay, Gujarat, Rajasthan and Kutch is a long narrow piece of thin white or coloured cloth wound loosely round the head, covering up at least one of the ears and a good part of the brow, and sits on the head like a crushed basket. The better classes in these parts of India wear their turbans neater, but the design is the same and the turban must cover half of one ear and a good part of the brow. The Punjabi Hindus' turban, a model borrowed from the Muslim, is martial in appearance. It is of white or coloured muslin wound beautifully round a small peaked cap of bright material, one end of the muslin rising up in a flowery crest in front and the other end hanging at the back of the neck as a tail. When worn by a well proportioned man, it looks very impressive.

Before passing from the subject of head-dress, a word may be said about the Gandhi cap. This is a plain white cap made of thick Khaddar which, when not required, can be folded and kept in the pocket. Instead of pure white, some people prefer brown and dark hues but the shape and material are the same. The Gandhi cap is generally worn by Congressmen and those who profess sympathy for Congress ideals, and its use by Hindu clerks in government offices was, during the British period, considered by Englishmen an offence against official etiquette. It is the white cap that was objectionable, and not the dark and brown ones. The cap, it may be mentioned, was invented and popularised by Gandhiji as the best for the Indian climate and pocket, hence its name. Its one great advantage over other caps is that it can be washed while other kinds of caps are worn till they stink. Gandhiji, by the way, never wore the Gandhi cap.

The Hindus as a rule do not care much for tailored clothes. But in the Punjab some Hindus have adopted the Salwar or the baggy trousers of the Muslims. Throughout northern India, out-of-doors the Hindus wear tight jackets or loose shirts. In Bengal and the United Provinces, in spite of centuries of Muslim domination, the preference for the Dhoti prevails. The Rajputs wear tight breeches of thin linen. The Sikhs do not care much for Dhotis They wear loose shirts, breeches and turbans. For the Sikh the turban has a religious significance, and no Sikh is allowed to discard his turban for a cap Well-to-do Hindus who wish to appear aristocratic wear long coats like the Rajahs and Nawabs. The long coat, known as Sherwani, has been standardized and is the dress recognized by the Government of India for official and ceremonial wear.

WOMEN'S DRESS

The dress of a middle class lady in the Mahratha countries and the South is a bodice and a Sari. The Sari may be of silk or of cotton according to the purchasing power of the wearer. The conventional Sari is a coloured robe with bright borders twenty to thirty feet in length and three to four feet broad. The orthodox method of wearing the Sari is to pass it round the waist so as to divide it into two unequal parts. The longer part falls as a skirt and its end is drawn between the legs and tucked behind the waist; the shorter part is passed across the upper part of the body and thrown over the shoulders. When worn well, the lower portion has the appearance of breeches falling in graceful folds when viewed from the front, but the back view is not equally attractive. For obvious reasons, a Sari so worn does not permit of the use of a petticoat and a Hindu lady walking in this attire often exposes her legs upto the thighs. Among the lower classes this is always the case; but the better classes, by dexterously arranging the lower part, manage to expose nothing above the knees while walking.

Among the poorer classes, and the old women of the middle classes, a bodice is not worn but the upper end of the Sari is made to serve this purpose. In this case the Sari is very long and the upper half is passed across the front portion of the body, brought behind the back and the end tucked to a convenient spot. Widows manage to cover their heads also with their Saris.

Among modern ladies, it is considered inartistic to draw the lower end of the Sari between the legs, and the Saris they wear are of different design. The modern Sari is smaller, five to six yards long, made of silk, with bright detachable or printed borders along its whole length on either side and at one of the ends. It is worn over a petticoat, half the portion falling as a skirt, and the other half rising in graceful folds, supported by the shining borders, from the left foot to the right shoulder across the whole figure of the lady. The modern Sari, well worn, can compare favourably with the fashionable clothes of European women. The Parsis and the Indian Christians have been the leaders of fashion in the matter of wearing the Sari, and educated young Hindu ladies follow their lead. The Hindu lady is extremely loyal to her Sari. While most of the modernized Hindu males have adopted the European costume in their outdoor life, no Hindu lady, however emancipated from conventions, has known to have given up her

Sari for the European frock. A modernized Hindu lady may move freely in the society of Europeans, but always in the Sari.

In Rajasthan and Uttar Pradesh, women wear skirts and jackets with wrappers to cover the head and, if need be, the face. The Sari, however, is slowly ousting the skirt. Among Purdah-observing Hindu ladies one end of the Sari is used as a veil to cover the head and face. In the Punjab, mainly through Muslim contact, young ladies consider it fashionable to wear long shirts and breeches with a coloured muslin wrapper to match. Those who wish to appear modest use the wrapper to cover their heads, others throw it over the shoulders. The Punjabi costume, because of the freedom of movement it gives, is becoming fashionable among unmarried young ladies, and very well suits a slim figure. Sikh ladies set the fashion in this costume and they seldom wear anything else, except when some modern Sikh lady shows a preference for the Parsi or Indian Christian Sari.

In North India, including Bengal, for a lady to appear in public without covering her head is considered immodest. Hence a wrapper or the end of the Sari is invariably used for covering the head. Young coquettes who are proud of their hair leave it bare, but if they happen to come across some elderly personage they immediately draw the wrapper or Sari over the head. On the other hand, if her head is covered and if she meets some young gallant whose attention she wishes to attract, she, as if by accident, drops the wrapper or the Sari from her head. The convention regarding covering the head is not observed in the Mahratha countries where young ladies decorate their hair with flowers, and strut about like dancing peacocks. In South India only widows with shaven heads are expected to cover their heads.

Inside and out of doors, the generality of women in South India walk barefoot. In North India they wear slippers. None except the modernised lady wears high-heeled shoes, and even these would not care to wear stockings. Poor women all over India walk barefoot.

ORNAMENTS

The craze for ornaments is common to all Hindus. This applies even to the male of the species. In addition to the ring, which men all over the world love to wear, a Hindu gentleman delights to wear wrist-chains and bangles. In most parts of India, men wear ear-rings, studded with glittering stones, and for this purpose the ears of a Hindu boy is bored at an early age. Boys and grown up men, when they can afford it, wear gold chains and lockets round their necks. The craze for ornaments is greatest among South Indians, and here many an ebony coloured, pot-bellied male may be seen in the street with his bare trunk adorned as a black idol of Krishna. He wears glittering ear-rings, gold wrist-chains in many folds, a huge locket round the neck hanging from a massive gold chain, and a gold girdle worn round the waist over the Dhoti.

The Hindus will starve themselves in order to buy ornaments for their womenfolk. Among orthodox classes, as mentioned elsewhere, what is most admired in a woman is not good looks, figure or health but ornaments. A middle class Hindu lady carries a fortune about her person by way of ornaments. She may not have enough to eat or feed her children, but she must have her trinkets. The minimum equipment of jewellery a middle class Hindu lady is expected to possess are two ear-rings of good size studded with diamonds, a nose stud, ten rings for the ten fingers, an additional ten for the toes, two or three gold chains for the neck and a dozen gold bangles for the wrist, and anklets for the ankles. With this paraphernalia she can appear in society as a properly clad person. In South India, the ladies of the upper classes wear girdles made of gold over their Saris, which when worn by a slim-waisted lady, beautifully divides the figure into two. The nose rings worn by orthodox ladies in Sind are too massive to be supported by the nose, and to prevent the ring from tearing the nose they bring down a few hairs from the crown of the head across the brow and tie the nose rings.

Ladies of the aristocracy and courtezans wear ornaments on their heads. These consist of pearl or gold chains worn at the sides and centre of the head, after the hair has been properly dressed. A jewelled crest go with these chains and is worn at the front of the head. By far the most lavishly adorned person is the Hindu bride. The wedding is a Hindu lady's day of days and the most burning thirst for jewellery is quenched on this day. From head to foot, a Hindu bride is literally loaded with gold and precious stones.

The poorer classes imitate the rich. Among them, the males have to be contented with two cheap silver ear-rings and a silver or brass locket tied from a string. But his wife must have all the ornaments her more fortunate sisters wear. As it is impossible for her to have them made of the same metal or stone, she goes in for inferior quality. Glass bangles are greatly admired by them and the poor Hindu woman has often her arms covered with them from wrists to the elbows. As ear-rings, she hangs two small iron hooks from the lobes of her ears. Around her neck she wears a twisted metal bar. In addition she has garlands of cowries and the inevitable locket hung from a string. The ankles and toes must also be adorned with metal even if base. Nor should the nose be neglected. A small iron hook, like her ear-rings, adorns the nose. Lower class women in the Mahratha countries and North India have small green marks tattooed at the centre of the brow and at the wrists. The mark on the brow serves the purpose of the Pottu, the small caste mark adopted by the ladies of the South to beauty their brows.

METHODS OF DRESSING HAIR

To the Hindu, as noticed in a previous chapter, the mode of dressing hair has a deep religious significance. Shaving is something of a ceremony and the barber a priest. The caste and religion of a man is known mainly by the manner he dresses his hair.

The easiest way to recognize a Sikh is by his long hair and beard. The generality of Hindus in North India shave their heads and faces clean, leaving a small tuft of hair, known as the Chhoti, at the back of the head. The Chhoti is dear to the Hindu and even those who crop their hair in Western fashion take care to see that the Chhoti is not cropped off.

Hair dressing among men has not developed into so elaborate an art in North India as in the South. The Brahmins of South India shave the front portion of the head but grow long hair on the back which is tied into a knot at the back of the neck. Others think this practice unclean; hence while they shave the front part of the head, they crop the hair at the back low. The Brahmins and Nayars of Malabar are contemptuous of the taste of the Tamils in the matter of hair dressing; they shave the back of the head and leave the hair to grow long at the front of the head in a circle, shaving off the sides which fall beyond the radius of the circle. Men in the South are as much proud of their hair as women, and take great care in combing and oiling it, and assiduously practise the art of tying the end of the hair into a beautiful knot.

During days of mourning, and certain periods of ceremonial impurity the Brahmin will not shave. But when this period is over, he shaves from head to foot excepting his Chhoti or its equivalent. The only persons who are allowed to shave off their Chhoti are Sannyasins who, as a sign of having attained emancipation from all bonds, may discard both the sacred thread and the Chhoti. Some Sannyasins, on the other hand, show their spirit of emancipation by not shaving at all, and leave the hair and beard to grow into dirty glued locks. Among the ordinary run of Hindus, the Western method of cropping is becoming exceedingly popular, and in cities and towns ninety per cent of young Hindus crop their hair and grow their Chhotis short.

Hindus shave their beards but some of them keep moustaches. Among certain communities, moustaches are shaved off in times of mourning. The Hindus of Bengal and Malabar love to shave their faces clean.

Her hair is the pride of a young Hindu lady. Black, glossy, luxuriant hair is the delight of the Hindu. Hindu women anoint their heads with oils and rub the hair with herbs at the time of bathing which promotes the growth of the hair and keeps it black. Some young ladies have hair which, when left loose, reaches down to the heels. Such long hair is greatly valued and considered the principal symbol of feminine attraction. Bobbing the hair is an abomination to the orthodox.

The usual method of dressing hair among Hindu ladies is to comb it well and tie it behind the neck. The method of tying the knot differs with different communities but a casual observer will find all knots alike. The ladies of South India adorn the knot with petals of jasmine or some other sweet smelling flower which adds much to the beauty of the hair. The ladies of the Mahratha countries make regular garlands of flowers which they pin to the knot of the hair, and these give the head the appearance of gaudy over-decoration. In other parts of India the hair being generally covered, women wear no flowers on the head.

Children and unmarried girls plait their hair and let it fall to the back and tie the tail end with bright pieces of ribbon. Those who follow Western methods bob the hair of their children, and this practice is at times continued by the ultra modern even after marriage. Such cases are very rare. Among the lower classes too, long hair is much valued. But they tie it in stiff knots, for better freedom of movement, and as they have very little time to attend to their hair. Hence the hair of the working class women often gets glued up, and is a regular forest teeming with insect life. On holidays these poor women may be seen at the doors of their huts sitting in a circle and hunting in each other's heads with knives and sickles.

SOME POPULAR SUPERSTITIONS

The folk of India, like their brethren all over the world, are superstitious. In the vast religious literature of the Hindus there is a place for everything and the superstitions of the Hindus can be made to appear more religious than those of other civilised peoples. But as a matter of fact, the superstitions of the Hindu folk are more ancient than their religion, and what some writers did was only to incorporate them in their works and pass them on as revealed wisdom.

No people of the modern world have such firm a belief in astrology as the Hindus. Astronomy and astrology are indistinguishable in India. The astronomer is often the astrologer too. On the birth of a child its horoscope has to be cast. Every Rajah had his official astrologer and without this gentleman's advice, His Highness never embarked upon any serious enterprise. The time for an important ceremony, religious or otherwise, is fixed by an astrologer. This applies not only to the Rajahs and the rich but to all Hindus worth the name. Every village has its astrologer and he fixes the time for every undertaking, whether of the individual or of the community. In the villages, when anybody falls sick, the first person consulted is the astrologer as the malignant influences of evil planets are believed to be the primary cause of diseases. The village astrologer is a powerful dignitary; but he is often ignorant and malicious and may not have even an elementary knowledge of the ancient Sanskrit authorities on astrology. These hoary sages, by the way, do not appear to have been infallible in their predictions.

Among the Hindus, the right side is considered more lucky than the left. While entering a house, a conscientious Hindu puts his right foot first. No gift is received or given with the left hand. If the gift is too big to be held by one hand alone, both the hands may be used, but never the left hand alone. A gift accidentally dropped while giving, is believed to have been given grudgingly, and considered unlucky to the receiver. The left hand is not only unlucky, but unclean. This is mainly because the Hindus use the left hand for washing after attending the calls of nature. It is probably this sense of ceremonial uncleanliness that led to its being considered unlucky. No orthodox Hindu will eat anything with the fingers of his left hand.

Belief in omens is universal among the Hindus. An omen seen on getting up in the morning is believed to be an index to the day's happening. On going out of the house, the Hindu looks for omens which are supposed to give an indication of what is in store for him. The method of determining the desirability or otherwise of an omen is somewhat arbitrary. A crow on the left side or a kite on the right, a snake, hare, an empty vessel, smouldering fire, a widow or a man with one eye or a big nose, is a bad omen. A cow, a horse, elephant, a parrot, a lizard on the east wall, a clear fire, a virgin, two or more Brahmins, etc., are good omens. Sneezing once is good; twice, evil. A pregnant woman must not go inside an empty house or one with an upper storey; nor should she sit with her feet turned back, or sleep during daylight or lie awake at night. Her husband must be equally cautious. "He must not build a house; for that might rouse the wrath of the earth spirit. He must no bathe in the sea for the sea shore is thick with ghosts. He must not attend at funeral." Nor should he travel or shave his head.

In Malabar the craze for good omens has developed into an art, and for Vishu, the New Year Day, every Hindu household prepares the Kani or good omen at night for the members to look at as they get up in the morning. The Kani is prepared in a spacious room, close to a wall facing east. A mystic design is drawn on the floor and a circular metal plate with rice in it is placed inside the design. Behind the plate a mirror is placed with its back propped up against the wall. Flowers and fruits are strewn on the floor on all sides of the design and a wick lamp is lighted on either side of the mirror. The Kani is now ready to be gazed on. To see this early in the morning is believed to bring luck for the whole year.

The worst omen a Hindu can possibly imagine is a cat crossing one's path. It portends death and destruction. Even those Hindus who have discarded most of the religious beliefs of their community, are mortally frightened of a cat crossing their path while going on a journey; they would rather give up the journey or postpone it to some other date than continue it after being forbidden by so terrible an omen.

Some individuals often get a notoriety in the localities they live for bringing bad luck to people. Every enterprise they engage in is believed to end in failure. Their very sight is obnoxious and portends evil. While employed in the Indian railways, I once noticed that one of the guards headquartered at a particular place was avoided and detested by every one at the station including other guards. Somehow or other a belief got currency at the station that he could never take a train to its destination on time. He had one or two accidents to his discredit. Drivers used to report sick as soon as they came to know that the 'unlucky guard' was to be in charge of the train they were booked to work. I took the trouble of ascertaining the percentage of trains he worked to destination on time. This was five against the average of forty-five for the month over the section. Probably the extra caution drivers used to observe while working this guard's trains was responsible for this low percentage obtained by him. But the point is how he ever came to be known as an unlucky guard!

The fear of unlucky persons is common to all Indian villages. Such persons are shunned by the villagers and their presence at a social gathering is resented. Mothers keep their children away from them. These persons may be of respectable families but they are not less obnoxious on that account.

The evil eye is as much dreaded as the ill omen. Crops are protected in Indian villages by putting up scarecrows which may divert the attention of evil-eyed individuals. It is the first look that is deadly and if the scarecrow manages to catch it, the crop is saved. Good crops, good looking children, beautiful young men and women, are all believed to be particularly amenable to the influence of the evil eye. While crops are usually protected by scarecrows, living beings are protected by lockets and charms specially prepared to ward off the evil eye. Cattle, dogs, in fact any desirable or beautiful thing is apt to be destroyed by the evil eye. But every weapon has its counter weapon and the Hindus have many preventives against the evil eye. The astrologer or the necromancer is always ready to perform, on payment of a small fee, certain magic rites to prevent the influence of the evil eye or to remedy its ill effect when affected.

The black tongue generally goes with the evil eye. The word of the man with the black tongue is believed to be more deadly than the sword. If a person afflicted with this malady remarks, on seeing a child, that it looks sweet or healthy, the child is feared to fall ill and die. If he casually mentions, on seeing a mango tree in blossom, that the flowers appear to promise a good crop, the tree is feared to wither away in a couple of days' time. The words of the evil-tongued person should be unintentional to have the deadly effect. There is the story of such a person in South India who was cleverly engaged by a farmer to get his field rid of the weeds that were growing thick with the seedlings. The evil-tongued person was invited by the farmer to his house and treated to a sumptuous repast; after which he took his guest for a walk in the fields. The farmer expected that the guest would notice the weeds and pass some remarks about their thick growth, but unfortunately the evil-tongued person appeared to interest himself in everything except the weeds. After many unsuccessful attempts to attract his guest's attention to the weeds, the farmer as a last resort casually pointed out to him how thick the weeds were growing in his fields. Upon this the evil-tongued person observed that though the weeds were growing thick, the few seedlings appeared extraordinarily strong. The result was, the next morning the seedlings were found withering away and the weeds flourishing; so at any rate the story goes.

Because of this universal fear of the evil tongue among the Hindus, it is bad manners for a stranger who happens to visit a house to speak well of anything. If, for instance, a visitor to a Hindu household were to remark of the guest's baby "how sweet," it will be an unpardonable insult to him. If a good meal is praised it will be no compliment to the cook. A good piece of furniture should not be spoken of with admiration, a promising young lad should not be mentioned as such. In all these matters, as well as in everything else, it is best not to express one's admiration at all. Nor should they be condemned. When visiting a Hindu, the golden rule is to observe all but speak little.

The Hindus believe that it is lucky to have a look at kings, saints, heroes and other well-known persons. Seeing such persons is known as 'Darsan.' Darsan is supposed to bring good luck in the spiritual as well as the material sphere. When any important personage visits a city or town, the crowds that gather to have 'Darsan' are enormous. The nearer a person approaches the great man, the better is the effect of the 'Darsan'. Hence the efforts people make to get near him are such that with the best police precaution the crowds in India often get out of control and lead to utmost confusion. It may, however, be mentioned that the eagerness to have a close view of a great man is universal among mankind and the Hindu idea of 'Darsan' is but an exaggeration of this.

The wall lizard is a prophet among the Hindus. The noise it makes, its position on the wall or ceiling, its fall from the wall by accident, are all capable of revealing the future. If a lizard falls on one's head, the happening is indicative of death. If it falls on the right part of a person's body, it brings him luck; if on the left, mishaps. There is an elaborate literature on wall lizards, and many Hindus carefully study it and daily consult the omens. The classical literature on the subject is known as Gowli Sastra or the science of the wall lizard.

CHAPTER IX

CEREMONIES

THE main concern of a Hindu gentleman about his children is not whether or not he would be able to educate them properly, or to look after their health and well-being, but whether he would be able to provide money for the various ceremonies that have to be performed till male children become 'householders,' and girls are married. Providing feasts and paying Brahmins are indispensable to all ceremonies, and the generality of Hindus spend more than they can afford on these occasions.

The principal ceremonies prescribed for a boy by ancient Hindu law-givers are twelve. These are called Samskaras or purificatory rites. The Samskaras are: (1) Garbha-lambhana (impregnation); (2) Pumsavana (male production); (3) Simantonnayana (hair parting); (4) Jata Karman (birth ceremony); (5) Nama Karna (name giving); (6) Nishkramana (carrying out); (7) Anna Prasana (food-giving); (8) Kshaura (shaving); (9) Kesanta (tonsure); (10) Upanayana (initiation); (11) Samavartana (return from the house of the preceptor); and (12) Vivaha (marriage). Some orthodox castes in certain regions still perform all these ceremonies, the methods of performing them varying in details in different states and among different subcastes.

It can be seen from the above list that among the Hindus a person's purificatory rites begin before his birth. The first ceremony, Garbha-lambhana or impregnation, is to be performed on the fourth day of marriage. Only after the performance of this ceremony is a man supposed to have sexual union with his wife. One of the incantations to be repeated on the performance of this ceremony reads as follows: "Let Vishnu prepare her womb; let the Creator shape its forms; let Prajapati be the Impregnator; let the Creator give the embryo." This ceremony is not usually performed nowadays except by very orthodox people. Nor do the generality of the Hindus wait for four days after marriage to enjoy conjugal rights.

Every Hindu loves to have sons and considers it a misfortune to have daughters. The main reason for this is that all Hindu scriptures teach that only male issues are competent to perform funeral rites without which no ordinary soul can hope to go to heaven. The Sanskrit word for son is 'Putra' meaning "he who delivers one from Put or hell." Even saints are believed to have been sent to hell for the crime of not having sons and suffered age-long agonies till they were saved by miracles. With these stories constantly dinned into his ears, it is no wonder that every Hindu ardently prays for sons. Apart from this religious incentive for begetting sons, there is a very material disadvantage in having daughters. Every Hindu is expected to provide a dowry for his daughters, usually more than what he can afford, so as to get them respectably married into a family of his social standing. A Hindu with half a dozen daughters is a doomed man. Hence the Pumsavana (male production ceremony) is even now performed by the pious who believe in its efficacy.

Pumsavana is performed "in the third month of gestation and before the period of quickening. According to Asvalayana the wife was to keep a solemn fast. She was then fed by her husband with two beans and a grain of barley mixed with a handful of curds, and made to pray three times for the production of male offspring. A further supplementary rite for the prevention of miscarriage was customary in some localities. It was performed by sprinkling the juice of a stalk of fresh Durba grass in the wife's right nostril, with the repetition of certain Mantras. This ceremony was called Anavalobhana."*

The Hair-parting ceremony (Simantonnayana) is nowadays performed in the Mahratha countries and by Brahmins of South India where it is known as Simantham. The prescribed rule for performing it is to pour scented oil on the head of the expectant mother and part the hair centrally from forehead to the crown by means of three stalks of Kusa grass bound into one. The Kusa stalk should be drawn from the forehead three times, each time the officiating priest repeating the three sacred words, Bhur, Bhuvar and Svar, and the mystic monosyllable AUM representing the Hindu trinity. In South India a feast is provided on the occasion for near relatives, and musicians are engaged. The object of the ceremony is the consecration of the woman for the great event. This ceremony is believed to make her impregnable against attacks of malevolent spirits looking for a chance to enter her womb and harm the unborn child.

The Jata Karman (birth ceremony) is performed immediately after the baby is born and before severing the umbilical cord. It is a simple ceremony performed by the father who touches the lips of the infant with a golden spoon containing a mixture of honey and clarified butter. On this act being performed, the father repeats the Vedic text: "O long-lived one, mayst thou live a hundred years in this world, protected by the Gods." After touching the lips, the ears are also touched with the following prayer: "May Savitri, may Sarasvati, may the Asvins grant thee wisdom." Finally the shoulders are rubbed and this blessing uttered. "Become firm as a rock, sharp as an axe, pure as gold, thou art the Veda called a son, live thou a hundred years. May Indra bestow on thee his best treasures."

There are many superstitions among the Hindus connected with child-birth. In the Mahratha count-

---

* Monier Williams, *Religious Thought and Life in India*.

ries and in many other parts of India, as soon as labour pains start, the pregnant woman is taken to the darkest room of the house of which all the windows and doors are shut. Only the village midwife and one or two other women remain with her. The object of closing the doors and windows is to shut out evil spirits. As an additional precaution, the family priest sits near the door of the room and repeats sacred verses to scare away malevolent imps.

In the Mahratha countries the Jatakarma ceremony is done in the following manner: "A square is drawn with quartz powder (in the women's hall) and inside the square two wooden stools are set. The father bathes in water in which a gold ring has been dropped. He dons a rich silk waistcloth, bows before the household gods and the elders and sits on one of the stools. He takes a little water in the palm of his right hand and throws it on the ground. He says aloud: "I throw this water to cleanse the child from the impurity of its mother's body." The mother is then brought in with the baby in her arms and is seated on the second stool. Blessings are called down on the day, the mother and the good spirits who bring happiness. The father takes a gold ring and through it lets fall a drop of honey and ghee into the child's mouth. He presses the ring against both its ears, smells its head three times, repeats some holy verses and withdraws. The midwife cuts with a knife the umbilical cord and buries it outside the house. The father returns, sprinkles water on his wife's right breast and she may now, for the first time, suckle the baby. Money is distributed to the Brahmins and the birth ceremony is over."*

On the sixth day the dedication of the baby to Shashti, the goddess of children, takes place. This deity is more popular in Bengal and the Mahratha countries than in the South. Shashti means 'sixth', so called either because she is the presiding deity of the sixth day of a child's birth or because she has five sisters who together with her, form a minor pantheon of six. Shashti's sisters are Jivanti, Kuhu, Raka, Sinivali and Skanda. All these are worshipped together with Shashti, and offerings of rice and areca nuts are made to them. Malevolent spirits are also appeased on the day by offerings so that they may not harm the child. The women of the house keep vigil throughout the night and the family priest repeats verses so that this night, supposed to be very dangerous for the child, may pass without evil befalling the child. The Hindus believe that evil spirits are more active when humans sleep, and seldom haunt places where lamps are lit and people keep vigil.

THE NAMAKARANA (NAME-GIVING) CEREMONY

This ceremony is popular among Hindus all over India. It is usually performed on the tenth or twelfth day of a child's birth. A family in which a child is born is considered ceremonially unclean for ten days and the Namakarana is preceded by a minor purificatory ceremony. "The mother is bathed, the walls of her room are cowdunged and her bathroom is carefully washed, adorned with red flowers, powder, and a lighted lamp. A present of money, rice, a bodice and a sari complete the ceremony (purificatory ceremony) and the family is deemed duly purified."

The Hindus attach great importance to names. The name is suggested by the family astrologer. Usually he makes a pretext of studying the child's horoscope and suggests three or four names from which the father of the child may choose. In the case of ordinary people, the astrologer who has been intimated about the exact time of the child's birth, comes for the name-giving ceremony armed with the horoscope. Very wealthy Hindus and noblemen of high lineage commission famous astrologers for the purpose and these take months to prepare the horoscope as they have to study the influences of all possible stars. The name-giving ceremony is not, however, postponed on this account. If the name indicated by the horoscope does not coincide with the name given on the tenth day, the child receives a horoscope name. This name must have a letter of the word referring to the Nakshtra or asterism under which the child is born. The real name of the child, however, is neither the name given to it on the Namakarana ceremony, by which he is commonly known, nor the horoscope name but a secret name whispered into his ears by his Guru or preceptor. A person knowing this name is believed to possess power over the child.

The name given to a child is usually that of a god, in the case of a boy, and of a goddess in the case of a girl. Krishna, Rama, Gopal, Shiva, Ganesh, Sankara, etc., are common names for boys. Very often combined names of two gods are used such as Hari-Hara, Shiva-Rama, Gopal-Krishna, Lakshmi-Narayana. A very popular practice is for a boy to be known as the Das or slave of some god or goddess, such as Hari-das, Kali-das, Gopal-das, Durga-das. Boys are also named after the heroes of the epics, Arjun, Bhim, Hanuman, for example.

Girls are named not only after goddesses (Sarasvati, Parvati, Lakshmi, etc., for instance) but are also called by the name of flowers, rivers, or precious stones or certain virtues. The common appellations of this category are Kamal or Kamalam (lotus), Kusum (flower), Moti (pearl), Vimal (pure), Sundari (beautiful), Prema (love), Mohini (charming), Vasanti (joyous as the spring); of the rivers Ganga, Yamuna, Godavari and Kaveri are popular as suitable names for girls. Pet names differ in different regions and are derived from the language of the place. But written names, especially among the higher castes, have a classical background derived from Sanskrit.

At times a very handsome young man or charming girl may be found to possess an obnoxious name. A fair girl may be called Kali meaning black. These exceptions are caused by the fear of the evil eye. When the parents of some attractive child fear that

---
* Kincaid, *Our Hindu Friends*.

the beauty of the child may catch the eye of some evil-eyed person or spirit, they give it an obnoxious name thereby making it less attractive.

After the name-giving ceremony, it is customary for the father to distribute presents to his friends. Clerks in government offices usually distribute sweetmeats to their fellow workers thereby announcing the happy event. If, however, the child happens to be a female, the fact is not mentioned to anybody and no sweetmeats are distributed. The birth of a daughter is an occasion for mourning to the Hindu and not for rejoicing.

Almost all Hindus bore the ears of their children. The ear-boring ceremony is generally performed on the day of the name-giving ceremony. Among some communities ear-boring takes place later. In the case of girls the nose also must be bored. This is done by a goldsmith with a gold wire, for which operation he receives a small fee.

The sixth Samskara, "the carrying-out ceremony" is an unimportant affair. It is performed in the fourth month of a baby's birth. On an auspicious day the mother carries the baby in her arms and goes out in the open followed by her husband. The child is presented to the sun and the following verses are repeated: "That eye-like luminary, the cause of blessings to the gods rises in the east; may we behold it for a hundred years. May we hear, may we speak, may we be free from poverty for a hundred years and more." After this prayer and presentation of the child to the sun, the mother carries it to the village temple, and prayers are addressed to the presiding deity of the village to be kind to the child.

In the sixth month after birth, Anna Prasana (food-giving ceremony) is performed. On this occasion a few friends are invited and the child is fed with solid food for the first time. A priest repeats sacred verses, and after the child is fed, the guests are treated to a feast.

The twin ceremony of tonsure and cutting off the hair is very important. As already mentioned on page 75 the Hindus attach religious importance to shaving which they believe has the power to clean the body and the soul. "In the case of a Brahmin the ceremony of tonsure was performed in the third year, but was often delayed, and sometimes did not take place till the seventh or eighth year. According to Asvalayana the child was to be placed on the lap of its mother to the west of the sacred fire. The father was to take up his station to the south of the mother, holding in his hand twenty-one stalks of Kusa grass. He was to sprinkle the head of the child three times with a mixture of warm water, butter and curds. He was to insert three stalks of Kusa grass seven times into the child's hair on the right side, saying: 'O divine grass protect him!' Then he was to cut off a portion of the hair and give it to the mother, with recitation of various texts, leaving one lock (sikha or cuda) on the top of the head or occasionally three or five locks, according to the custom of the family. The operation of shaving was sometimes regarded as a different ceremony from that of hair cutting."*

In certain regions, the car-boring ceremony followed the tonsure ceremony.

UPANAYANA

Upanayana (initiation) is one of the most important of all Hindu ceremonies. It is also called the "Sacred Thread Ceremony" because the boy is invested with the sacred thread which alone entitles him to be recognized as an Aryan. Before this ceremony and the investiture with the sacred thread, a boy of any of the three higher castes is not recognized as belonging to his proper caste but a Sudra. Before the Upanayana, an orthodox Brahmin will not allow his son to eat with him. The boy is not permitted to participate in the rites exclusively performed by the twice-born and he is not allowed to repeat any of the verses of the Vedas. Only male children are entitled to be initiated into the fold of the twice-born, the religious status of a woman of the three higher castes always remaining, in theory, that of a Sudra.

The Upanayana takes place between the age of seven and ten; if circumstances are not suitable it may be deferred till the age of sixteen. A good number of friends and relatives are invited for the occasion. The larger the number of Brahmins present, the better the ceremony is, and hence all Brahmins in the neighbourhood are requested to attend, which they do with alacrity; for it is a sin to send away a Brahmin who attends the ceremony empty handed. The day for the ceremony must be auspicious and an astrologer fixes the date and time. "The day must fall in one of the five auspicious months, in which the sun is moving northwards towards the Ecliptic. The time of the day must be between six a.m. and noon, since that is the most fortunate part of the twenty-four hours."

Prior to the ceremony, the boy is shaved, anointed with perfumed oil and is bathed. The officiating priest now takes charge of the boy and he presents him to the household gods. The boy bows down to his parents and the guests who shower blessings upon him. After this, he is seated on a wooden stool, with the father sitting opposite, and the priest repeats sacred verses. When this is over, the boy bows down to his father and touches his feet with folded hands. The father blesses his son and the guests shower rice or some other grain on the boy for luck. A fire is now lit with sacred twigs and is continuously fed with clarified butter.

Now everything is ready for the thread-girding. The sacred thread consists of three white cotton threads each consisting of three finer threads intertwined into one. The three threads represent the trinity and the white colour purity. The thread must be consecrated by Brahmins before girding the boy. The boy is seated on a wooden stool and the priest hangs the cord on the left shoulder of the boy and passes it across the body and the ends are tied under the right arm into a sacred knot called Brahma-

---
* Monier Williams. *Religious Thought and Life in India.*

LXV

141 SCULPTURE OF SHIVA DANCING,
MADURA TEMPLE
(Photo: S. S. Aiyar)

LXVI

142 **A SOUTH INDIAN TEMPLE TOWER, CARVINGS**
(India Pictorial Features)

143 **SHIVA TEMPLE, KULU**
(*Journal of Indian Art and Industry*)

LXVII

SCULPTURE IN A CAVE TEMPLE
(Forbes' *Oriental Memoirs*)

LXVIII

INTERIOR, DILWARA TEMPLE, MT. ABU
(Photo: B. B. & C. I. Railway)

LXIX

146 RAMA'S TEMPLE, PUSHKAR
(Rousslet's *India*)

147 TEMPLE OF JAGANNATH, PURI
(Rousslet's *India*)

LXX

148 CEREMONIAL ABLUTIONS
(India Pictorial Features)

149 A VAISHNAVA BRAHMIN OF SOUTH INDIA
(India Pictorial Features)

150 BRAHMIN SPINNING YARN
FOR SACRED THREAD
(India Pictorial Features)

151 CEREMONIAL SHAVING OF A HINDU BABY
(India Pictorial Features)

LXXI

152 THE SACRED THREAD CEREMONY
(Photo: S. S. Aiyar)

153 ABLUTIONS IN A TEMPLE TANK DURING A FESTIVAL
(Photo: S. S. Aiyar)

154 WEDDING OF THE TULSI PLANT AND VISHNU
(Photo: Stanley Jepson)

155 A HINDU GOD-MAKER AT WORK
(India Pictorial Features)

156 VILLAGERS WITH OFFERING OF FLOWERS AND COCOANUTS FOR IDOLS
(India Pictorial Features)

157 WORSHIP OF SANKARA, THE FAMOUS PHILOSOPHER SAINT
(Photo: S. S. Aiyar)

grandhi. Verses from the Vedas are repeated by the priest and the Brahmins present. After the girding of the thread, the boy has to repeat the mysterious Gayatri. As this celebrated Vedic incantation is not repeated in presence of others, all the guests leave the room, and the priest or the father whispers the Gayatri into the boy's ear, both being wrapped up in a shawl. The Gayatri is whispered three times into the boy's ear and the latter repeats it as many times. After the Gayatri is repeated the guests come back and take their seats.

In ancient times the Upanayana immediately preceded the boy's education, and soon after this ceremony the boy was led into his preceptor's house (hence the name Upanayana, meaning leading one to one's Guru). A student in ancient India had to beg for his food, and symbolic of this, a staff is given in the boy's hand in modern Upanayana ceremonies.

The sacred thread is the distinguishing mark of the twice born. It is the symbol of regeneration. It is believed to have mystic powers, and in all forms of worship and daily life, the sacred thread is given an important place and its position altered according to variations in the ceremonial. "For example, when a Hindu worships the gods he puts it over his left shoulder and under his right, being then called Upaviti; when a Hindu worships his departed ancestors he suspends it over his right shoulder and under his left, being then called Prachinaviti; and when he worships the saints he hangs it round his neck like a long necklace, being then called Nivitti."

The sacred thread is never taken away from one's body. If the thread is worn out, another one duly consecrated must be worn. No public ceremony is, however, needed for this. Some Brahmins change their sacred threads once a year and a small feast is provided on the occasion.

The eleventh ceremony of Samavartana (return home) has little meaning as it is performed at present. The ceremony had much importance in ancient times when the boy, after his education in the preceptor's house, returned home. The education of a Brahmin lad in those days was a laborious and protracted affair and entailed the continuous absence of the boy for several years from his home. Hence his arrival was eagerly awaited by the parents and relatives and we can very well imagine how happy the parents in those days were to see their son back home. But now the ancient system of education has been discarded, but the ceremony is not. What is being done at present is to perform the Samavartana ceremony immediately after the Upanayana before the priests and guests go away. After the Upanayana the boy is dressed like a householder and the beggar's staff is removed from his hand. Instead of the staff he holds an umbrella, the insignia of prosperity and dominion. After the inevitable repetition of the sacred texts, the officiating priest addresses the boy thus: "Till now you have been a Brahmachari, now you are a Snatak or householder."

A feast for the guests and gifts for the Brahmins close the double ceremony of Upanayana and Samavartana.

MARRIAGE AND CONNECTED CEREMONIES

The last of the Samskaras, marriage, is the most important of all, from a social point of view. It is decidedly the most expensive.

Among some communities not practising child marriage, a ceremony is performed on girls attaining puberty and a feast provided for guests. This ceremony takes place after the girl's menstruation for the first time. Among the lower classes the ceremony is performed with much show. The occasion is something of a public announcement that the girl has come of age and the parents are willing to consider offers for her marriage. Even among communities practising child marriage, a girl's reaching puberty is a suitable occasion for performing some ceremony or other as the consummation of marriage usually takes place only after the girl shows signs of puberty.

The Hindus have many superstitions connected with menstruation in women. Women are considered ceremonially impure during this period. Even a Brahmin woman, we are told, degenerates into a Chandali, the lowest of the low, once her period starts. It is only proper that such a woman should be excluded from decent society during her uncleanliness. Hence she is not allowed to enter the house, cook meals or touch a clean person. She lives in solitude during this period. In villages, every Hindu household has an outhouse set apart for this purpose and women, during their periods of uncleanliness, live in these houses. Their meals are served here and they are expected not to show themselves about as their sight may bring calamity to all people. In the cities this seclusion is not possible among middle classes who live in small flats and they usually set apart a corner of a room for unclean women. Such women are not allowed to use clean clothes or good furniture but must squat on torn or dirty mats as untouchable outcastes. In houses which have no servants, the male member or children do the cooking as the unclean woman is not allowed to enter the kitchen or cook food. It is very common for school boys and girls to stay away from classes and for clerks to ask leave on the ground that the lady of the house is "out of home" which is the euphemistic way of expressing the monthly troubles of women in India. So much for ceremonial uncleanliness of women.

As mentioned elsewhere, among the Hindus marriages of boys and girls are arranged by their parents. The young people before their marriage do not meet each other except accidentally. It is considered highly improper for a young man or woman to take the initiative in the matter of his or her marriage. A well bred boy is expected to abide by the decision of his parents in this matter. Nowadays, child-marriage being prohibited, the general tendency is to defer marriages till boys and girls attain ages between sixteen and twenty and with this raising of the marriageable age, educated young men and women are beginning to show an independent spirit in the matter of their marriages. Even among these classes those who go against the wishes of their parents are few; the parents, on the other hand, now allow, after a marriage proposal has been made and accepted, the young people to meet once only and talk to each other in other people's presence so that the prospective couple may confirm their parents' decision. This confirmation is but formal, and if the young people have complaints, they are usually coaxed or bullied into submission, and it is rarely that a marriage once fixed by the parents breaks up.

The marriage proposal always comes from the girl's party. The father of a boy is a proud person and is sure of a match for his son; the father of a daughter, on the other hand, is never sure of a husband for his daughter and the humiliation of the bargain should be his. Anyway, he never goes direct seeking for a bridegroom for his daughter. He sends his family priest for the purpose, if he has one. In most parts of India there are professional matchmakers who travel up and down the country looking for bridegrooms for girls and brides for boys. They pretend to know all the young men and women of the neighbourhood, their lineage and character, and the income of their parents. These match-makers are called Ghatakas. Among the higher castes Brahmins take up this profession and among the lower, barbers. In certain provinces professional match-makers are old widows who, because of their easy access to women folk, are usually more successful than their male compeers. Whatever their caste or sex, all matchmakers thrive on lies and flattery. Their main object being to collect their fees from both parties as soon as a marriage is fixed, the sole ambition of the Ghatakas is to make as many matches as possible in the shortest possible time. Hence their job is to flatter every boy and girl they come across and give wide publicity to their virtues. All Hindus know them and their services are requisitioned only in the initial stages. When there is some chance of a proposal maturing into a marriage, either the family priest or some common friend of both families takes the matter in hand and negotiations proceed through him.

According to Manu, a marriageable girl should be "free from bodily defects, should have an agreeable name, should be of graceful gait like a swan or an elephant, should have a moderate quantity of hair on the body and on the head, small teeth and soft limbs." "A maiden with reddish hair, who has a redundant member, who is sickly, garrulous or with red eyes, or one with no hair or too much hair" is to be avoided. But the money question often vitiates the marriage transaction and a decent dowry is considered a good compensation for many shortcomings a girl may have.

Once the negotiations begin, the horoscopes of the boy and the girl are consulted. The Hindus have always had an exaggerated idea of the influence of planets on the destiny of individuals, and a marriage is believed not to lead to success if the horoscopes of the boy and girl are unharmonious. Many promising marriages have been prevented by astrologers because of incompatibility in horoscopes. If the horoscopes agree, the family priest and astrologers get busy checking up the genealogies and pedigrees of the two families. If everything goes well and the dowry question is settled, a date is fixed for the betrothal ceremony.

The betrothal ceremony is more or less a solemnization of the forthcoming marriage contract. The astrologers and the priests of the two families, the male parents of the boy and the girl and a few friends congregate on the occasion. The parents in presence of the friends who act as witnesses give their solemn word that they are willing to perform the marriage of the boy and the girl on a date to be fixed later, and the priests ratify the contract by repeating sacred verses. In certain cases a written contract is drawn up, in others a promise by word of mouth is considered sufficient. The ceremony is called Vag-dana in Sanskrit and Nisbet in Hindi. In the Punjab, it is known as Mangini. Once the betrothal is performed, the parties are expected to stick to their contract, but under extraordinary circumstances it can be broken up. A betrothed girl, however, is not widowed by the death of the person to whom she is betrothed and there is no objection to her being married again.

The season usually preferred for performing the marriage ceremony is spring. The Hindu months of Magha, Phalguna and Vaisakha corresponding to February, March and April respectively, are considered the most auspicious. But it is not enough to know the auspicious month; the lucky hour and the lucky minute must be ascertained. This is usually done by astrologers after consulting the stars. Once the time is fixed, the next important item is to invite friends and relatives. In some parts of India this is done by the parents, uncles and aunts of the bride or the bridegroom going in a procession, accompanied by musicians and drum players, to the houses of the guests and inviting them, each individual separately. The women invite the ladies and the men menfolk. Relatives living away from the village are invited by special messengers, usually close relatives of the parents of the bride or bridegroom.

The marriage ceremony takes place in the presence of all the assembled guests, in a hall or porch built for the purpose. The details of the ceremony differ according to localities but the essentials are the same. The most important point in the marriage ceremony is that it should be witnessesd by Agni, the god of fire, the most truthful and straight-dealing of the Hindu gods. For this purpose a sacred fire is lit in the centre of the marriage hall and is kept continually fed by clarified butter. The moderns nowadays substitute lamp burning scented oil for the fire pit. The bride and bridegroom sit side by side, both gaily decorated, the bride's face usually veiled. Prior to the beginning of the ceremony Ganesha, the remover of obstacles, is worshipped for the smooth progress of the ceremony. The officiating priest now takes a piece of consecrated linen, fastens one end of it to the bridegroom's clothes and the other to the bride's. The priest then starts chanting sacred verses. While repeating parts of the text, he joins the hands of the bride and bridegroom under the consecrated cloth; on reciting certain other verses, the assisting priest takes a consecrated cord and winds it round the necks of the boy and the girl. At times he asks the bride and bridegroom to throw rice, cocoanut kernel, etc., into the fire pit in front of them, at other times he does so himself. The marriage ceremony is a long and tedious affair, the texts to be repeated on the occasion being many. Sprinkling of water, throwing of red powder, and similar actions mark certain definite stages of the proceedings. The role of the bride and bridegroom is passive; they do, however, repeat texts, throw rice about or clasp each other's hands under instructions from the priest who chants texts from the very beginning of the ceremony to the end. All these long verses do not, however, solemnize the ceremony. This is done by taking the irrevocable "Seven Steps" known as Saptapadi. The bride and bridegroom under instructions from the priest, get up and take seven steps round the sacred fire, the groom leading and the bride following. This seals the marriage contract and it has now become a sacrament. The text repeated while taking the seven steps is this: "Take thou one step for the acquirement of force; take thou two steps for strength; take thou three steps for the increase of wealth; take thou four steps for well being; take thou five steps for offspring; take thou six steps for the season; take thou seven steps as a friend; be faithfully devoted to me; may we obtain many sons; may they attain to a good old age." The words are uttered by the bridegroom to the bride.

After the marriage ceremony, there is the usual feast, already described in a previous chapter. In the case of very wealthy people the marriage festivities last for about ten days, the Brahmins being never at a loss to point out the efficacy of subsidiary and supplementary ceremonies which may be performed prior to and after the main ceremony. People belonging to the nobility are expected to prolong the festivities for at least four days. The poor, and the miserable among the middle classes wind it up in a day.

The marriage concludes the principal ceremonies connected with a man's life. In the case of children married before maturity, the consummation ceremony takes place after the girl's first period when she is allowed to share her husband's bed. This is a minor ceremony, and there is little feasting. After marriage, a man's duty is, generally speaking, to store up wealth for the various ceremonies he will have to perform in connection with his children who are expected soon. A man may, however, celebrate his sixtieth birthday in right royal fashion, and is at liberty to feed as many Brahmins as he likes and give them gifts. According to Hindu conceptions, the age of man is hundred and twenty, and the sixtieth birthday marking off half his life, known as Shashitipurti, is an occasion for rejoicing. Wealthy people feed many Brahmins and give feasts to guests and relatives and some ceremonies are performed in gratitude to the gods who have granted the host sixty years of life.

FUNERAL RITES, SHRADDHAS AND BONE-GATHERING CEREMONIES

In the Vedic times, the Indo-Aryans, it appears, buried their dead. The following verses repeated at the time of disposing of the dead body clearly indicate that burial was the Vedic custom.

"Open thy arms, O earth, receive the dead
With gentle pressure and loving welcome.
Enshroud him tenderly, e'en as a mother
Folds her soft vestments round the child she loves."

Again:

"Return to thy mother earth, may she be kind to thee and lie lightly on thee, and not oppress thee."

Later on, however, cremation replaced burial and it continues to the present day. Ceremonies connected with death, cremation and after life are very important to the Hindu.

The Hindus consider it essential that a man should be free from all sins before his death. Hence old people, on the point of death, make long journeys to Benares or some other sacred city on the banks of the Ganges so that they may either wash their sins away in the stream or die in its waters. A dying man is often carried by his relatives to the Ganges and is held immersed knee-deep in the waters of the river. The banks of the Ganges at Benares is as sacred as Ganges itself and people of the neighbourhood, who fall sick and are not expected to survive, are made to live in huts on the banks of the river till they die.

This method of absolving sins cannot, for obvious reasons, be practised by all. Those living away from the Ganges perform atonement ceremonies, when they are on their death beds. The usual methods of performing this ceremony is to invite a number of Brahmins to the sick man's house. The sick man is made to sit upright or in a reclining position and the Brahmins ask him why he invited them. He tells them that from his birth he had been living in sin till that hour, and he prays for atonement for his sins. He gives the Brahmins gifts of coins. They accept the gifts and choose a representative. This person now steps forward and proclaims that he is willing to have all his patron's sins transferred on to him except certain major offences such as murder and adultery. He receives the wages of sin from the sick man and leaves the house. Loaded with another man's guilt the primary concern of the Brahmin is to take a purificatory bath and wash away the sins.

The details of death and funeral rites vary according to places, but general instructions for their performance are on the following lines: "A dying man, when no hopes of his surviving remain, should be laid on a bed of Kusa grass in the open air, his head sprinkled with water from the Ganges and smeared with clay brought from the same river. A Salagrama (the sacred ammonite representing Vishnu) should be placed near him, holy strains from the Vedas should be chanted aloud and leaves of holy basil scattered over his head.

"When he expires, the corpse must be washed, perfumed and decked with wreaths of flowers, and carried by the nearest relatives to some spot in a forest or near water; the funeral pile is lighted from the consecrated fire maintained by the deceased; the nearest relation applies the flaming brand to the pile, hung round with flowers and the attendant priests recite the appropriate invocations: 'Fire! thou wast lighted by him; may he therefore be reproduced from thee that he may attain regions of celestial bliss. May this offering be auspicious!' All who follow the corpse walk round the pile but may not view the fire. They then proceed to the river and, after bathing, present oblations of water from the joined palms of their hands to the manes of the deceased saying, 'May this oblation reach thee.' Elegiac verses, such as the following, are then recited: '(1) Foolish is he who seeks for permanence in the human state, insolid, like the stem of the plantain tree, transient like the foam of the sea. (2) When a body, formed of five elements, to receive the reward of deeds done in its own former person reverts to its five original principles, what room is there for regret? (3) The earth is perishable; the ocean, the gods themselves, pass away. How should not that bubble, mortal man meet destruction? (4) All that is low must finally perish; all that is elevated must ultimately fall; all compounded bodies must end in dissolution; and life be concluded with death.'"*

The Hindus do not use a coffin to carry the dead to the cremation ground. The dead body is wrapped up in linen, tied to a stretcher of bamboos constructed for the purpose and taken in procession. The chief mourner who is the eldest son or some very near relative of the dead person leads the procession. He carries a firepot in his hand. The widow never accompanies her husband's funeral procession. In some parts of India funeral processions are accompanied by musicians and drumplayers. In North India a few people walk in front of the corpse repeating the words "Ram, Ram" or "Ram Nam Sach Hai" (The name of Ram is truth itself).

In the dead man's house there is incessant wailing of women. In the Tamil countries wailing has developed into an art, and women sit round the corpse and relate in long verses all the greatness of the departed person. They vie with one another in producing the best melody and rhyme while wailing over the dead. In certain parts of India it is customary to engage professional mourners to wail in the dead man's house for a number of days. These mourners (usually women) are hirelings clad in black who come to the house, sit at the doorstep, wail for an hour or two each day, and go home. Wailing in India is accompanied by beating of the breast with both hands. A near relation whose grief is real may beat the breast violently, but professional mourners merely make a show of doing so. But to return to the cremation ground.

Prior to the burning of the dead body, a priest has to perform a petty ceremony. This priest can be hired for a small sum at the cremation ground. The occupation is considered very low among the Brahmins and the better classes of them do not engage themselves in it. After performing the death ceremony, the winding sheet is cut and the body placed on the pyre. The chief mourner lights the pyre on the head side in case of males, and on the side of the feet in case of women. Those who attend the cremation see to it that the skull of the dead person bursts while the body is burnt. The Hindus believe that the soul of a person, on his death, gets locked up in the skull, and if the latter does not break, the soul gets trapped in it. If the skull does not burst by fire, it is broken into pieces by a blow from a cudgel. After this, the relatives and mourners leave the cremation ground to have a purificatory bath, and return home.

On the third day of the cremation is the bone-gathering ceremony. It is the fond hope of every Hindu to drop the bones of his departed parent in the Ganges or some other sacred spot as, by so doing, he believes that the parent is assured of a passage to heaven. For the bone-gathering ceremony, a few close relatives of the dead person repair to the cremation ground where the priest performs the bone-gathering ceremony by uttering sacred texts, and by sprinkling sacred water on the spot. Then he collects the calcined bones in a vase and presents them to the son or the nearest relative of the deceased. In the case of very poor people who cannot take the bones to any sacred place, the bones are thrown in the nearest stream, as every stream is believed to be mystically connected with the Ganges, the mother of all waters. When the bones are to be taken to the Ganges or some distant place, the vase containing the gathered bones was buried near the place of cremation whence it is unearthed on the tenth day or on the day of the Shraddha, and made over to the family.

For ten days the family in which a death occurs is considered unclean. On the first day they are not allowed to cook any food in the house, but relatives may send them food. Most of the adult members of the household fast on the first day. The family is allowed to cook and eat certain kind of food for the other nine days. The reason why the first ten days are so important is that it is on the tenth day that the soul of the departed is believed to get a complete subtle frame. All the ten days ceremonies are performed. If these are properly performed, the first day the soul gets a head; on the second, a neck; on the third, a heart; on the fourth a back; on the fifth a nave; on the sixth the private parts; on the seventh thighs; on the eighth knees and on the ninth and tenth hands and feet. If the funeral ceremonies are not performed properly the soul gets no body or gets but a partial body and wanders in space as a deformed evil spirit. The

* Moor, *Hindu Pantheon*.

readers will now see why a Hindu ardently prays for a son to perform his funeral rites.

The subtle frame, completed on the tenth day, must be nourished before it can travel to its celestial abode. For this purpose the Shraddha ceremony is performed. The Shraddha is one of the most important and expensive of Hindu ceremonies. The gifts and feasts given on this occasion are believed to reach the soul of the departed ancestor, and every Hindu is expected to give freely to Brahmins who attend the Shraddha.

The Shraddha is performed between the tenth and the thirty-first day of the cremation. The person performing the ceremony is expected to go to the houses of his relatives barefoot and invite them for the Shraddha. For the performance of the ceremony a large number of metal vessels are required, which, after the ceremony, are presented to the Brahmins. The very wealthy use a good number of silver vessels and the less fortunate brass vessels. Musicians are engaged to entertain guests at intervals between the performance of one ceremony and the other, the Shraddha being constituted of a series of minor ceremonies. These rituals begin early in the morning, and end in the afternoon when the Brahmins receive their gifts. "The first in the list gets, in ordinary cases, about five rupees in cash, and one brass vessel valued at four or five rupees; the second, third, and others in proportion. The Guru or religious teacher and the Purohita or officiating priest carry off the lion's share."

In the case of poor people the feast is given on the same day, and the Shraddha is over, and with it the period of mourning. But the wealthier classes defer the feasting till the next day. They set apart one day for the feasting of Brahmins and the succeeding day for the feeding of other castes. This, however, does not end all the ceremonies connected with death. In fact the manes, like humans, are not satisfied with one meal, but can digest what they eat, and hunger for more. Hence every conscientious Hindu is advised to perform as many Shraddhas as he can afford. Shraddhas may be performed annually, monthly, weekly or daily. These minor Shraddhas, however, are not very expensive and can be performed by a single Brahmin in presence of a few guests. It is usual to make balls of boiled rice, called Pinda, at the time of the Shraddhas and throw them out of the house. The idea is that the manes feed on them, though visibly the crows eat them.

The bone-throwing ceremony may be said to conclude the rituals connected with death. The bones of the departed, as mentioned elsewhere, are kept in a safe place, and within a year are to be thrown in some sacred stream. Those lucky persons who live near the Ganges have little difficulty in performing the bone-throwing ceremony, and they do it soon after the cremation. Those who live away from the sacred stream have to carry the bones all the way to the Ganges. The most efficacious places for performing the Shraddhas and the bone-throwing ceremony are Haridwar, Benares and Gaya. In these cities, on the banks of the Ganges, there are hundreds of professional priests who can be seen performing the ceremony for the pilgrims who daily throng to these places with the bones of their ancestors. Nasik, near Bombay, at the source of the Godavary, is also a hallowed spot for performing bone-throwing ceremonies, and the middle class people of the Western region, who cannot afford to carry the bones of their ancestors to the Ganges, go on a pilgrimage to Nasik and perform the ceremony here.

SACRIFICES

Vedic religion, when it was systematized, became mainly a religion of sacrifices. The Brahmanas attached to the Vedas give detailed instructions on how to perform sacrifices, what hymns are to be repeated at each stage of the proceedings, what types of altars, and sacrificial pits are to be constructed for each kind of sacrifice. The Purva Mimamsa, as we have seen, gives the philosophic explanation of the sacrificial and ritualistic religion of the Vedas. The killing of animals constituted an important item of Vedic ritual, and the materialists and the Buddhists successfully revolted against it. On the regeneration of Hinduism after the decay of Buddhism, animal sacrifice lost much of its importance. Vaishnavism set its face against animal sacrifice, and only in some unimportant shrine of Shiva were victims sacrificed. The worship of the female deities, however, was and is connected with bloody rites, but the sacrifices of the Saktas are very different from those of Vedic Aryans. These derived their authority mainly from the Vedas, and sacrifices were considered by them the very essence of their system, the highest Brahmins and Kshatriyas taking part in the ceremony. The Saktas, on the other hand, draw their inspiration from the Tantras, and the better class of Hindus generally dissociate themselves from some of the Sakta rites.

The greatest of the ancient Vedic sacrifices, which was performed even in medieval times, was the Asvamedha or horse-sacrifice. This sacrifice could be performed only by kings who established world dominion, according to Hindu conceptions of the world of course. The sacrificial animal was to be a white horse with certain royal signs, and prior to the ceremony the animal was to be let loose to wander at will. An army followed the horse. Whoever stopped the horse challenged the claims of world supremacy of its owner and had to be defeated in battle and the horse reclaimed. From the ancient literature of the Hindus it appears that the title to world supremacy was more or less formal, and powerful neighbours were often won over to recognize the claim of the owner of the horse by means other than that of the sword.

After the horse had wandered at will for a definite period, it was led back to the city of its owner and the Asvamedha took place. The horse had to be sacrificed and the consecrated meat offered to the gods, after which the priests partook of it. No need to say that enormous sums were spent in feeding Brahmins and giving them presents. The Asvamedha usually took place after some great victory in battle and the looting of some unfortunate country, and the performer of the sacrifice was in a favourable position to spend large sums of money on the occasion.

Another celebrated Vedic ritual was the Soma sacrifice. This too was attended by the killing of animals, usually goats, but the chief item of the ceremony was the offering of the Soma liquor to the gods and the drinking of large quantities of it by all present. The ceremony started very soberly, but probably ended up in riots. At present there is hardly any Brahmin in India who knows the details of the ceremony. Even the identity of the plant, from which the Soma liquor was extracted in Vedic times, is lost.

As Brahmins became vegetarians and teetotallers, sacrificial religion lost much of its importance. At present no decent Brahmin will openly associate himself with cutting the throat of sacrificial beasts or drinking spirituous liquors. There are, however, certain great sacrifices performed at present, symbolic of the ancient Vedic rites. These great Yagas, as these are called, are directed towards some object of great importance such as world peace or the general well-being of humanity. I remember one such Yaga performed by the mercantile community of Karachi during the world depression of 1929-32. At times wealthy individuals perform these Yagas for the sole purpose of obtaining salvation for themselves. These big Yagas cost enormous sums of money, running into several lakhs of rupees. Hundreds of priests are engaged for the ceremony which lasts for weeks. Huge sacrificial pits are constructed and a burning fire maintained in them, constantly fed by clarified butter. So elaborate is the ritual connected with these Yagas that a separate ceremony has to be performed by several Brahmins, at the expense of a huge sum, for the sole purpose of expiating the sins committed, due to oversight, in performing the main Yaga.

Though Brahmins now generally disapprove of animal sacrifices (except in Tantric rites, for which see page 27), these are widely prevalent among the lower castes and the aborigines. In annual village festivals known as 'Jatras' it is customary to sacrifice a buffalo. The blood of this animal is particularly relished by the goddess Durga who is fabled to have killed a demon named Mahisha (buffalo) in a terrible single combat. During the Dasara celebrations (see Ch. XIV), held in her honour it is meritorious to sacrifice buffalos. In Indian States ruled by Hindu kings who used to celebrate the Dasara festival as the most important to their caste, it was obligatory on the officiating priest to cut a Kalabash fruit imagining it to be a buffalo, as the actual killing of the animal had gone out of fashion among the higher castes after the rise of Vaishnavism.

Again, the shrines of Kali even now claims a large number of victims in several parts of India, the animals generally sacrificed being sheep or goats; of the meat of birds the goddess has a preference for chicken, and cocks are sacrificed in large numbers at her shrines.

CHAPTER X

LITERATURE AND LANGUAGES

THE sacred language of the Hindus is Sanskrit. It is more ancient than Latin and Greek, but has close affinity to both. It is, however, doubtful if Sanskrit was ever the spoken language of the people. Its high polish and strict rules of grammar are intended for literary expression. Sanskrit was, however, the common language of the intellectuals and philosophers who held their learned discussions in this language. The people used its dialect known as Prakrit; and Hindi, the current language of North India, now recognized by the Indian Government as the lingua franca of India is believed to be a derivation of Prakrit.

Sanskrit literature can be broadly divided into two: sacred and secular; of these, the latter mainly derives its inspiration from the former. Sacred literature consists of two main divisions, Srutis and Smritis.

SRUTIS

Sruti means what is heard. This is the revealed wisdom of the Hindus; it consists of the four Vedas, and the Brahmanas and Upanishads attached to them. The four Vedas are Rig, Yajur, Sama and Atharva. The Rig Veda embodies the earliest literature of the Hindus and is more interesting than the other Vedas. It is in the form of hymns addressed to the great Vedic deities such as Indra, Varuna, Maruts, etc. In the Rig Veda is also expressed the wonder of a people newly awakened to the beauty, grandeur, majesty and mystery of nature. Here is a hymn addressed to Ushas, the goddess of dawn:

"Hail! Ruddy Ushas, golden goddess, borne
Upon thy shining car, thou comest like
A lovely maiden by her mother decked,
Disclosing coyly all thy hidden graces
To our admiring eyes; or like a wife
Unveiling to her lord, with conscious pride,
Beauties which, as he gazes lovingly,
Seem fresher, fairer each succeeding morn.

Through years on years thou hast lived on,
   and yet
Thou art ever young. Thou art the breath and life
Of all that breathes and lives, awaking day by day
Myriads of prostrate sleepers, as from death,
Causing the birds to flutter from their nests,
And rousing men to ply with busy feet
Their daily duties and appointed tasks,
Toiling for wealth or pleasure or renown."*

Some of the hymns of the Rig Veda are believed to have been composed some five thousand years ago. These hymns were orally transmitted from generation to generation till the invention of the alphabet. Even after the invention of the Indian script, Vedic texts were for a long time committed to memory and not written down as this procedure was feared to involve loss of sanctity of the hymns. The prejudice, however, was overcome and the Rig Veda was eventually reduced to writing.

The Sama Veda and Yajur Veda have little originality about them. These consist mainly of the hymns of the Rig Veda arranged in particular ways for recitation during ritual sacrifices. The Atharva Veda, however, is different. This work is of much later origin than the other three, and many ancient books of the Hindus mention the Vedas as three and not as four. The Atharva Veda, as it stands at present, is a curious mixture of sublime wisdom, witchcraft, beautiful poetry and silly charms for exorcising evil spirits. Of the better class of hymns, the following verse in praise of Time is a typical example:

"Time, like a seven-wheeled, seven-naved car
   moves on.
His rolling wheels are all the worlds, his axle
Is immortal. He is the first of gods.

We see him like an overflowing jar;
We see him multiplied in various forms.
He draws forth and encompasses the worlds;

He is all future worlds; he is their father;
He is their son; there is no power like him;
The past and future issue out of Time,
All sacred knowledge and austerity.

From Time the earth and waters were produced;
From Time the rising, setting, burning sun;
From Time the wind; through Time the earth is
   vast;
Through Time the eye perceives; mind,
   breath and name
In him are comprehended. All rejoice
When Time arrives — the monarch who has
   conquered
This world, the highest world, the holy world,
Yea, all the worlds — and ever marches on."

Here is a charm for luck:

"Oh dice, give play that profit brings,
Like cows that yield abundant milk;
Attach me to a streak of gain,
As with a string the bow is bound."†

The four Vedas are considered by the Hindus as eternal, indestructible, infallible. They are greater than the gods. When the gods perish the Vedas survive. The great cataclysm that destroys even Brahma, Vishnu and Shiva is powerless against the Vedas. These are coeval with the Supreme Being, above the ravages of Time.

---

* M. Williams, *Indian Wisdom*.
† K. Saunders, *A Pageant of India*.

The Brahmanas are ritualistic precepts attached to the hymns of the Veda. The Rig Veda has two Brahmanas, namely, Aitareya and Kaushitaka; the Sama Veda has eight, of which the best known are the Pancha Vimsa, the Tandya and the Shad Vimsa; the Yajur Veda has two well known Brahmanas, i.e., Taittiriya and Satapatha; and the Atharva Veda has one Brahmana called Go-patha. In between much that is dry and ritualistic, the Brahmanas contain many interesting stories and shrewd observations. The plots of many of the great stories of the epics can be traced to the Brahmanas. It is interesting to read the following passage in the Aitareya Brahmana written about 2,000 years before the birth of Copernicus:

"The sun never sets nor rises; when people think to themselves the sun is setting, he only changes about after reaching the end of the day, and makes night below and day to what is on the other side. Then when people think he rises in the morning, he only shifts himself about after reaching the end of the night, and makes day below and night to what is on the other side. In fact, he never does set at all. Whoever knows this, that the sun never sets, enjoys union and sameness of nature with him and abides in the same sphere."

The Upanishads attached to the Vedas contain, as we have mentioned elsewhere, mystical and philosophical doctrines. The Upanishads are the mainstay of the philosophical systems. The better known Upanishads are: The Aitareya and Kaushitaka of the Rig Veda; the Taittiriya, Brihad-aranyaka and Isa belonging to the Yajur Veda; the Chhandogya and Kena of the Sama Veda; and the Prasna, Mundaka, Mundukya and Katha of the Atharva Veda. A few passages quoted at random from the Upanishads will show the nature and spirit of this bold and interesting branch of Vedic literature:

"Beyond the darkness I know Him, the Great Spirit, shining in the Sun;
Knowing Him is immortality; that only is the Path by which men escape Death:
Naught is there so high, so intangible, so powerful:
As a tree He standeth in the heavens firmly rooted:
His spirit filleth all the Universe.

Without form, sorrowless, is the Most High:
Knowing this, man escapeth Death; knowing it not, he cometh utterly to grief.
Pervading all things He dwelleth within; He the Lord whose
Countenance is in all places, the gracious One whose Presence is everywhere.
Within the heart, as the heart and mind conceive Him, dwelleth He in the inward soul of all.
To know this is Immortality.
Himself void of sensation, He revealeth Himself in all
Senses, Lord of all, of all Ruler and Refuge....
Handless, He holdeth, footless He speedeth....
Eyeless seeth He, earless He heareth. Knowing all
Himself unknown: yet known of man as the First, the Great Spirit....
All-soul pervading all things, birthless, eternal".*

Says the Brihad-aranyaka Upanishad:

"Those who know him as the life of life, the eye of the eye, the ear of the ear, and the mind of the mind, have comprehended the eternal pre-existing spirit.

"By the mind is he to be perceived, in him there is no variation. Whoever sees variation in him obtains death after death....

"'I am Brahma.' Whoever knows this, 'I am Brahma' knows all. Even the gods are unable to prevent his becoming Brahma."

In the Chandogya Upanishad is a passage which condemns as futile the widest knowledge of the scriptures without a true knowledge of Brahma.

"The knowledge of these works (the Vedas, Puranas, etc.) is a mere name. Speech is greater than this name, Mind than Speech, Will than Mind, Sensation (or the capacity of feeling) is greater than Mind. Reflection is higher than Sensation, Knowledge than Reflection, Power than Knowledge, and highest of all stands Prana or Life. As the spokes of a wheel are attached to the nave, so are all things attached to Life.

"This Life ought to be approached with faith and reverence, and viewed as an immensity which abides in its own glory. That immensity extends from above and below, from behind and from before, from the south and the north. It is the Soul of the universe. It is God Himself. The man who is conscious of this divinity incurs neither disease nor pain nor death."†

For the contemplative mind no study is more enthralling than that of the Upanishads, and all great Hindu mystics from time immemorial have drunk deep of the knowledge the Upanishads impart. The four Vedas together with their Brahmanas and Upanishads are believed to have been compiled by the mythical sage Vyasa to whom is attributed more works than is possible for one individual to compose.

SMRITIS

Smriti or what is remembered form the larger part of the sacred literature of the Hindus. The authority of any part of a Smriti cannot be valid if it is in contradiction with the teachings of the Srutis. But where there is no such contradiction the authority of the Smriti is as binding as that of the Sruti.

The Smritis consist mainly of (1) the two epics, (2) the eighteen Puranas, (3) the Dharma Sastras, (4) the Smartha Sutras, (5) the six Vedangas, and (6) the Niti Sastras. The six Darsanas (treatise on philosophy; see page 37), stand as a class apart, being considered neither as regular Smritis nor as Srutis.

THE EPICS: The two great epic poems of the

---

* M. Williams, *Indian Wisdom*.
† *Ibid*.

LXXIII

158 **FACADE OF TEMPLE OF KALI, KHAJURAHO**
(Rousslet's *India*)

159 HARIDWAR, A CENTRE OF PILGRIMAGE
(Elliott's *Views in India*)

LXXIV

160 JUGGLERS
(Rousslet's *India*)

161 INDIAN BOXING, MAHRATHA STYLE
(Rousslet's *India*)

LXXV

162 SNAKE GODS AND GODDESSES
(*The Indian Antiquary*)

LXXVI

163   **SACRIFICIAL IMPLEMENT: IMAGE OF GANESHA**
(Moor's *Hindu Pantheon*)

164   VISHNU   165   VARAHA (BOAR INCARNATION OF VISHNU)
(After Sculptures in Badami Cave)

LXXVII

166   SARASVATI AND GANESHA

167   NAGANANDI LINGA, A SACRIFICIAL IMPLEMENT

168   KHANDEHRAO, A FORM OF SHIVA, AND HIS WIFE

169   HANUMAN CARRYING RAMA AND SITA

(Moor's *Hindu Pantheon*)

LXXVIII

170 SHIVA, PARVATI AND THEIR SON, THE WAR GOD KARTIKEYA

171 BRAHMA, THE CREATOR

172 KRISHNA ABOUT TO DESTROY THE SERPENT KALIYA, WHEN HIS WIVES INTERCEDED

(Moor's *Hindu Pantheon*)

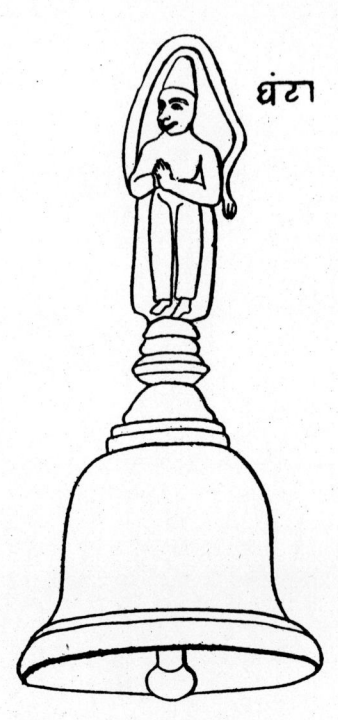

173 A SACRIFICIAL IMPLEMENT: THE BELL

LXXIX

174   IDOLS OF JAGANNATH
(Rousslet's *India*)

175   KRISHNA RIDING ON AN ELEPHANT IMPROVISED BY THE
MILKMAIDS OF GOKULA:
DRAWN FROM A PHOTOGRAPH OF AN INDIAN PAINTING IN
ATKINSON'S *HINDU PANTHEON*
(*Journal of Indian Art and Industry*)

LXXX

177 RANGOLI: DECORATING THE FLOOR WITH MYSTIC SYMBOLS DRAWN IN FLOUR
(Photo: B. F. Ferreira)

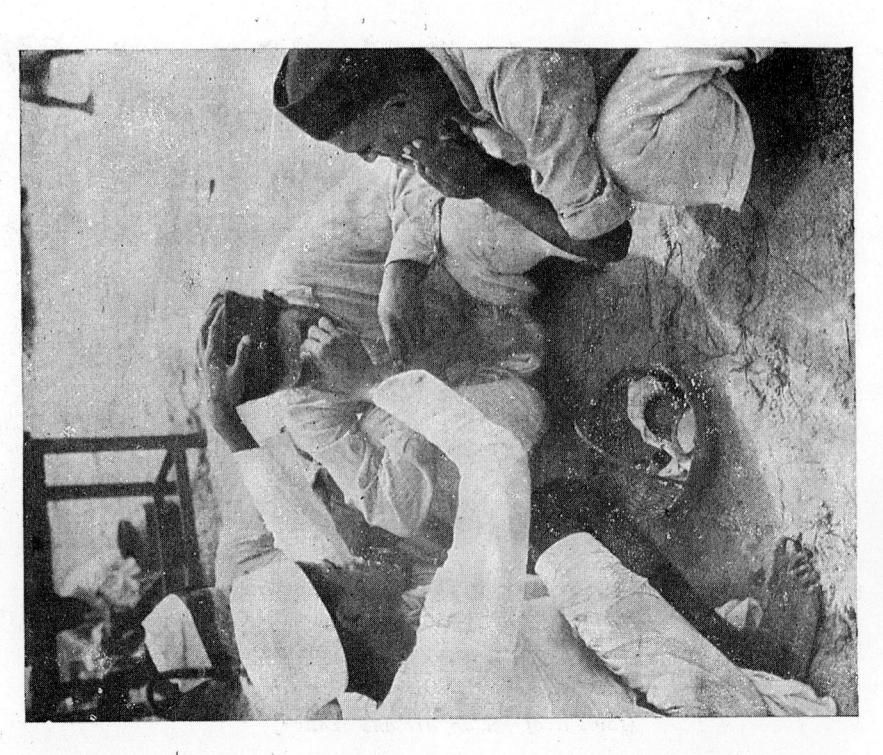

176 COCOANUT DAY INTERLUDE: PUTTING THE CASTE MARK ON THE FOREHEAD
(Photo: B. F. Ferreira)

Hindus are the Mahabharata and the Ramayana. Of these the Mahabharata is the more ancient but it deals with a later epoch than that of the Ramayana.

The incidents narrated in the Mahabharata are said to have occurred in the Dwaparayuga (see page 1) the third age of the Hindu cycle. The original was a small work which treated of a war of succession between Kauravas and Pandavas (of the lunar dynasty of kings) of whom the Kauravas were depicted as persecuted heroes and the Pandavas as murderous villains. The claimants were first cousins. This work was, however, re-written, obviously by the partisans of the Pandavas. Later writers made many additions and the Mahabharata, as it stands today, is a voluminous work of about 100,000 stanzas, the longest single poem in the world. The main story, as in the original, treats of the war of accession between the Pandavas and Kauravas, but in the present form the Kauravas are the villains and the Pandavas the persecuted heroes. Besides the main story, the work contains many digressions which deal with statecraft, the art and science of war, philosophy, rules of conduct for the four castes, etc; side by side with these profound subjects are fairy tales, mythical geography and history, and idle passages which teach nothing. The Bhagavadgita, a philosophical gem we have already noticed, is found in the Mahabharata. More than this, the whole Hindu tradition can be found in the Mahabharata, and on this account it is revered by the Hindus as "the fifth Veda." Vyasa, the compiler of the Vedas, is believed to have composed the Mahabharata. This sage dictated the work and Ganesha, the elephant-headed god of prudence, is fabled to have written it. The sanctity of the work can very well be imagined from these beliefs.

The main story of the Mahabharata is briefly this:

In the lunar dynasty of kings, there was once a prince named Vichitravirya. He had two sons, Dhritarashtra and Pandu. Dhritarashtra was the elder, but he was born blind and was hence disqualified to rule. Pandu, after a few years' reign, died leaving his five sons (Pandavas) very young. Dhritarashtra ruled as regent for the Pandavas. He had one hundred sons (the Kauravas) of whom Duryodhana was the eldest and most ambitious. The Pandavas and the Kauravas were of about the same age, and Duryodhana could not see how the Pandavas were to be the heirs to the throne when his father was the elder brother of Pandu. He was jealous of the Pandavas from very childhood and prevailed upon his weak and aged father to plot their ruin. In the court of Dhritarashtra intrigues started and parties were formed; but all the machinations of Duryodhana and his brothers could not destroy the Pandavas. These princes, however, had to go into exile and lived for many years in forests unknown to Duryodhana who thought them dead. During their wanderings in the forests the Pandavas made secret alliances with friendly monarchs, especially with Krishna (the eighth incarnation of Vishnu, and the ruler of Dwarka) and the king of the Panchalas. When they found themselves strong enough to challenge Duryodhana, they made known their identity and sent an envoy to Duryodhana to return to them their paternal possessions. Duryodhana wished to wage a war, but the elders in his court prevailed upon him to divide the kingdom equally between the cousins. Yudhishtira, the eldest of the Pandavas was accordingly crowned king of Indraprastha and Duryodhana remained the ruler of Hastinapur.

The Kauravas again became jealous of the fame and glory of the Pandava princes. Many petty causes for quarrel soon ensued. Once when the dignified Duryodhana went on a visit to Indraprastha, Panchali (also known as Draupadi), the common wife of the Pandavas, laughed at him when he fell into a magic tank of water which he mistook for crystal. Mockery by a woman was worse than death in those ancient days. This insult and many other things convinced Duryodhana that there was no place for the Pandavas and Kauravas in this world, and one party had to be destroyed. Hence he invited Yudhishtira for a gambling contest. Ancient rule of chivalry demanded that no invitation for gambling should be refused; besides, Yudhishtira himself was fond of gambling. Duryodhana's uncle Sakuni was notorious for sharp practice in the game and this man played on behalf of Duryodhana. Yudhishtira began to lose heavily in the game. A madness seized the king and he gambled away his kingdom, his brothers and himself. His only possession that remained was his wife Draupadi, and this lady was offered as a stake and lost. Not content with this, Duryodhana asked for a last throw of dice which was to decide the final issue; if Yudhishtira were to lose, his brothers and himself together with their wives and children, were to wander fourteen years in the forests as exiles; if Duryodhana was to lose he would do likewise. The challenge was accepted, the fatal dice was thrown, and Yudhishtira lost.

Now was Duryodhana's turn to insult Draupadi. She was denuded in public, and the Pandavas, together with her, were sent into exile. They wandered for fourteen years in the forests during which period Duryodhana made many unsuccessful attempts to kill them. After the term of exile was over, the Pandava princes felt themselves strong enough to demand their kingdom. Duryodhana not only refused to listen to their demands but even threatened to horse-whip Krishna who went to him as the envoy of the Pandavas. All attempts at a peaceful settlement having failed, the Pandavas sent word to their allies that their claim could be enforced only through force. Many powerful monarchs sided with them, and war was declared. The great battle was fought on the field of Kurukshetra near Delhi. The struggle lasted for eighteen days. At the end of the battle, of the hundreds of thousands of active combatants on either side none was left alive except the five Pandavas. Shortly after the battle, the disillusioned heroes gave up all ideas of dominion and after installing a younger member of the family on the throne, started on a long and perilous journey towards the heaven of Indra. Four of the five brothers perished on the road. Only Yudhishtira, the most righteous of the princes, could reach the abode of bliss.

The Mahabharata depicts Indo-Aryan society at the zenith of its glory. The conquest of India was complete and not only in the north but even in South

India the principal kingdoms were all ruled by Aryan kings. The original inhabitants lived in servility to them and those who preferred independence to peace inhabited forests and hilly tracts inaccessible to city-dwelling Aryans.

The original Mahabharata is a work of great antiquity. But the present compilation is considered not older than the fourth century A.D. In fact, a good part of it is of much later origin.

The Ramayana is a smaller work than the Mahabharata, and consists of 24,000 couplets. The incidents narrated in it are believed to have happened in Thretayuga, the second age of the Hindu cycle. The work is attributed to Valmiki, a sage greatly venerated by the Hindus. The date of the Ramayana, as that of the Mahabharata. is uncertain, but the spirit of the whole work indicates that it is of much later origin than the Mahabharata though treating of a more ancient age.

The fortunes of Rama, prince of Ayodhya (he was the seventh incarnation of Vishnu) form the main theme of the epic. The prince, virtuous, brave and kind, was the eldest son of king Dasaratha and beloved of the king and his subjects. Dasaratha growing old, he decided to crown Rama ruler of the kingdom, and to live a retired life. On the eve of the coronation day, Kaikeyi, the youngest wife of Dasaratha and stepmother of Rama, asked the king for a favour, and before knowing its nature he promised to grant her whatever she would ask. Kaikeyi now wanted the king to cancel all preparations for Rama's coronation, to install her son Bharata as king in place of Rama, and send this prince into exile to the forests of the Deccan for fourteen years. Neither threats nor entreaties could detract Kaikeyi, and the miserable old king had to accede to her requests. Rama was exiled. His young wife, Sita, and half-brother Lakshmana followed him.

When these things happened in Ayodhya, Bharata, Kaikeyi's son, was away on a visit to his uncle's kingdom. On hearing of Rama's exile, he hurried back to Ayodhya, but before reaching this city his father Dasaratha had died of grief. Bharata, like Lakshmana, was much attached to Rama and had no desire to usurp his throne. He reviled his mother for her selfishness and cruelty, and set out in search of Rama. He met this prince in the forests of Dandaka wearing the garb of a hermit and living on jungle fare. The meeting of the brothers is described with much pathos and tenderness. But all the coaxing and pleading of Bharata could not detract Rama from the promise he had given his father, and he had to order his weeping half-brother back to Ayodhya to rule the kingdom as his regent.

From this point the real saga begins. Ravana, the demon-king of Lanka (Ceylon) came to hear of the extraordinary beauty of Sita and abducted her. He took her away in his aerial car, Pushpaka, and interned her in his impregnable castle at Lanka. Rama and Lakshmana were out in the forests when this happened and they set out on a search for Sita. After long wanderings in the forests of the Deccan they found out the whereabouts of Sita by the help of the bear and monkey tribes that inhabited the hills. Under Rama's leadership an army of redoubtable monkeys was raised who built a bridge across the gulf and stormed Lanka. After many bitter and bloody battles the ten-headed Ravana was slain and Sita reclaimed. The termination of the battle coincided with the end of the fourteen years' exile and Rama, Sita and Lakshmana returned to Ayodhya with many of the monkey chiefs. Of these, Hanuman was considered the most loyal and brave, and he is worshipped at present by the Hindus as a god.

In the Ramayana period the Aryans had only partly conquered India. In the north, they were quite powerful, but South India was inhabited by wild tribes whom the Ramayana describes as demons, monkey-tribes, bear-tribes, etc. The whole work is highly artificial when compared to the Mahabharata. The heroes of this work are full-blooded humans, with all human weaknesses and passions, drunk with the joy of living. Rama, the hero of the Ramayana, on the other hand, is a detached and unreal figure, more or less a passive spectator of the life that passes past him. A similar difference is also discernible in the heroines of the two epics. Draupadi, the chief feminine character of the Mahabharata is an independent and high spirited lady representing the ancient Aryan womanhood; but Sita, wife of Rama, has no opinions and no status of her own; her greatness lies in her complete self-surrender to the will of her lord. Sita is too idealistic to be real, and she appears as an invention of the author to emphasize the tendencies of his times to bring women under the subjection of men.

THE PURANAS

These are eighteen in number and all of them are believed to have been written by Vyasa. Their object is to convey to the ignorant and the dull, the teachings of the Vedas. Each Purana is supposed to treat of five principal subjects (known as its Lakshanas), namely, (1) the creation of the universe, (2) its destruction, (3) principal gods and patriarchs, (4) Manvantaras or the reigns of the Manus (the fourteen world-teachers), and (5) the history of the two great races (Solar and Lunar) of Indo-Aryan kings. The Puranas are metrical compositions with occasional passages in prose.

The present day religion of the generality of the Hindus is inspired by the Puranas. On this account, the Arya Samajists, as we have noticed elsewhere, call orthodox Hindus Puranics, and they treat the Puranas as mere fiction which has no Vedic authority.

"The Puranas are properly the history of the gods themselves, interwoven with every variety of legendary tradition on other subjects. Viewing them as a whole the theology they teach is anything but simple, consistent or uniform. While nominally tritheistic, the religion of the Puranas is practically polytheistic and yet essentially pantheistic. Underlying their whole teaching may be discerned the one grand doctrine which is generally found at the root of Hindu theology whether Vedic or Puranic — pure uncompromising pantheism. But interwoven with the radically pantheistic and Vedantic texture of these compositions, tinged as it is with other philosophical ideas (especially the Sankhya doctrine of Prakriti), and diversified as it is with endless fanciful mythologies, theogonies, cosmogonies and mythical genealogies, we have a whole body of teaching on nearly every subject of knowledge." Thus religion is not the only subject of which the Puranas treat. Some of them speak with divine authority on everything from the genealogies of gods down to the origin of insects and even give medical advice for the minor ailments of men. In its wild imagination the only work in the English language which remotely resembles the Puranas is Milton's Paradise Lost. But the Puranas have nothing of the compactness and sense of proportion of the English poem. They are loose meandering works, the teachings being conveyed by dialogues between sages. In a congregation of sages, some minor sage is doubtful of some abstruse point of religious law or doctrine and he asks of a greater sage for a clarification of the subject. This personage with necessary preliminaries begins to elucidate the point when doubters again ask questions, and what with one subject leading to another the whole realm of human knowledge is covered by the dialogues.

The eighteen Puranas are grouped into three, each group exalting one of the members of the Hindu trinity. The six Puranas which relate to Brahma are believed to be predominated by the quality by Rajasa (active virtues), those that relate to Vishnu by Sattva (fineness) and those that relate to Shiva by Tamasa or coarseness. The Rajasa (of Brahma) Puranas are: (1) Brahma, (2) Brahmanda, (3) Brahma-vayvarta, (4) Markandeya, (5) Bhavishya, and (6) Vamana. The Satvika (of Vishnu) Puranas are: (1) Vishnu (2) Bhagavata, (3) Naradiya, (4) Garuda, (5) Padma, and (6) Varaha. The Tamasa, Puranas (of Shiva) are: (1) Shiva, (2) Linga, (3) Skanda, (4) Agni, (5) Matsya and (6) Kurma. Of the eighteen Puranas the Vishnu Purana is the most interesting and complete. Markandeya is quite unsectarian in character and is believed to be the oldest Purana, and the Bhagavata, which exalts Krishna, the most recent. The dates of these works are unknown, but the earliest of them are believed to be of later origin than the epics.

Before leaving the subject of the Puranas, a word may be said about the Tantras, as these works are to the Saktas what the Puranas are to the other sects. The Tantras are little known works, but they too like the Puranas treat of five subjects: (1) Creation of the universe, (2) destruction of the universe, (3) worship of the gods, (4) attainments of super-human faculties, and (5) the four modes of union with the Supreme Spirit. In addition to these, the following subjects are also dealt with in the principal Tantras: "Praise of female energy; spells for bringing people into subjection; for making them enamoured; for unsettling their minds; for fattening; for destroying sight; for producing dumbness, deafness, fevers, etc; for bringing on miscarriage; for destroying crops; for preventing various kinds of evil; modes of worshipping Kali; methods of breathing in certain rites; language of birds, beasts, etc.; worship of the female emblem, with the adjuncts of wine, fish, meat, women, etc."

The principal Tantras are: Rudrayamala, Kalika Maha-nirvana, Kularnava, Syama-rahasya, Sarada-tilaka, Mantra-mahobodhi, Uddisa, Kamada and Kamakhya.

DHARMA SASTRAS

Dharma Sastras is the collective name for the various law books of the Hindus, which regulate their political, religious and social life. According to one authority there are forty-seven ancient sages who have given laws to the Hindus. All of them, however, have not been recognized as such by all sects. Yagnavalkya, himself a law-giver of no little importance, mentions twenty law-givers, including himself. They are (1) Manu, (2) Yagnavalkya, (3) Atri, (4) Vishnu, (5) Harita, (6) Usana, (7) Angiras, (8) Apastambha, (9) Yama, (10) Brihaspati, (11) Parasara, (12) Samvarta, (13) Katyayana, (14) Daksha, (15) Vyasa, (16) Likhita, (17) Sankha, (18) Gautama, (19) Shatatapa, and (20) Vashishta. The works of these law-givers as well as those of some later legislators are still extant.

Of all the law books, the code of Manu is the most ancient, comprehensive and authoritative. Manu is a mythical personage, believed to be the progenitor of mankind and the originator of law. There are several Manu's mentioned in Hindu sacred literature and the name appears to be an epithet rather than a proper noun. For instance, the Puranas mention that each Kalpa or Day of Brahma (see page 1) is divided into fourteen Manvantaras over each of which reigns a Manu. Here Manu means a world-teacher. The code of Manu is believed to be revealed to each Manu by the original Manu (the celestial patriarch of mankind) at the beginning of a Manvantara and made known to the world by him. At the time of the destruction of the universe the code gets dissolved into chaos but is not destroyed. It reappears when order is restored. Myths apart, Manu seems to have been the first law-giver of the Indo-Aryans, and all later law-givers accept his authority as unquestionable.

The code of Manu is of great antiquity, only less ancient than the three first Vedas. Later writers made additions in the name of Manu, and some passages in the code breathe the spirit of medieval writers. The social theory on which the code is based is founded on caste. The whole design of the code is to perpetuate the supremacy of the Brahmins to whom even kingship is subordinate. The discipline imposed on Brahmins themselves by Manu is very rigid and the life of a Brahmin is to be a duty towards himself and to others.

Next in importance to Manu comes Yagnavalkya. Parasara is, however, considered the most reliable authority for the Kaliyuga (present age). Says the code of Parasara: "The laws of various ages are different, Manu's law-book belongs to the Kritayuga, Gautama's to the Threta, that of Sankha and Likhita to the Dwapara, and Parasara's code to the Kaliyuga."

Besides the twenty law-givers above referred to, there are various other legislators; as many as forty-eight of these are mentioned in some of the Hindu scriptures. Most of these minor law-givers have but local importance, and where their laws are in conflict with those of the greater law-givers their authority is rejected.

SMARTHA SUTRAS

This branch of Smriti falls under two heads: Grihaya Sutras or aphorisms connected with domestic rites and Samayacharika Sutras or aphorisms relating to "conventional practices." Smartha is the adjective of Smriti and Sutra means aphorism, hence the name Smartha Sutra for this part of sacred literature. These Sutras are even more ancient than the Dharma Sastras and even Manu refers to some of them; the Sutras dealing with Vedic ritual are at times referred to as Srauta Sutras as distinct from those based on Smriti.

The Sutras are generally attached to the Vedas and the best known of them are: Asvalayana's Grihya Sutras attached to the Rig Veda, Gobhila's Sutras attached to Sama Veda, and the Sutras of Paraskara, Baudhayana, Apastambha and Bharadwaja attached to the Yajur Veda. The Sutras order in great detail each and every act of a person from the time he gets up from bed till he goes to sleep, and give elaborate instructions for performance of rituals and ceremonies. The following is a description of how to perform the cremation of a dead body: "When a man dies, a piece of ground is to be excavated in a Smasana or burning ground south-east or south-west of his abode. His relations are to carry the fires and sacrificial implements to the excavated place. Those of them who are most advanced in years are to walk behind in single file—the men separated from the women—bearing the corpse, the hair and nails of which have all been cut off or clipped, and leading the sacrificial animals, either a cow or a black she-goat. The remaining relations and connexions are to follow with their garments and sacrificial cords hanging down, and their hair dishevelled—the elder in front, the younger behind. When they reach the prepared ground, the performer of the ceremony is to sprinkle water on it with a branch of the Sami tree, repeating Rig Veda X 14.9, etc"*

While the Smartha Sutras still remain the final authority in most of the ceremonies performed by the Hindus, the details vary according to localities. Besides, any deviation in present day ceremonial is excused on the ground that the Smartha Sutras refer to social codes of the second or third Yuga and are not applicable in its entirely to the present Kaliyuga.

THE VEDANGAS

Vedanga means the limb of the Veda. The study of the Vedangas is considered necessary for the proper understanding of the Veda and hence the Vedangas are said to support the Veda. Those who are not acquainted with Hindu notions of sanctity may fail to appreciate why such subjects as grammar and metre which form part of the Vedangas are considered sacred at all. The answer is that to the Hindu, formalism is of greater importance than emotions or intentions. The written word is more powerful than the most heartfelt cry. Ceremonial religion is a matter of correct pronunciation, correct grammar and correct accents. And the structure of the Sanskrit language is such that an accent in the wrong place may lead to an entirely different meaning. There is a serious story of an ascetic who, while begging of Brahma for a boon of immortality, laid accent on the wrong vowel and found himself condemned to eternal sleep. Even slight mistakes in repeating texts are believed to derange sacrifices and ceremonies performed at the cost of much time and money. Besides the person who repeats the texts wrongly is himself feared to be thrown into hell. Says one of the ancient authorities on the Vedas: "He who shall cause anyone to repeat or shall himself repeat any hymn of the Veda without having acquainted himself with the name of the Rishi to whom it was revealed, the metre in which it was written, the deity to whom it was addressed, and its application, is the worst of sinners." Hence the importance of the Vedangas and their sanctity.

The Vedangas are six: (1) Kalpa or ceremonial directory, (2) Siksha or phonetic directory, (3) Chandas or metre, (4) Nirukta or exposition, (5) Vyakarana or grammar, and (6) Jyotisha or astronomy.

Each Veda has its own Kalpa Sutras; the Rig Veda has three, the Sama Veda three, the Yajur Veda thirteen, and the Atharva Veda one. The burden of the Kalpa Sutras is to instruct the student in all the elaborate general rules for sacrifices and ceremonies.

Siksha treats of the laws of correct pronunciation and the science of "letters, accents, quantity, the right use of the organs of articulation, and phonetics generally." The Pratisakhyas attached to the Vedas, together with a later work attributed to Panini, the grammarian, are classified under the Siksha Sutras. The most important of the Pratisakhyas are four: One attached to the Rig Veda, two to Yajur Veda and one to Atharva Veda; the Sama Veda has none.

The most important work on Chandas or metre is the Chanda-Sastra (the science of metre) ascribed to Pingala who appears to have flourished in the 2nd century B.C. This work mainly refers to Vedic literature, but later writers have invented many metres not found in this ancient text.

On the Nirukta part of the Vedanga we have only one important work, a compilation attributed to a little known author named Yaska, believed to have lived in the fourth century B.C. There are many commentaries and classical glossaries on Yaska by later writers, of which the Amara Kosa of Amara Simha is the best known.

Of the sixth Vedanga, grammar, the most celebrated work is that of Panini. His work is even now the last word on Sanskrit grammar. For lucidity, conciseness and originality of classification there are few works on the subject that are comparable to Panini's. Yet his work cannot be strictly termed a Vedanga, for it treats of Sanskrit literature in general and only exceptionally of the Vedas. Yet such is Panini's greatness that he is regarded as a seer and his work a revelation.

NITISASTRAS

This department of Smritis can be classed under two heads, i.e., the regular, moral and ethical teach-

---

* M. Williams, *Indian Wisdom*.

ings strung together in verse as a complete guide to conduct and styled Nitisastras, and the numerous beast fables and stories found in Hindu literature which are designed to drive home a moral.

Of the Nitisastras proper, most of the verses are attributed to some wise ancient like Chanakya or Bhartrihari; and the moral sentiments expressed can be found in the epics or in the Puranas though not in the same words. Nitisara by Kamandaki is a complete list of maxims for everyone from the prince to the peasant designed to be a guide to conduct. The author acknowledges as his master, Chanakya (see page 4) and this has made the work repugnant to some orthodox Hindus though, because of the worldly wisdom it teaches, it is classed under the Smritis. Other well-known works classed under Nitisastras are the Sayings of Bartrihari, Vridha-Chanakya or Rajniti Sastras, and Sarn-gadharapaddhati (a collection of sententious verses from various sources with the author's name given with every verse). The following examples selected at random will give some idea of these works:

"The archer's arrow may slay one, or it may not; the cunning of the wise man slays foes ere they are even born." — Nitisara.

The attribute most noble of the hand
Is readiness in giving; of the head
Bending before a teacher; of the mouth
Veracious speaking; of a victor's arms
Undaunted valour; of the inner heart,
Pureness the most unsullied; of the ears
Delight in hearing and receiving truth—
These are adornments of highminded men
Better than all the majesty of Empire.
— Bhartrihari

Now for a little while a child, and now
An amorous youth; then for a season turned
Into a wealthy householder; then stripped
Of all his riches, with decrepit limbs
And wrinkled frame, man creeps towards the end
Of life's erratic course; and like an actor,
Passes behind Death's curtain out of view.
— Bhartrihari

Of the fiction part of the Nitisastras, it may be mentioned that the invention of animals and birds as characters in moral tales originated in India. The Jataka tales of the Buddhists in which the Blessed One, during his various incarnations, appears as a wise animal, bird or insect were probably the model from which the Hindu authors of the Panchatantra and Hitopadesa copied. The object of these fables, according to their authors, was to teach the foolish sons of a king some wisdom, as they would read no books and listen to the preaching of no wise man. So the cunning author took them under his charge and started telling them stories which so interested the princes that they never got tired of listening to them; and the author so managed to put moral and political teachings in the mouth of his characters that at the end of his story-telling all the foolish princes were found to be extremely wise and able to rule kingdoms.

The Indian fables were borrowed by the Greeks and the Arabs. The wise Aesop is believed to have learnt his fables from Indians. The Tales of Bidpai which were popular in medieval Europe point to an Indian origin. Even now the charming beast fables of the Hindus are found to have a perennial appeal to all men, especially in their young age, and Kipling in his "Jungle Book," has copied with advantage ancient Indian sages. The Panchatantra never loses its moral and didactic character and the beasts ably represent the human kingdom with its various types. The fox is always wise, and the crow cunning; the stork is a hypocrite, and the donkey a fool; the monkey is meddlesome and the lion brave.

Side by side with the plot of the story, which, though simple, is often interesting, are found moral teachings and wise sayings, such as the following:

No man of sense should take as his adviser
A barber, dancer, mendicant or miser.

* * *

Give women food, dress, gems, and all that's nice
But tell them not your plans, if you are wise.

* * *

Even a foe, if he perform a kindness,
Should be esteemed a kinsman; e'en a kinsman,
If he do harm, should be esteemed a foe.
A malady, though bred within the body
Does mischief, while a foreign drug that comes
From some far forest does a friendly work.

* * *

Praise not the goodness of the grateful man
Who acts with kindness to his benefactors.
He who does good to those who do him wrong
Alone deserves the epithet of good.

Before leaving the subject of sacred Sanskrit literature, a word may be said about the literature of the Buddhists. Early Buddhists wrote in Pali or Magadhi, the dialect of ancient Magadha, as they treated Sanskrit as essentially the language of the Brahmins. Later, however, Mahayana Buddhism showed a preference for Sanskrit and its canonical works were written in this language. The ancient Pali language and the Buddhist scriptures written in it were carried by early missionaries to Ceylon and Burma, where to this day Pali remains the sacred language of the Buddhists. The Sanskrit canon is preserved in Nepal and other countries following Mahayana Buddhism.[*]

The religious literature of the Buddhists is classified into the Tripitaka or Three Baskets: The Vinaya, dealing with the discipline and rules of conduct for monks and nuns; the Suttas or stories and sayings; and Abhidhamma or higher philosophy. Many works attributed to different authors in different ages are extant under each of the above heads. The Lalita Vistara is an important work, the date of which is uncertain,

---

[*] A more detailed account of the Buddhistic canonical literature will be found in the author's work *The Story of the Cultural Empire of India*.

containing a legendary history of the Buddha and his works. It is written partly in Sanskrit and partly in a mixture of Sanskrit and Prakrit. The celebrated Asvaghosha who was a Brahmin convert to Buddhism wrote many works in Sanskrit including the Buddhacharita (the history of the Buddha); but only fragments of his works exist at present. Asvaghosha is believed to have lived in the reign of emperor Kanishka.

SECULAR SANSKRIT LITERATURE

Strictly speaking there is hardly any secular literature in Sanskrit. We have seen that the Hindu genius for mysticism is such that even purely mundane subjects such as grammar, metre and fable have been treated by them as sacred literature. The same may be said to be true of drama, poetry and even scientific works on subjects such as medicine and mathematics. The themes of plays and lyrics were usually borrowed from the epics, and authors of scientific works claimed infallibility for themselves on the ground that the knowledge contained in their works was revealed to them by the Almighty. What interested literary men in India was not what humans did but what the gods and demi-gods did. Hence there are few important works in Sanskrit which are purely secular.

Yet a line must be drawn somewhere and we shall treat the following works as secular.

KALIDASA

Of all Sanskrit playwrights and poets, Kalidasa in undoubtedly the greatest. The work that won him immortality is his great play "Shakuntala." Goethe pays the following tribute to this work:

Wouldst thou the young year's blossoms, and the fruits of its decline,
And all by which the soul is charmed, enraptured, feasted, fed,
Wouldst thou the earth or Heaven itself in one sole name combine?
I name thee, O Shakuntala! and all at once is said.

The story of Shakuntala was borrowed from Mahabharata and adapted for the stage by Kalidasa with necessary embellishments. Shakuntala, the heroine of the play, was born of a casual love affair of King Vishwamitra with the celestial dancer Menaka. Both the parents disowned the babe and she was exposed on the bank of a forest stream and found by the hermit Kanwa who brought her up in the hermitage as his own daughter. Shakuntala grew up into a beautiful maiden and King Dushyanta, in a hunting expedition, happened to stray into the hermitage of Kanwa where he met the lovely maiden and fell in love with her. Shakuntala requited his love and the young lovers, drunk with love, spent some hours in sport. Kanwa was not in the hermitage at the time and before his arrival Dushyanta had departed promising Shakuntala that he would come back shortly and take her to his kingdom; as a ratification of the promise, he put his signet ring on Shakuntala's finger.

After the departure of Dushyanta, Shakuntala sat dreaming of him when the ill-tempered sage Durvasa visited the hermitage. The love-lorn maiden forgot to welcome him and the irascible old man, knowing by his occult powers the cause of her inattention, cursed that the man she was thinking of should forget her for good. Shakuntala's companions begged for mercy and the sage was won over so far as to declare that on seeing the signet ring the lost memory would be restored to Dushyanta.

Months passed and Dushyanta did not return. Shakuntala showed signs of pregnancy and her condition could be hidden from no one. At this stage, the hermit Kanwa was informed of all that had happened between Dushyanta and Shakuntala and he sent her with two companions (one of them a lady) to the court of Dushyanta.

On the way to Dushyanta's court, Shakuntala happened to pass a lake where she stopped to wash her hands, and while doing so lost the signet ring in the lake without her noticing it. Thus the only thing that could have restored his lost memory to the king was irretrievably lost. In the court of Dushyanta, this king very naturally disowned Shakuntala and swore that he had never met her. Neither the wailings of the unhappy woman nor the pleadings of her companions were of any avail. Kanwa's instructions were, however, clear and Shakuntala's companions left her in the king's court. The king drove her out of the palace. While the wretched Shakuntala was standing outside the palace not knowing what to do, her mother Menaka descended from heaven and carried her off to her own abode midway between heaven and earth. Here a son was born to Shakuntala.

The lost ring was swallowed by a fish and the fish was caught by a fisherman who, on cutting it open, found the king's signet ring. This was taken to the king who, on seeing it, regained his memory, and began to wail over the loss of Shakuntala. A vain search was made for the lady throughout his kingdom.

Years passed, and while Dushyanta was living in sorrow, a messenger came to him from Indra, king of the gods, who requisitioned his help in a war he (Indra) was engaged in with the Asuras. Dushyanta was taken to heaven and the enemies of Indra were defeated by him. On his way back to earth in Indra's car, Dushyanta happened to stray into the house of Menaka where he met his son and wife. After the rejoicings proper to the occasion, the three returned to the kingdom of Dushyanta.

The story, though highly artificial, is handled with supreme skill and appears almost natural. "Vikramorvasi" or Urvasi won by valour, and the "Malavikagnimitra" or story of Malavika and Agnimitra, are two other important plays by Kalidasa. Of his other works "Kumara Sambhava" or birth of the war-god, "Megha-duta" or cloud-messenger, "Raghuvamsa" or dynasty of Raghu and "Rutsamhara" or collection of seasons, may be mentioned. Of these, the cloud-messenger has few equals in wild fantasy and originality in expressing the pangs of separation from one's beloved.

Kalidasa's fame as a poet and dramatist has

woven round him many legends. One is that he was extremely stupid as a young man and by a special favour of the goddess Kali (hence his name Kalidasa meaning slave of Kali) was suddenly transformed into a wit and a poet. He is believed to have been the most precious of the nine gems (the nine geniuses called Navaratnas) of the court of king Bhoja, a semi-mythical figure considered by some authorities the same as Vikramaditya of the legend and by others as Samudragupta (he is also identified as Vikramaditya by some writers), the great Hindu emperor of the Gupta dynasty under whom Hindu culture reached the zenith of its glory. Samudragupta reigned in the fourth century A.D. and available evidences support the view that Kalidasa lived in his time.

Unlike most of the great Hindu poets, Kalidasa was a lover of life and beauty and was never enamoured of dry philosophy and asceticism. The theme that appealed to him most was love; not the mystic love of the soul for God, but the very mundane love of man for woman and of woman for man. It was fresh, newly awakened love of youth that he loved to dwell upon. For him sex love was not the symbol of divine love, but divine love was the symbol and sex love the real stuff. When he wrote on the loves of gods (as in Kumara-sambhava) he brought them down to the level of men. The form of marriage that appealed to him most was Gandharva, the consummation of mutual love (as in "Shakuntala") which the law-givers treat with contempt.

BHAVABHUTI

This poet is mentioned in some works as a contemporary of Kalidasa and another of the nine gems of king Bhoja's court. This does not appear to be correct. His date is now fixed as the eighth century A.D. Bhavabhuti's fame as a dramatist is only second to that of Kalidasa. He wrote three plays, Malati-Madhava, Uttara-Rama-Charita and Mahavira-Charita, of which the first is considered the best. His style is somewhat laboured, but in his plots he often excels Kalidasa himself. He is a master in describing weird and horrible scenes. In Malati-Madhava there is a scene in which the heroine held as captive in the temple of the demon-goddess Chamunda and about to be sacrificed, is rescued by Madhava who slays the priestess. This is considered the most gripping scene in the whole field of Sanskrit drama.

Bhavabhuti, when he pleases, can be tender and pleasing, as is evident from the following description of Sita in Uttara Rama Charita:

" 'Tis Sita; mark
How lovely through her tresses dark
And floating loose, her face appears,
Though pale and wan and wet with tears,
She moves along, like Tenderness
Invested with mortal dress."*

* Rawlinson, *India*.
† K. Saunders, *A Pageant of India*.

SOME OTHER SANSKRIT POETS AND THEIR WORKS

Of the other Sanskrit poets mention may be made of Bharavi, Bhatti, Kumaradasa and Magha. Bharavi's most important work, now extant, is Kiratarjuna (the hunter and Arjuna) the subject of which is borrowed from the Mahabharata. Arjuna, one of the Pandava princes, while engaged in the worship of Shiva for a certain boon, happens to be provoked by a hunter whom he fights. At the end of the fight, the hunter transforms himself into Shiva, and this god now reveals to Arjuna that he assumed the form of the hunter to test Arjuna's skill in arms. Pleased with Arjuna's valour, Shiva grants him the desired boon.

Bhatti's important work is Ravana-vadha (the destruction of Ravana), otherwise called Bhatti Kavya. Its theme, as the title suggests, is borrowed from the Ramayana. Kumaradasa's Janaki-haran (rape of Sita) is also based on the Ramayana.

Of all Sanskrit Kavyas (artificial single poems), Magha of the poet Magha is considered the greatest. The theme is borrowed from the Mahabharata and describes the destruction of king Sishupala by Krishna. Magha is in his element in the battle-field, and describes with supreme skill the battle between the armies of Sishupala and Krishna. Here are some of the stanzas which depict the scene:

"As the hosts of the king with unbroken flow, with unceasing clamour in their proud onslaught, advanced against the vast armies of Krishna, there arose a battle swaying to and fro as when the waters of the streams mingle with the foaming waves of ocean."

"The roar of the chariot, matching the thunder of the raincloud and filling the air, was eagerly echoed by the peacocks, who stretched out their necks and redoubled their loud calls."

"Over a corpse that danced blindly moving its hands amidst the loud roll of the drums and the trumpet's clangour, the conch rang shrill as it laughed aloud."†

Magha was a keen student of grammar and metre, and his work shows him as a master of Sanskrit.

MRICHHAKATIKA (OR CLAY CART) AND MUDRA RAKSHASA

Mrichhakatika is a delightful play which unlike other Sanskrit works is conspicuously free from the religious element. It deals with ordinary men and women and not with gods and demi-gods. The play opens with a scene of a busy street in the city of Ujjain. The chief characters in the play are Vasantsena, a courtesan, a gambler, a noble but simple-minded Brahmin named Charudatta, and a villainous courtier, Samstanaka. There is a court scene where Charudatta is falsely accused of murder, and here is the decription of a law-court:

"The court looks like a sea: its councillors
Are deep engulfed in thought; its tossing waves
Are wrangling advocates: its brood of monsters
Are these wild animals, Death's ministers.

Attorneys skim like wily snakes the surface;
Spies are the Shell-fish cowering midst its wheel,
And while informers, like the hovering curlew,
Hang fluttering o'er and pounce upon their prey."

This charming play is ascribed to a royal personage named Sudraka, none of whose other works has come down to us.

The Mudra Rakshasa (seal of the minister) of Visakhadatta is a historical play dealing with Chandragupta Maurya's usurpation of the throne of Pataliputra. The author was obviously a partisan of the Nandas whom Chandragupta overthrew, and he depicts Chandragupta and his wily minister Chanakya as the villains of the piece. The minister of the Nandas thus wails the misfortunes of his party:

"Fortune in all befriends
The cruel Chandragupta. When I send
A messenger of certain death to slay him,
She wields the instrument against his rival,
Who should have spoiled him of one-half his kingdom,
And arms and drugs and strategies are turned
In his behalf against my friends and servants."

PROSE WORKS

Ancient Sanskrit writers almost always used poetry as the medium of expression; they loved the artificial more than the simple and the plain, and hence mere prose was considered unfit for literary expression. Some writers, however, did use prose but their language was artificial and style laboured. Of Sanskrit prose works the best known are Dasakumaracharita (the story of ten princes) by Dandin, and Kadambari and Harsha-charita (story of Harsha) by Bana. Bana is considered the greater of the two writers, but his style is highly artificial. Here is a description of a maiden from Kadambari: "Her form was lovely, yet dreaded, even as a sandal plant wherein lurks a snake, by reason of the sword which she wore at her left side, belying her womanhood; she was, as it were, the Ganges, her bosom whitened by sandal showing the temples of Airavata (Indra's elephant) as he emerges from his bath; through her reflection in their crest jewels she was, as it were, an embodiment of the king's order, borne on the heads of obedient princes; by the whiteness of her robe which vied with the swans, she resembled the autumn when they return home; she conquered all the assembled kings as did the edge of Parasurama's axe; with the cane wand which she bore she resembled the Vindhya forest land, and she seemed none other than the guardian deity of the realm in human shape."

Among other Sanskrit writers we may mention Somadeva, the great story teller of Kashmir, whose work, the Kathasaritsagara (ocean of story), is known as the Indian Arabian Nights. Somadeva wrote these interesting stories of gods, heroes, devils, fools and sages, of love, hate, treachery, devotion, in fact of all human passions, for the entertainment of queen Suryamati. The stories of Somadeva have been translated into almost all Indian languages, and are also current among the folk who often while away their idle hours listening to some story-teller or bard of gifted memory.

HISTORICAL AND SCIENTIFIC WORKS

History is a subject which did not interest the Hindus. There are certain works which their authors claim to be history; but most of these are panegyrics of kings and their ancestors whom the authors wished to extol. There is, however, one work which has considerable historical merit and that is Raja-Taringini (river of kings) of Kalhana. Kalhana was born in Kashmir and wrote his work in the 12th century A.D. He is not completely free from the superstitions of his age and race, but with all that, his work is the only one in Sanskrit literature which can lay some claim to be history.

The one branch of science in which the Hindus have done exceptionally well is medicine. The indigenous Ayurvedic system of medicine is as old as the race and still competes successfully with the Allopathic system. In every town and village a good Ayurvedic doctor commands as much popular respect as an Allopathic physician. If anything, Indians, as a rule, have better faith in the Ayurvedic system than the Allopathic. The name of the system itself suggests the sanctity and greatness of the science of medicine; for Ayurveda is considered an Upaveda (auxiliary Veda) of the Atharva Veda. The sage who revealed it is believed to be Dhanwantari, though other seers are also mentioned. Some of the ancient writers on medicine were Atreya, Susruta and Charaka; Charaka is believed to have lived in the court of Kanishka. Of later writers mention may be made of Vagbhata (who wrote Astangasamgraha and Ashtangahridayasamgraha), Madhavakara (author of Rugviniccaya), Dribhabala, Vrinda, Bhava Misra and Surapala.

For the Hindus even today astronomy and astrology are inseparable, and this has always been the case with them. The earliest work of importance on these subjects is the Panchasiddhantika of Varahamihira who wrote in the sixth century A.D. The Panchasiddhantika gives a summary of five systems (hence the name) of astronomy which were probably in vogue at that time. One of the Siddhantas (systems) is called Romakasiddhanta (the system of the Romans), thus clearly indicating that the Hindus had a very good knowledge of the astronomers of the West. Greek influence is also traceable in some of the Siddhantas. The Romaka makes calculations for the meridian of Yavanapura (city of Greeks) and the Paulika Siddhanta gives the difference in longitude between Yavanapura and Ujjain. Of later writers on astronomy Aryabhata (fifth century A.D.) and Brahmagupta (seventh century A.D.) may be mentioned.

The astronomers were also mathematicians, and wrote on geometry and mathematics which formed part of their works on astronomy. A work of considerable importance dealing solely with mathematics was written by Mahaviracharya in the ninth century A.D., and has come down to us under the title of Ganitasarasamgraha (collection of the essence of mathematics). In the tenth century Shridhara wrote his Trishati, dealing mainly with geometry. By far the greatest Sanskrit writer on mathematics was Bhas-

LXXXI

179 YUDHISHTIRA'S FEAST PRIOR TO THE HORSE SACRIFICE: A SCENE FROM THE *MAHABHARATA*
(*Razmnamah*: *Journal of Indian Art and Industry*)

178 BHIMA DRINKING THE BLOOD OF HIS ENEMY DUSSASANA: A SCENE FROM THE *MAHABHARATA*
(*Razmnamah*, Jeypore: *Journal of Indian Art and Industry*)

LXXXII

181 TRIUMPHAL PROCESSION OF THE WHITE HORSE BEFORE ASWAMEDHA SACRIFICE: A SCENE FROM THE *MAHABHARATA*
(*Razmnamah: Journal of Indian art and Industry*)

180 BHISHMA, GENERALISSIMO OF KAURAVAS ENTHRONED BEFORE COMMENCEMENT OF THE MAHABHARATA WAR
(*Razmnamah: Journal of Indian art and Industry*)

LXXXIII

182 EFFIGIES OF THE DEMONS RAVANA, KUMBHAKARNA AND MEGHNATH BEING SET FIRE TO: RAMLILA CELEBRATIONS
(India Pictorial Features)

183 IMAGE OF BHIMA, THE PANDAVA HERO
(Photo: G. N. Aiyar)

184 YUDHISTIRA, THE PANDAVA KING
(Photo: G. N. Aiyar)

185 BATTLE ARRAY OF THE KAURAVAS: THE *MAHABHARATA*
(*Journal of Indian Art and Industry*)

186 **BATTLE ARRAY OF PANDAVAS: THE *MAHABHARATA***
(*Journal of Indian Art and Industry*)

187 RELIGIOUS DANCE: THE DANCERS ARE DRESSED AS HEROES OF THE *MAHABHARATA*
(India Pictorial Features)

188 BRAHMINS ATTENDING UPAKARMA CEREMONY
(India Pictorial Features)

189 DIVALI CELEBRATIONS AT HOME
(India Pictorial Features)

190 TEMPLE PRIEST ON CEREMONIAL RIDE
(National News Photo Service)

LXXXVII

191. DOMESTIC WORSHIP OF THE GOOD KING BALI
(Photo: Stanley Jepson)

192. CIRCUMAMBULATION IN TREE WORSHIP
(Photo: S. S. Aiyar)

LXXXVIII

193 SCULPTURE OF HINDU DEITIES, KESAVA TEMPLE, SOMNATHPUR
(India Pictorial Features)

194 LAKSHMI TEMPLE AT PUSHKAR, AJMER
(B. B. & C. I. Rly.)

kara Acharya who lived in the 11th century. His work Lilavati is acknowledged as the most authentic work on mathematics, while his Bhijaganita gives a systematic exposition of algebra. The Hindus appear to have been the inventors of this branch of mathematics.

This completes the list of the more important classes of works in Sanskrit. There are minor works on every conceivable subject from elephant-training to the study of omens, and it is impossible to give even a short account of these works in a book like this. Some important works on Hindu erotics will, however, be mentioned in chapter XIII.

MODERN INDIAN LANGUAGES

The living languages of modern India can be broadly divided into two groups: the Aryan and the Dravidian. The Aryan group of languages use the Devanagari script or some modified form of it, and is, more or less, allied to this language; the Dravidian group, on the other hand, use the Tamil script and its modifications. Both groups have Sanskrit for their classics; in fact, except some ancient Tamil works, no book of any importance in any Indian language can be found which does not owe much to Sanskrit.

THE ARYAN GROUP

The more important of the Aryan group of languages are Hindi, Mahrathi, Bengali and Gujarati. Of these, Hindi can be said to be the lingua franca of India. The home of the language is the Gangetic plain, but it is spoken and understood in all the great cities of North India. The language is probably the lineal descendant of Prakrit, the dialect of ancient India. The Rajputs had Hindi for their court-language. The court bards of Rajput princes sang the praises of their patrons in Hindi, and of these bards, Chandbardai, author of Prithwirajrasou, was the greatest. It was the heroic that appealed most to the Rajput, and the bards always chose for their themes the deeds of valour performed by their patrons. Here is a description of how Prithwiraj carried away the fair princess Padmavati from the marriage hall:

> "Then, on seeing King Prithwiraj,
> She smiled bashfully, hiding her face through shame.
> Seizing her hand, putting her on horseback,
> The king, the Lord of Delhi, took her away.
> The rumour spread that, outside the city,
> They were carrying off Padmavati by force.
> Drums are beat, there is saddling of horse and elephant,
> They ran, armed in all direction.
> Seize! seize! shouted each warrior.
> Rage possessed the heroes and the king.
> On the field fell heads, and headless trunks of the foe.
> The foe fell on the field of battle;
> Turning his face towards Delhi,
> Having won the battle, went Prithwiraj,
> All the chiefs were glad."*

* Tr. Beames.

Another valued work in Hindi is the Prem Sagar (ocean of love), a free rendering of the Bhagavata Purana into Hindi. But the greatest Hindi work universally admired for beauty of expression, style and religious fervour is the Ramayana of Tulsidasa, a free rendering into Hindi of Valmiki's original work in Sanskrit. Tulsidasa has even eclipsed Valmiki, and the Ramayana which is most valued in India is that of Tulsidasa.

Hindi was adopted by the Moghuls for the use of the army. They introduced many Persian and Arabic words and changed the script into Arabic. This language has developed a copious literature and is known as Urdu. It is the lingua franca of Indian Muslims. The British adopted the language for use in the Indian Army but changed the script into Roman, and they called it Hindustani or Roman Urdu.

Mahrathi is spoken by the Mahrathas and the script is purely Devanagari. It was the court language of the Peshwas and has a classical and modern literature more copious than any other Indian language excepting perhaps Hindi and Tamil.

Bengali is spoken in Bengal and the script used is a modified form of Devanagari. Other languages of India owe much to Bengali for their modern literature. This is mainly due to the fame of writers like Bankim Chandra Chatterjee, the novelist, and Dr. Rabindranath Tagore, the poet and playwright.

Gujarati is the language of Gujarat and the script is a modified form of Devanagari. The genius of the Gujaratis for literature is not so marked as for commerce, and the literary productions which enjoy all India fame in this language are few, if any.

Ooriya is the language of Orissa. The dialect of the Punjab, known as Punjabi, has no script of its own. The literary genius of the Punjabis is expressed either in Urdu or in Hindi. The Sikhs, however, write Punjabi in Gurmukhi, their sacred script, which is a modified form of Devanagari. Sindhi, the language of Sind, is written in Arabic script, but the Hindu writers depend upon Sanskrit for the classical background and Muslims on Persian and Arabic.

THE DRAVIDIAN GROUP

The languages that constitute the Dravidian family are Tamil, Telugu, Canarese and Malayalam. Of these Tamil is the most important and ancient.

Tamil literature is almost as ancient as Sanskrit. Some authorities even tell us that the Aryans borrowed the alphabet from the Tamils. This may be an exaggerated claim but there is no doubt that the Tamils had an ancient culture of their own independent of the Aryans. The most ancient Tamil work that has come down to us is the well-known Kural of Thiruvalluvar. Its date is uncertain but it was probably written in the first century of the Christian era. "The Kural consists of 2,660 couplets dealing with the three stock subjects—virtue, wealth and pleasure. It has been described as the 'most venerated and popular book south of the Godavari...the literary treasure, the poetic mouth-piece, the highest type of verbal excellence among the Tamil people'." Thiruvalluvar was low born, but to the credit of the Brahmins it must be mentioned that they recognized his genius and canonized him. Another ancient writer who is much respected among the Tamilians is Naladiyar. The writings of both Thiruvalluvar and Naladiyar show a high moral sense seldom found in Sanskrit works.

On Vaishnavism becoming popular in South India, poets arose who sang the praises of Vishnu. These Vaishnava poets were known as Alvars and twelve of them are considered the most famous. Their hymns have been collected into what is known as the Vaishnava Prabandham, or the prayer book of South Indian Vaishnavas. It contains 4,000 verses. Here is a typical hymn by Nammalvar, considered the greatest of the Alvars:

Eternal Lord of Angels, who dost deign to veil
    Thy form
In all Creation's varied state, to save poor souls:
Vouchsafe in all Thy grace to stay and hear Thy
    servants' cry
That we be saved the dire return to former
    wretchedness,
When we mistook the body for the soul and
    sinned all sins,
Which clung to us and fixed us ever more to
    mortal frames.*

Of the Shaiva poets Manikka Vasagar, who lived in the tenth century, is worthy of note. His Thiruvasakam (sacred utterance) shows him not only as a saint but as a great poet as well. The following will give some idea of his poetic genius:

Now anigh Indra's East
    Draws the sun; dark flies apace
At the dawn; and the sun
    Of the kindness in Thy face
Rise in high'r, ever high'r,
    As like fair flowers opening,
Eyes unclose from their sleep,
Eyes of Thee our beauteous king.

Hear how now clouds of bees
    Humming bright fill all the air.

Siva, Lord, dweller in
    Holy Perundarai fair,
Thou wilt come to bestow
    Favours rich. Oh show Thy face!
Mountain-joy, Ocean-bliss,
    From the couch rise in Thy grace!†

Tamil has a script of its own and the alphabet is similar to that of Sanskrit. It has few hard consonants and is a musical language. In South India, Tamil is the most widely spoken language.

Telugu was the court language of the Vijaynagar kings and it is spoken in the Telugu districts. In Mysore and Canara districts, Canarese is the current language. Both Telugu and Canarese have the same script, a modification of the Tamil. Malayalam is spoken in Kerala. It has a script of its own, very much like the Tamil.

The British rule had brought about many changes in the world of Indian literature. English literature has greatly influenced the literature of all modern Indian languages. Prior to British contact, writing in prose was a neglected art, but at present poetry is suffering this fate. The novel forms an important department of the literature of all Indian languages at present. Most of these are translations of well-known novels of the West or imitations. Prose works on history, sociology, politics and philosophy are also considerable.

The publishing of magazines and newspapers is another development for which contact with the British was mainly responsible. At present every Indian language which has a script has newspapers which reach even remote villages. The arrival of the daily newspaper is awaited with great interest in village teashops and coffee houses, and discussions on international topics is the favourite hobby of young men of fashion in the village. Present Indian journalism, however, leaves much to be desired. What interests the average reader is personal attack on those in authority, and most of the lower class journals pander to this taste of the public. There are certain journals, however, which maintain a higher standard and some of these compare favourably with many of the journals of the West.

---

* Rawlinson, *India*.
† *Ibid*.

CHAPTER XI

MUSIC AND DANCING

THE Hindus are a musical people. They seem to be unable to work or worship without the aid of melody. Boatmen at the oar, peasant women in the fields, dock workers heaving a beam or girder, shepherds tending their flocks and the priest performing the Puja must sing as they work or worship. The cowboy in the Indian village has always a reed in his hand, as Krishna of old, and the countryside often resounds with the notes from his reed. The beggar in the street begs in music, and the hawker advertises his wares in songs he composes as he goes along.

Both music and dancing were scientifically studied in India from the earliest period of Indo-Aryan history. The hymns of the Vedas were chanted in a particular way, and, later, with the rise of Shaivism and Vaishnavism, music and dancing were adopted in temple worship and rituals. Most of the well-known temples of Shiva and Vishnu had a number of Devadasis attached to the temple whose main duty was to dance and sing before the idols. These girls were adopted by the temple priests in childhood and were trained by experts in the art of dancing and singing. In the medieval times they added considerably to the attraction of a temple and a good number of pilgrims used to visit the shrines for purpose other than pure worship.

In most of the temples there were regular Bhajans or Kirtans (songs addressed to the gods) by famous musicians, and some of the greatest songs of the Hindus were composed by saints who found in music full expression of their religious fervour. These saints have done not a little to give Indian music its classical background. Side by side with the religious and scientific music, there developed the song and dance of the folk, rich and varied as the multitude of races and communities Hinduism has assimilated.

MUSIC

The most ancient authority on Indian music is Bharata, whose Natya Sastra is an elaborate treatise on the twin art of dancing and music, and on drama. He is believed to have lived in the third century A.D. The author claims that his work was revealed to him by Brahma the creator and hence most sacred and infallible. There is an excellent commentary on Natya Sastra by Abhinava Gupta, a Kashmiri Brahmin who lived in the 11th century A.D. Bharata mentions other authorities on music with whose opinion he disagrees, which shows that much before his time the study of music was prevalent in the country.

From very early times to the present day, two schools of music have flourished in India: The northern school and the southern school; the latter is also called Karnataki school. Due to contact with various other races, especially the Muslims, the northern school has deviated far from the orthodox tradition but has gained much by adopting Persian forms and by allowing individuality to express itself unhampered by the choking rules of the science of music. The southern school, on the other hand, has kept up its purity of classical spirit.

The chief notes of the Saptak, as the Octave is known in India, are twelve. Of these seven are called Shuddha Swaras or sharp notes from which the other five known as Komal Swaras or flat notes are derived. By varying combinations of these twelve notes of the Octave, seventy-two Thathas or parent scales are formed. These seventy-two, in the opinion of one authority on Indian music, "can neither be increased nor decreased even by god Shiva himself."

The seven Shuddha Swaras or sharp notes are: Shadj, Rshabh, Gandhara, Maddhyam, Pancham, Dhaivat, and Nishad. The "tonic-solfa" names of these notes are Sa, Ri, Ga, Ma, Pa, Dha, Ni. For the benefit of the uninitiated, these notes are further explained to represent the characteristic sounds produced by certain animals and birds. The peacock crows in Shadj, the bull bellows in Rshabh, the goat bleats in Gandhara, the heron cries in Maddhyam, the cuckoo sings in Pancham, the horse neighs in Dhaivat and the elephant trumpets in Nishad.

The main difference between Western and Indian music is that the latter attaches more importance to melody than to harmony. The chief Ragas or melody-modes of Indian music are six and these are called Janaka Ragas or parent Ragas. But writers on Indian music found these Ragas too prosaic, aloof and masculine, and married each of them to five Raginis or female melodies. Later on when the science of music developed further, even this number did not include certain very subtle melodies and it was found necessary to bestow six sons on each of the Raginis. These sons are called Putras (literally sons). So, in all, the family consists of 216 members. All these Ragas, Raginis and Putras are derived from the 72 Thathas or parent scales we have already mentioned.

It is one thing to write with mathematical accuracy on all possible Thathas and Ragas, Raginis and Putras, but quite a different thing to sing in all these. So even the best musicians in India cannot sing in more than a hundred Raga-Ragini-Putras. Similarly, of the seventy-two Thathas or parent scales a score are more than what a musician is expected to know as those will embrace all the Ragas he will require in practice. The artists of the North have reduced Ragas and Raginis into charming paintings and have elaborate rules as to what Raga or Ragini should be sung at what time of the day and at what season of the year.

The Six Ragas are: Megha Raga, Sri Raga, Hindola Raga, Bhairava Raga, Dipaka Raga, and Kaisika Raga. Some of the well-known Raginis are: Kedara, wife of Sri Raga, Gunakali of Bhairava, Devagandhari of Hindola, Purvi of Dipaka and Kamoda again of Sri.

Each of these Ragas, Raginis and Putras are believed to possess certain essential characteristics.

Some are said to produce heat, which naturally must be sung in the cold season; others are cool melodies which may be sung on a hot day. There are, in fact, stories current in India of famous musicians who have set fire to rivers and frozen boiling water by singing the proper Raga with the required amount of intensity. Such a story is told of Naik Gopal of Akbar's time. This musician's favourite Raga was Dipaka which is believed to have fire-producing effect. The emperor wished to hear this Raga sung in the perfect manner, and commanded the Naik to sing it. The musician tried his best to avoid singing the Raga but under compulsion had to do it. He, however, took the precaution of standing in the Jumma immersed in water upto his neck. But this did not save him. As he sang the tune to perfection, flames burst forth from his body and consumed him! From Bengal comes the story of a dancing girl who, by singing the Megha Raga, produced rain and saved crops.

Similar to Tan Sen's fame in the North (Tan Sen lived under the patronage of Akbar and is believed to be the greatest musician of North India) is Thyagaraja's fame in the South. Thyagaraja was an ardent devotee of Rama, and the songs he composed in honour of that god are considered even today as the most perfect Kirtans (devotional songs) of South India. This gifted musician and saint was born in the Tanjore district in 1759; from an early age he showed a religious bent of mind and a talent for music. Though his mother-tongue was Tamil, he composed his songs in Telugu as he thought this language more suitable for composing his great songs. In the North another Vaishnava composer, Jayadeva, became equally famous, but his Gita-Govinda, singing of the love of Radha and Krishna, is marked by strong erotic tendencies. We will have occasion to deal with this work in a later chapter.

From the earliest times music was valued in India as a great art, and princes, both Hindu and Muslim, were ardent patrons of the art. For the Hindu kings music has a religious significance and they have always been munificent to musicians. Akbar, the great Moghul emperor, was particularly fond of music and some of the greatest musicians of India, like Tan Sen and Naik Gopal, lived under his patronage. Aurangazeb, however, disapproved of music. He considered life too serious a trust from God to be whiled away in singing and dancing. Shortly after his coronation, the puritanic emperor issued peremptory orders for the dismissal of all musicians, singers and dancers from the palace. The Moghul nobles and chiefs were also asked to do likewise. This threw a large number of people out of employment and these men, reduced to starvation, played a practical joke on the emperor. One day when the emperor was proceeding towards Juma Musjid, he noticed a procession of mourners carrying numerous biers towards the public cemetery. Apprehending that riots had taken place in the city, he stopped his palanquin and sent a messenger to find out the cause of the tragedy. The messenger came back with a dozen spokesmen from the crowd. They told the emperor that the procession consisted of the orphans of the Muses whom the emperor had executed and the biers contained their corpses! The grim tyrant ordered the dead to be buried deep enough to prevent their resurrection.

SOME MUSICAL INSTRUMENTS OF INDIA

Indians, as a rule, prefer stringed instruments to wind instruments. Of all stringed instruments, the Vina is a favourite of the Indian musician. Sarasvati, the goddess of music, and her son Narada, the musician of the gods, are represented in Indian art as carrying Vinas in their hands.

"The Vina is a fretted instrument of the guitar kind. The finger board is $21\frac{3}{4}$ inches long. A little beyond each end of the finger-board are two large gourds, and beyond these are the pegs and tail-piece which hold the wires. The whole length of the instrument is 3 feet 7 inches. The first gourd is fixed at 10 inches from the top, and the second is about 2 feet $11\frac{1}{2}$ inches. The gourds are very large, about 14 inches in diameter, and have a round piece cut out of the bottom, about 5 inches in diameter. The finger-board is about 2 inches wide. The wires are seven in number, and consist of two steel ones, very close together in the right side; four brass ones on the finger-board; and one brass one on the left side."*

"In shape the Vina is supposed to represent the body of goddess Parvati, by reason of the curved neck, the gourds or breasts, and the frets or bracelets".

Similar to the Vina in construction is the Sitar. It is a simpler instrument with no gourd attachment and no curved neck. Like the Vina it has seven strings, but some Sitars have sympathetic understrings which vibrate with the main strings. The Sitar is more popular in the North than in the South. The reason for this can be found in the fact that the instrument was invented by Amir Khusru, the famous musician who lived in the court of Allaudin Khilji (fourteenth century A.D.), the great Pathan king of Delhi. The Sitar is often used as an accompaniment to vocal music. But the most popular instrument used for this purpose is the Tambura. The Tambura is a stringed instrument very much like the Sitar. Its special value is in the rich droning accompaniment it supplies.

The Dilruba is very much like the Sitar, but smaller. It is popular in Bombay and the Deccan. The Sarangi is the Indian equivalent of the violin. The Sarangi is of about two feet in length and has four strings. Some Sarangis have many understrings. The Sarangi is popular with the professional and the amateur alike. Smaller than the Sarangi is the Sarinda, usually noticed in Bengal and certain other States of North India.

Of wind instruments, the flute is the most popular in India. It is the symbol of love all over India, the instrument dear to Krishna, the god of playful love, who captivated the hearts of the maids of

---

* Fawke, quoted in *Indian Music and Instruments* by Ethel Rosenthal.

Vrindavan by his irresistible notes on the flute. Krishna is usually represented in art as playing on his flute. His notes on the flute are also symbolized as the expression of God's love for humanity. As mentioned elsewhere cowherds and shepherds all over India learn to play on the flute. Serious students of music also practise on the flute, and in South India there are masters who claim to charm even birds and beasts by the perfect melodies they play on the flute.

Another wind instrument very much appreciated in the South is the Nagaswara. "The Nagaswara has twelve holes, of which seven are utilised for fingering and the remainder for the regulation of the pitch. Expert players render every variety of grace on this instrument." The Pongi provides the drone for the Nagaswara. It has only one note the pitch of which can be varied by means of the few holes bored in it. The Indian band, usually met with in street processions, either on occasions of marriage or religious festivals, consists mainly of the Nagaswara played to the accompaniment of the Pongi and a couple of small drums. The music played by the Indian band usually sounds monotonous to Europeans. This is mainly because of the fact that the great masters of India have never cared much for harmony but have always paid greater attention to melody. Hence the Indian band suffers greatly from neglect, and only third-rate musicians can be found to play in the band.

Drums are the favourite instruments of the common folk and the number and variety of them are too many to be described. The jungle folk and primitive tribes value the drum for the loud noise it makes, and much skill is not needed in making it. The Indian kettle drum, known as Nakara has been a favourite instrument with warring princes from time immemorial, and even now in temple processions it is carried in a bullock cart, two muscular men beating it with all their might. In Malabar, the drummers with trumpets lead all religious processions and the peculiar notes of the Malabar drum can be heard for a radius of two miles. All these noisy drums of course do not appeal to those with superior musical tastes. For them the Mridanga and the Tabla, which, together with the Tambura and one or two wind instruments, form the chief instruments of the Indian orchestra, appeal most. The two heads of the Mridanga are covered with parchment and are tuned by means of braces. "A mixture of flour and water is frequently applied to one head to increase the resonance, and the plaster is removed with care after each performance whereas on the other drum head 'the eye' as it is sometimes called, consisting of boiled rice, dust and juice is permanent. Similar pastes are applied to the tabla or pair of drums, which has been likened in appearance to a pair of cups, one of large and one of medium size."*

Indian musicians have been famous for their originality in producing excellent music out of seemingly unmusical objects. I have seen some players producing beautiful music by rubbing a brass vessel with a gong. Others strike brass gongs with small sticks and produce remarkably pleasant musical effect. Some Indian musicians are adepts in playing on the Jalatarang, a number of small metal bowls containing water, over which they run a stick.

DANCING

The greatest ancient authority on dancing, as on music, is Bharata. His Natya Sastra gives the fullest exposition of the art of dancing. Acting and dancing, according to Bharata, "yield the fruit of righteousness to those who follow the moral law, pleasure to those who follow lust, a restraint for the unruly, a discipline for the followers of a rule, creating vigour in the impotent, zeal in warriors, wisdom in the ignorant, learning in scholars, affording sport to kings, endurance to the sorrow stricken, profit to those who seek advantage, courage to the broken willed; replete with the diverse moods, informed with the varying passions of the soul, linked to the deeds of mankind, the best, the middling and the low, affording excellent counsel, pastime, weal and all else†". This wonderful art as already stated, was revealed to Bharata by Brahma himself. Brahma, by the way, is the theorist; the most tireless dancer of the Hindu pantheon is his compeer Shiva and the popular form in which he is worshipped in South India is as Nataraja or king of dancers.

Dancing, from the earliest times, was connected with worship in India. In Vedic rituals dancing played an important role. In later times, dancing before idols formed part of daily worship in all well-known temples. Some of the great saints of India (like Chaitanya and Thukaram) used to dance in ecstasy before idols. It is in the temple that the classical dance of India developed. In the mythology of the Hindus, the celestials have their professional dancing girls (Apsaras) and musicians (Kinnaras and Gandharvas).

In the classical dance of India, gestures and facial expressions have as great an importance as rhythm. To achieve perfection in Indian dancing, the student must undergo a rigid course of training. To provide pleasure to others, he must deny it to himself, so at least the great authors of works on dancing say. "Indian acting or dancing—the same word Natya covers both ideas—is a deliberate art. Nothing is left to chance; the actor no more yields to the impulse of the moment in gesture than in the spoken words... Precisely as the text of the play remains the same whoever the actor may be... so there is no reason why an accepted gesture language should be varied with a view to set off the actor's personality. It is the action and not the actor which is essential to dramatic art. Under these conditions, of course, there is no room for any amateur upon the stage. In fact the amateur does not exist in Oriental Art."‡ From this it should not be supposed that the actor does not count at all.

---

* E. Rosenthal, *Indian Music and its Instruments.*
† *Tandava Lakshanam.* ‡ A. K. Coomaraswamy.

The connoisseurs of Indian dancing are very particular about the figure and personal appearance of those who take to dancing. "The danseuse (Nartaki) should be very lovely, young, with full round breasts, self-confident, charming, agreeable, dexterous in handling the critical passages, skilled in steps and rhythms, quite at home on the stage, expert in gesture, with wide-open eyes, able to follow song and instruments and rhythm, adorned with costly jewels, with a charming face, neither very stout nor very thin, nor very tall nor very short."*

The Indian stage was meant exclusively for the cultured. Like the actors, the audience too were expected to know the language of gestures. As far as classical dancing is concerned even now this is the case, and those who witness Indian dancing without first mastering the meaning of gestures will derive no more pleasure out of the show than an illiterate from a highly entertaining book.

The Bharata Natya enumerates 108 Karanas (primary poses of the limbs) and 32 Anghaharas (difficult poses in which a number of Karanas are combined). The names of some of the Karanas are Talapuspaputa (flower-handful), Swastika Recita (whirling cross), Katicchhinna (split waist), Bhujanga Trasita (serpent fright), Lalita (graceful), Lata Vrischika (scorpion creeping down), Avarta (whirpool), etc., and are suggestive of the poses. Some of the Anghaharas are: Mattakrida (drunken dance), Madavilasita (dallying in lust), Parivrita Recita (circling about), Acchurita (taunting laughter), Sambhranta (bewilderment), etc. The dancer who aspired to appear on the Indian stage in ancient India had to master all the thirty-two Anghaharas and the 108 Karanas together with numerous other poses. This often meant years of training and the Indian actor or dancer truly lived for his art.

Bharata Natya (classical dancing) is an exacting and highly evolved art which only the cultured and instructed could appreciate. The common people, however, had their own dances and some of them reached a high degree of excellence and these have been adopted for the stage by well-known exponents of classical dancing.

SOME POPULAR INDIAN DANCES

Most of the folk dances of the Hindus have a religious background. It is the temple festival or some holiday that occasions dancing and singing, and naturally the theme is some episode from the Mahabharata or Ramayana. Though the themes may be the same, the genius of the different races has expressed itself in various ways. The primitive myths and legends of the various folk who were assimilated in the Indo-Aryan religious system, are clearly expressed in their folk-lore and dance, and give a diversity to the folk dances of India which cannot be found among peoples of other countries, though they may be following the same religion.

An interesting and very peculiar dance which has recently won all India fame and is being popularised even overseas is the Kathakali of Malabar. This is a pantomime dance closely following Bharata Natya for its language of gesture. The folk element is in the costume and make up with the exuberant wealth of ornamentation and details. The head-gear usually indicates whether the character is a king, sage, god or demon. The Kathakali dancer is not allowed to make a single articulate sound on the stage. He must express himself in gestures and by miming. A background of music is provided by an orchestra consisting of the Chenda (the drum peculiar to Malabar noted for its shrill sound), the Muddalam (a small drum played with the hand) which goes with the Chenda, Chengalam (gongs) and Elathalam (a pair of big cymbals); vocal music and a pair of wind instruments complete the Kathakali orchestra.

For the leisured classes of Malabar pleasure is a whole time job, and a Kathakali performance which begins shortly after sunset is continued throughout the night till dawn. "From sunset till about nine or ten o'clock the approaching performance is proclaimed for miles around by the incessant and hypnotic rhythms of the huge temple-drum, after which the full orchestra begins its overture on a stage conventionally facing south and lit with an enormous lamp holding perhaps as much as twenty seers of oil. After this overture the chorus begins, the wording of which is supposed to be in Sanskrit slokas, but is often a mixture of Sanskrit and Malayalam; then the curtain, 'Trishila,' which is beautifully decorated, is removed. The dancers appear and dance with the accompaniment of chorus and orchestra. The chorus is sung to invoke the gods and goddesses, and after their invocation, known as 'Totayam,' follows the 'Vandana slokam' in praise of the gods. Then the chief dancer enters the stage and begins the main theme."†

The theme is generally some episode from the Ramayana or the Mahabharata. Usually stories with a moral are chosen.

The control a good Kathakali dancer has over the muscles of his face must be seen to be believed. The Navarasas (the nine emotions) are most accurately portrayed by facial expressions, supported by appropriate gestures, and even the uninitiated cannot but be struck by the performance of a really good Kathakali dancer. I must, however, warn the readers against some North Indian dancers who go to Malabar for a week and come back with the claim that they have mastered Kathakali and are competent to give an exposition of it on the stage. Kathakali must be seen in Malabar with its natural background of the Malabar night, the brass lamps and other surroundings native to the art, to be appreciated fully.

One of the popular dances in which women alone take part is the (Garba). Gujarat is the home of this dance, but it is now fairly well-known all over India. The Garba is danced in honour of the goddess Durga during the Navaratri festival. During the nine days of this festival (hence Navatri) in every household in Gujarat a Garbi, or earthen pot, beautifully painted with designs, is kept in a place of honour with a wick

---

* A. K. Coomaraswamy.
† P. Banerji, *Folk Dances of India.*

burning scented oil in it. The girls carry these earthen pots on their heads and go from house to house and dance in every household, the womenfolk of the house joining them. "During the dance, the leader of the group of performers sings the first line of the Garba song, which is repeated by the rest in chorus, the whole song being accompanied by the movements of the ritual dance, and time being stressed by clapping their hands rhythmically on every 'tal' or beat. They bend sideways gracefully at every clap, the hands sweeping in beautifully formed gestures, upwards or downwards or to the side in order to make the clap." There is very little of the classical element in the Garba dance. The Kathak dance, on the other hand, is classical and is designed to appeal to the intellect as well as to the emotions.

The Rasa-lila is a popular dance of the Vaishnavas all over India. The theme is the Gopis' love for the sporting god Krishna. It is a mixed dance with one boy in the centre playing the flute and girls dancing around him. In another form of the dance, while the central figure remains the same, men and women dance in pairs around him to the accompaniment of music. Mathura, the city most sacred to Krishna, is the home of this dance, and during the many festivals held in honour of Krishna, Rasa-lila and various dances similar to it, all reminding of the loves of Krishna and the Gopis, are danced daily in this city for the entertainment of pilgrims and for the pleasure of the gods. The old prejudice against mixed dances in India led to boys dressed in women's costumes acting the part of women in Rasa-lila. While this remains still the case in the dances held in honour of the god, stage performers often employ women dancers in Rasa-lila.

Dances organized in honour of Rama and to commemorate his great victory over the demon king Ravana are known as Rama-lila, and the Diwali festival is considered the appropriate occasion for the performance of these dances. These dances are most popular in the Gangetic plain. Both the Rasa-lila and the Rama-lila dances have been evolved out of folk dances, the former, however, being adopted nowadays for the classical stage.

Of all the folk of India, the Manipuris inhabiting the North-East Frontier are the most jovial, and rhythm loving.

The Manipuris are worshippers of Krishna and every village has a temple dedicated to this god of love, dance and song. Attached to the temple is the inevitable dance hall for celebrating the love-dances of Krishna during festivals held in honour of him. The Manipuri dancers pay particular attention to costumes; beautiful, many coloured skirts, tight jackets, necklaces, bangles and an ornamented headgear form the principal costume of the girls who play the part of the Gopis. In Rasa-lila dances, the Gopis are matched by a Krishna adorned with a yellow dhotie below the waist, a bare trunk and a beautiful crown crested with peacock feathers.

The Lai-haroba (merry-making of the gods) of the Manipuris is of primitive origin, pointing to the times when they were animists, not yet assimilated into the Hindu fold. "The dances are performed in the open space before the temple; and although the occasion is one of religious solemnity, it is nevertheless marked by a good deal of merry-making and fun... The celebrations begin with a dance offering of fruit and flowers, performed by gaily dressed girls, who are led by the 'maibis,' priestesses of the older religion. This having been performed, the youths select dance partners from among the girls for the ensuing entertainment. The more expert dancers assume the lead, and they dance the story of Khamba and Thaibi, the tale of the love of a poor but noble youth for a princess, a story of which there are versions in the folklore of every land."*

The Chow dances of Orissa are a series of dances performed for a number of days in honour of Shiva during the annual festival of this god. The festivities last for a week. "The traditional patrons of these dances are the Maharajahs of Seraikala and even the members of the royal family take part in the dance. The themes are religious, drawn from the mythology of the Shaivas. Some of the dances of the Chow series are the Tandava depicting the mad grief of Shiva on his consort's immolating herself in fire, the Mayura or the peacock dance, and the Sabara or hunter's dance." All these three dances of the Orissans have been adopted for the classical stage and are usually performed by well-known exponents of Indian dance.

Many of the wild tribes of India, like the Nagas of the North-East Frontier and the Bhils, have dance festivals in which war dances form the chief attraction. The Nagas especially have war-like and barbarous costumes and adorn themselves with such doubtful embellishments as skulls and bison horns. Actual hurling of spears takes place in these dances. Wild men, by the way, are not the only people who indulge in war dances. Almost all the communities of India have some kind of war dances or other. The Punjab, Bengal, Deccan and South India have their own war dances, each one peculiar to the traditions and legends of the people.

More primitive than the war dances of hill tribes, are the devil dances of the low classes of South India. The devil dances are connected with witchcraft, and are performances meant to exorcise evil spirits. "The possessing Yakshas or demons are summoned by the beating of drums and the highly complex gestures of the dance, and when their invocation is complete, are commanded to depart from the body of the affected person. Every gesture of this violent and somewhat terrifying ritual has a special significance, and even the slightest change in the prescribed ritual would violate the efficacy of the spell. The remarkable position of the thumb and first finger of the dancers' bejewelled right hands are particularly important."† A good deal of yelling accompanies this dance, and the dancers at times carry pots of burning fire on their heads or torches in their hands. Night, naturally,

* P. Banerji, *Folk Dances of India.*
† Ibid.

is the most favourable time for the performance of the devil dance.

Although music and dancing are believed to have been originated and patronised by gods themselves, professional musicians and dancers have been held in contempt by the Hindus especially in the middle ages. Manu, the law-giver speaks of them as persons not fit to be associated with decent Aryans. In the mythology of the Hindus the Apsaras and Gandharvas (celestial dancers and musicians) are depicted as "impure persons" inhabiting the mountains and valleys bordering on the celestial regions, and in matters moral they are a law unto themselves. This low social status of professional dancers and musicians has given rise to a caste among the Hindus known as the dancers, whose main occupation is to provide pleasure to men not only by singing and dancing but by abandoning their persons also.

Even at the time of the author of the Natya Sastra, the status of dancers was not high. The Natya Sastra mentions that the progeny of the sage to whom the art of dancing was revealed degenerated the art and fell under the curse of celestial saints. The dancers thus lost their high social position and were condemned to "eke out a living by their women and children." The Natya Sastra says that even the art was cursed by the saints, but on being addressed on the matter they cancelled the curse as far as the art was concerned, but the lot of the dancers had to remain the same.

The institution of Devadasis, it must be mentioned, did nothing to elevate the social position of dancers. These dancers of the temple degenerated into mere prostitutes and their quarters adjoining the temple into brothels. Chastity among the Hindus was a virtue of the women of the three higher castes, and among the women of some of the other classes and the unowned Devadasis, prostitution was, if anything, encouraged by the State and the Temple. We are, perhaps, unduly harsh on the Hindus; dancers all over the world have held a low social position and even in the highly civilised nations of the West, respectable people fight shy of sending their daughters to act on the stage or for the screen. All the blame for this, however, does not appear to lie with society. The conduct and behaviour of professional actors and dancers have also something to do with it.

Of the professional Nautch girls of India, the best known are those of Uttar Pradesh. These dancing girls have combined in themselves the traditions of the Hindus and the Muslims. Some of the Europeans who have seen the performances of these girls have paid them high compliments. Says one: "I thought I could dance, but compared with your girls, I know nothing." Again, "it should be understood that the dance women of India pique themselves entirely on the gracefulness of their positions and motions. They have no variety of steps, the feet being kept parallel and close; one foot advancing or moving only a few inches, and the other always following it. This, however, is done with remarkable exactness as to time, which, on all occasions, is regulated by the instruments played by men attached to the set." For the most difficult feat which the Nautch girls have to perform is the walk. "The perfect walk is the ne plus ultra of the Nautch, and to watch a Nautchwali glide effortlessly across the floor is the personification of art."*

---

* Quoted in *Folk Dances of India*, by P. Banerji.

LXXXIX

195 LESSONS IN STICK FIGHTING
(India Pictorial Features)

196 A MEDITATING DEVOTEE
(Photo: B. F. Ferreira)

197 THE CEREMONIAL OIL BATH
(Photo: S. S. Aiyar)

198 THE BANGLE CEREMONY
(Photo: B. F. Ferreira)

199 GANESHA BEING WORSHIPPED ON GANESHA CHATURTHI DAY
(India Pictorial Features)

200 EXHIBITION OF DOLLS IN A HINDU HOME FOR NAVARATRI FESTIVAL
(India Pictorial Features)

201 A BRAHMIN BOY LEARNING SACRIFICIAL DUTIES
(India Pictorial Features)

XCI

203 A SADHU AT A WAYSIDE SHRINE
(Photo: Stanley Jepson)

202 DURGA TAKEN IN PROCESSION IN A CAR:
DASARA CELEBRATIONS
(National News Photo Service)

XCII

204 NAGA, A SERPENT DEITY
(*Journal of Indian Art and Industry*)

205 NAGPANCHAMI, FESTIVAL OF SERPENTS
(Rousslet's *India*)

206 MENDICANT ADORNED WITH LEMON GARLANDS
(India Pictorial Features)

XCIII

207   A CARTMAN WORSHIPPING HIS BULLOCKS
AND THE CART ON NAVARATRI DAY
(India Pictorial Features)

208   A NAYAR GIRL, MALABAR
(Photo: Stanley Jepson)

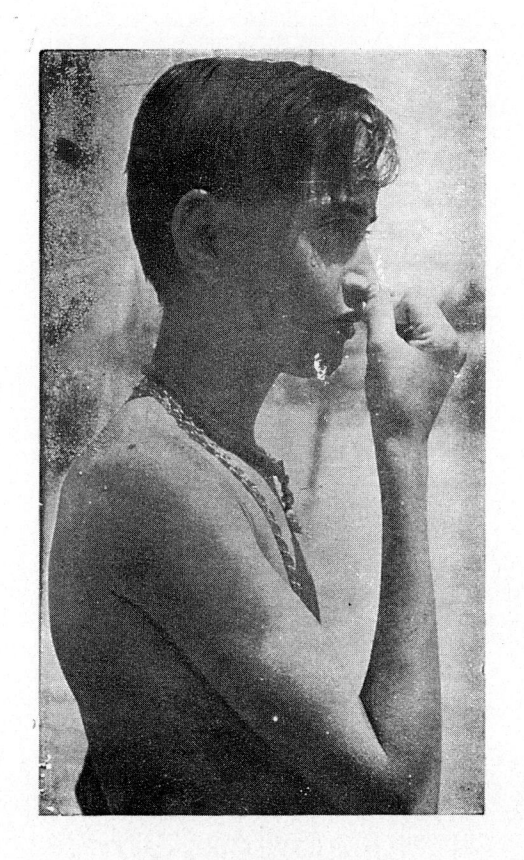

209   SANDHYA PRAYERS
(India Pictorial Features)

210   GANESHA BEING CARRIED IN PROCESSION FOR
IMMERSION
(Photo: Stanley Jepson)

XCIV

212 DECORATED IMAGES BEING TAKEN IN PROCESSION
(Photo: S. S. Aiyar)

211 RATI, GODDESS OF LOVE
(Belur. Photo: India Pictorial Features)

XCV

213 CHANGING OF THE SACRED THREAD
(India Pictorial Features)

214 BRASS LAMP WITH FIGURE OF GANESHA ON THE RIM OF RECEPTACLE FOR OIL
(Journal of Indian Art and Industry)

215 MAKING CAKES OF COW DUNG FOR FUEL
(India Pictorial Features)

216 WHITE CLAY FOR SALE
THE CLAY IS USED BY VAISHNAVAS FOR PUTTING CASTE MARKS
(India Pictorial Features)

217 DOMESTIC WORSHIP OF SHIVA AS THE LINGAM
(India Pictorial Features)

218 A VILLAGE GOD MADE OF CLAY
(India Pictorial Features)

219 GIVING ALMS OF COOKED RICE
(Photo: S. S. Aiyar)

CHAPTER XII

ARCHITECTURE, SCULPTURE AND PAINTING

VEDIC Aryans were nomads who were constantly on the move in search of pastures for their flocks. Hence their habitations had nothing permanent about them. In course of time they subdued the original inhabitants of India and began to settle down in the counrty. Villages grew into towns and towns into cities, when city planning and architecture became a necessity. The houses, temples and palaces in those early days were built of wood. This was certainly not due to lack of knowledge of more permanent building material. For the Indus valley civilisation that preceded the Indo-Aryan, was noted for its buildings in bricks. The racial arrogance of the Aryans probably forbade them to borrow anything from the peoples they conquered. We know that the Mongols under Chengiz Khan disdained to build cities but loved to destroy fortresses and castles and preferred their tents to palaces. It was probably a similar spirit that prompted the ancient Indo-Aryans to use wood as building material in preference to stone and bricks.

In Vedic India the carpenter held a high place of honour. He constructed the altars on which the priest-king performed his sacrifices, and the carpenter's craft was believed to have been inspired by the gods themselves.

The earliest structural work in masonry was connected with the rise of Buddhism. Stone was at first used exclusively for buildings meant for worship. The earliest form of Indo-Aryan religious buildings was the Buddhist Stupa. The Stupa was unpretentious in construction. It was a circular tumulus of brick erected to enshrine some relic of the Buddha. The idea of the Stupa was no doubt existent before Asoka, but it was this emperor who decided to adopt it as a permanent structure to commemorate the Master's life and works. He had them erected in many parts of India; the Stupa was the principal structure in a number of buildings constituting a Buddhist monastery, and it was a centre of pilgrimage as well as a shrine of daily worship.

Most of the monuments of early Buddhism have either been destroyed or fallen into ruins, and very little remains at present of the ancient glory of Buddhism. No Stupa has come down to us as a living shrine, but a number of them have been discovered in the ruins of ancient cities or excavated from debris and accumulation of rubbish. Of such Stupas, the one at Sanchi deserves particular mention. The Stupa at Sanchi (in the present Madhya Pradesh) consists in fact of two Stupas, one designed to enshrine the other. The original Stupa was a small affair believed to have been built by the emperor Asoka in the 3rd century B.C. A century later, the shrine gained so much importance that it was necessary to have it enlarged. It was a sacrilege to demolish a living shrine, and when the Stupa was enlarged Asoka's brick tumulus was not removed but enclosed in a bigger structure of similar appearance. The diameter of the Stupa as it stands at present is 120 ft. and its height 54 ft. Circumambulation of the shrine was the principal act of worship performed by devotees, and for this purpose every Stupa had an ambulatory passage built round it. This Medhi, as it is called, of Sanchi is 16 ft. above the ground built round the Stupa with railings for protection. The Medhi is reached by a double stairway on the southern side. At the crest of the dome is a square structure known as the Harmika or pedestal which supported the triple umbrella (the insignia of royalty) which adorned every Stupa signifying the universal sway of the Buddha.

The Sanchi Stupa is enclosed in a railing of stone and there are four gateways at the four cardinal points. The prodigality of the embellishments of the gateways must be seen to be believed. Each of the gateways consists of "two square upright posts 15 feet high, prolonged vertically and connected above by three separate lintels between each of which is a row of ornamental balusters. The total height of this erection is some 34 ft. with a width of 20 ft. at the broadest part. When it is understood that the thickness of the whole averages only two feet and that it stands alone without any struts or similar support, it is a matter for astonishment that any of these gateways should have remained in position for some two thousand years. Few portals in any style of architecture can excel the array of rich symbolism and imagery which has been portrayed with such dramatic intensity on the Sanchi toranas (gateways), the result entirely of Indian tradition and genius."*

The pillars Asoka had erected for publishing his edicts also deserve mention. These were monoliths with exceedingly polished surfaces on which were carved the edicts of the emperor. Each pillar was a free-standing monolith with no supporting base but rising from the ground and tapering towards the top with a capital signifying some Buddhistic symbol. The pillar with capital often rose to a height of fifty feet from the ground. Asoka had erected some thirty of these pillars in various parts of his empire, mainly in places of pilgrimage or highways where people used to congregate. A few of these pillars are still existent, while the capitals of many others have been found.

Along with structural architecture, the early Buddhists developed what is known as the rock cut architecture. The idea was simple: to hew out of living rock, caves, Stupas and cells for purposes of worship and meditation, and as residences for the monastic communities. The cave with its darkness and mystery has a perennial appeal to the religious.

---

* Percy Brown, *Indian Architecture*.

and to the essential mysticism of Indian religions nothing could be dearer than cave temples and monasteries. Of the many cave monasteries of the Buddhists those of Ajanta (in Maharashtra State) and Karli (near Bombay) are the most important. The two majestic pillars at the entrance of the Karli cave are each fifty feet in height. The main hall of the cave is 124 ft. long, 46½ ft. wide and 45 ft. in height. Besides this main hall there are numerous cells for the monks, corridors and passages for the pilgrims. The pillars and walls are adorned with sculptures of no mean artistic merit, and the whole place is superbly designed to inspire awe and religious emotion. "There can be nothing but admiration for those who, urged by their passionate devotion for the Great Teacher could conjure out of the bare hillside such a majestically imposing and at the same time supremely artistic place of worship." The Karli caves were excavated and completed in the first century B.C.

Of later origin than the Karli cave but more famous are the cave temples and monasteries of Ajanta. The site chosen for the excavation of these caves is exceedingly beautiful and romantic. The rocky hillside out of which the caves were hewn, overlooks a pretty stream and commands a beautiful view of the country. The Ajanta group consists of a series of Viharas or monasteries and Chaityas or halls of worship which extend to over a third of a mile. There are in all twenty-eight of these halls and monasteries and they are numbered in serial order from west to east. These caves were not planned by a single person but grew out of the needs of the religious community that chose the site as a monastery some two hundred years before the beginning of the Christian era. Some of the caves belong to the Hinayana or Puritanic phase of Buddhism and others to the later Mahayana or theistic phase. The work of the last group of caves was completed in the seventh century A.D. under the famous Chalukyan king Pulakesin II. Shortly after, the country was invaded by the Pallava king Narasimhavarman and in the confusion that followed this event, Ajanta caves were abandoned.

Rock cut architecture reached its final phase in Ellora, where magnificent temples of exceptionally skilled workmanship were carved out of huge monoliths and were, to all outward appearances, as well proportioned and even more beautiful than some of the famous structural temples. The rock cut form of architecture, originated by the Buddhists, was adapted by the Hindus who even improved upon it as the temples of Ellora clearly show. From the rocky hillside at Ellora the workmen hewed out sixteen temples extending for the distance of half a mile, thus turning a dead and uncouth hillock into a fairy land. The most important of these temples are Kailasa or Shiva's paradise, Ravana-ka-khai or the abode of Ravana, Dasa Avatara or the ten incarnations of Vishnu, Rameshwara or god Rama, Sita's Nani or Sita's bath. Of all these, the Kailasa temple is considered a marvel of rock cut architecture.

The Kailasa combines in itself the style of the Buddhists and of the Dravidians. It is believed to have been executed in the reign of Krishna I (eight century A.D.), the Rashtrakuta monarch who subjugated the Western Chalukyas. The temple is sculpture on a grand scale rather than architecture. What the workmen did was to cut into the hillside three deep trenches about fifty feet wide, each at right angles to the adjoining one and reaching down to the base of the hill, obtaining by this operation a solid piece of rock 200 feet in length, 100 feet in width and 100 feet in height, surrounded on three sides by courtyards (the trenches) and the fourth side open to the country. Out of this solid rock was carved out the Kailasa temple.

The temple itself is composed of the entrance gateway, a small shrine of Nandi (Shiva's bull) and the main shrine. "Much of the imposing character of this portion of the composition (the main shrine) is obtained by the lofty and substantial plinth, which is twenty-five feet high, and at first sight has the appearance of a ground story. Above and below, the structure is heavily moulded, while the central space of the sides is occupied by a grand frieze of boldly carved elephants and lions. Standing high on this plinth is the temple proper, approached by flights of steps leading to a pillared porch on its western side and it is here that its designers rose to the greatest heights. There is no pronounced departure from the conventional combination of the mandapa (hall) and the vimana (the cell enshrining the idol) but the manner in which the various architectural elements, all definite and sharply outlined, such as cornices, pilasters, niches and porticos, have been assembled in an orderly and artistic manner to form a unified whole, is masterly. Then over all rises the stately tower in three tiers, with its prominently projecting gable front, and surmounted by a shapely cupola, reaching up to a total height of ninety-five feet. But this is not all. Around the wide space of the platform at the base of the vimana, five subsidiary shrines have been fashioned out of the rock, each an elegant reproduction to a reduced scale of the main theme, to which they serve as a refrain."*

On the walls or rock surrounding the courtyard are cloisters for the dwelling of the priests and temple dignitaries. There are two free standing pillars with capitals on either side of the Nandi shrine. All told, "the temple of Kailasa of Ellora is not only the most stupendous single work of art executed in India but as an example of rock-architecture it is unrivalled. Standing within its precincts and surrounded by its grey and hoary pavilions, one seems to be looking through into another world, not a world of time and space, but one of intense spiritual devotion expressed by such an amazing artistic creation hewn out of the earth itself."

* Percy Brown, *Indian Architecture.*

SOME NORTH INDIAN TEMPLES

Compared to the gigantic temples of South India, which we shall describe presently, North India, where Hinduism established itself long before its journey to the South, is sadly devoid of ancient or medieval buildings of outstanding beauty or magnificence. The reason for this is not the want of architectural genius on the part of the Hindus of the north, but rather the iconoclastic zeal of early invaders.

We know for a fact that a flourishing school of architecture and sculpture existed in the north-west of India, known as the Gandhara school, in which the Indian and Hellenic ideals met and fused; and it is quite probable that many temples built in this style were destroyed by invaders, especially as the Punjab and the North-West Frontier lay in their direct route. Besides the Gandhara school there was a pure Indo-Aryan school of art and architecture, the chief centre of which was Muthra. This city became famous for its magnificent structures, and Mahmud of Ghazni, iconoslast as he was, was profoundly affected by the beautiful temples of the city and wrote home to Persia that it was with the greatest reluctance that he destroyed the city. The celebrated temple of Somnath in Gujarat, which too he destroyed, contained many wonders of which we know but little at present.

Although most of the ancient and important temples of the north have been lost to us, there are still a few especially in Orissa, Central and Western India, which have much that is admirable in them.

The structural temples of the Hindus have a definite plan. The most important part of the temple is the sanctuary called Vimana, for the enshrinement of the idol. The idol is installed in a cella inside the Vimana and this cella is known as Garbha Graha or 'the womb.' The upper part of the sanctuary rises into a pyramid or tapering tower called Sikhara. The Garbha Graha is entered by a doorway to its east, towards which side the idol usually faces. In front of the doorway is the Mandapa or pavilion for the worshippers. Some of the temples have a Pradikshana Patha or processional passage around the Vimana as circumambulation of the sanctuary often forms part of worship. These essential features of the structural temples of the Hindus vary according to the size and location of the temple, but all the better class temples are constructed on this plan.

The group of temples at Bhuvaneswar in Orissa are much valued for their architectural excellence. The most important temple in this group is the Lingaraja or Great Temple dedicated to Shiva. The outstanding feature of the Lingaraja temple is the stately tower built over the Sri Mandir or Vimana. The base of the tower measures some 56 feet inside. It rises vertically to a height of about 50 feet when the contours of the structure begin to incline slightly inwards and produces, at the height of 125 feet, the neck of the tower over which "is the ponderous fluted disc or amila sila, supported by sedent gryphons, the whole being crowned by a vase-shaped finial (Kalasa) bearing the trisula or trident of Shiva." The total height of the tower from the ground to the Trisula is 150 feet. The Lingaraja temple was built in the tenth century A.D.

Another important temple of Orissa is the shrine of Jagannath in Puri. This is a famous centre of pilgrimage for the Vaishnavas but the structure is not architecturally beautiful.

The famous temple of the sun-god at Konarak in Orissa speaks of an obsolete cult now not publicly practised. The structural peculiarity of this shrine is that it is built mainly of blocks of laterite without the use of mortar. The blocks are held together by a system of poise and balance, "the weight of one stone acting against the pressure of another, much of the stability being a matter of balance and equilibrium." The temple was built in the thirteenth century A.D., but was abandoned for some unknown reason. At present there is an annual feast at the temple for which pilgrims from various parts of the country flock to the place after which the site is again deserted till the festival starts again the next year.

A group of shrines almost as famous as those of Bhuvaneswar, are the Khajuraho temples of central India. These temples were built in the 10th century A.D. and the group consists of a dozen temples, none of them of imposing dimensions. The largest is the Kanderiya Mahadev temple dedicated to Shiva, and it is only 109 feet in length, 60 feet in width and 116 feet in height. But the Khajuraho temples are not admired for their dimensions but for their architectural and sculptural excellence. Their spires are considered the most refined and elegant of their kind and the sculptures are on a lavish scale, the ideals of the flesh and blood school predominating over the mystic. The erotic scenes, a marked feature of the Khajuraho sculptures are, from an aesthetic point of view, some of the most beautiful in India.

In Gujarat and Western India there were magnificent temples but most of them are now in ruins. Efforts were made to repair and reconstruct the famous shrine of Somnath Mahmud of Ghazni had destroyed; but in spite of the recent, determined efforts of well-known Indians in the matter, the temple has not regained its lost glory nor its original appearance. Of other great temples of Western India, now in ruins, mention may be made of the Surya temple at Modhera and the Rudramala temple of Siddhapur, both in Gujarat. Gujarat and Western India were strongholds of the Jains for many centuries and they have numerous temples to their credit in this part of India. But Jain architecture has few outstanding features that distinguish it from the architecture of the Buddhists and the Hindus. The Jain temple of Vimala, at Mount Abu in Rajasthan, however, deserves particular mention as it is one of the few structures of the period that have come down to us intact. This temple is dedicated to Adinath, the first Thirthankara of the Jains, and was built in the 11th century A.D. It is a structure in white marble measuring 98 feet long and 42 feet wide with a courtyard, at the sides of which are cells for the monks to dwell. There is little ornamentation on the exterior of the temple, but the interior is full of sculptures depicting scenes from Jain mythology. "The Vimala temple is a notable achievement, its fame resting not so much on its architecture which has few conspicuous virtues, but on the infinite caprice and inventiveness of its sculptured decoration which seems to be a reflection of the intense religious fervour then existing among the Jain community."

TEMPLES OF SOUTH INDIA AND THE DECCAN

The Dravidians were great builders, and there is nothing in North India now existing to compare with the great temples that have risen under the Pallavas, Cholas and the Pandyas. The temple in South India occupied the central place in city planning. The four main streets of the city took off from the principal gateways of the temple and the area surrounding the temple naturally formed the busiest part of the city. The temple was, and in many parts of the country still is, the centre of life in a South Indian city.

Of all the great temples built in what is known as the Dravidian style, the temple of Meenakshi (fish-eyed) wife of Shiva, at Madura is the greatest and most famous. The Madura temple is a double shrine, one dedicated to Meenakshi and the other to her consort, built inside a larger shrine. The main temple is enclosed in a wall about 850 feet by 725, and at the centre of each wall is a Gopuram (pyramidical structure built over the gateway) which is a distinctive feature of Dravidian temple architecture. The main entrance is by the eastern gateway "which communicates with a fine pillared avenue two hundred feet long and nearly one hundred feet wide. This leads directly to a smaller Gopuram, forming the eastern entrance to the second Prakaram, a rectangular enclosure measuring 420 feet by 310 feet, also having four gateways, one in the middle of each side, but all smaller than the preceding. Most of this second enclosure is covered in with a flat roof, but is partly open on the northern side. Within, there is again another covered court, its sides 250 feet by 160 feet, and with only one entrance, a doorway on the east. Only so far are the uninitiated allowed to proceed, but it is outside this entrance, in what may be termed the nave and transept of the temple that the most elaborate part of the scheme and most intricate grouping of pillars are to be found."* The Madura temple was built in the seventeenth century A.D. and marks the final phase of the Dravidian style. The prominence given to the Gopurams, which, in a South Indian temple, dominates the countryside for miles around, appears to be a later development, earlier temples having towers built over the Vimana or sanctuary. The great temple of Tanjore built under the Cholas in the 11th century A.D. is a conspicuous example of this. The tower of the Tanjore temple is considered the "finest single creation of the Dravidian craftsman, ...also a touch-stone of Indian architecture as a whole."

The largest South Indian temple, larger than the Madura temple but less compact and unified, is the great Vaishnava temple of Srirangam. It is a meandering structure, built during many centuries and completed by the seventeenth century A.D. The outermost wall protecting the group of buildings is a rectangle measuring 2,880 feet by 2,475 feet, "enclosing an area of over half a square mile, and including, large and small and also unfinished, 21 Gopurams, 13 of which may be seen in an axial line of the temple from one point of view." The main architectural features of the temple are the "hall of thousand pillars," a flat-roofed structure 500 feet by 160 feet, and "the horse court" within, containing 900 carved granite monoliths. "Considering the amount of labour expended in this hypostyle hall, it is a somewhat uninspiring production."

Conjeevaram and Chidambaram are other temple cities of the South, the former a stronghold of Vaishnavism and the latter of Shaivism. The temples, though large and famous, are similar to other Dravidian temples, differing only in details. In fact, all Dravidian temples conform to the same style, and to a layman they may all look alike. The temple at Rameswaram, however, is a notable exception. The distinctive feature of this temple is the pillared corridor which completely surrounds the whole temple and forms avenues leading up to it. The aggregate length of the corridor is calculated to be 3,000 ft. "The breadth of these fine columned passages varies from seventeen feet to twenty-one feet, and their height from floor to roof is about twenty-five feet. Richly decorated pillars of good proportions and closely set, continue along the entire length, each pillar being twelve feet in height and rising from a moulded stylobate five feet high. In almost every direction, therefore, there is an unending perspective of columned halls those on the north and south sides being particularly effective as they are over 700 feet in length."†

The temples described above are all living shrines where images are worshipped as of old, and pilgrims and devotees come daily with their offerings to the gods. In these temples can still be heard the blowing of the sacred conch, the chimes of bells, Kirtans and Bhajans performed to the accompaniment of wind instruments; and shaven priests can still be seen attending to the needs of the idol, and an unending stream of devotees daily come in and go out of the shrine.

There are, however, a few temples in the South which have been deserted but deserve mention on account of their architectural excellence. Of these the most noteworthy are the temples of Belur, Halabid and Somnathpur in the modern Mysore state, built in what is known as the Chalukyan style which combines in

---

* P. Brown, *Indian Architecture*.
† *Ibid.*

itself the technique of the Dravidians and the Indo-Aryans. Early specimens of this style are believed to be the temples of Aihole and Badami built in the seventh or eighth centuries of the Christian era. The Chalukyans were masters of the Deccan during this period and their influence lasted in this region for a number of centuries.

Of the three temples mentioned above, Halabid is the most important. The glory of Halabid is not in its proportions or architectural excellence but in the sculptures that adorn it. The Chalukyans appear to have been liberal patrons of art but the sculptures at Halabid are so profuse that connoisseurs accuse the originators of the Halabid plan as lacking in restraint. All the fourteen worlds of Hindu mythology and the beings that inhabit them are sculptured on the walls of the temples of Halabid. As if this were not enough, scenes from the Mahabharata and Ramayana are also represented.

The temples of Halabid, Belur and Somnathpur were built between the 11th and 13th century A.D. and they have the appearance of unfinished structures. This may be due to some calamity which usually overtakes an Indian king unawares; or the work might have been completed but later destroyed by some iconoclast.

Before leaving the subject of South Indian temples, mention must be made of the famous Seven Pagodas built by the Pallavas. These are a group of eight monoliths, known as Rathas carved out of granite and having the appearance of small temples. These Rathas are not isolated shrines, but form part of a group of temples, structural and rock-cut, which were probably the pride of the city, in the prime of its life. The site is Mamallapuram at the mouth of the Palar river, now a deserted spot. In the eighth century A.D. Mamallapuram was probably a flourishing port teeming with population, from where Indian artists and architects embarked for distant Java and Bali and carried to these islands the ideals and forms of Indian art.

The reader may rightly wonder why no mention has so far been made of any secular buildings. The answer is that there is no secular building of any antiquity that has come down to us. The Hindus were content to live in hovels and gaze in admiration at the stupendous houses of their gods. Even kings were no exception to this rule. No palace of a king survived his dynasty. There appears to have been a convention among the Hindus that only gods should have houses of stone erected for them. Hence palaces of kings and nobles were usually built of wood and brick, and few of these have survived the ravages of time. Only after Muslim domination became permanent did Hindu princes begin to build their palaces in sandstone and marble after the manner of the Muslims, and a few of these palaces still exist. But there is nothing distinctive about the architecture of these palaces and none of them even remotely approaches in grandeur the stately palaces of the Moghuls in Delhi, Agra, Lahore and other cities.

The faith that had inspired the great temples of the middle ages seems to have died out among the Hindus. The commercial and utilitarian spirit of the West has invaded India too. After the British occupation no temple of even moderate size has risen in India. The architects and workmen who built into the sky the gigantic Gopurams of Madura and the lofty spires of the Orissan temples, and the patient toilers who carved out of the living rock the marvellous temples of Ellora have disappeared for good. The modern buildings of India are dedicated to commerce, industry and convenience and have very little to distinguish them from similar buildings in the West. In fact, it is the West that now sets up the standard in architecture for India, and Indian architects closely study the styles of the West and follow them.

SCULPTURE

Indian sculpture is as old as the country itself. The earliest specimens of sculpture that have come down to us are works of the sculptors of the Indus valley civilization. The torso of a statuette of red stone discovered at Harappa shows remarkable artistic merit and speaks well of the artist's knowledge of human anatomy. The effort has been evidently to copy nature and not to idealize. Another torso of a statuette of grey slate, also discovered at Harappa, suggests a slender figure of a dancer probably of Shiva, the Dancer, who seems to have been the popular deity of the Indus valley people. A bronze figurine of a dancing girl discovered at Mohen-jo-daro completes the list of the three great art-treasures, so far unearthed, which depict the human form by the Indus valley craftsmen.

Nor was the human body the only subject that interested the artists of the Indus valley. Numerous seals and terracotta impressions unearthed at Mohenjo-daro and Harappa show skilful representations of animal and plant life, and of celestial beings. The plastic art of the Indus valley, according to one authority, "is mainly conspicuous for its ponderosity and its naturalism, i.e., innervation. Animals chiefly, but also trees, with their sinuous stems suggestive of vegetation, occupy exalted positions. Associated and combined with them, the human figure becomes divine. It also transcends human limits by such devices as multiple heads and limbs, indicative of superhuman potentialities. In the case of animals with multiple heads, super-animalic potentialities are suggested. Nature and the supernatural are experienced as dynamically connected."

Passing from the little known Indus valley civilisation to the art of the Indo-Aryans, the Buddhists were, as in architecture, pioneers in sculpture. The themes that interested the Buddhists were, naturally, the Buddha and his life. Episodes from the Buddha's life and scenes from the Jataka tales were favourite subjects for decorative art, and the lintels of gateways and railings of Stupas were profusely adorned with such sculptures. But the subject that attracted the artist most was the figure of the Buddha himself. As a result of efforts of probably centuries, the Buddhist sculptor succeeded in perfecting the figure of the Blessed One as conceived by the sages of Buddhism. For supreme calmness born of the perfect union of the soul and body, and for a suggestion of divine imperturbability there is nothing in the world of art to excel some of the seated images of the Buddha of Indian art.

The Greek ideal of mere muscular strength did not appeal to the Buddhist sculptors. The body of the Buddha was certainly human, and the early Buddhists did not try to produce an effect of divinity by giving him extra arms and heads as the Hindus did later when they sculptured images of their gods. What they did was to give him a perfect body as evolved through Yoga, neither too muscular nor too smooth, but conforming to the conventional Indian standard of a deep leonine chest, slender waist and erect pose. The divine touch was given by a majestic calmness of expression, and a poise suggestive of illimitable energy ready to break forth at any time.

The Buddhists, though pessimists, were moralists and not ascetics. Hence they did not believe that an emaciated body necessarily enshrined an exalted soul. Yet one sculpture of the Buddha as an ascetic has come down to us. It may be mentioned that while undergoing the various conventional methods of enlightenment advocated by the Hindus of the time, the Buddha once tried asceticism to find out a solution to the mystery of life. The statue in question depicts this phase of his search after truth, but it is a horrible piece intended by the sculptor to be a caricature and a warning.

Some of the statues of the Buddha discovered in the north-western regions of India show clear traces of Greek influence. As we have seen in an earlier chapter, the Greeks ruled over this part of India for quite a long period, and they exercised considerable influence on the life of the people even after their departure from India. But as far as sculpture was concerned, the Indian never gave up his cherished ideals for the cult of the Greeks who were worshippers of physical beauty. The Greek had to remain content with having his own way about the head-dress, wrapper and other external adornments of the Buddha, but the "barbarian" was not allowed to touch the person of the Blessed One. In fact many schools of Buddhist sculpture have flourished in various parts of the country, but any good statue of the Buddha, of whatever school, will show the essential qualities of the Blessed One.

With the rise of the Mahayana or theistic Buddhism, the mythology of the Buddhists grew richer and artists found many themes to work on. The Buddha was exalted to the position of the god of gods, and his doings in the various heavens, the might of his bodyguards, the various gods and goddesses who interceded on behalf of humans, supplied plenty of material for the imagination of the sculptors to work on. Thus we find statues of Kubera, the bodyguard of the Buddha, and of his wife Hariti, of the famous goddess Tara, the madonna of the Buddhists, and of numerous gatekeepers and sentries, sculptured on the walls, gateways, and halls of Buddhistic shrines. No artist is, however, entirely content to depict the gods only; ordinary men and women, animal and plant life also interested the Buddhist sculptor and on the railings and gateways of the Stupas of Sanchi, Amaravati, Barhut and other ancient centres of Buddhism, scenes depicting the life of the common folk, and carvings of animals and trees are occasionally met with. The Jataka tales deal with various lives of the Buddha, mostly in the animal kingdom, and hence the sculptors of animals had to study their subjects as part of their religious duty and many of the carvings of the beasts show an intimate knowledge of the anatomy of animals and their ways of life. The lion capitals of some of the Asokan pillars speak very highly of the skill of Mauryan sculptors.

The art of the Buddhists was highly symbolic, and one who knows the mystic signs and language of gestures is able to see more in a well-executed piece of sculpture than the uninitiated can.

While the Buddhists excelled in chiselling out of granite the majesty of stillness, the Hindu sculptors aimed at achieving perfection in depicting in stone the poetry and terror of motion. They too have ideals of stillness and even inactivity in their religion. The ascetic Shiva practising meditation in his mountain abode of Kailas is a figure as still and majestic as the Buddha. But it is not this Shiva that interested the Hindu sculptor, but Shiva, the dancer of the gods, dancing either for grief of his lost spouse or for joy of conquest over his foes. The motif of the dancing Shiva was most popular with the sculptors of South India and some of their figures in stone and metal are masterpieces of Indian art.

Krishna, the popular dancer of the Vaishnavas, was a favourite subject for the sculptors of the North. The youthful Krishna sporting with his favourite Gopi Radha, and the boy Krishna dancing on the hood of the evil serpent Kaliya are popular themes. Krishna is generally depicted as playing on his flute, standing with one foot crossed over the other suggesting a poise of graceful rhythm. Sculptures of the child Krishna and his mother are also common.

The Hindus, again, like the Buddhists, rejected the ideal of mere muscular strength, but sculptured the bodies of Shiva and Krishna as gracefully evolved through dancing and rhythm — neither too muscular nor too effeminate, but of slender waist, deep chest and smooth limbs. In fact, the bodies of some of the male figures may easily be mistaken for those of females but for the absence of breasts.

Of the goddesses of the pantheon, the wife of Shiva in her various manifestations appears to have interested the sculptor most. Images of this goddess in her terror aspect as Kali are not uncommon, but in her active form she is best depicted as Durga killing the buffalo demon Mahisha. As Kali she is sculptured as dancing on the prostrate body of her husband. In some sculptures, Shiva and Parvati, as constituting the ideal couple of the pantheon, are shown as seated side by side, Shiva lovingly holding her with his left arm passed round her waist. As a rule the female figures of the Hindu sculptors are more true to nature than the male figures, the idea probably being that the body of the female is meant to create desire rather than to inspire spirituality.

The Hindus never believed that love-making was a sin. Nor did they think that love-scenes were indecent objects unworthy of holy places. On the other hand, Maithuna (sexual congress) was considered one of the main objects of life, and religion not only recognized it as such but even encouraged the pursuit of this prime pleasure of life. Hence erotic scenes formed part of the scheme of decorative art, and were sculptured on the walls and pillars of most of the Hindu temples. In some shrines given over to the practice of sex cults, these scenes were the main subjects for the sculptor and some of the postures mentioned in Kama Sutra (see page 114) and improved upon by the imagination of the sculptor were depicted on the walls and pillars.

A fine work of sculpture executed in relief on the face of a rock at Mamallapuram (see page 109) is worthy of particular mention. This consists of a group of men, animals and mythical beings, some of the human figures suggesting sages practising austerities. For a long time the theme could not be identified but was believed to be Arjuna's Penance, in the forests among animals, sages and birds. But now the sculpture is recognized as depicting the fall of the Ganges from the celestial regions to the earth in the forests of the Himalayas.

There appears to have been some convention among the Hindus against making images of mere men and women. In the Sukra Niti (belonging to the Nitisastra branch of Smriti) we are told "the images of the gods, even if deformed, are for the good of men. But the images of men, even if well formed, are never for human good." Again "the images of the gods yield happiness to men, and lead to heaven; but those of men lead away from heaven and yield grief." But no law has ever been respected to the letter and, in spite of the foregoing belief, there were sculptors, though few, who were bold enough to make images of men. In certain shrines, both Buddhist and Hindu, appear sculptures of patrons; Karli, for instance, has the figures of a couple, full-blooded, mature and decidedly of the earth. The figures are alive, dynamic and almost breathing. Side by side with the "idealistic school" there grew to be sure, in India a flesh and blood school, although this was given a subordinate position.

The ideals of Indian art were not confined to India. The art of Ceylon, Java, Burma and Cambodia owes much to India. Indian influence is so well marked in the sculptures of Borobadour in Java that we may safety conclude that either Indian workmen executed them or they were done under the direction of experts from India. Similarly, the famous statue of the Buddha at Anuradhapura in Ceylon was clearly the work of an Indian master-sculptor. The statue conforms to the Indian style in all its details.

Like architecture, sculpture is a lost art in India. Budhism has died in the land of its birth, and modern Hindus show little interest in Shiva the dancer and Krishna the flute-player. There are few artists in India at present who engage themselves in the comparatively unprofitable art of sculpture. The only human figures that can be credited to the modern sculptor are the marble statues and bronze casts of politicians and public bores that disfigure the street corners of Indian cities.

PAINTING

Painting, like sculpture is an ancient art, but because of the impermanence of the material used, few good paintings of antiquity have come down to us. Sanskrit literature speaks highly of painting, and kings and nobles are mentioned as having Chitra Shalas (art galleries) full of paintings in their palaces. In Kalidasa's Shakuntala there is an interesting scene in which king Dushyanta appreciates a picture of his beloved. After his vain search for Shakuntala (see page 94) the king paints a picture of her. In a moment of grief he calls for the picture to draw what consolation he could by looking at her likeness.

King: (Gazing at the picture). It is a beautiful picture. See!
A graceful arch of brows above great eyes;
Lips bathed in darting, smiling light that flies
Reflected from white teeth; a mouth
As red Karkandhu-fruit, love's brightness shed
O'er all her face in bursts of liquid charm—
The picture speaks, with living beauty warm.

Clown: (Looking at it). The sketch is full of meaning. My eyes seem to stumble over its uneven surface. What more can I say? I expect to see it come to life, and I feel like speaking to it.

Mishrakesi: The king is a clever painter. I seem to see the dear girl before me.

Clown: There are three figures in the picture, and they are all beautiful. Which one is the lady Shakuntala?

King: Which do you think?

Clown: (Observing closely). I think it is this one, leaning against the creeper which she has just sprinkled. Her face is hot and the flowers are drooping from her hair; for the ribbon is loosened. Her arms droop like weary branches, she has loosened her girdle, as she seems a little fatigued. This, I think is the lady Shakuntala; the others are her friends.

King: You are good at guessing. Besides, here are proofs of my love.
See where discolorations faint
Of loving handling tell;
And here the swelling of the paint

Shows where my sad tears fell.
(The king finds the background not painted to his satisfaction. And he gives directions to an artist:)

The King: Listen, my friend.
The stream of Malini, and on its sands
The swan-pairs resting; holy foot-hill lands
Of great Himalayas sacred ranges, where
The yaks are seen; and under trees that bea.
Bark hermit-dresses on their branches high,
A doe that on the buck's horn rubs her eye.

* * *

And another ornament that Shakuntala loved, I have forgotten to paint.

* * *

The siris-blossom, fastened o'er her ear,
Whose stamen brush her cheek;
The lotus-chain like autumn moon light soft
Upon her bosom meek.

Clown: But why does she cover her face with fingers lovely as the pink water-lily? She seems frightened. (He looks more closely.) I see. Here is a bold bad bee. He steals honey, and so he flies to her lotus face.

King: Sting that dear lip, O bee with cruel power. And you shall be imprisoned in a flower.

Clown: Well, he doesn't seem afraid of your dreadful punishment.

King: Will he not go, though I warn him?

Clown: (Aloud). It is only a picture, man!*

This portrait of Shakuntala with its idyllic background is certainly a pleasing one. That unreal idealism usually associated with Indian art is conspicuously absent here. The bee mistaking the ruddy lips of Shakuntala for a fresh blossom adds to the sense of physical beauty of the youthful maiden, and "a modern lover examining the photo or oil painting of his darling could not be more realistic." But then we must remember that Kalidasa was an ardent advocate of the youthful, the beautiful and the lovable in life, and was a delighter in the joy of life. It is doubtful if the artists of his period conformed to his views of art any more than the moralists of the period accepted his standard of Gandharva as the most noble form of marriage.

The earliest Indian paintings that have come to us are the frescoes of the Ajanta caves done by Buddhist artists. The paintings were not executed by one or a group of artists at one period, but belong to different periods, generation after generation having engaged themselves in producing them. The earliest paintings are believed to belong to the first century of the Christian era and the latest to the eighth. Many of the paintings were defaced through neglect and the ravages of time, but enough have been preserved to convey to us the skill of the masters of Ajanta. The fact that the caves were abandoned in the eighth century A.D. and were discovered only in the nineteenth century speaks well of the material used.

The Indian painter has always shown a wider interest in the selection of subjects than the sculptor. Celestial beings and saints were not the only subjects he loved to paint. The Ajanta frescoes depict a wide variety of scenes drawn from the daily life of the people, in addition to the usual religious subjects. Paintings of dancing girls, of lovers, of boats sailing in the seas, of bull-fights, of beggars and monkeys have been discovered at Ajanta. As regards the quality of the paintings I can only quote the following passage of a European art critic who had copies of the paintings made: "The painters were giants in execution. Even on the walls, some of the lines, drawn with one sweep of the brush, struck me as wonderful; but when I saw long, delicate curves traced with equal precision on the horizontal surface of the ceiling, their skill appeared to me nothing less than miraculous. For the purposes of art education, no better examples could be placed before an Indian art student. The art lives. Faces question and answer, laugh and weep, fondle and flatter; limbs move with freedom and grace, flowers bloom, birds soar, and the beasts spring, fight or patiently bear burdens."

From Ajanta to the Moghuls is a far cry. But either through want of patronage or lack of interest painting suffered much during this period. No great school of painting appears to have flourished during this gap and no picture of any worth has come down to us. Akbar, however, took a keen interest in the art and under his liberal patronage, what is now known as the Moghul school grew up. Muslims very naturally introduced Persian forms into Indian paintings. The greatest works of the artists of the Moghul school were those exquisite miniatures valued all over the world. Some of the Moghul paintings, it is true, suffer greatly by overcrowding of subjects. But others are charming works by masters of colour, harmony and line.

The interest Akbar took in art is thus eulogized in the Ain-i-Akbari by Abul Fazal: "His Majesty, from his earliest youth, has shown a great predilection for this art (painting) and gives it very great encouragement as he looks upon it as a means both of study and amusement. Hence the art flourishes, and many painters have obtained great reputation. The works are weekly laid before His Majesty by the Darogahs and the clerks; he then confers rewards according to excellence of workmanship or increases the monthly salaries. Most excellent painters are now to be found, and masterpieces, worthy of a Bihzad, may be placed at the side of the wonderful works of the European painters, who have obtained world-wide fame. The minuteness in detail, the general finish, the boldness of execution, etc., now observed in pictures is incomparable; even inanimate objects look as if they had life. More than a hundred painters have become famous masters of the art, whilst the number of those who approach perfection, or those who are middling is very large. This is specially true of the Hindus: their pictures surpass our conception of things. Few indeed in the whole world are found equal to them ... I have to notice that the observing of the figures of

---

* B. K. Sarkar, *Hindu Art: Its Humanism and Modernism*.

XCVII

220 A HINDU MENDICANT OF THE
PICTURESQUE TYPE
(Photo: Stanley Jepson)

221 HERALDING THE TEMPLE PROCESSION
(Photo: A. S. Aiyar)

XCVIII

222 PAINTING AN ELEPHANT FOR A FESTIVAL
(Photo: Stanley Jepson)

223 STATE ELEPHANT DECORATED FOR PROCESSION
(Photo: A. L. Syed)

XCIX

224 BANGLE OR BRACELET OF PLAQUES EMBOSSED WITH MYTHOLOGICAL FIGURES
(*Journal of Indian Art and Industry*)

225 SHIVA DANCING AS VIRABHADRA
(South India; Photo: India Pictorial Features)

226 THE MENDICANT SHIVA
(From a South Indian Temple; Photo: India Pictorial Features)

227 SIGNS OF THE ZODIAC
(Maurice's *Hindustan*)

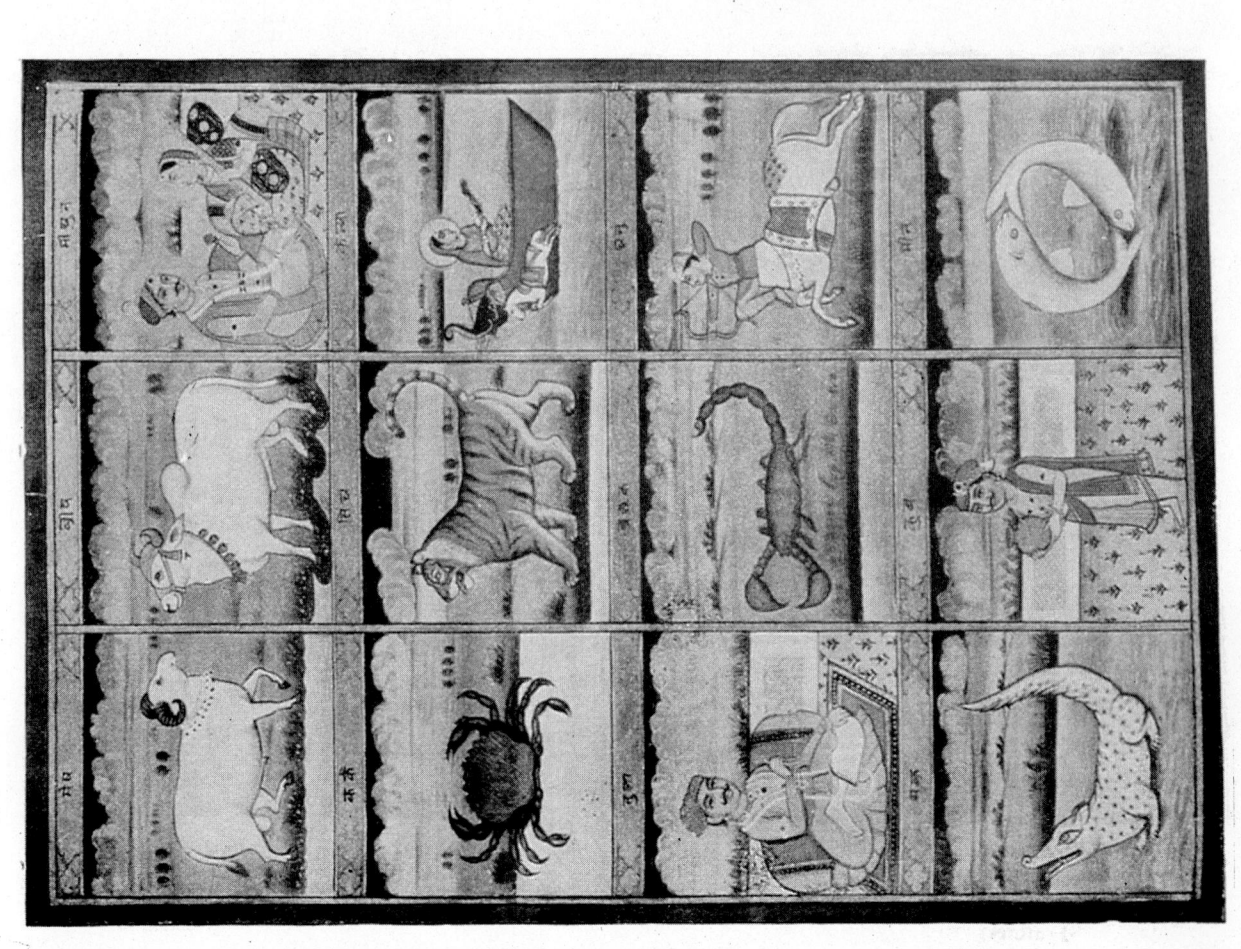

228 CAR FESTIVAL, KANCHIPURAM, MADRAS
(Photo: S. S. Aiyar)

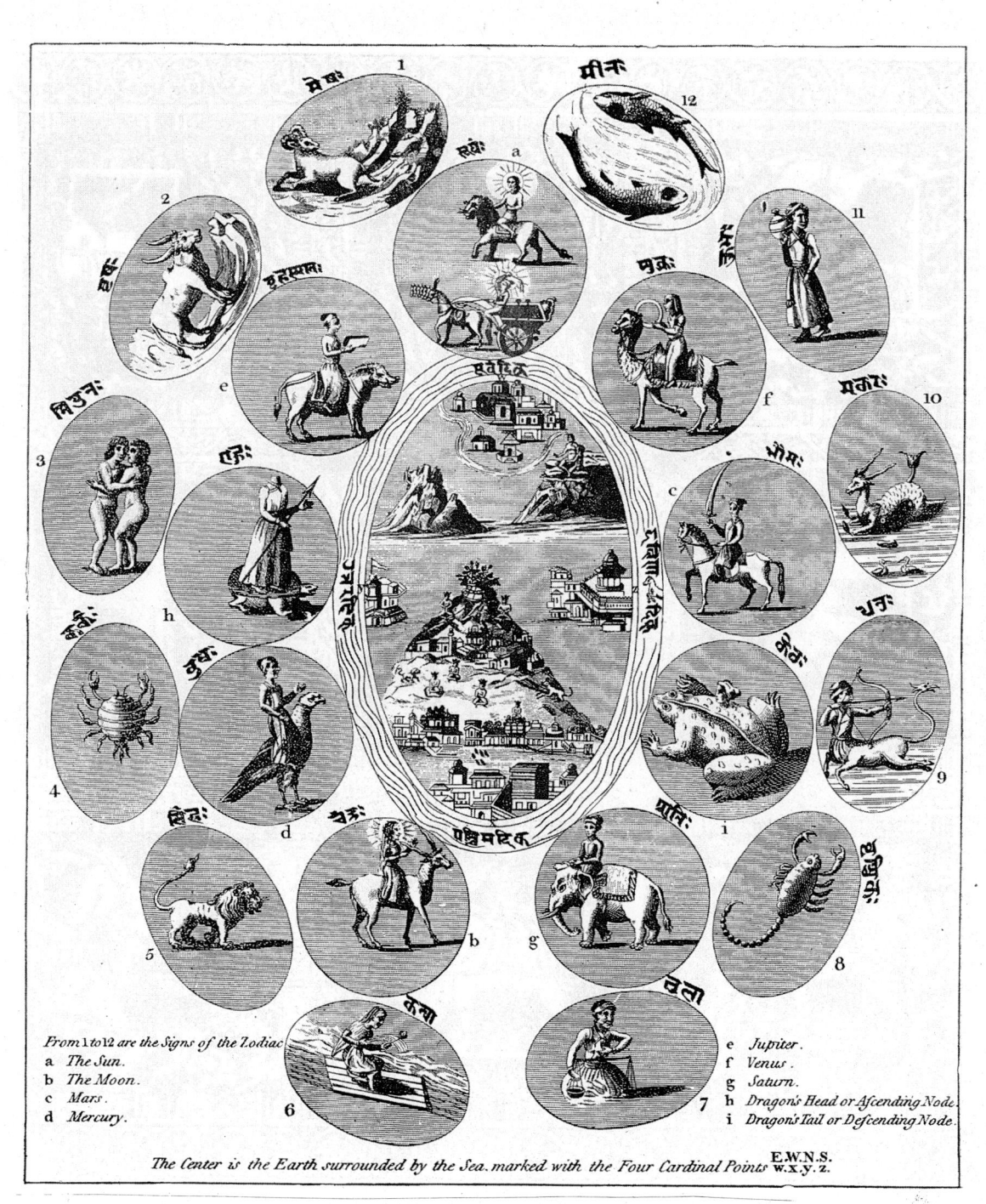

From 1 to 12 are the Signs of the Zodiac
a *The Sun.*
b *The Moon.*
c *Mars.*
d *Mercury.*

e *Jupiter.*
f *Venus.*
g *Saturn.*
h *Dragon's Head or Ascending Node.*
i *Dragon's Tail or Descending Node.*

The Center is the Earth surrounded by the Sea, marked with the Four Cardinal Points E.W.N.S. w.x.y.z.

229 THE EARTH, THE PLANETS AND THE SIGNS OF THE ZODIAC
(Maurice's *Hindustan*)

CII

230   **GUARDIANS OF THE UNIVERSE**
North: Kubera on horse: N.E.: Isha (Shiva) on bull; E.: Indra on elephant: S.E.: Agni on ram; S. Yama on buffalo
S.W.: Nirriti on man; W.: Varuna on fish; N.W.: Vayu on deer.
(Carved stone ceiling in a Hindu temple, *Journal of Indian Art and Industry*).

CIII

231 WORSHIP OF BOOKS
BY SCRIBES ON NAVARATRI DAYS
(India Pictorial Features)

232 HINDU GIRL ADORNING
HER FOREHEAD WITH THE EXQUISITE
CASTE MARK KNOWN AS 'POTTU'
(India Pictorial Features)

233 A SACRED COW DECORATED
FOR A PROCESSION
(India Pictorial Features)

234 BREAKING A WHITE PUMPKIN
TO SCARE AWAY EVIL SPIRITS
(India Pictorial Features)

GANESHA
(Photo: Indrajit N. Nalawala)

objects and the making of likenesses of them, which are often looked upon as an idle occupation are, for a well-regulated mind, a source of wisdom and an antidote against the poison of ignorance. Bigoted followers of the letter of the law are hostile to the art of painting; but their eyes now see the truth."

Royal patronage of painting continued under Jehangir and Shah Jehan, but Aurangazeb was a "bigoted follower of the letter of the law," hostile to the art of painting. The army of painters mentioned by Abul Fazal disappeared from the Moghul court during Aurangazeb's reign and were reduced to starvation. Many of them however found their way to the Hindu princes of Rajasthan who gave them a ready welcome. Under the patronage of these princes, the painters built up what is now known as the Rajput school of painting. The themes of the painters of the Rajput school were drawn largely from Hindu epics. But following the Moghul tradition, they also painted portraits of kings and queens, and manuscripts were profusely illustrated with miniatures. The best works of Rajput painting have come mainly from Jaipur.

The Rajput school had many offshoots of which the most important was the Kangra school that flourished in this valley.

Unlike architecture and sculpture, painting is a flourishing art in India. Towards the latter half of the nineteenth century a wave of Westernism swept over India, and Indian painters thought the art of their own country and its idealism were unnatural and decadent. There was a clamour for deviation from the traditional Indian style in favour of the flesh and blood school of the West. Ravi Varma was the leader of this revolt and his paintings commanded great respect in his time. He did, if nothing else, much to dispel the notion some European artists had that Indians were incapable of painting like the Westerners. But a storm of protest arose against Ravi Varma, especially from Bengal, for the sin of degenerating Indian art to the level of the "photographic," standard of the West. The modern tendency in Indian painting is to draw inspiration completely from the past but the masters of the present day go even a step further than their predecessors of Ajanta, and paint pictures some of which only saints and sadists can appreciate.

CHAPTER XIII

THE ART AND SCIENCE OF LOVE

ACCORDING to ancient Hindu sages, the prime objects of life are four: Dharma (duty), Artha (acquisition of wealth), Kama (pleasures of sex) and Moksha (salvation or release). The copious sacred literature of the Hindus, as we have seen, explains Dharma and the methods of obtaining Moksha. On Artha, we have no important work. The Arthasastra of Kautilya, though dealing as its title indicates with Artha, is much wider in scope. Brahaspati is said to have written a treatise on Artha, but his work has not come down to us. Generally speaking the individual was left to earn wealth as best as he could, and no guidance was thought necessary for those engaged in the pursuit of wealth. Kama, however, had able exponents and many interesting works have come down to us on the subject of sex love.

The Hindus were probably the first of the ancients to study sex love as a natural emotion. The greatest ancient authority on the subject was Vatsyayana, whose Kama Sutra (aphorisms of love) are even now thought by the Hindus to be a priceless work on the art and science of love. Vatsyayana claimed his work to be a revelation and he was canonized by the Hindus as a saint and a seer. Later writers drew inspiration from Vatsyayana, and every Hindu gentleman of the middle ages was expected to know something of the great master of love. Poets and artists studied Vatsyayana, and the erotic sculptures of the temples show that the sculptors had a thorough knowledge of the Kama Sutra.

THE SCIENCE OF LOVE*

Vatsyayana is believed to have lived in the 3rd century A.D. Later, two well-known sexologists, Koka Pandita and Kalyanmalla, wrote works similar to the Kama Sutra. Both these writers, drawing mainly from Vatsyayana, are agreed upon a classification of women into four: Padmini (lotus woman), Chitrini (aesthetic woman), Sankhini (conch woman), and Hastini (elephant woman). Of these Padmini is said to be the most desirable. Her distinguishing characteristics are: Eyes beautiful and bright as a fawn's, face like the full moon; bosoms well-developed and elevated; and body soft and smooth. Padmini has a sweet voice with the Madhyama note of the octave predominating (see page 99). She is slim and slender and her gait is like the swan's. Her neck is well-shaped and nose straight and proportioned. Her complexion is rosy. She has "three folds or wrinkles round about the umbilical region," and is bashful, docile and guileless, loyal and religious. Her bodily secretions are said to be sweet-scented.

Chitrini is less religious than Padmini, but her physical attractions are greater. She has a slender waist, heavy breasts, and well developed hips. Her beautiful eyes are restless and always on the look out for adventure. Her ruddy lips appear luscious as Vimba fruits. She has glossy, black hair. The predominating note of her sweet voice is Panchama. Her gait is majestic like the elephant's. She is always anxious to display her youth and beauty to the best advantage. She is not the spiritual type, but a lover of music and poetry and takes delight in the legitimate pleasures of the world. She loves wealth, a beautiful well-furnished home and the company of the cultured. She is loyal to her husband and loves children, birds and pet dogs.

Sankhini is not much to look at. She has a heavy frame, lean limbs, a small head and underdeveloped breasts. She is ill-tempered and suspicious. She has a shuffling gait, a long face and a tilted nose. She is selfish but cunning enough to understand the advantage of making a pretext of selflessness. Hence she is courteous and well-mannered. She is slow in the game of love, but once roused, is capable of sadism and hurting her partner with her nails. Sankhini, however, is not without attractions. She is fond of flowers, good clothes and ornaments and tries to make up by decoration what she lacks in good looks.

Hastini is the worst type of woman. She is tall, stout and ugly. She has red eyes, a sign of wickedness. Her mouth is broad, lips thick, and teeth discoloured. She is spiteful, jealous, faithless, cruel, voluptuous, unrelenting and extremely selfish. She has a pale and unattractive complexion, crooked toes, a short, thick neck and appears a hunch-back while walking. She is shameless, and often courts her mate whom she hurts and overpowers while engaged in lovemaking.

But every woman has her mate and there are four classes of men to go with the four classes of women. Men are classified into: (1) Shasha (hare men), (2) Mriga (buck men), (3) Vrisha (bull men) and (4) Asva (horse men).

Shasha is handsome. He is well built, of medium stature, and well-proportioned. "His face is round, his teeth short and fine, his hair silky and eyes large." He is of light complexion but his thighs are darkish. He is unselfish, religious and faithful to his wife. He is the natural mate for Padmini.

The Mriga has a larger frame than the Shasha. Broad-shouldered, tall and handsome, he is a soldier by nature and resents insults and injuries. He is not so religious as the Shasha but has a high sense of honour. He enjoys good health and a keen appetite. His gait is manly and steady. Honest, straightforward and faithful, he is unselfish and ever ready to champion the cause of the downtrodden and the poor. He is fond of music and literature. He is the correct mate for Chitrini.

* The author's work *Kama Kalpa* deals with the subject in greater detail.

More powerfully built than either the Shasha or the Mriga, the Vrisha is essentially a worldly type. He has few intellectual pleasures. He loves an active life and is contemptuous of the refined and the contemplative. "He claims a brawny chest, sinewy arms and a hard peritoneal region. His forehead is high, eyes large with pink shade in the corners and the palms of his hands are red."* He is not religious, but a pleasure seeker. He loves the company of the gay and the frivolous and is not very fastidious in the choice of a mate. He will make a good husband for Sankhini.

The lowest type of man is Asva. He is meant to be the hewer of wood and the drawer of water for his superiors. He has an undeveloped intellect and delights in animal pleasures. His complexion is brown and his skin rough. Built for toiling, he is not well-proportioned, though strong. His voice is harsh and unpleasant. He loves to stare at people. Vulgar songs appeal to him more than refined music. He is contemptuous of delicate and graceful women, but loves the big and passionate type. Caring little for courtship he is violent in love-making. He is naturally the fit mate for Hastini.

It can be easily seen that this four-fold classification closely follows the division of society into castes. For lovers, however, it is not enough to know the types; for the erogenous zones of the four classes of women shift according to the waxing and waning moon. Koka Pandita in his Rati-Rahasya (mysteries of passion) and Kalyanmalla in his Ananga Ranga (theatre of the love god) give detailed descriptions of how the zones change from one part of the body to another in the different types of women according to the changing digits of the moon. Nor is it enough to know the day on which one mates. The time is also important; for Padmini is most excitable during the first Prahara (6 to 9 A.M.), Chitrini during the fifth Prahara (6 to 9 P.M.), Sankhini during the 7th (midnight to 3 A.M.) and Hastini throughout the night. Padmini may, however, be approached at any part of the day but she hates dalliance in the dark. Hastini, as a rule loves the night but the third Prahara (midday to 3 P.M.) is also a suitable time for having sexual congress with her.

It is true that the above classification of men and women is somewhat arbitrary, and the truth of the observations regarding the shifting of the erogenous zones and the like remains to be proved. But as an attempt to reduce the wildest instinct in man to a scientific basis, they are certainly interesting.

COURTSHIP

Hindu sexologists classify courtship into three: pre-marital, post-marital and extra-marital. In Vatsyayana's time, it would appear, child-marriage had not become general in Aryan society, and the Kama Sutra dwells at length upon pre-marital courtship.

Man, naturally, is to take the lead in courtship. Among the Hindus social intercourse between young men and women was not permitted even in Vatsyayana's time and this sage emphasizes the need for a go-between for establishing contact. A man is to be careful in his choice of the go-between. A mutual friend, a class mate or play mate, a dancing girl, a barber or his wife, a hawker of trinkets, a jester or buffoon and an elderly widow are mentioned as reliable go-betweens. These people are to be paid for their services either in cash or, when the status of the person does not permit of cash payment, by presents, and are thus to be kept loyal to the suitor. After the intermediary has started on his delicate mission, the lover must try to meet the lady, as if by chance, near a temple, riverside or some other place frequented by her. He must carefully watch her, without giving suspicion to others, and note by her behaviour whether his suit is progressing well. If the lady blushes on seeing the suitor, the sign is good. Restlessness, a tendency to tease children or her friends, and exposing any part of the body under the guile of adjusting her garments, are better signs. A girl who has requited one's love takes care to decorate her person when attending functions in which the suitor is likely to be present, and lingers about him without an ostensible reason. When the suitor departs she casts wistful glances at him.

When, by these signs, a lover knows that the lady has softened, he may arrange a secret meeting. He must take full advantage of such meetings and must always go to her armed with presents of flowers, scents and sweetmeats. In such meetings he is to sit close to her. If he is not quite sure of her he may touch, as if by accident, different parts of her body. If this is not resented, he may take it for granted that she has no objection to further advances and shall press and caress the tender parts of her body. Night time is best for secret meetings, as women are bolder in the dark than in daylight. Going to extremes is to be avoided till the lovers are married.

Marriage, however, does not give a man power over his wife's body. Courtship is said to be essential every time one approaches one's wife, and forcing is rape in or out of wedlock. According to Hindu conventions, sexual union between newly-weds is prohibited for the three days following marriage, and is allowed on the fourth. The bride and bridegroom are conducted on the fourth night to a room furnished with luxurious couches and decked with sweet smelling flowers.

The first step in post-marital courtship is the embrace. The bridegroom must ingratiate himself into the confidence of the bride by sweet speech, smiles, and caresses and the yielding bride may then be embraced and her bosom pressed against his chest. Very young girls are likely to fight shy of bright light and the bridegroom will be well-advised to have a dim light in the bed-room. After the bride has yielded to his embrace, he may prepare himself for the kiss. The best method of extracting a kiss from one's newly-wed wife is said to be for the man to hold a betel leaf or chip of areca-nut between his lips and request the lady to push it with her lips into his mouth! If she shows reluctance, the bride-groom must coax her by sweet words. If sweet words fall

---

* N. K. Basu, *Art of Love in the Orient*.

on deaf ears, he may use threats and pretend that he may desert her and renounce the world or commit suicide. If the bride is not perturbed by this, the lover, by a show of frenzy, must fall at her feet and implore her to accede to his request. This master-stroke, we are told, is bound to succeed; for no woman can be indifferent to a man who falls at her feet.

After the embrace and the kiss, the lover may start taking further liberties. He may gently coax the bride, by caresses to permit him to open her jacket and pass his hand round her bosom, and must by clever manipulation of the mammae, work her up to that pitch of emotion when she begins to forget herself and abandon her person to her husband. At this stage, he may cleverly pass his hands round her waist, loosen the girdle and initiate her into the mysteries of advanced love.

Vatsyayana, Kalyanmalla and Koka Pandita are respectors of convention. Hence, as a rule, men are allowed to have sexual relations only with their wives or concubines. The courtezan, however, is fair game for all, and when her fee is paid it is no great sin to seek the pleasure of her company. A virgin whom a man has no intention of marrying is not allowed to be courted or made love to. Other peoples' wives are forbidden to be approached, but the following cases are considered permissible exceptions.

A married woman of loose character known to have relations with many men may be courted with impunity. A man may have sexual relations with another man's wife if, through her, he can get back the money he has lent to her husband when there is no other means of collecting it. A person having no ostensible means of livelihood, and reduced to starvation, may earn a living by making love to another man's wife if this lady lusts after him and is willing to pay for his services. If a man is so desperately in love with another man's wife that he may die of his hopeless love, he is permitted to have union with her once only, on the principle of self-preservation. Notwithstanding the above, no man is allowed to have sexual union with the happily married wife of a sincere friend, the wife of his teacher, preceptor or disciple, the king's wife, a lunatic, or a woman suffering from some incurable disease, the wife of a near relative, a pregnant woman, a shameless woman and a woman older than himself.

In extra-marital courtship, the woman courted is not a virgin but one experienced in love, and many of the preliminaries of courtship may be dispensed with. But the lover has to watch and study his subject carefully, much more carefully than when courting a virgin, as adultery, if discovered, may lead to grave consequences. No woman, we are told, whether married or unmarried, can fail to yield to a lover who has mastered the technique of courtship and approaches her in the proper way. All women, however, are not equally amenable to overtures. The types that can be easily seduced are officious women, women who love to talk to strangers and stare at them as if inviting them, women of society who mix freely with young men, cultured women fond of publicity, singers and dancers, neglected and illtreated women, barren women, talkative women, wives of misers, young widows, wives of impotent, pot-bellied, ugly or deformed men, wives of goldsmiths, jewellers and of men with a plurality of wives. It is not enough for a man to know his women; the seducer must know himself. For men who are most successful with women are: men well-versed in the art of love, good conversationalists and clever gossipers, handsome and well-built dandys, musicians, popular neighbours, well-known personalities moving in cultured society, a spendthrift, an actor, jester or magician, a brave and courageous man, a young bridegroom, "an employer of the father, brother or the husband of the courted woman," a lover of garden parties and a wealthy man living in a luxurious style. The reasons that prevent a lady from yielding herself to the seducer, are said to be twenty-five. Some of these are: "Consideration for children, a deep love for the husband," low vitality, sorrow on the death of some near relative, fear of detection by the husband or neighbours, doubt about the real intentions of the lover, "a strong suspicion that her husband may be testing her fidelity through the agency of the so-called lover," and fear of punishment in the life to come. "Anxiety, hesitation and scruples," says Vatsyayana, "are to be assuaged by means of proper technique. The man who is confident of success with a particular woman, understands the favourable and unfavourable hints through which she may communicate her feelings and takes adequate measures to remove the possible grounds for refusal, always wins in the long run."* Lovers are reminded that boldness pays and he who hesitates is lost.

After a lover has won over the lady for extra-marital pleasure, he may arrange a secret meeting through a very trustworthy intermediary. The choice of the place of meeting is important. In the absence of the husband, the lady's own house may be chosen provided there are no people there who are likely to frustrate the plans. Otherwise, a more convenient place such as the house of a lady-friend in the confidence of both will be more suitable. In these meetings it is not necessary for the lover to waste his time in preliminaries. He may take presents with him, to be sure; for every woman loves presents. The fact of the meeting itself is proof that the lady has yielded and she knows what to expect. Hence the lover may deal directly with her without any preliminaries. In fact, lingering on preliminary courtship is likely to irk an experienced woman, as she loves the more serious part of the game.

Vatsyayana holds out a warning to unwary lovers seeking illicit connection with a married woman: "One should not approach a second woman in the house where he is carrying on with another. If there is an old chaperon or matron in the house who had tasted the fruits of the forbidden tree in her younger days, she should be brought round by greasing her palm, otherwise she will certainly frustrate the whole project. An intelligent man should better not consider approaching a woman who is chicken-hearted,

---

* N. K. Basu, *Art of Love in the Orient*.

distrustful, capricious, incorrigibly scrupulous, guarded by armed attendants, and to crown all, by a vigilant mother-in-law."*

SOME OBSERVATIONS ON COURTSHIP AND LOVE

Hindu erotologists were masters of classification and detail. There are, according to Vatsyayana, eight stages in love-making, beginning with the embrace and ending in the pleasant lassitude following coitus. Each of these eight are again subdivided into eight and to drink the cup of love to the dregs the lover has to drain all these sixty-four ingredients of love. For the generality of men a knowledge of all these sixty-four stages is not essential. Some of them may, however, be mentioned.

The names of the eight forms of the embrace are: Ballari-reshtitaka (creeper-twinning), Vrikshadhirudha (the tree-climbing), Teela-Tandulaka (rice-seasamum), Kshira-Niraka (milk-and-water), Upagudha (thigh-pincer), Jadhanupaguhana (hip-thigh embrace), Stanalingana (bosom embrace), and the Lalatika (the forehead embrace). The names are suggestive of the postures or the harmony of the embrace. In the tree-climbing embrace, for instance, "the woman puts one of her feet on the opposite of her lover, while both are standing and the other she twines round his waist. She passes one arm behind his back and with the other tries to bend his neck, all the time imitating the climbing of a tree, and making different cooing sounds." In the milk-and-water variety, the lovers lie face to face and embrace in so harmonious a way that they become indistinguishable like milk and water in a mixture of the two.

Some of the kisses are named Adharapana (lip-drinking kiss), Jihwajuddha (the tongue-tilting kiss), Sphuritaka (the tremulous kiss), Sama (the straight kiss) and Vakra (the crooked kiss). The places most suited for administering the kiss are said to be the eyes, cheeks, lips, forehead, the hair, neck, breasts and the tongue. Some authorities go a step further and include the arm-pits and remoter regions as fit places to be kissed. The Hindus have always recognized that a certain amount of sadism is indispensable to successful love-making, and include scratching and biting as two of the eight stages of love. These are applicable both to men and women and can be sufficiently violent to cause slight bleeding. Scratching and biting of the milder type are recommended in all forms of love-making, but the virulent types are to be reserved for the exceptional occasion when the love-making precedes the separation of the husband from his wife for a number of days. The names of the eight forms of biting are: Gudhaka-dashana (the hidden bite), Uchhunduka-dashana (the swollen bite), Pravalamani-dashana (the coral bite), Manimala-dashana (the pearl bite), Vindu-dashana (the bead bite), Vindumala-dashana (the rosary bite), Khandabhaka-dashana (the cloud bite) and the Kolacharcha-dashana (boar bite).

It is hardly necessary to mention that the last named is a violent form; it leaves teeth marks on the breasts of the woman and even causes bleeding; for obvious reasons this must be strictly avoided when dealing with virgins or other peoples' wives.

The various coital postures are also described by Hindu erotologists. Yasodhara, Vatsyayana's commentator, maintains there are 729 possible coital postures. Some of them are extremely difficult, and cannot be practised by any one who is not a contortionist. In spite of their elaborate technique, Hindu sexologists are broad-minded enough to recognize spontaneity, and the lover is allowed to do anything the occasion demands.

We will conclude the subject of the science of Indian love with what the ancient Hindus thought an ideal wife ought to be. According to them a model wife is a drudge at home, a minister in adversity, the earth herself in patience, a mother in affection and a harlot in bed.

MYSTIC LOVE

In a previous chapter we have noticed certain tendencies in Vaishnavism which treated sex-love as the symbol of love between soul and God. The ecstasy experienced by the devout followers of this cult in contemplating their favourite personal God Vishnu could not be compared to anything on earth except to an ardent lover's feeling when pressing his beloved to his bosom. A similar tendency in Islam gave rise to Sufism. Nor is the idea altogether foreign to Christianity. The Song of Songs of Solomon is pervaded by the same spirit, and Roman Catholic mysticism recognizes the relationship between the bride and the bridegroom as the most appropriate symbol of the soul's yearning for the presence of God. But while Christianity finds in sensuous love an unholy passion unworthy of spiritual life, the Vaishnavas have no such horror of human love and some of their poets have given free play to their imagination in their treatment of mystic love. Hindu gods, in their various incarnations, are said to have enjoyed the company of the daughters of men, and the Vaishnava poets could find no harm in a god having made love to a woman in the sense ordinary humans understand love.

The lover-god of the Vaishnavas is Krishna, the eighth incarnation of Vishnu. While he lived in Vrindavan he is believed to have captivated the hearts of the Gopis (milkmaids), married and unmarried, and on many occasions, on hearing the love notes of his flute, the women of Vrindavan are said to have deserted their husbands, children and parents and followed him. In a spiritual sense, the behaviour of these women represents the renunciation of the world and the breaking of all ties that bind the soul to the world. The Hindus are, however, aware that all men are not spiritually gifted enough to see it in this light and may view the love of the Gopis as sensuous and carnal. But the Vaishnavas are not perturbed

---

* N. K. Basu, *Art of Love in the Orient*.

by this. A peculiarity in Hindu religious belief justified the behaviour of the Brij girls. The contemplation of the deity from any angle is believed to elevate the soul irrespective of the motives, "just as the water of life makes the drinker immortal, without question whether he knows or does not know its virtue." Shishupala, the mortal enemy of Krishna, for instance, is said to have obtained salvation on his death, because even in sleep he contemplated the destruction of Krishna ! Hence the Brij girls who loved Krishna in a sensuous way also had their reward.

Of all the Brij girls, Radha, wife of Ayanaghosha, loved Krishna most, and the love of this lady is the favourite theme of song for Vaishnava poets. The most widely known work on the subject is Jaya Deva's Gita Govinda. Jaya Deva lived in the 13th century A.D. in the court of Lakshmana Sena of Bengal and he wrote in Sanskrit. He was a great musician and poet, and a few extracts from his work will be of interest as typical of this branch of Hindu literature.

In the Gita Govinda we are introduced to Radha and her maid watching the playful Krishna sporting with the girls of Vrindaban. The spot selected for Krishna's sport is:

Where the breath of waving Madhvi pours
    incense through the grove,
And silken Mogras lull the sense with
    essences of love—
The silken-soft pale Mogra, whose perfume
    fine and faint
Can melt the coldness of a maid, the
    sternness of saint.

*   *   *

Where—as if warm lips touched sealed eyes
    and waked them—all the bloom
Opens upon the mangoes to feed the sun-
    shine come;
And Atimuktas wind their arms of softest
    green about,
Clasping the stems, while calm and clear
    Jumma spreadeth out.

Here, Radha and her maid see Krishna with the Gopis, and the maid says :

See, Lady ! how thy Krishna passes these
    idle hours
Decked forth in fold of woven gold, and
    crowned with forest flowers
And scented with the sandal, and gay with
    gems of price—
Rubies to mate his laughing lips, and
    diamonds like his eyes :—
In the company of dancers, who dance and
    sing and play,
Lies Krishna, laughing, toying, dreaming his
    Spring away.
One with star-blossomed champak wreathed,
    wooes him to rest his head
One the dark pillow of her breast so tenderly
    outspread;
And o'er his brow with roses blown she fans
    a fragrance rare,
That falls on the enchanted sense like rain
    in thirsty air,
While the company of damsels wave many
    an odorous spray,
And Krishna, laughing, toying, sighs the soft
    Spring away.

The sight of Krishna thus sporting with other girls, forgetting his beloved Radha, naturally rouses jealousy in the latter. Her heart is heavy-laden on seeing Krishna proving so wantonly disloyal. But still she can't help loving him. Mourns Radha :

Must love thee—cannot choose but love thee
    ever,
My best beloved ! set on this endeavour,
To win thy tender heart and earnest eye
From lips but sadly sweet, from restless
    bosoms,
To mine, O Krishna with the mouth of
    blossoms !
To mine, thou soul of Krishna ! yet I sigh
Half hopeless, thinking of myself forsaken,
And thee, dear Loiterer, in the wood
    o'ertaken
With passion for those bold and wanton
    one's
Who knit thine arms as poison-plants gripe
    trees
With twining cords—their flowers the
    braveries
That flash in the green gloom, sparkling
    stars and stones.*

Radha, heart-broken, withdraws from the scene, but her companion undertakes to convey a message of love to Krishna with a view to bring him back to his beloved.

In the meantime the love-dance in Vrindavan has ended and the Brij girls have departed. Krishna, left alone, repents of his rash behaviour and his disloyalty towards Radha. His yearning to see Radha becomes a frenzy and he raves :

"Grant me but a sight of thee, O lovely Radha ! for my passion torments me. O god of love, mistake me not for Mahadeva ! wound me not again, approach me not in anger; hold not in thy hand the shaft barbed with an Amra flower. I am not the terrible Mahadeva; a garland of water lilies with subtle threads decks my shoulders;—not serpents with twisted folds—the blue petals of the lotus glitter on my neck —not the azure gleam of poison; powdered sandal wood is sprinkled on my limbs—not pale ashes. For pity's sake, wound me not, O god of love. My heart is already pierced by arrows from Radha's eyes, black and keen as those of an antelope; yet mine eyes are not gratified by her presence. Her's are full of shafts; her eye-brows are bows, and the tips of her ears are silken strings: thus armed by Ananga, the god of desire, she marches, herself a goddess, to ensure her triumphs over the vanquished universe. I meditate on her delightful embrace; on the ravishing glances darted from the fragrant lotus of her mouth; on her nectar-dropping speech; on her lips ruddy as the berries on the Vimba."†

---

* *Tr*: Edwin Arnold.   † Sir William Jones.

Radha's messenger now comes to Krishna and tells him that Radha is pining for love of him. The maid tells Krishna of Radha's plight: "Radha paints you in her tears; she burns with passion and the breeze from the Jumna cannot cool her; her eyes are heavy with weeping and her face is like the hidden full moon veiled by a dark cloud. She has spread a rose couch for thy reception and sits by its side and weeps; the empty couch is wet with her tears. O lord of Radha! come," she pleads, "thy Radha is sick with love of thee." This news emboldens Krishna and the repentant sinner is led back to his beloved. On seeing her lord Radha, woman like, though happy, pretends to be angry with him. Krishna is apologetic and craves for pardon; he makes many protestations of love and expresses regrets for his past behaviour. Radha, half pacified, thus tenderly reproaches him: "Alas! alas! Go, Madhava: depart, Kesava; speak not the language of love; follow her, O lotus eyed god, follow her who dispels thy care. Look at his eyes, half-opened, red with waking through the pleasurable night, yet smiling still with affection for my rival. Thy teeth, O cerulean youth, are as azure as thy complexion, from the kisses thou hast imprinted on the beautiful eyes of thy darling, graced with dark blue powder; and thy limbs marked with punctures in love's warfare exhibit a letter of conquest, written in polished sapphire in liquid gold."

Krishna pleads guilty. Says he: "Irate Radha! punish me for my sins. Wound my heart by thy glances, deadly as Kama's shafts; lock me up in the gaol of thy bosom with your delicious arms; let the silk soft manacles of thy wrists and hands be the ropes that bind me; and kill me by the pressure of thy breasts!" Radha agrees to this, and a reconciliation takes place; and Krishna makes Radha his.

Two other well-known bards of Bengal sang of mystic love. These were Chandidasa who composed his songs in Bengali and Vidyapathi who sang in Maithili, a mixture of Hindi and Bengali. Both lived in the fifteenth century A. D. and followed Jayadeva closely; in certain respects, however, their songs are more sensuous than the Gita Govinda, as the following passages from Vidyapathi will show; Vidyapathi depicts Radha as a maiden unskilled in the art of love, quivering at the touch of the Prince of Lovers. He describes Krishna's dalliance with her thus:

> Taking her hand, he sets her by his side,
> And she in shame and anger veils her face:
> When he unfolds her face and kisses her upon her mouth
> She hides the shamefast face in Madhav's breast.

* * *

> She cries: Oh no, no, no! and tears are pouring from her eyes
> She lies outstretched upon the margin of the bed,
> His close embrace has not unloosed her zone,—
> Even of handling of her breasts has been but little.

* * *

> When Kanu lifts her to his lap, she bends her body back.
> Like a young snake, untamed by spells.

Radha thus narrates her first experience in love to her lady friend:

> How can I tell of what was done that night?
> Unhappily the hours were spent with Madhava:
> He clasped my breasts and drank the nectar of my lips,
> Laying his face on mine, he killed my life.
> He held me close, with pinioned arms,
> And then my heart was beating wildly;
> I let him see my streaming eyes,
> But even then Kanu had no pity.
> My wicked lover parched my lips—
> Abetted by the night, Rahu devoured the moon;
> He tore my twin breasts with his nails,
> Just as a lion tears an elephant.*

It must be admitted that it is difficult to see anything very spiritual in these lines. One could only wish that Krishna had looked up his Vatsyayana before he approached Radha!

A poetess of a different order who sang of the same theme was Mira Bai, the revered Vaishnava saint of Rajasthan. Of royal birth, Mira renounced the world to devote herself to Krishna, and ran away from her home, to the horror of her highly placed relatives. She openly sang and danced before idols of Krishna, a thing unheard of among ladies of rank. And her songs, unlike those of the poets described above breathes a spirit of love free from the taint of gross sensuousness. Mira sings:

"Ah, my lord maddened am I with love of thee, but to whom shall I tell of my suffering? My bed is made of thorns, how then can I sleep on it? The couch of my beloved is in the firmament and mine on earth, how then can we be united?

"One who has suffered knows the pangs of love, but not one who has not. He who has quaffed poison knows its bitterness; others do not.

"Wounded, I wander from forest to forest, but I have not found the healer yet. O Mira's lord, I will get relief only when thou shalt be my physician."

* * *

"My lord, thou kindled the flame of love, and now where art thou fled? Thou lit the lamp of love and then fled away leaving her who knows nought but thee.

"Thou launched the boat of love and then left it to drift in the wild sea. O Mira's lord, when wilt thou come? No longer can I live without thee."

Mira's prayer is heard: For,

"Hark! The footsteps of Hari! From the terrace

---

* Translation by A. Coomaraswamy and Arun Sen.

of my palace I can see my king coming.

"The frogs, and the peacock cry in delight, and the cuckoo sounds her sweet notes. The clouds rain nectar in sheer delight, and the earth has decked herself with emerald garments to meet her lord!

"Oh darling Giridhar! Mira's lord and beloved, come quick and be one with thy slave."

VENAL LOVE

From what we read in Hindu scriptures and law books, the Hindus will appear as a most exacting race as far as fidelity of women is concerned. A wife, as Manu lays down, is to worship her husband as a god even if he is a worthless person. Adultery is deprecated as the most heinous sin a woman is capable of committing. Until recently a widow was even expected to die with her husband. With all this, we find that the Hindu state and religion have always tolerated and even encouraged prostitution and venal love. Kings were patrons of courtezans, and the temples were the sanctuary of sacred prostitutes. This apparent contradiction of precept and practice may appear inexplicable to the reader who is not well-acquainted with Hindu notions of morality.

Among the Hindus, there is one standard of morality for the three Aryan castes and quite a different standard for the others; and all the rules of fidelity and chastity, laid down in the codes, are applicable only to the women of the Aryan castes. For the Sudras, marriage is not a sacrament and for the women of this caste there are no marriage vows to be broken. Fidelity among them is certainly appreciated, in the sense that this virtue is universally appreciated; but the women of the Sudras are ruled by traditions and customs, many of which do not enjoin loyalty to the husband as one of the prime social virtues. Women of a good many sub-castes are allowed to divorce their husbands as they like, have a plurality of husbands and entertain paramours in the house known and unknown to the husbands. In fact, there are certain castes among the Sudras whose traditional occupation is prostitution, and deviation from this is considered sinful by them. These castes supply courtezans in India.

Prostitution was looked down upon by the Hindus, but prostitutes were not. They enjoyed special privileges, and even kings paid homage to well-known courtezans. The prostitutes' quarter was the pride of every medieval Hindu city. The harlots "were objects of sympathetic admiration, and were considered the glory and ornaments of the city. They were in evidence at all public festivities, in religious processions, at race meetings, at the cock-fighting, quail fighting and ram-fighting, and were the stars of each theatrical audience. Kings showered favours upon them and took councel with them, they come down to us as heroines of plays and romances."

"In the Jataka we read of them as receiving a thousand gold pieces for a night, and in the Taranga of Katha, one of them demands five hundred elephants for a single hour. In the latter work, too, a prostitute is so rich that she can buy an army to restore a fallen king."*

This is not literary exaggeration. Reliable witnesses who visited Vijayanagar (an important medieval Hindu state conquered by Muslims) at the zenith of her glory, testify to the high honour paid to prostitutes. "Prostitution was encouraged; every temple had its crowds of Devadasis or handmaids of the god, and the prostitutes' quarter was one of the sights of the capital. 'The splendour of these houses, the beauty of the heart-ravishers, their blandishments and ogles are beyond description,' says Abdul Razak with puritanical horror. These girls were skilled dancers and singers, and many of them amassed enormous fortunes. The revenues derived from the brothels were used to pay the police."†

The prostitute profited much by the social degradation of married Hindu women in medieval India. Bound and condemned to domestic drudgery, the role of married women among the respectable classes was to bear children and to look after them. They had neither time nor freedom to cultivate those refinements which make women attractive to men. The prostitute, on the other hand, lived only for attraction; every successful harlot had to gain proficiency in dancing, singing and literature, and in adorning her person to the best advantage. Free and unowned, the prostitute could refuse her charms as she liked, and she alone could provide that sense of conquest (though by money) which is essential for all successful courtship. And as men of the higher castes had a morality different from that of their wives, they assiduously sought the favours of the gay women of the city as a relief from the boredom of the company of their uninteresting wives. Thus gained ground in Hindu society, the idea of two legitimate classes of women; those fettered to domestic drudgery in holy wedlock, and the free courtezan who lived for the pleasure of men.

All prostitutes, however, were not alike. The types with whom "kings took counsel" were known as Ganikas. The Ganika was an accomplished woman, proficient in the sixty-four arts, well-mannered, exceedingly beautiful, a patroness of men of letters and of philosophers, a wonderful conversationalist, intelligent, sensible, liberal towards the poor and reverent towards her superiors. Princes, nobles, poets and philosophers sought her company. She was the jewel of the city in which she lived. A well-known Ganika was able to build up the fame of a city, and ancient literature speaks of kings who tried to attract Ganikas of neighbouring kingdoms by special favours so as to enhance the reputation of their own kingdoms.

An amusing story of intrigue is told of Kalidasa and his patron, both of whom were in love with a Ganika. The story is worth narrating, as it illustrates the position the Ganika held in Hindu society. King Bhoja, Kalidasa's patron was so enamoured of the charms of a Ganika that he jealously kept her other lovers away from her. She was, however, of a literary turn of mind, and was exceedingly fond of the witty Kalidasa whom she used to entertain in her apartment unknown to the king. One day, as ill luck

* E. P. Mathers, *Eastern Anthology.*

† Rawlinson, *India.*

would have it, the king paid a surprise visit to her, and Kalidasa had just enough time to hide himself behind her wardrobe unnoticed by the king. It did not, however, take the king long to find out that the Ganika was sporting with some lover when he entered the premises. In her confusion, she confessed her guilt, and the king, in his wrath, ordered her head to be shaved.* Upon this, Kalidasa emerged from his hide-out to point out that there was a serious miscarriage of justice in the king's order. The head of the lady, he told the king, was innocent, and the punishment of shaving was misplaced! The king, it is said, burst out laughing, and left the irrepressible wit to continue his dalliance with the courtezan.

Due mainly to Muslim and British influence, the Ganika has disappeared from public life in India. But prostitution, though not encouraged, is even now tolerated as a necessary social evil. The Hindu, it must be mentioned, has still a soft corner for the prostitute. On occasions of festivities, the service of a prostitute, proficient in dancing and singing, is often requisitioned. Among the wealthier classes, it is still "fashionable" to keep mistresses, and in some parts of India, the social position of an aristocrat is judged by the number and notoriety of the women he keeps.

DAMODARAGUPTA AND KSHEMENDRA

Venal love had its bards. Two well-known works on the subject have come down to us. These are the Kuttanimatham (lessons of a bawd) of Damodaragupta and Samayamatrika (harlot's breviary) of Kshemendra. Damodaragupta lived in the eighth century A.D. and Kshemendra in the eleventh.

Except Kuttanimatham, no work of Damodaragupta is extant. Before discussing this work, a word may be said about the Indian bawd. This person is often an old woman, who had been gay in her young days but whom age has disqualified from taking active part in the profession. Her position in disreputable society is the same as that of the mother-in-law in respectable society. She instructs the young women under her charge in the art of venal love, and sternly rebukes any girl who shows tendencies of softening towards a young gallant and of making a free gift of her charms. She studies her customers carefully and takes pains to forbid entry to those who develop a tendency to ask for credit. She collects the fees in advance at the desk before the customer is let in. She is the object of ridicule of all those who know the ways of harlots. Customers detest her, and young women fear her. But she has control of the purse and stays in the market against the wishes of both buyers and sellers.

It is this personage Damodaragupta has selected to give instruction to his heroine Malati. This courtezan of the holy city of Benares, young and new to the profession, wishes to get instruction on the subject and approaches the oldest bawd in the street. The old sinner, when Malati meets her, is seated on a stool in the street at the doorway of her house, and around her are a number of young women who had sought her advice like Malati. Here is a picture of the bawd: "Her thin sown teeth rose up within her mouth, and her chin had fallen away; her pug nose was flattened broadly, and her belly, with its soft and bloated flesh, was hidden beneath a mass of ruinous breasts; her sunken eyes, under their fallen lids, were bleared and red, and the lobes of her ears hung down unjewelled; her rare white hairs dropped on too long a neck, ploughed with a knot of veins. She wore a robe of glittering white, her collar bore an amulet, and she carried a ring on her finger, portraying a slim girl."†

This individual now starts her lectures on the trade of love. The first thing a successful courtezan is to learn is to cultivate hard-heartedness. She must have a heart of granite but honeyed lips. Scorning real love, she must so successfully feign it as to delude her lover into mistaking it for a passion for him. No lover, however handsome or well-meaning, must be admitted into the house of a courtezan if he has no money; and no one who brings money to her house must be permitted to take even a small amount of it back. If a customer shows reluctance to part with cash at the desk, a successful courtezan must see to it that he surrenders it in the inner apartments. Rings, wrist chains and other ornaments vain men love to wear, may easily be acquired by the clever courtezan while playing the game of love. If, after working a man up, the girl suddenly develops coldness and withdraws her favours, the lover, we are told, can be made to yield anything he possesses, even his soul!

Damodaragupta shows an intimate knowledge of Vatsyayana and the bawd instructs her young students on the art of pleasing men, her lectures on this branch of the trade being based on the Kama Sutra. It is, however, worthy of note that Damodaragupta has a few passages addressed to foolish men who frequent the houses of harlots. "They (the harlots) are as unpitying as the ichneumon for the snakes, yet smile and smile; although they are lamps of love, in the sweetness of oil they nothing participate.

"They practise the expediency of princes; they studiously avoid, that is to say, relation with the penniless; they are man-eating birds.

"Women and bees first coax their victims open; then leech them to the dregs.

"What things have power of attraction and a hard exterior? Woman and lodestones.

"Harlots and elephants have this in common: they are ridden by men, and loved for their lying devotion; they are well-beaten about the hinder parts and go from one owner to another."‡

Damodaragupta's work is fragmentary, and some of the passages are incoherent. He was not much of a literary genius and his work is somewhat sentimental.

Kshemendra was, on the other hand, an accomplished and brilliant writer. His Samayamatrika is a masterpiece, compact and unified, bristling with cruel

---

* Shaving the head was the usual form of punishment meted out to courtezans for minor offences.
† Tr. E. P. Mathers.
‡ Tr. E. P. Mathers.

wit, marked by cynicism and possessing much literary merit. In many respects his work can be compared to Voltaire's Candide.

The heroine of the Samayamatrika is a young courtezan, Kalavati by name, who lived in the city of Pravarapura in Kashmir. This city was "the sensuous court of Kama, the fortunate house of games and laughter, the place of the waves of the lascivious sea which women rule." The old street barber, who knew all the women of the city, happens to meet Kalavati, and finding in the lady the promise of a great life, tells her to seek instruction at the feet of Arghagharghatika, the richest and oldest courtezan of Pravarapura. On Kalavati wishing to know something about this woman, the barber gives her a short biography of Arghagharghatika.

This lady entered the profession while very young. Her first adventure was with a wealthy merchant. She so well plied him with wine that he did not notice the loss when she, hanging about his neck, removed his ear-rings and seals. After this she cried Help! Help! as if she had discovered a thief in her bed-room, which brought the neighbours with cudgels and knives at her door, and the foolish merchant fled for life.

Arghagharghatika sold the gold at a good price, and migrated to another city where she set up a house and continued to practise the trade. She was an indefatigable worker and toiled day and night. "What with the lovers who went in, and the lovers who came out, and the lovers who waited at the door, there were as many men about her house as there were wandering dogs in the city." When money was to be made, she never hesitated to go out of doors. The guardian of the city temple was particularly fond of her and she used to visit the shrine very often. One night, after she had sported with the holy man, he fell fast asleep and she walked stealthily into the sanctuary and bolted away with all the jewels of the goddess. She left the city that very night, changed her name and for some time lived a retired life in a new city.

She did not remain single for long. For a rich farmer took a fancy for the cut of her face, and he was fool enough to waste half his fortune on her. This antagonised the relatives of the farmer, and he was, one day, found clubbed to death in one of his fields. Not daunted by this calamity, our heroine immediately went to the farmer's father, who was so moved by the tale of her woes that he took her under his protection. She gave the old man many herbs and tonics which restored to him his lost vitality to such an extent that he clung to her like a leech. His life became a public scandal and he could neither abandon his mistress nor face his people; in this predicament he cut his own throat, and his mistress laid hold of what cash and gold she could collect, and left the place for another city.

In her new city she lived as a widow, wearing white garments of silk and looking very pretty in them. Living a reserved life, she kept her distance from men, which made her all the more attractive to fools. One day, however, while attending a religious function "she snared a rich knight named Bindusara as a heron takes a fish." After living for some time with him, she murdered him and went into deep mourning for him. After establishing her legal claim to his wealth she resumed her gay life, and then the royal steward fell for her. As she started robbing this person, his sons revolted, and this led to a lawsuit in which she engaged a rich lawyer who could not resist her charms. She managed to put herself in possession of all his wealth including what she had paid him by way of fees.

She had a few more adventures of a like nature, but in one instance she was caught red-handed by the minions of law, convicted and jailed. But she made friends with the gaoler and escaped from the prison.

By now our heroine had grown somewhat old, but she managed to look pretty by make-up and there were many fools who mistook paste for flesh. As the income from her body began to decrease, she supplemented it by running a public house where every man who got drunk lost something. When this game was played out she tried astrology and palmistry. Finally, even this failed to bring her money, and she took up the position of a bawd.

The barber introduced Kalavati to this infamous person and she gave a lengthy discourse on the greatness of her profession and on how to achieve success in it. I do not wish to quote it at length, but a few typical passages may be cited.

The need for making the best of a courtezan's youth is emphasized, for "men are like palm-trees in their strength and have a durable youth; but she who yesterday was a child, is a girl today, and tomorrow an old woman." A lover who has lost his wealth must be immediately discarded, as one spits out the chip of the sugarcane once it is well-chewed and the juice drunk; for "when the flower has withered and spoils its place among the hair, how quickly the hair itself will let it fall!" Young courtezans are warned against pregnancy. "Pregnancy means this for a young woman; a blight upon the graces of youth, a muddy maturity for the body's stem, an unforgivable sin against the pride of breasts. When a love-seller finds that the youth of her breasts has died in the disgraceful disaster of child-bed, what may she expect to fetch in the open market?"

In his epilogue, Kshemendra says that he wrote his work as a warning to foolish men against the dangers of the brothel. Says he: "Now you have learned that ancient benefits mean nothing to a bawd, and have seen how she cheats her daughter's lovers." But Kshemendra has no illusions on the subject. For "although the gazelles in the forest well know how game is taken, they run head-down into the snare." So indeed it has proved. In spite of all the preachings of saints, all the threats of punishments in this world and the life to come, all the warnings of moralists, men walk into the snares of the courtezan with their eyes wide open.

CHAPTER XIV

HINDU CALENDAR AND HOLIDAYS

ALL Hindus do not follow the same calendar. More than a dozen eras are in use among the Hindus, each one based upon some myth or fable the real significance of which is now lost. The reckoning followed in all these different eras is either purely solar or luni-solar. Pure lunar reckoning is not now in use. It is probable that the most ancient form of reckoning among the Hindus was lunar, and foreign influence was responsible for the adoption of the solar reckoning.

The obvious natural division of time is the day and the lunar month; the latter is divided by the Hindus into two Pakshas or fortnights called the Shukla Paksha (bright half) and the Krishna Paksha (dark half). The fourteen days of each Paksha are: Prathama (first), Dwitiya (second), Trithiya (third), Chaturthi (fourth), Panchami (fifth), Shashti (sixth), Saptami (seventh), Asthami (eighth), Navami (ninth), Dashami (tenth), Ekadasi (eleventh), Dwadasi (twelfth), Thrayodasi (thirteenth) and Chaturdashi (fourteenth). The full moon day is called Purnima (full), and the new moon day, Amavasya (living with).* These names are important because a good many Hindu holidays are known by the name of the day and that of the deity in whose honour the day is observed as holy, such as, Ganesha-Chaturthi, Ram-Navami, Naga-Panchami, etc. The lunar month begins with the full moon according to some reckonings and with the new moon according to others.

The months of the lunar year are: Chaitra (March-April), Vaisakha (April-May), Jyeshta (May-June), Ashadha (June-July), Sravana (July-August), Bhadrapada (August-September), Asvina (September-October), Karthika (October-November), Margashirsha (November-December), Pausha (December-January), Magha (January-February), and Phalguna (February-March). The moon in each month is believed to pass through twenty-seven Nakshatras or asterisms and these constitute the lunar mansions of the Hindu calendar.

The most obvious advantage of solar reckoning is the definite relation obtained between the months and the season. The reader may have had occasion to notice that the Muslims who follow purely lunar reckoning, have their Ramzan fast sometimes in winter and at other times in summer. This is obviously due to the month Ramzan not corresponding to any definite season. Europeans who follow solar reckoning, on the other hand, always have a cold December and a warm July. The Hindus recognized this advantage of the solar reckoning and some of them adopted it for their calendar while others fitted the lunar year into the solar. Now, a lunar year falls short of the solar by about 11 days, and to catch up with the solar reckoning, Hindu astronomers add one month to a lunar year every three years or so. This intercalary month is called Adhikamasa (extra month). The Adhikamasa does not occur at regular intervals, but is added on those occasions when a lunar month falls between two Sankrants (the time the sun leaves one sign of the Zodiac and enters another) and passes without one.

The solar reckoning of the Hindus closely follows the Greek system. The Sanskrit names of the signs of the Zodiac are: Mesha (Aries), Vrishabha (Taurus), Mithuna (Gemini), Karka (Cancer), Simha (Leo), Kanya (Virgo), Tula (Libra), Vrischika (Scorpio), Dhanus (Sagittarius), Makara (Capricorn), Kumbha (Aquarius) and Meena (Pisces). The solar months of the Hindus are named after the signs.

The Hindu names of the days of the week bear closer affinity to Greek names than English names do. Sunday is called Ravi-var, Monday Soma-var, Tuesday Mangal-var, Wednesday Budh-var, Thursday Brahaspati-var, Friday Sukra-var, and Saturday Sani-var. Ravi means Sun, Soma Moon, Mangal Mars, Budh Mercury, Brahaspati Jupiter, Sukra Venus, and Sani Saturn. There are elaborate astrological treatises dealing with the influence of the planets on the destiny of individuals on each day, and what must and must not be done every day of the week. The solar day or Divasa of the Hindus is divided into sixty Ghatikas, each Ghatika being equivalent to 24 minutes. A Ghatika is sub-divided into sixty Palas, a Pala into sixty Vipalas and a Vipala into sixty Prativipalas. The Prativipala is the smallest Hindu division of time and is equivalent to about 0.006 seconds.

The Hindus call an almanac "Panchanga" (of five limbs), because it deals mostly with the five main divisions of time. These divisions of time are: Vara (week), Thithi (lunar day), Nakshatra (the lunar mansion which is the twenty-seventh part of the lunar month and is equivalent to 24 hrs. 18 min.), the Yoga or conjunction, and the Karana; the Yoga and the Karana are time-divisions based on the joint motion of the sun and the moon, the former being equivalent to about 22 hrs. 34 min. and the latter to half a Tithi.

HINDU ERAS

There are in use among the Hindus a dozen eras, while the number of obsolete ones are about as many. The following are the more important of the eras, now in use.

(1) THE KALI ERA: This is based on the mythical astronomy of the Hindus. We have seen in Chapter I that the Hindu cycle consists of four Yugas or ages constituting a Mahayuga or great age. The Kaliyuga is the last of the four ages and its length is said to be 43,200 solar years, at the end of

---

* Amavasya is so called because on this day the moon is supposed to be living with the sun.

which this world is to perish. The Kali era is calculated to have begun "at midnight on Thursday corresponding to 17-18th February, 3102 B.C. old style." So we are now living in the sixth millennium of the Kali era, the year, 1900 A.D. corresponding to 5002 of the Kali era.

The Kali era is the classical era of the Hindus, and is even now used all over the country mainly for religious and literary purposes. Hindu writers have an ingenious system by which they denote the date of an event by its description alone (mainly in poetry), each letter of the alphabet having a definite numerical value, and a stanza denoting the date. In such literature the Kali era is commonly used.

The years of the Kali era are luni-solar.

(2) VIKRAM ERA: This era is extensively used in North India except Bengal. In Gujarat it is the sole era in use. The era is traced to the semi-mythical king Vikramaditya, from the date of whose coronation it is believed to have begun. But it is interesting to note that upto the eighth or ninth century of the era it was not called Vikram era at all, but merely Samvat meaning a year. It is probable that some king, to whom the Vikramaditya legends were later attributed, introduced innovations in an era already existing in his time, and the era thenceforth came to be known by his name.

The Vikram era follows the luni-solar system of reckoning. It is older than the Christian era, the year 1900 A.D. corresponding to 1958 of the Vikram era.

(3) THE SAKA ERA: Like the Vikram era this is in extensive use in India. A good part of North India, the Mahratha countries and the greater part of South India use this era. Like the Vikram era it follows the luni-solar method of reckoning. It is of later origin than the Vikram era, the year 1900 A.D. corresponding to 1823 of the Saka era.

The era is believed to mark the accession to the throne of king Salivahan. According to one legend, he killed Vikramaditya and seized the Kingdom of Ujjain, while another story mentions the vanquished king as one Somakrant; considering the dates, the latter story is the more probable. The legend of Salivahan says that he was of miraculous birth. Vikramaditya, or Somakrant, so goes the story, was to be killed, according to a prophecy, by a boy not older than his mother. The king becoming apprehensive of this danger sent the Vetal (his demon-slave) to find out if such a boy existed anywhere in the world. The Vetal came across a little girl and a boy playing in a potter's house, and on enquiry found that the boy was the girl's son. The boy was born of no man, the Vetal was told, but of a powerful serpent king. The Vetal reported the discovery to his master and the king immediately set out in search of the potter's house. Here the little boy killed the king in single combat and seized the throne of Ujjain.

(4) The BENGALI SAN: An era used exclusively in Bengal. The years of this era are purely solar. It is of later origin than the Saka era, the year 1900 A.D. corresponding to Bengali San 1408.

(5) THE MADI SAN: Current in Chittagong. It is similar to the Bengali San, but commenced 45 years after the Bengali San.

(6) THE SAPTARSHI KALA: An era current in Kashmir. The era is so called because it is based on an assumption that the Saptarshis or seven sages (Ursa Major) "move through one Nakshatra in one hundred years."

(7) THE KOLLUM ERA: In use in Kerala State and certain adjoining regions. It is believed to have commenced when the country was reclaimed from the sea by Parasurama. Tradition has it that to expiate the sins committed by him, especially in the campaigns against the Kshatriyas (see page 14). Parasurama prayed to the sea god Varuna for a piece of land which he wished to give as a gift to Brahmins. Upon this, the sea is fabled to have receded from the foot of the Western Ghats and presented Parasurama with the Malabar Coast.

The Kollum era runs into cycles of 1000 years. After each cycle the era starts afresh. The astronomers of Malabar maintain that three cycles have already passed and we are now living in the fourth. The fourth cycle, however, is allowed to run over a thousand, and the year 1960 A.D. corresponds to Kollum 1136. The years of the Kollum era are purely solar.

HINDU HOLIDAYS

The Hindus have no weekly day of rest. But astrology, ritualism and a vivid imagination have supplied the Hindus with numerous holidays in the year, and a pious Hindu can find sufficient text to observe every day of the year as a holy day and abstain from useful work. The main controlling factor in the observance of holidays is astrology. The sun, moon, the planets and the countless stars of the heavens are, to the Hindu, deities exercising definite influence on the daily life and destiny of men. Some of these deities are malevolent, others benevolent. But each has his moods, and a malicious planet in an auspicious conjunction of stars may be in a pleasant mood, while a benevolent planet in an inauspicious conjunction may lose his temper and cause harm. Hence every day, every hour, nay every minute of the day, has to be studied carefully and the proper deity propitiated. Only then can a conscientious Hindu escape the wrath of the gods, and hope to obtain salvation. This belief is general among the Hindus and accounts for the extraordinary position the astrologer has held in Hindu society throughout the ages.

Each day of the week is, in a sense, holy since it is dedicated to a deity, and certain observances are indispensable to those who wish to keep peace with the gods on that day.

Sunday or Ravi-var is sacred to the sun. The sun, in Hindu mythology, is known as a luminous red person driving in a chariot drawn by seven horses. His charioteer is the lame Arun or morning. According to Hindu astrologers the Sun is a malefic and a man born under his influence "will possess an anxious mind, be subject to diseases and other sufferings, be an exile, a prisoner, and suffer the loss of wife, children and property." All the more reason why the sun should be propitiated on the day sacred to him. Sunday, however, is considered propitious for beginning an undertaking, such as building a house, starting a business, etc. The colour sacred to the sun is green, and it is considered good to wear a green robe on Sunday.

Monday or Soma-var is sacred to the moon. The moon, in Hindu mythology, is a male deity, handsome and active. He rides an antelope. The full moon is benefic and a man born under his influence "will possess elephants, horses and palanquins; will be honourable and powerful; and will live on excellent food and rest on superb couches." As the moon forms part of Shiva's adornments, Monday is also sacred to this god. Shiva being an ascetic, it is good to fast on Mondays. Monday is not an auspicious day for shaving, as a man shaved on a Monday is feared to lose his son, if he has one. It is an act of merit to kill vermin on Mondays, and the victims are considered an offering to Shiva. The moon is partial to no particular colour, and the wise man, so as to avoid exciting the ire of other deities, is advised to wear a multicoloured robe on Monday.

Mangala-var or Tuesday is sacred to the planet Mars. In Hindu mythology he is known as Kumara or Kartikeya, second son of Shiva, and the god of war. In some myths he is mentioned as the husband of Devasena (army of the gods), in others he is said to be a misogynist and a hater of women. In certain parts of India women are not allowed to worship at his shrine, and a woman transgressing this rule is feared to lose her husband. It is considered unlucky for a girl to come of age on Tuesday. According to astrologers, the planet Mars is a malefic. A person born under his influence "will be full of anxious thoughts, will be wounded with offensive weapons imprisoned, oppressed with fear of robbers, fire, etc., and will lose his lands, cattle and good name." Hence the planet may be worshipped on Tuesday so that he may refrain from malevolent activities. Needless to say it is lucky to start a war on Tuesday. But it is inauspicious to begin any other undertaking on this day, such as going on a journey, building a house, etc. Red, the colour of blood, is dear to the war-god, and it is good to wear a red robe on Tuesdays.

Budh-var or Wednesday is sacred to the planet Budh (Mercury). He is the son of moon, born of an intrigue. The moon abducted Tara (star), wife of Brahaspati (Jupiter), who approached all the gods of heaven with a request to prevail upon the sinning god to return to him his wife. The gods were sympathetic, but the moon refused to return Tara. Upon this, Indra, king of the gods, declared war on the moon but the latter enlisted the support of the demons and met Indra on the battle-field with a formidable army of fiends. To avoid bloodshed, Brahma the creator, came upon the scene and asked the rash moon if he was not ashamed of himself to behave in this manner. He preached to him at length on the sin of adultery, and the moon, half-converted, reluctantly agreed to return Tara to her husband. Now another difficulty arose. For when Tara was returned, she was found pregnant, and Brahaspati refused to accept her till the birth of the child. Nor would the moon take her back. In this predicament, Brahma forced Tara to deliver the child immediately. The new-born babe was, however, so beautiful that both Brahaspati and Chandra (moon) claimed him. Brahma now asked Tara who the real father of the child was. Tara, out of delicacy, hesitated to answer when the babe suddenly found speech and commanded her to speak the truth. The lady now admitted, before all the gods, that Chandra was the baby's father. The moon was so pleased with his son's wisdom in speaking to his mother in that fashion that he called him Budh or wise.

Budh is neutral as far as astral influence is concerned. Persons born under him will have their destiny decided by the position of other planets in relation to Budh. Yellow is the favourite colour of Budh. The worship of Budh and feeding of Brahmins on Wednesday are believed to bring prosperity.

Brahaspati-var or Thursday is also called Guruvar; for Brahaspati (Jupiter) is said to be the Guru (spiritual preceptor) of the gods. His favourite colour is white. He is a Brahmin by caste and good-natured by disposition. He is a benefic. A person born under his influence "will be endowed with an amiable disposition, will possess palaces, gardens, lands, and be rich in money and corn. He will possess much religious merit, and have all his wishes gratified. Brahmins, however, will not be so fortunate as members of other castes, for Brahaspati, being a Brahmin, does not wish to exalt those of his own caste." A girl coming to womanhood on a Thursday will be the mother of many sons.

Sukra-var of Friday is sacred to the planet Sukra (Venus). According to the Hindus, Sukra is not a beautiful lady like Venus but a kindly old Brahmin, very wise and very learned. He is the preceptor of the Asuras or demons, but is not a bad person on that account. On the contrary, he is the most auspicious of all the planets. A man born under his influence "will have the faculty of knowing things past, present and future. He will have many wives, a kingly umbrella (an emblem of royalty) and other kings will worship him." Sukra is believed to know the magic formula which can bring the dead back to life. He is blind in one eye. This affliction was caused by Vishnu because of Sukra's extraordinary loyalty to his king.

The favourite colour of Sukra, like that of Brahaspati, is white, and on Fridays, the wearing of white robes is recommended. It is good to fast on Fridays.

Sani-var or Saturday is the day of Sani. Sani (Saturn) is the most malicious of the planets. He is painted by the Hindus as a lean, ugly, lame old man whose very appearance portends evil. He rides a vulture. All misfortunes are traced to him, so much so that periods of misfortune are usually termed by the Hindus Sani-Dasa (the period of Sani). It is not necessary for Saturn to plan or will evil. He just exudes evil. Once, out of sheer curiosity, he is said to have looked at the new-born baby of the goddess Parvati, and this resulted in the head of the baby flying off from its trunk. The head was irretrievably lost and no god could regain it. Hence an elephant's head was grafted to the trunk of Parvati's son. Thus the origin of Ganesha (according to one of the many legends), the elephant-headed deity of the Hindu pantheon.

The favourite colour of Sani is black. Saturday is auspicious for doing evil. Thieves and murderers may choose this day for their nefarious activities. The planet may, however, be worshipped on Saturdays so that his evil influence may be mitigated. There is even a legend to the effect that once he enriched a poor Brahmin household, where he went begging for food, disguised as a leper and was served with dainties.

VRATAS

Vratas may be described as days of fasting and prayer. Brahmin house-holders, wholly devoted to a religious life, usually observe all the Vratas prescribed by the texts. But those Hindus who are engaged in outdoor activities keep very few of these Vratas. Women, however, are very scrupulous in the observance of Vratas and spend such days in fasting, praying and performing the prescribed Pujas. The most characteristic feature of the Vrata is complete fasting or abstention from cooked food.

Hindu sacred books, especially the Puranas and certain other works which deal exclusively with rituals, give in great detail the methods of keeping the Vratas, their origin and the benefits that accrue from their observance. By observing even some of the minor Vratas, depraved sinners are said to have obtained salvation and poor wretches gold and diamonds; persons afflicted with incurable maladies, miraculous cure of their diseases, men and women with no children many sons; and so on. On the other hand, through neglect of keeping the prescribed Vratas, affluent persons are said to have lost their wealth, saints to have gone to hell, fertile women to have become sterile, and healthy persons to have suffered various afflictions. It may be noticed that giving presents to Brahmins is doubly efficacious on a Vrata day, and it is no wonder that we have a copious literature dwelling upon the merits of the Vratas.

Of all Vratas, the most commonly observed is the Ekadasi or the eleventh day of the fortnight (see p. 122). In every part of the country, women of the three higher castes fast on this day. Men whose work and inclination permit of it also do likewise. On the day previous, only a limited quantity of food is allowed to be taken. Before breaking the fast on the twelfth day a Brahmin has to be fed. If the person who observes the fast is of a caste from whom a Brahmin cannot accept cooked food, it is enough to give the Brahmin, ghee, rice, cocoanuts, fruits and other uncooked edibles.

The folklore of the Vrata traces its origin to a lady named Ekadasi who destroyed the Asura Mrudumanya. This demon, by virtue of his severe austerities, obtained a boon from Shiva by which he made himself free from death through natural causes, and from destruction by any one born of a female. Imagining himself thus immortal, he started terrorizing heaven itself and drove all the gods from their celestial abode. Brahma, Vishnu and Shiva himself, who had granted him the boon of immortality, had to flee for life. These members of the triad, with their wives, hid themselves in the hollow trunk of an old tree. Space was limited, the weather was hot, and the gods and their wives, huddled together in their uncomfortable hide-out began to perspire. From this perspiration sprang forth a maiden, Ekadasi, born of no woman, who waged war on the unreasonable demon and destroyed him.

The two Ekadasis falling in the month of Ashadha are celebrated with much pomp at Pandharpur, a Vaishnava shrine popular among the Mahrathas, and pilgrims flock to the great fairs held at the temple on these occasions. At Jagannath, the famous Vaishnava shrine of Orissa, Ekadasi, however, is in disgrace. No one is allowed to fast at Jagannath on Ekadasi, the day of universal fast among Hindus. It appears that the god of fast (in Orissan mythology Ekadasi is mentioned as a male deity) protested to Jagannath (Vishnu) against the pilgrims at his shrine who did not fast on Ekadasi day. Vishnu tried to reason with him, but the god of fast lost his temper and assumed an insolent attitude, upon which Jagannath asked his minions to capture the impertinent god and chain him near the entrance of his shrine. Pilgrims who visit the temple of Jagannath may see an image of Ekadasi, thus disgraced.

The importance of Vratas is at no time greater than during the four months of the Indian monsoon. The reason for this is that Vishnu, the preserver of the universe, goes to sleep on the tenth day of Ashadha and wakes up on the eleventh day of Kartik, and incessant vigil on the part of humans is needed to keep at bay the ferocious demons who are ever on the prowl to find an opportunity to destroy the good work done by the gods. It was, in fact, during one of these long slumbers of Vishnu, that the demon Hiranyaksha stole the Vedas and deprived the world of the wisdom and knowledge that support it. To regain the Vedas, Vishnu had to incarnate himself as the boar, delve into the ocean abode of Hiranyaksha and destroy him.

It may, however, be said that Vishnu does not enjoy undisturbed sleep for the whole period of four months. The god, who goes to sleep on the 10th of Ashadha, turns to his right side on the 11th of Bhadrabad (exactly after two months) and wakes up on the 11th of Kartik. Hence these three days are particularly important and should be spent in fasting and prayer. During the four months of Vishnu's slumber, it is considered meritorious to worship the print of a cow's hoof daily.

The full moon day of the month of Vaisakh is sacred to Ganesha. Ganesha is usually worshipped as the remover of obstacles and all who desire their ambitions to be fulfilled and wishes gratified are recommended to observe this day as a Vrata. Ganesha is a jovial god who is very fond of his dinner and the main items of the Vrata consists in offering plenty of food to the god. After offering him cooked food, fruits may be served. All this consecrated food may then be eaten by members of the family or distributed to Brahmins who may be given a feast and presents.

The third day of the month of Bhadrapad is dear to unmarried girls as by worshipping Parvati on this day, they hope to get married to the men they love. Parvati, whom her father wanted to give away in marriage to Vishnu, loved Shiva and ran away from home and engaged herself in austerities which so pleased Shiva that he appeared before her and promised to marry her. The girl who observes the Vrata is not permitted to eat anything but plantains on this day. She must spend the day in prayer and in performing the prescribed Pujas. Brahmins may be invited and fed, and a copper, silver or gold image of Shiva, according to the social and financial position of the performer of the Vrata, may be given to them. Girls who do not observe the Vrata are feared to remain unmarried for seven successive lives. Married women are also advised to observe the Vrata, as failure, in their case, may lead to widowhood in seven lives. The Vrata is known as Haritalika (abducted), as Parvati who ran away from home was suspected by her father to have been abducted.

Makara Sankrant is the winter solstice when the sun enters the sign Makara or Capricorn. It falls either in the month of Margashirsha or Pausha. As the sun now begins to move northwards, the Hindus naturally feel happy over the favourable course of the sun and believe that the day of the gods begin with Makara Sankrant. For the demons, on the other hand, the day marks the beginning of the night. On Makara Sankrant the sun is worshipped. It is a day of fast. Brahmins may, however, be fed sumptuously and given presents. Sexual congress is prohibited on this day. Other taboos include "using harsh language, cutting grass, plucking leaves, milking cows, sheep, goat or other animals."

Every Sankrant (see page 123) is a holy day and it is good to observe it as a day of fasting and prayer. But the Sankrant falling on Tuesday of every even month of the calendar is called Mangal Sankrant and is very holy. The deity of Sankrant is usually described as a goddess and her worship is recommended on these days. Sankrant Vrata, if properly kept, has "the power to wash away the sin of touching a Brahmin, a conch-shell, a cow, or a copper basin during a woman's recurring monthly illness."

A Puja sacred to the god Vishnu and performed not on a fixed day of the calendar but on any convenient day with a definite object in view is the Satyanarayan Puja. This Puja is somewhat expensive and involves the inviting of a large number of Brahmins, friends and relatives and treating them to music and light refreshments. An eloquent Kathak (teller of sacred stories), describes to the audience the exploits and greatness of Vishnu. Songs are sung in praise of the deity and the performer of the Puja is even required to dance. An important item of the Puja is the partaking, by all the assembled people, of a consecrated pie made of flour, ghee and slices of plantain. The ingredients of the pie must be of equal weight, one and a quarter being the lucky weight for each. The Puja of Satyanarayan, if properly performed, is believed to grant the performer not only the particular prayer for which the Puja is performed, but salvation. The Puja is most popular in the Mahratha countries and Uttar Pradesh.

Hindu women fast on the full moon day of the month of Jeshta in honour of Savitri. The Vrata is called Vat Savitri (Banyan Savitri) or Vat Purnima (Banyan full moon.) Savitri is the paragon of conjugal fidelity and she is fabled to have brought her dead husband back to life by her devotion and loyalty to him. Hence women who observe this Vrata are assured of the longevity of their husbands. Worship of the Banyan tree forms part of the rituals, hence the name Vat Savitri.

The above list of Vratas is not exhaustive, but indicates only a few of the important ones. There is enough in the Hindu texts, as mentioned elsewhere, to make the pious householder and his wife observe every day of the year as a Vrata, and it is impossible to describe all the Vratas and their folklore in a work like this. I may, however, mention two extraordinary days of the Hindu calendar which do not recur every year but fall only on rare occasions. One of these is Kokil Vrata and the other Kapila Shashti. Kokil Vrata is observed on the full moon day of the intercalary month when it falls in the month of Ashadha. This happens only once in twenty years. The day is sacred to Sati, wife of Shiva. It is known as Kokil Vrata (Kokil means cuckoo) because Sati is believed to have once been converted into a cuckoo for the sin of polluting a sacrificial fire. The story goes that Daksha, Sati's father, gave her in marriage to Shiva much against his will, and was never on good terms with his son-in-law. One day, Daksha gave a feast to the gods and did not invite his daughter and her husband. Sati went to the feast uninvited, and while arguing with her father on the pointed omission, Daksha made some disparaging remarks about Shiva. To vindicate her husband's honour, Sati immediately jumped into the sacrificial fire, and burnt herself to death. Shiva appeared on the scene and in a terrible combat, destroyed a good many of the partisans of Daksha, and this person himself lost his head. Sati, however, had to atone for the sin of having polluted the sacrificial fire and she was reborn as a cuckoo. For the proper observance of Kokil Vrata, a person must take but one meal a day for the whole of the intercalary month, and on the last day nothing at all. A live cuckoo may be worshipped if one is found by chance or procurable on payment of money; otherwise, an image of the bird may be worshipped.

The other extraordinary day, Kapila Shashti, occurs on a certain conjunction of planets and stars which, according to Hindu astronomers, happens only once in sixty years. The necessary conditions for this auspicious conjunction are seven: (1) The day must fall in the month of Bhadrapad. (2) It must be the dark half of the month. (3) It must fall on a Tuesday. (4) The sun must be at Hasta, the thirteenth lunar sign. (5) The sun and moon must be in the opposite Ayana, the sum of their longitudes being 180 degrees (this conjunction is known as Vyatipati). (6) The moon must be at the fourth sign, Rohini. (7) It must fall on the sixth day of the Paksha. If this rare conjunction occurs at night, it is considered abortive.

Because of this extraordinary conjunction which falls once in sixty years, both the Saka and Vikram eras run in cycles of sixty years. The last Kapila Shashti fell on 1st October 1912.

The mythology of Kapila Shashti is interesting. The sage Narada, the favourite son of Saraswati, dedicated his life to the promotion of literature and music and remained a celibate. But after some years, he began to feel tired of single life and longed for the company of the fair sex. He requested his friend Krishna, husband of 16,008 wives, to spare one of his wives for him as it was obviously impossible for Krishna to manage so many women. Krishna agreed to this, and asked Narada to take that wife of his whom he found alone. Narada went to the palace of every queen but found her enjoying the company of her husband. Tired of wandering from house to house in search of a wife, Narada gave up the pursuit and went to the Ganges for his ceremonial bath. Coming out of the waters of the river, the sage was disconcerted to find himself converted into a woman! Standing on the banks of the Ganges, not knowing what to do with himself, or rather herself, the woman was led into a hut by a hermit. The hermit married her, and every year she gave birth to a son till she had sixty sons. By now the prolific mother became sick to death of the cares of child-birth and of her domestic life, of which she had thought so highly as Narada. She prayed ardently to god Vishnu to restore her lost manhood and swore that once converted to her original self, he would never wish for domestic happiness again. Upon this, the hermit stood before her as god Vishnu and the woman was converted into Narada again.

As far as Narada was concerned, this was all right. But the hungry sons of Narada now started crying for food, and the helpless sage appealed to Vishnu. This god gave each of the sons kingship over the world to be enjoyed in turn. Hence each of the sixty years of the Hindu cycle is supposed to be presided over by one of the sons of Vishnu and Narada, and is named after him. The last day of the cycle is Kapila Shashti, believed to be the day on which Narada was reconverted into a male.

FEASTS AND FESTIVALS

HOLY: Of the Hindu festivals which have an all India importance, Holi is the most popular. It is essentially a festival of the people, and the whole country puts on a holiday atmosphere during at last three days of the festival. Holi is a fertility festival which has its origin in the aboriginal orgies of some powerful tribe, and even now retains many of the characteristics of the fertility festivals of savages. The processions are usually composed of drunken crowds who dance and sing lewd songs, and carry phallic emblems. The Holi, for obvious reasons, is dearer to the lower classes than to the upper. An interesting feature of the festivities is the squirting of coloured water on one another. Even men of rank, and women of the higher castes, indulge in this innocent pastime and grave men and women who look sternly on the frivolities of the clownish are often held down by a number of gay fellows and poured coloured water on. Children parade the streets with syringes and bottles containing coloured water and threaten to discolour the clothes of passersby who are, however, allowed to go unmolested on payment of a small sum. Mischief and frivolity reign the day.

In most parts of India, Holi is appropriately connected with some of the activities of Krishna, the god of many loves. Effigies of Putana, a female demon whom the child Krishna killed, is made and destroyed. In South India the songs sung by women include the lamentations of Rati, wife of Kama the love-god, on the destruction of the latter by Shiva whose asceticism Kama disturbed. In Mathura, the centre of Krishna worship, Holi festivities last for several weeks and pilgrims flock from all over India to take part in the celebrations.

Holi falls on the full moon day of the month of Phalgun (February-March) which heralds the spring.

DIVALI: The word Divali is a corruption of the Sanskrit Deepavali meaning "cluster of lights." The festival is so called because of the illuminations that form part of the celebrations. It is a four-day festival which includes the last two days of the month of Asvin and the first two days of Kartik. It is the new year festival of those Hindus who follow the Vikram era and begin the year with Kartik as the first month. King Vikram is believed to have ascended the throne on this day. Another legend of the origin of the festival is that Rama, after the conquest of Lanka and the return to Ayodhya, was crowned king on this day. The two legends are not, however, mutually exclusive. Rama might have ascended the throne on this day and king Vikram probably selected this auspicious day for his own coronation. In the Mahratha countries there is yet another story explaining the origin of the festival. The good King Bali, who ruled the three worlds justly, and under whom this world attained unheard of prosperity, is believed to have been dethroned by Vishnu, out of sheer jealousy of his power on this day. Hence the Divali celebrations of the Mahrathas include making images of Bali and worshipping him. "In Bengal it is believed that the night of the Pitris (departed souls) begins at this time and lamps are lighted on long poles to serve as a guide to these benighted souls." Vishnu, again, is believed to have destroyed Narakasura, the demon of filth, on the first day of the Divali festival and effigies of this demon are erected and burnt in certain parts of the country. Vishnu, his wife Lakshmi, his eighth incarnation Krishna, and his sacred mountain Govardhana are worshipped during the Divali festival by Vaishnavas.

Divali is the most important festival of the trading classes of Western India. These wealthy merchants spend lavishly on this occasion, and beautifully illuminate those quarters of the city in which they dwell or conduct business. They send presents of sweet-meats to friends and relatives, and children are supplied with a good stock of crackers which they use all the four nights of Divali and turn nights into days. The trading classes begin everything afresh on New Year Day. They discard partly used account books of the previous year and start fresh ones; the houses are neatly whitewashed and the cushions and upholstery of furniture are changed; all don new clothes and generally begin a new life.

It is auspicious to gamble on Divali, and even respectable women indulge in this deep-seated human vice on this occasion.

DASARA: This royal festival of the Hindus is the culmination of the Navaratra (nine nights) festivities which begin on the first night of the month of Asvin. The Navaratra and the Dasara are held in honour of Durga, the warrior-goddess of the pantheon, and are particularly sacred to the fighting castes and ruling clans. The nine nights being observed as occasions of fasting and prayer in honour of Durga, Navaratra is also known as Durgapuja or Durgotsava. The rituals of the nine nights include the worship of a virgin on each day. The virgin selected to represent the goddess "should be healthy, beautiful and free from eruptions. She should be of the same caste as the devotee." The worshipper has the option of worshipping a girl on each of the nine days or nine girls in one day. In the latter case, the day selected is the fifth, particularly sacred to Durga, known as Lalita Panchami.

The wife of Shiva, as we have seen, is the most widely worshipped goddess of the Hindu pantheon, and her names and manifestations are many. During the Navaratra holidays, the goddess is worshipped in her nine warlike manifestations. The first of these manifestations is known as Mahakali, who, through her power for creating illusions, caused the death of two demons named Madhu and Kaithabha whom Vishnu could not vanquish in a battle that lasted 5,000 years. In the second manifestation of Durga, known as Mahishamardani, the goddess killed the buffalo-demon of immense might who troubled the inhabitants of the three worlds. The third manifestation of the goddess is known as Chamunda, as she killed two brother demons Chanda and Munda in this form. As Kali, the fourth manifestation, she destroyed Raktabija whom she killed by sucking his blood. In her fifth manifestation, the goddess was born as the daughter of Nanda, the herdsman, and was called Nanda on this account; as a babe, she predicted the destruction of Kansa, the demon whom Krishna was destined to kill. The sixth manifestation is known as Raktadanti (of bloody teeth) because she bit to death a ferocious demon. In the seventh she fought the demons of famine and protected the world from the ravages of this calamity for a hundred years; this manifestation of the goddess is known as Sakhambari. In the eighth she killed a demon called Durga and hence got her popular name Durga. In the ninth she destroyed the demon Aruna and is known as Labhramari.

The first seven days of Navaratra are usually spent in domestic and public worship of the goddess and there is very little of festivities. On the eighth day, however, feasting and merry-making is allowed. On the ninth day is the Dasara and it is an occasion for offering animal sacrifices to the goddess. Among the lower classes animals are still sacrificed; the upper classes, however, cut a cucumber or some other equally innocent vegetable symbolic of the animal sacrifice. The animal most dear to the goddess as already mentioned, is the buffalo, and in certain places a buffalo is still sacrificed at the shrine of Durga.

The Dasara used to be celebrated in right royal fashion by the princes of Hindu states. In the olden days, most of the military campaigns of Hindu kings against their neighbours started on the Dasara day; these activities were stopped by the British during the British period, but a great procession of infantry, cavalry, elephants headed by the prince, started from the palace and crossed the boundary of the city in memory of the olden days when the king left his kingdom for the invasion of others. The Dasara processions of Hindu princes were truly oriental in their pageant, colour and noise. Durga was ceremonially worshipped outside the boundary of the city, in a previously selected spot, and then the procession returned to the palace. With the coming of independence, and the disappearance of princes these ancient pageants are dying out.

The Shami tree (Prosopis spicigera) is worshipped on the Dasara day and its leaves, supposed to be gold on this day, are 'looted' after the worship. A legend says that in the reign of Raghu the famous ancestor of Rama, the leaves of all the Shami trees that stood in the city of Ayodhya were turned into gold by god Indra. Raghu, so the story goes, promised to make a costly gift to a sage but found himself short of money. So he decided to raid Amaravati, the wealthy city of Indra and made preparations for the invasion. Indra came to know of this and to avoid a battle with so powerful a king as Raghu, showered gold on all the Shami trees in Raghu's city of Ayodhya.

Of all the Dasara processions of India, that of the modern state of Mysore is the most famous.

MAHASHIVARATRI or Shiva's Great Night falls on the thirteenth day of the month of Magh and is to be observed as a fast in honour of Shiva. Every one is expected to keep vigil at night. The next day, however, is spent in feasting and gaiety. The fasting and vigil of the night are believed to bring great merit. The story is told of a hunter who, due to anxieties connected with his occupation, had to keep vigil on this particular night without even knowing that it was sacred to Shiva, and was converted into a saint and carried by Shiva himself into his Paradise.

Mahashivaratri, so called to distinguish it from the ordinary Shivaratri that falls on the thirteenth day of the dark half of every month, is a festival of all-India importance. The main feature of the festival is the large fairs held on river beds or sea-shores to which pilgrims flock in thousands. It is considered meritorious to bathe in the water near which the fairs are held. In some parts of India lower classes sing obscene songs at the fairs in honour of Shiva and his wife.

GANESH CHATURTI or Ganesh's Fourth falls on the fourth day of the month of Bhadrapad. Ganesh was born on this day. Although worship of Ganesh is fairly general all over India, the folk of the Western Region are particularly attached to this god. The main features of the festivities are the buying of a clay image of Ganesh by individual householders, worshipping it in the house and taking it in procession to be drowned in a river, a lake or sea as most convenient. The image is bought on Ganesh Chaturthi and taken to the house in a palanquin or on the devotee's head. Images to suit all pockets are available, from miniatures costing a few annas to life-size works worth well over a couple of hundred rupees. The image is kept in the house for four to seven days and worshipped daily. At the end of this period it is carried in a procession, accompanied by musicians and drum players, to the sea-side. Here the god is taken out of the palanquin, placed on the ground and worshipped, and a lamp is waved round his head as a sort of farewell. Then a paid menial takes the image, wades through the water and drowns it in waist-deep water.

As every householder takes his image in procession, the number of processionists and images increases as the journey progresses; and during the week following Ganesh Chaturthi, at the sea-side of Bombay can be seen vast crowds engaged in bidding farewell to the god before drowning him.

It is unlucky to look at the moon on Ganesh Chaturthi. Once, when Ganesh was out riding on his mouse, he fell off his charger, and Chandra (moon) who happened to see this laughed at the god. The irate Ganesh immediately pronounced a curse on Chandra who became an object of evil. Everyone who saw Chandra thereafter got into trouble and gods and men shunned him. Having thus become repugnant to all, Chandra hid himself in a lotus. Now the worlds became devoid of moon-light, and the gods approached Ganesh, and requested him to cancel his curse on the moon. Chandra too repented of his rash act and begged to be pardoned. He worshipped Ganesh in due form, and the god, accepting the prayers of the penitent sinner, cancelled the general effect of the curse but maintained that Chandra's insolence should be perpetuated and the curse should have effect on Ganesh Chaturthi. Hence, those who see the moon on this day are feared to be slandered. Even Krishna, the eighth incarnation of Vishnu, is said to have been maligned and spoken ill of, for the sin of looking at the moon on this day. The evil effect of the curse may, however, be avoided by getting oneself abused by one's neighbours. Hence those who see the moon on Ganesh Chaturthi provoke their neighbours into using bad language against them.

JANMASHTAMI, falling on the eighth day of the month of Shravan, is an important festival among Vaishnavas. Krishna was born at midnight of the 8th day of Shravan. The main items of the worship are feeding Brahmins, listening to sacred stories and performing Pujas in honour of Krishna. Janmashtami is also known as Gokulashtami, Gokul being the birth place of Krishna. Mathura, Krishna's birth-place, celebrates the festival on a grand scale.

NARALI PURNIMA or Cocoanut Day is celebrated on the full-moon day of the month of Shravan. The day marks the end of the monsoon and the chief festivities consist in people flocking to the river or sea-side and throwing cocoanuts to Varuna the sea-god (hence cocoanut day). The cocoanut is particularly sacred to the Hindus and is considered a symbol of Shiva, the three-eyed, because of the three 'eyes' of the nut. It is auspicious to break cocoanuts before starting any enterprise and the kernel of the nut forms part of the objects offered to the gods at the time of worship.

Narali Purnima is also called Rakhi Purnima because of the Rakhi or amulet girls tie round their brothers' wrists for luck. Any lady who wishes to show favour to a friend and adopt him as her brother may tie the Rakhi round his wrist, and he is in honour bound to remain her protector without having any other intentions towards her. The ladies who thus honour their brothers are entitled to receive presents of money from them. Members of the three higher castes renew their sacred threads on this day. On this account, Cocoanut Day is more important to the higher castes than to the lower.

RAMA NAVAMI or Rama's Ninth is the birthday of Rama, the seventh incarnation of Vishnu. Among the Vaishnavas, the festival begins on the first day of the month of Chaitra and continues till the ninth (hence Rama Navami) on which day, at noon, Rama was born. The birthday of Rama is celebrated in all important Vaishnava temples, the priest, when the sun reaches the meridian, publicly exhibiting a cocoanut, putting it in a cradle and announcing the birth of the god. The main features of the festival are organizing congregations and regaling them with stories of the exploits of the great Hindu hero who conquered the island of Ceylon and destroyed the demon king Ravana. Religious dances and plays depicting episodes from Rama's life are also organized. These dances and plays are known as Rama Lila, plays of Rama, and are particularly popular in Uttar Pradesh where was situated the ancient kingdom of Ayodhya where Rama was born.

HANUMAN JAYANTI, falling on the full moon of Chaitra, is the birthday of the great monkey chief Hanuman, who was a devoted ally and friend of Rama. Hanuman, according to some myths, was an incarnation of Shiva himself who took this form to help Rama in his war on Lanka. The loyalty and might of Hanuman are extolled in the Ramayana. He is so dear to the Vaishnava that wherever idols of Rama and Sita are installed, Hanuman's images are invariably placed by their side. Hanuman is the symbol of physical strength, ungrudging service and unquestioning loyalty, and the lower classes are particularly devoted to his worship. Hence his birthday is more popular among the lower classes than among the upper.

NAGAPANCHAMI or the Fifth Day of Snakes is sacred to Nagas or snakes. The snakes according to the Hindus are powerful gods, some well-disposed towards humans, others malevolent. The fifth day of Shravan (hence Panchami) is dedicated to them and they are worshipped in various ways. In South India, where snake worship is very common, the householder feeds live snakes which have a shrine in the compound. Some temples are dedicated to snakes and giving them fruits and milk at the shrine form the main item of worship. In Bengal, Manasa is the goddess of snakes and she is worshipped on this day. The Hindus have a copious serpent lore and each region has its own legends supporting the worship of snakes. On Naga Panchami day it is forbidden to plough a field. A legend says that a farmer ploughed his field on this day, and the ploughshare accidentally entered a hole and killed some young serpents living in it. The mother of these serpents came on the scene and bit the farmer. Not content with this, she went to the farmer's house and killed all the members of his family except a young girl who was engaged in the worship of serpents. Seeing the girl's devotion to her tribe, the serpent was much pleased, and repenting of her rash act, revived the farmer and all his dead relatives by a charm she possessed.

GUDI PARWA is the first day of Chaitra, the New Year Day of those who follow the Salivahan era. Salivahan is believed to have ruled in Maharashtra, and hence the day is celebrated mostly in the Mahratha countries. On this day, they raise a banner (hence Gudi Parwa or Banner First) of silk and gold cloth on a long pole and pay homage to it. Feasts are given by those who can afford them. It is lucky to eat a few bitter leaves of the Neem tree on this day, as this is believed to prevent diseases for the whole year. Every one is enjoined to speak in the most polite terms on this day; showing signs of anger or using violent language is strictly prohibited.

VAMAN DWADASHI (Vaman Twelfth) is sacred to Vaman, the fifth incarnation of Vishnu (see page 24). The worship of Vishnu and Bali is recommended on this day. It is said that those who observe the day in due form and give freely to Brahmins, will be reborn as kings who will possess the celestial kingdom, like Bali who conquered and ruled the kingdom of Indra. Vaman Dwadashi falls on the twelfth day of the month of Bhadrapad.

VASANTA PANCHAMI which falls on the fifth day of Magh is sacred to Sarasvati, the goddess of literature and fine arts. She is the purest and most lovable of the deities of the Hindu pantheon. She has no extra arms, indulges in no martial expoits like her sister-in-law Durga; nor is she worshipped for lucre as Lakshmi is. Sarasvati is the goddess of the intellectual and the refined, and in art she is represented as a pleasant faced lady holding the Vina, the popular musical instrument of the Hindus. On Vasanta Panchami day the goddess is worshipped and books, brushes and pens are placed before her images. In some parts of India dedication of books, etc., is done during the Navaratra holidays. Sarasvati being the goddess of the intellectually gifted, the celebration of her day is not marked by popular processions, dances and the like which form the main features of other Hindu holidays.

This list covers most of the holidays that have importance all over India or over a fairly large part of the country. But there are certain festivals which have only local importance, but are celebrated in the particular locality as a greater festival than any mentioned above. The Onam festival of Malabar, for instance, is the most important festival of the Malabar coast, celebrated in honour of Bali, the king whom Vaman dethroned, but nowhere else is this festival observed. Again, among the lower classes and aborigines, there are a number of festivals which do not conform to any of the important dates of the Hindu calendar, but are based on the tradition and lore of the tribe or sub-caste.

CHAPTER XV

CONCLUSION

IN the foregoing chapters my main attempt has been to give the reader a fairly representative picture of the Hindus and their way of life; hence, as far as possible, I have refrained from making comments, adverse or otherwise. The views expressed in this chapter, on the other hand, are entirely personal, and if any reader finds them not to his or her taste, I can only say in defence that opinions differ.

THE BURDEN OF THE PAST

The Muslim scholar and traveller al-Beruni wrote of the Hindus of medieval India: "They are by nature niggardly in communicating that which they know, and they take the greatest possible care to withhold it from men of another caste among their own people; still much more, of course, from any foreigner. According to their beliefs, there is no country on earth but theirs, and no created being beside them has any knowledge of science whatever. Their haughtiness is such that if you tell them of any science or knowledge in Khorassan or Persia, they will think you both an ignoramus and a liar. If they travelled and mixed with other nations, they would soon change their minds, for their ancestors were not so narrow-minded as the present generation is."*

This sound observation is true of the generality of the Hindus of the present day. Except those who have broadened their outlook by travel and proper study, the Hindus even now believe that there is little good outside their country and little knowledge outside Sanskrit literature. Ancient Hindus were originators of philosophy, arts and sciences, and they did not consider it derogatory to their national or communal pride to study the literature and scientific achievements of their neighbours and adopt what good could be found in other people. Indian astronomers, as we have seen, studied Roman and Greek astronomy, and incorporated what was desirable in these systems into their own, magnanimously acknowledge the sources. Further, from the time of Asoka (3rd century B.C.) till the Arab expansion under Islam, India was the inspiring source of culture in Asia, and her missionaries, Brahmins, colonists and adventurers carried Indian religions, social and political institutions, ideals of art and architecture to all Asian countries east of Persia; the admirable part India played in civilising the primitive peoples of South East Asia was particularly important.†

In medieval times, specially after the Muslim conquest, the cultural expansion of India ceased and her people slid into a narrow conservatism which shut out all outside influences and gradually degenerated into a worship of the past. Hindu thinkers could look only to their dead ancestors for guidance and inspiration. Seclusion and separatism became the watch words of Hindu society. Continued foreign aggression and the fear of annihilation in a hostile world were probably responsible for this extreme conservatism and social rigidity adopted by medieval Hindus. Whatever the causes, the result was not happy. Thought became stagnant and progress reactionary. It is no exaggeration to say that Hindu thought did not far advance from the time of the Upanishads, Hindu poetry from the time of the Mahabharata and Ramayana, and Hindu drama from the time of Kalidasa.

This is true to some extent of the present generation too. No theme in drama or cinema is so well appreciated as a story from the epics or the old Sanskrit masters. Even well-known painters of the present day can find no better subjects for their pictures than the meditating Buddha, the dancing Shiva and scenes from the epics. As regards thought, the best modern philosophers among the Hindus can do no better than interpret the teachings of their ancestors.

But so large a community as the Hindus could not have possibly existed for the last 3,000 years without a certain amount of adaptability; there have been in India, as we have seen in Chapter V, various reform movements intended to bring the religion and social institutions of the community in line with altered environments.

The younger generation in modern India is, again, in active revolt against the old order, and enlightened members of the Hindu community support it. It should not be imagined that religious leaders always combat these reform movements. Though the priests of the old school view all reforms with suspicion, there is at least one religious organisation which stands for the widest possible scope for individual and communal development and fearlessly denounces those ancestors who made the Hindus a narrow-minded and ineffective race. This organisation is the Rama Krishna Mission. The members of the mission are advocates of the Advaita philosophy and seek unity of the human race through incessant activity. One of the objects of the mission is to give the widest publicity to Hindu culture and thought. We have already had occasion to mention the celebrated missionary Swami Vivekananda. It will be interesting to quote what another well-known Swami says of the degeneration of Hinduism and the need for upheaval. "The Brahmins and social leaders of the middle ages," he writes, "were short-sighted and superstitious; they had love of power, they wished to rule over the people and keep them under their control. Today India would be one of the mightiest nations in the world if these short-sighted orthodox

---

* Quoted from Rawlinson's *India*.
† The subject is the main theme of the author's book, *The Story of the Cultural Empire of India*.

social leaders had not pursued a policy of seclusion and isolation, which resulted in absolute disunion among the members of the different classes of the Hindus. England could not have held her dominant sword over the heads of three hundred millions of people in India if there had been unity among the isolated communities and clans of the four divisions. Well has it been said by Sir Monier Williams: 'Certainly the antagonism of these caste associations and trade leagues has helped us to govern the country by making political combinations impossible.' "* The reader may wonder whether these are the utterances of a religious leader or a political rebel. But to the Hindu, politics, sociology and religion are inseparable from one another.

Swami Abhedananda, however, is hopeful of the future. "The conditions are changing. India of today is different from what she was fifty years ago. Education and intellectual progress are opening the eyes of the nation. The cry for social reform is to be heard in every corner of this vast country. People are beginning to see the defects of the existing social organism. The educated classes are now convinced that if the present conditions are allowed to continue, the absolute disintegration and complete annihilation of the national life will be the inevitable result. Thinking people are no longer satisfied with the seclusion and isolation of the different communities by the iron barriers of superstition. They wish to unify all communities into one homogeneous whole, to make every member feel that he is a part and parcel, not merely of a family, clan or community, not merely a part of a section of the Hindu nation which is limited by colour or caste, but a most important part of the Indo-Aryan nation as a whole. The solidarity of all classes and all communities is the aim of the social reformers. The work has begun, but it will take a long time to make this reform effective and universal." There is, no doubt, a great political and social awakening among the Hindus. But it remains to be seen whether or not the present reform movements will also die out, as so many have done before, leaving Hinduism little affected.

PSEUDO-SPIRITUALITY

It has become a fashion among the Hindus to speak of their culture as essentially spiritual and to treat the achievements of the nations of the West as merely materialistic. In their condemnation of the West they overlook the fact that the West has almost as great a spiritual heritage as India, in the teachings of Christ, St. Paul, Thomas Aquinas, and the numerous saints of the middle ages. Two of the four avowed objects of life, according to the Hindus, on the other hand, are Artha and Kama, meaning enjoyment of sexual pleasures and the acquisition of wealth. Nor are these neglected aims, for a great many Hindus are employed in the pursuit of wealth and of the legitimate pleasures of sex. I am afraid the Hindu condemnation of the civilisation and culture of the West, especially of the great heritage of Europe as essentially materialistic

* Swami Abhedananda, *India and Her People*.

was the solace of despair of a subject race who considered themselves not inferior to their masters. With the attainment of political freedom now, the Hindus will no doubt get over this inferiority complex.

Anyway, it must be admitted that the present day Hindus as a rule admire the passive more than the active. To a great many Hindus, inaction appeals as a sort of spiritual excellence, but in this they belie their own traditions; for the great heroes and sages of the Hindus like the legendary Rama and Krishna and the historical Sankara Acharya were men of exuberant energy and ceaseless activity. We have seen that the Bhagwad Gita, considered a perfect piece of revelation by all Hindus, teaches a philosophy of action rather than of passive meditation. The ignorant among the orthodox (these can be counted in millions), however, confuse inertia with spiritual perfection, and this has led to the breeding among the Hindus of an army of parasites who, under the pretext of piety and renunciation, idle their lives away and prey upon the community. The confusion of inaction and self-torture with spirituality has also produced a great many maniacs who assiduously court pain, privation or death as an end in itself. Although Western travellers and writers are usually attracted by these men, no fair-minded observer of Hinduism can say that these represent the Hindu best.

In fairness to the meditative outlook it must be admitted that the Hindu attitude towards life is more or less philosophic. Pessimism being the predominant note of his philosophy, the Hindu considers suffering as the necessary condition of life and is hence less impatient of his troubles than his Western brother. This had led the Hindu to a fatal reconciliation to all forms of suffering, preventible or otherwise, and he is less eager to improve his social and political status than the Westerner who often wonders at the bovine contentment of the Hindu. This state of mind, however, has its compensations. For in many cases the Hindu is quite happy when a Westerner considers him miserable, happiness being essentially a condition of the mind.

SOME HINDU CHARACTERISTICS

The Hindus strike the Europeans as an exceptionally docile race. Of the present day Hindus this is somewhat true. But that the Hindus had not always been so is evident from their history and literature. Continued foreign domination is mainly responsible for the docility of the Hindus. From the 12th century of the Christian era to the present day, the Hindus have been a subject race and nothing so thoroughly induces docility as long-standing dependence upon others. The decay of the Kshatriyas and the martial ideal they stood for also added to the inertia of the Hindus. Under the supremacy of the Brahmins, intellectual and spiritual attainments came to be considered superior to the martial. The martial philosophy of the Gita was interpreted by Brahmins as a school of thought rather than as a guide to conduct. Its importance was shifted from the battlefield to the study rooms and discussion halls of philosophers.

In his daily life and as a rule of conduct, what appeals most to the average Hindu is the philosophy of Ahimsa or non-injury. Even those Hindus who eat meat will often shrink back in horror if asked to kill. In this matter, every Hindu is a Jain at heart. Those Hindus who are non-vegetarians are such because of the weakness of the flesh.

Excepting the hardy races of the Punjab, the Hindus are diminutive in appearance when compared with the peoples of Europe. The sole reason for this is often pointed out as the climate of the country. This is not quite correct. The climate has probably something to do with it, but the main cause of the poor physique of the Hindus is the poverty of the lower classes and the stupidity of the higher. The average Indian worker does not eat as much nourishing food in a month as an average British workman does in a week. Poor Hindus live on a starvation diet all the year round. Those who are worst off in this respect are the people of the Southern States. The majority of the population of this area live on nothing more nourishing than rice gruel of poor quality and tamarind water.

The higher classes, on the other hand, indulge in gluttony and avoid all work involving physical exertion. A Hindu who has enough money to maintain himself and his family thinks it demeaning to do any kind of manual work. Sports being considered childish, the tendency among the better classes of Hindus is to sit idle, sleep or gossip. The trading classes of the cities are the worst sinners in this respect. The Bania usually starts work at about eight o'clock in the morning and leaves his shop at about nine in the evening. During this period he squats all along on a cushion or reclines on it and never leaves it except to answer calls of nature. He lunches and takes tea on the same cushion. Very naturally he develops a paunch and is unable to move about without the help of an automobile or a horse. For the hard-worked, famished Hindu labourer, the pot-bellied Bania is the embodiment of ease, comfort and material prosperity.

I have read many books written by Englishmen accusing the Hindus of dishonesty and underhand dealings. These accusations were mainly based on Englishmen's experience of their Hindu domestic servants. The first thing a European will do well to note is that no Hindu of the four higher castes will serve a beef eating Christian as a domestic servant. The Englishman no doubt was the ruler of the country, but the fact remains that he was an untouchable to a respectable Hindu. Hence the servants of Europeans were drawn mainly from the Panchamas who, as mentioned elsewhere, were treated by the Hindus themselves as the scum of society. These people cannot be expected to show a very high moral standard, and any observation based upon their behaviour cannot be applicable to the generality of the Hindus.

It is true that subtlety is a Hindu characteristic. During the Muslim and British domination the Hindus, a subject race, had to strain their wits to the utmost to be able to live in peace with their rulers. Hence they had developed a characteristic evasiveness towards all strangers. Among themselves, however, they are more outspoken and straight-forward. Hindu mercantile communities, it is true, do not always believe that honesty is the best policy; but then merchants all over the world are subtle, secretive and evasive, though courteous and polite.

The best types of Hindus are the higher classes of the villages. Agriculturists by occupation, they are free from the wiles of the city and take pride in the ancient virtues of the race. Seldom coming into contact with strangers, the simple Hindu villager is honest, outspoken and reliable.

GLOSSARY AND INDEX

Abdul Razak, a Muslim Scholar; 120.
Abhedananda, Swami; 133
Abhidamma, a Branch of Buddhist literature; 93.
Abhinavagupta; 99.
Abhishekapatra, a sacrificial vessel; 29.
Absolute Monism; 26.
Abu, Mount; 16, 107.
Abul Fazal; 112.
Achara, duties; 14.
Adhikamasa, intercalary month; 123.
Adigranth; 51.
Adinath or Adinatha; 107.
Adishura; 13.
Advaita, a system of philosophy; 41, 43, 132.
Advaitins; 42.
Aesop; 93.
Afghanistan; 50, 51.
Aghori, a sect; 26.
Agni, a *Purana*; 91.
Agni, the fire god; 22.
Agnikula Rajputs; 16.
Ahimsa, non-injury; 134.
Ahmad Shah Durrani, a prince; 8, 52.
Aitareya, a *Brahmana*; 88.
Ajanta; 106, 112.
Akali, a Sikh sect; 51.
Akasamukhins, a sect; 26.
Akbar; 16, 51, 112.
Akhada, wrestling and boxing ground; 60.
Al Beruni; 132.
Alexandria; 47.
Allah; 50.
Alvar, a Vaishnava poet; 98.
Amarakosa; 92.
Amarasimha, an author; 92.
Amaravati; 110.
Amarnath, a centre of pilgrimage; 35.
Amavasya, new moon; 123.
Amherst, Lord; 53.
Amils, a Hindu community of Sind; 17.
Amir Khusru, a musician; 100.
Amra, a flower; 118.
Amritsar; 51.
Ananga, a name of the god of love; 115.
Anandpal, a prince; 8.
Ananga Ranga; 115.
Anavalobhana, a ceremony; 78.
Andhras, a Brahmin sub-caste; 13.
Angaharas, poses; 102.
Angiras, a legislator; 91.
Anglo-Vedic College; 55.
Animism; 30.
Annaprasana, a ceremony; 78, 80.
Anuradhapura; 111.
Anusuman, a prince; 34.
Apastambha, a legislator; 91.
Apsaras, celestial dancers; 101.
Aquinas, Thomas; 133.
Aranyaka, an *Upanishad*; 89.
Arghagharghatika, a courtesan; 122.
Arhat, the enlightened one; 48.
Arjun, Guru; 51.
Arjuna, a Pandava prince; 44, 95, 111.
Arnold, E; 118.
Artha, acquisition of wealth; 37, 114.
Arthasastra; 4, 114.
Aruna; 129.

Aryan; 3, 4, 17, 19, 23, 97.
Aryabhatta; 96.
Arya Samaj; 54, 55.
Asana, posture; 39, 40.
Ashad or Ashadha, a Hindu month; 123, 127, 128.
Ashrama, order of life; 12.
Ashtami, a day of the lunar month; 123.
Ashtanga-hridaya-samgraha; 96.
Ashtanga-samgraha; 96.
Asia; 47, 48.
Asoka; 4, 5, 47, 105.
Assam; 27.
Asura, a demon; 24, 32.
Asva, horse-man; 114, 115.
Asvaghosha; 93.
Asvalayana, a legislator; 78, 80.
Asvamedha, horse sacrifice; 85.
Asvin or Asvina, a Hindu month; 123, 129.
Atharva Veda; 88, 96.
Atimukta, a tree; 118.
Atman, soul or First Cause; 38, 42, 43.
Atri, a legislator; 91.
Aum, a mystic monosyllable; 30, 79.
Aurangazeb; 8, 51, 100, 113.
Avatar, incarnation; 25.
Avidya, ignorance; 41.
Ayana; 127.
Ayodhya; 6, 90, 128, 129, 130.
Ayurveda, Hindu system of medicine; 96.

Baconian philosophy; 53.
Badarayana, a philosopher; 41.
Balarama; 34.
Bali, a king; 24, 131.
Bali, an island; 109.
Bana; 96.
Banerji, P; 103, 104.
Banias; 17, 134.
Bankim Chandra Chatterjee; 97.
Banyan, the Indian fig tree; 31, 67, 127.
Baptism of the sword; 51.
Barhut; 110.
Barygaza, an ancient port; 6.
Basu, N. K.; 115, 116, 117.
Baudhayana, a legislator; 92.
Besant, Mrs.; 33, 53.
Bellala Sena, a king; 13.
Belur temple; 109.
Benares; 30, 34, 51, 54, 83, 84.
Bengal; 27, 31, 53, 75, 79, 97, 118, 124.
Bengali; 97, 124.
Bengali San, an era; 124.
Bentinck, Lord William; 52.
Bhadrapad or Bhadrapada; a Hindu month; 123, 127, 129.
Bhadrinath, a place of pilgrimage; 35.
Bhagavad Gita; 44, 133.
Bhagavata, a *Purana*; 91.
Bhagiratha, a prince; 34.
Bhairava, a Raga; 99.
Bhajan, religious music; 98.
Bhakti, cult of devotion; 25, 43, 44, 49.
Bhandarkar, Sir Ramakrishna; 53.
Bharadwaja; 92.
Bharata, a mythical author; 99, 101.
Bharata, a prince; 89.

Bharatanatya, Indian classical dance; 102.
Bharavi; 96.
Bhartrihari; 93.
Bhaskara; 96.
Bhasya; 37.
Bhatti; 96.
Bhatti Kavya; 96.
Bhavabhuti; 95.
Bhavamisra; 96.
Bhavani, a goddess; 26.
Bhavisya, a *Purana;* 91.
Bhija Ganita; 96.
Bhils, a hill tribe; 32.
Bhoja, a king; 39.
Bhur, a mystic syllable; 79.
Bhuta, an evil spirit; 32.
Bhuvaneswar temple; 107.
Bhuvar, a mystic syllable; 78.
Bidpai; 93.
Bihar; 47.
Bilva, a sacred tree; 31.
Bindusara, a knight; 122.
Biting, in love; 116.
Bodhhisatva, Buddha elect; 46.
Bombay; 25, 130.
Bone-gathering ceremony; 83, 84.
Bone-throwing ceremony; 84.
Borbadour; 111.
Brahaspati; 37, 39, 91, 125.
Brahma, a god; 1, 10, 15, 17, 20, 23, 125.
Brahmacharya; 11.
Brahmin; 1, 10, 14, 37, 45, 80.
Brahminism; 45, 46.
Brahmagranthi; a sacred knot; 80.
Brahmagupta; 96.
Brahmanas, books dealing with rituals; 40, 87, 88.
Brahmanda, a *Purana;* 91.
Brahma, Nirguna; 41.
Brahmapurana; 91.
Brahma, Saguna; 41.
Brahmavaivarta, a *Purana;* 91.
Brahmo Samaj, a Hindu sect; 52, 53.
Brihad, an *Upanishad;* 87, 88.
Brij girls; 117, 118.
British; 8, 9, 53, 54.
Brown Percy; 104, 105.
Buddha 23, 24, 34, 45-47, 109, 110.
Buddhacharita; 93.
Buddhism; 5, 45-47.
Budh or Budha, a planet; 123, 125.
Bukhara; 50.
Burma; 17, 47.

Canarese; 13, 97, 98.
Candide; 122.
Caste; 10, 11, 19, 52, 54.
Catholic, Roman; 22, 27.
Central Asia; 47.
Central India; 105.
Ceremonial worship; 28.
Ceylon; 24, 47, 90.
Chaitanya, a Vaishnava saint; 25, 44.
Chaitra, a month; 123, 130.
Chaityas; 105.
Chakrapuja, circle worship; 27.
Chalukya; 7, 105, 108.
Chamunda, a goddess; 129.
Chanakya, an ancient statesman; 4, 5, 93, 96.
Chanda, a demon; 129.
Chanda, charioteer of the Buddha; 46.

Chanda, metre; 92.
Chandala, low caste man; 18.
Chandel, a Rajput clan; 15, 16.
Chandbardai; 97.
Chandidasa; 119.
Chandra, moon; 124, 125, 129.
Chandragupta II; 6.
Chandragupta Maurya; 4, 48, 96.
Charaka; 97.
Charvakas; 37.
Chaturdasi; 123.
Chaturthi; 123.
Chauhan, a Rajput clan; 16.
Chenda, the Malabar drum; 102.
Chengalam, a musical instrument; 102,
Chengiz Khan; 104.
Chera, an ancient kingdom; 7.
Cherumars; 18.
Chettiars; 17.
Chhandogya, an *Upanishad;* 88.
Chhoti, a small tuft of hair; 75.
Chidambaram; 35, 108.
Child marriage; 62.
China; 47.
Chitragupta, clerk of the god of death; 35.
Chitrasalas, art galleries; 111.
Chitrini, a type of woman; 114, 115.
Chittagong; 124.
Cholas, a dynasty; 7, 108.
Chow, a dance; 103.
Christ; 22, 43, 133.
Christian; 19, 22, 33, 43, 56, 134.
Christian era; 123.
Christianity; 43, 56.
Christians and Christianity in India and Pakistan; 7.
Christians, St. Thomas; 7.
Congress; 73.
Conjeevaram; 35, 108.
Coomaraswamy, A.; 101, 119.
Courtezan; 120, 121.
Cow; 30.
Cremation; 83, 84.
Cupid; 63, 68, 118.

Daksha; 91, 127.
Dakshinamargis, a sect; 27.
Damodaragupta; 121.
Dancers, status of; 104.
Dandaka; 90.
Dandapani; 46.
Dandin; 96.
Daroga, a Moghul Official; 112.
Darsan, auspicious sight; 77.
Darsanas, systems of philosophy; 88.
Dasakumaracharita; 96.
Dasami, a day of the lunar month; 123.
Dasara festival; 129.
Dasaratha, a king; 90.
Dasaratha Rama; 24.
Dasas, Vaishnava poets of South India; 25.
Dasyu, an enemy of the gods; 21.
Dayanand Sarasvati, Swami; 54.
Deccan; 7, 89.
Deepavali, Cluster of lights; 128.
Delhi; 8, 51, 89.
Deluge, the legend of; 2.
Demonology; 32.
Depressed classes; 21.
Devadasis, temple dancers; 100, 103, 120.
Devadatta; 46.

GLOSSARY AND INDEX

Devagandhari, a Ragini; 99.
Devi, a goddess; 27.
Devil dance; 103.
Dhaivat, a musical note; 99.
Dhanus, Sagittarius; 123.
Dhanwantari; 96.
Dharma, duty; 37, 40, 44, 91, 114.
Dharma Sastra, sacred law books; 15, 91.
Dhoti; 72.
Dhritarashtra, a king; 89.
Digambaras, a Jain sect; 48.
Dilruba, a musical instrument; 100.
Divali, a festival; 128.
Divasa, a day; 123.
Divine Mothers; 27.
Draupadi, a princess; 89.
Dravida Brahmins; 11.
Dravidian; 34, 97, 108.
Dravya, substance; 38.
Dribhabala; 97.
Dubois, Abbe; 56.
Durba, or Durva, a kind of sacred grass; 78.
Durga, a goddess; 24, 26, 27, 28, 51, 127, 129.
Durga Puja or Durgotsava, a festival; 129.
Durgotsava, a festival; see Durga Puja.
Durani; see Ahmad Shah Durani.
Durva; see Durba.
Durvasa; 94.
Duryodhana, a prince; 89.
Dushyanta, a prince; 94, 111.
Dwadasi, a day of the lunar month; 123.
Dwapara, an age; 1, 89.
Dwarka; 34, 89.
Dwitiya, a day of the lunar month; 123.

Ekadasi, a day of fasting; 123, 126, 127.
Elathalam, a musical instrument; 101.
Ellora; 105, 106, 108.
Elphinstone, Mountstuart; 18.
Embraces, forms of; 114, 115.
Englishman; 133.
Epics; 88, 89.
Eras, Hindu; 123-125.
Europe; 16, 64, 70, 133.

Fa Hian, the Chinese traveller; 6, 19.
Fergusson; 8.

Ganapatya, a sect; 25, 28.
Gandhara school of art; 107.
Gandharvas, celestial musicians; 101.
Gandhi; 21, 73.
Gandhi cap; 73.
Ganesha, a god; 24, 28, 29, 129, 130.
Ganesha Chaturthi, a festival; 129, 130.
Ganges; 33, 34, 53, 128.
Gangesa; 38.
Ganika, a courtesan; 120.
Ganita-Sara-somgraha; 96.
Garba dance; 102.
Garbhagraha, sanctum sanctorum; 107.
Garbhalambhana, a ceremony; 78.
Garuda, charger of Vishnu; 25, 31.
Garudapurana; 91.
Gauda, a Brahmin sub-caste; 11.
Gautama, a legislator; 91.

Gautama, the Buddha; 20, 24, 45, 46, 47.
Gaya, a centre of pilgrimage; 33, 83.
Gayatri, an incantation; 2, 8, 67, 74.
Ghat, burning; 33, 34.
Ghataka, a professional match-maker; 82.
Ghatika, a division of time; 123.
Ghee, clarified butter; 37.
Ghazni; 7, 8.
Ghori; 7, 8.
Giridhar, a name of Krishna; 119.
Gita; 44.
Gita Govinda; 118, 119.
Gobind, Guru; 51.
Gobhila Sutras; 92.
Godavari; 85.
Goethe; 94.
Gokul, birth place of Krishna; 25, 31, 33, 118, 130.
Gokulashtami, a festival; 130.
Golden Temple; 52.
Goloka, the heaven of the cow; 31.
Gonds, a hill tribe; 15, 32.
Gopal Naik, a musician; 100.
Gopatha; 85.
Gopis, milkmaids; 33, 34, 103, 118.
Gopuram, structure over temple gateway; 108, 109.
Gotras, clans 13.
Govinda, a name of Krishna; 30.
Gowli Sastra, science of the wall lizard; 77.
Grahastha; 11, 12.
Gramadevata, village deity; 29.
Granth; 51.
Greece; 47, 107.
Greetings, methods of; 71.
Grihyasutras; 91.
Gudi Parwa, a festival; 131.
Gujarat; 6, 73, 101, 107, 124.
Gujarati; 97.
Guna, quality; 38.
Gunakali, a Ragini; 99.
Guptas; 6, 94.
Gurjaras, a sub-caste of Brahmins; 13.
Gurjara tribe; 15.
Gurmukhi, sacred language of the Sikhs; 97.
Guru, teacher; 41, 50, 80.
Gurukula, section of Arya Samajists; 55.

Haj, pilgrimage to Mecca; 51.
Halebid temple; 109.
Hanuman; 31, 34, 130.
Hanuman Jayanti, a festival; 130.
Hara, a name of Shiva; 30.
Harappa; 109.
Hargobind, Guru; 51.
Hari, a name of Vishnu; 30, 118.
Haridwar; 35, 55.
Harijans; 18.
Harita; 91.
Haritalika, a feast; 126.
Hariti, a Buddhist goddess; 110.
Harmika; 104.
Harsha; 6, 7.
Harshacharita; 96.
Hasta, an asterism; 123.
Hastinapur; 89.
Hastini, a type of woman; 114, 115.
Hellenic ideals; 107.
Hemachandra; 49.
Himalayas; 24, 34, 45.
Hinayana Buddhism; 5, 46, 47, 104.
Hindi; 97.

HINDU RELIGION, CUSTOMS AND MANNERS

Hindola; a Raga; 99.
Hindu pantheon; 23, 24.
Hiranyakasipu; 24.
Hiranyaksha; 24, 126.
Hiriyanna; 43.
Hitopadesha; 93.
Hiuen Tsang, a Chinese pilgrim; 6, 7, 18.
Holi, a festival; 34, 128.
Holidays; 124.
Homa; 55.
Hookah; 66.
Huna tribe; 15.

Indo Aryans; 10, 23, 109.
Indra, king of the gods; 15, 23, 24, 125.
Indraprastha; 89.
Iravata, a mythical elephant; 96.
Isa, an *Upanishad;* 88.
Ishtadevata, personal god; 28, 29.
Islam; 7, 50, 55, 62.
Isvara, God; 41, 42.

Jagannath, a form of Vishnu; 34, 107, 126.
Jaichand, a Rajput prince; 8.
Jaimini, a philosopher; 40.
Jaina; 48.
Jainism; 47, 48.
Jains; 48, 107.
Jaipal, a Rajput prince; 8.
Jamadagni, a sage; 15.
Janakiharan; 95.
Janmashtami, a festival; 34, 130.
Jataka; 93, 109, 120.
Jatakarman, a ceremony; 78, 79.
Jati, caste; 10.
Jauhar; 7.
Java; 111.
Jayadeva, a poet; 118, 119.
Jehangir; 51, 100.
Jejury; 35.
Jews; 17, 35.
Ji, a term of respect; 72.
Jiva; 48, 49.
Jivan Mukta, the liberated; 44, 48.
Jnana, knowledge; 25, 26, 42.
Jnanakarma, enlightened activity; 41.
Jnanavapi, well of knowledge; 33.
Jnanayoga; 43.
Jnatri, a clan; 47.
Joint family; 64, 65.
Jones, Sir W.; 118.
Jumna; 33, 34, 118, 119.
Jupiter; 123, 124.
Jyeshta, a month; 123, 124.

Kaaba; 50.
Kabir; 50-51.
Kabirpanthis, followers of Kabir; 50.
Kacha, one of the five K's; 51.
Kadamba; a tree; 33.
Kadambari; 96.
Kaikeyi, a queen; 90.
Kailas, abode of Shiva; 24, 50, 106.
Kailasa temple; 106.
Kaisika, a Raga; 99.
Kaithabha; a demon; 129.
Kalari system of physical training; 60.

Kalavati, a courtesan; 122.
Kalhana, a historian; 96.
Kali, a goddess; 27, 28, 85, 91, 129.
Kalidasa, a poet; 6, 94, 111, 120.
Kali, era; 123.
Kalighat; 27.
Kalika, a *Tantra;* 91,
Kalinga, an ancient kingdom; 5.
Kaliya, a serpent; 110.
Kaliyuga, the fourth age of Kali; 1, 91.
Kalki, an incarnation of Vishnu; 1, 24.
Kalpa, an age; 1.
Kalpa, a Vedanga; 92.
Kalyanmalla; 115.
Kama, love; 114, 118, 128.
Kamadhenu, a mythical cow; 15.
Kamakhya, a *Tantra;* 91.
Kamandaki; 93.
Kamasutra; 111, 114, 115, 118, 122.
Kamoda; 99.
Kanada, a philosopher; 37.
Kanauj; 6, 8, 13, 14.
Kandali, a commentary; 37.
Kangha, one of the five K's; 51.
Kani, a prepared omen; 75.
Kanishka, an emperor; 5, 6, 47, 94.
Kankan, one of the five K's; 51.
Kanpathas, a sect; 26.
Kansa, a king; 24.
Kanwa, a sage; 94.
Kanya, Virgo; 123.
Kanyakubjas, a sub-caste of Brahmins; 13.
Kapalikas, a sect; 26.
Kapila, a philosopher; 38.
Kapila; a sage; 34.
Kapilashashti, a feast, 127.
Kapilavasthu; 46.
Karachi; 86.
Karana, a time division; 123.
Karanas, poses; 102.
Karka, Cancer; 123.
Karli; 106.
Karma, action; 39, 46, 51, 56.
Karmayoga, philosophy of action; 44.
Karna; 21.
Karnatakas, a sub-caste of Brahmins; 13.
Karnataki, school of music; 99.
Karthavirya; 15.
Kartik or Kartika, a month; 123, 127, 129.
Kartikeya; a god; 24, 125.
Kashmir; 5, 35, 47, 52, 122, 124.
Kasi, ancient name of Benares; 33.
Katha, an *Upanishad;* 88.
Kathak, a dance; 103.
Kathak, a story teller; 127.
Kathakali dance; 61, 102.
Kathasaritsagara; 96.
Kathiawar; 35.
Katyayana, a legislator; 91.
Kaula or Kaulika, sect; 27, 28.
Kaurava; 88, 89,.
Kausitika, an *Upanishad;* 88.
Kautilya, a name of Chanakya; 4, 93, 96.
Kaveri, a river; 35.
Kedara, a Ragini; 99.
Kena, an *Upanishad;* 88.
Kes, one of the five K's; 51.
Kesava, a name of Krishna; 119.
Kesdhari, a Sikh sect; 52.
Keshub Chandra Sen; 53.
Kevala; 48.

GLOSSARY AND INDEX

Khaddar; 73.
Khajuraho temples; 107.
Khalsa, a Sikh sect; 51.
Khandoba, a god; 35.
Khatri, a caste; 50.
Khusru, a Moghul Prince; 51.
Kincaid; 79.
Kinnaras, celestial musicians; 101.
Kipling; 93.
Kiranaval; 38.
Kirpan, one of the five K's; 51.
Kirtans, religious songs; 100.
Kisses, forms of; 115.
Koka Pandita; 116.
Kokila; 127.
Kollum era; 124.
Komal Swaras; 99.
Konarak temple; 107.
Koran; 51.
Krishna, an incarnation of Vishnu; 24, 25, 33, 34, 44, 103, 117-120, 128, 130.
Krishnamurti J.; 53.
Krishnapaksha, the dark half of the lunar month; 123.
Kritayuga, an age; 1.
K's the five; 51.
Kshatriya, the warrior caste; 1, 2, 6, 14-18, 20, 130.
Kshaura, a ceremony; 78.
Kshemendra; 121, 122.
Kubera; 110.
Kuladevata, tutelary deity; 29.
Kurlanava, a *Tantra;* 91.
Kulins, a sub-caste of Brahmins; 13.
Kumara, a name of Kartikeya; 125.
Kumaradasa; 95.
Kumarasambhava; 94.
Kumbha, Aquarius; 123.
Kumbhamela, a festival; 34, 35.
Kundalavana monastery; 5.
Kundalini Yoga; 40.
Kural; 97.
Kurma, tortoise incarnation; 24.
Kurma Purana; 91.
Kurukshetra; 89.
Kusa, a sacred grass; 31, 78, 80, 83.
Kushans; 5.
Kutch; 73.
Kuttanimatham; 121.
Kuttichathan, an imp; 33.
Kutub Minar; 8.
Kutub-ud-din Aibek; 8.

Labhramari, a form of Durga; 129.
Lahore; 8, 50, 52.
Lai-haroba, a dance; 103.
Lakshanas, distinguishing qualities; 90.
Lakshmana, a prince; 32, 90.
Lakshmana Sena; 118.
Lakshmi, a goddess; 24, 29, 31, 128, 131.
Lalita, Panchami, a feast; 129.
Lalitavistara; 93.
Lanka, ancient name of Ceylon; 24, 90, 128.
Likhita, a legislator; 91.
Lilavati; 96.
Linga, a *Purana;* 91.
Linga or Lingam, phallus; 3, 34.
Lingaraja temple; 107.
Lingasarira, subtle body; 39.
Livy; 15.
Lunar reckoning; 123.

Madhava, a teacher; 25.
Madhava, a name of Krishna; 117, 118.
Madhu, a demon; 129.
Madhvi, a tree; 118.
Madhyam, a musical note; 99.
Madonna; 22.
Madras; 108.
Madura; 7, 108.
Madya, sacramental liquor; 27.
Magadha, an ancient kingdom; 4.
Magadhi, an ancient language; 93.
Magh or Magha, a month; 123, 129, 130.
Magha, a poem; 95.
Magi San, an era; 124.
Mahabharata; 44, 88-90.
Mahadeva, a name of Shiva; 118.
Mahakali; 129.
Mahanirvana, a *Tantra;* 91.
Mahapralaya, the great cataclysm; 1.
Maharajah, a sect; 25.
Maharashtra; 13.
Mahars; 18.
Mahashivaratri, a festival; 129.
Mahavira; 47-49.
Mahayana Buddhism; 5, 47, 109, 110, 112.
Mahayuga, an age; 1, 123.
Mahendra; 47.
Mahipala; 7.
Mahishamardini, a name of Durga; 129.
Mahmud of Ghazni; 7, 8, 107.
Mahrathas; 8, 18, 29, 59, 74, 79, 124, 131.
Mahrathi; 13, 97.
Maithila; 13.
Maithili; 119.
Maithuna, sexual congress; 27.
Makara, Capricorn; 123.
Makarasankrant, a feast; 127.
Malabar; 7, 14, 19, 60, 124.
Malati; 120.
Malati Madhava; 95.
Malavikagnimitra; 94.
Malaya; 16.
Malayalam; 97.
Malini, a stream; 112.
Mamallapuram; 109.
Manasa, a goddess; 31, 130.
Mandapa; 107.
Mangal or Mangala, Tuesday; 125.
Mangal Sankrant, a feast; 127.
Mangini, betrothal; 82.
Manikarnika, a well; 33.
Manikkavasagar; 98.
Manipuris; 103.
Mansa, sacramental meat; 27.
Mantra, spell; 76.
Mantramahodadhi, a *Tantra;* 91.
Manu; 1, 2, 10, 18, 24, 91, 92.
Manwantara, reign of a Manu; 1, 90.
Mardana, a musician; 50.
Mardana, men's apartments; 62, 65.
Margashirsha; 123, 127.
Markandeya, a *Purana;* 91.
Marriage ceremony; 81, 82.
Mars; 123, 125.
Maruts, storm deities; 21.
Marwar; 16.
Mathers; E. P.; 120, 121.
Mathura; 33, 103, 130.
Matsya, fish incarnation; 24.
Matsya Purana; 91.
Mauryan; 4, 5, 16, 104, 110.

Maya, illusion; 41.
Mayura, a dance; 103.
Mecad, a serpent shrine; 31.
Mecca; 51.
Medhi, ambulatory passage; 104, 105.
Meena, Pisces; 123.
Meenakshi, a goddess; 35, 108.
Megasthenes; 4, 5, 7.
Meghaduta; 94.
Menaka, a celestial dancer; 94.
Mercury; 123, 125.
Mesha, Aries; 123.
Messiahship; 53.
Metempsychosis, doctrine of; 35.
Mewar; 16.
Mihiragula, a Hun; 6.
Milton; 91.
Mimamsa; 40, 41.
Mirabai; 44, 119, 120.
Mirs; 52.
Misrakesi; 111.
Mithila; 13.
Mithuna, Gemini; 123.
Modhera temple; 107.
Mogra, a tree; 118.
Moghul; 8.
Moha, illusion; 38.
Mohammed Ghori; 8.
Mohen-jo-daro; 104.
Moksha, salvation; 39, 114.
Mongols; 104.
Monkeys, worship of; 31.
Moor, E.; 84.
Mother goddess, worship of; 3.
Mricchakatika; 95.
Mridanga, a drum; 101.
Mriga, buck men; 114, 115.
Mrudumanya, a demon; 129.
M's, the five; 27.
Muddalam, a musical instrument; 101.
Mudra, corn; 27.
Mudra-rakshasa; 95, 96.
Muhammed, the Prophet; 22.
Mukti, liberation; 37, 38, 39, 41, 43.
Munda, a demon; 129.
Mundaka; 88.
Mundukya; 88.
Munja, sacred thread; 11.
Muslim; 7, 8, 9, 16, 50, 51, 52, 100, 112, 132.
Muzuris or Mushiri, an ancient port; 7.
Mysore; 4, 108, 129.

Naga Panchami, a festival; 31, 130.
Nagas, a tribe; 103.
Nagas, serpents; 31, 130.
Nagaswaram, a musical instrument; 101.
Nakara, kettle drum; 102.
Nakho-ka-kusthi, a form of boxing; 60.
Nakshatras, asterisms; 123, 124.
Naladiyar, a poet; 97.
Nalanda; 6.
Namakarana, a ceremony; 78.
Namaste, a form of greeting; 71.
Nambudiri, a sub-caste of Brahmins; 13, 14, 18.
Nammalvar, a poet; 98.
Nanak, Guru; 50, 51, 52.
Nanakpanthis, a sect; 52.
Nanda; 96.
Nandi, Shiva's bull; 24, 31, 106.
Narada, a sage; 99, 127.

Naradiya, a *Purana;* 91.
Narakasura, a demon; 129.
Narali Purnima, a festival; 130.
Narsimha, an incarnation of Vishnu; 24.
Nartaki, dancer; 102.
Nasik; 35, 85.
Natya, art of dancing; 101.
Natyasastra; 101, 104.
Nautch, a dance; 104.
Navadvaras, the nine orifices of the body; 32.
Navami, a day of the lunar month; 124.
Navarasas, the nine emotions; 102.
Navaratna, the nine gems; 94.
Navaratra or Navaratri, a festival; 124.
Nawab; 73.
Nayars; 14, 18, 75.
New Dispensation Samaj, a sect; 53.
Nicator; see Selucus.
Nirgranthas; 49.
Nirukta; 92.
Nisbet, betrothal ceremony; 82.
Nishad, a musical note; 99.
Nishkramana, a ceremony; 78.
Niti Sastras; 92, 93.
Nirvana; 47, 48, 49.
Nivitti; 81.
Nyaya, a system of philosophy; 38.

Omens; 76.
Onam, a festival; 60, 131.
Ooriya; 97.
Orissa; 4, 13, 34, 97, 103, 126.

Padma Purana; 91.
Padmavati; 97.
Padmini, a type of women; 114.
Pakshas; 123.
Pala, a time division; 123.
Palar; 109.
Pali, an ancient language; 93.
Pallavas, a dynasty; 7, 109, 111.
Panchakosi; 33.
Panchali; 89.
Panchamas, the fifth caste; 18, 33, 60.
Panchami, a day of the lunar month; 123.
Panchanga, calendar; 123.
Panchasiddhantika; 96.
Panchatantra; 93.
Panchavimsa; 96.
Panchayat; 56.
Panchayatana, a form of worship; 29.
Pandal, a porch; 59.
Pandava; 89.
Pandharpur; 35, 126.
Pandu, a king; 89.
Pandya, a dynasty; 7, 108.
Panini; 92.
Panipat; 8.
Parapathi; 43.
Parasara; 89.
Parasurama, an incarnation of Vishnu; 13, 15, 24, 124.
Pariah; 19.
Parihar, a Rajput clan; 15.
Parsi; 70, 73.
Parsva, a Thirthankara; 48.
Parvati, wife of Shiva; 24, 26, 129.
Pasu, an animal; 27

GLOSSARY AND INDEX

Pataliputra, an ancient city; 3, 5, 6, 96.
Patanjali, a philosopher; 39.
Pattar, a sub-caste of Brahmins; 18.
Paulika Siddhanta; 96.
Paul, St.; 133.
Paushya, a month; 123, 127.
Perumal, king of Chera; 7.
Peshawar; 5, 47.
Peshwas; 16, 97.
Phalgun or Phalguna, a month; 123.
Pilgrimages; 33.
Pinda; 84.
Pingala; 92.
Pipal, a sacred tree; 31.
Pisacha, a devil; 32.
Pitris, manes; 128.
Plants, worship of; 30.
Pongi, a musical instrument; 101.
Poona; 18.
Potti, an evil spirit; 32.
Pottu, a feminine adornment; 74.
Powar, a Rajput clan; 15.
Prachiniviti; 81.
Prahara, a time division; 115
Prakrit; 87, 97.
Prakriti, nature; 39.
Pralaya, cataclysm; 1.
Prana; 88.
Prarthana Samaj, a sect; 53.
Prasasthapada, a commentator; 38.
Prasna, an *Upanishad*; 88.
Pratap, a Rajput prince; 16.
Prathama, a day of the lunar month; 123.
Pratikshanapatha, ambulatory passage; 104.
Pratisakhyas; 92.
Prativipala, a time division; 123.
Pravarapura; 122.
Prayag, ancient name of Allahabad; 35.
Premsagar; 97.
Preta, an evil spirit; 32.
Prithwiraja, a Rajput prince; 8, 97.
Prithwirajrasou; 97.
Prostitution; 120.
Puja, worship; 28, 126, 127.
Pulaya; 18, 19.
Pulikesin; 106
Pumsavana, a ceremony; 78.
Punjab; 3, 4, 6, 8, 50, 51, 54, 97.
Punjabi; 97.
Puranas; 90, 91, 126.
Purdah; 8, 13, 74.
Puri; 107.
Purnima, full moon; 123.
Purusha, a hymn; 29.
Purushapura ancient name of Peshawar; 5, 47.
Purushas, souls; 39.
Purva Mimamsa, a system of philosophy; 40, 41.
Purvi, a Ragini; 99.
Pushpaka, an aerial car; 90.
Put, hell; 78.
Putras, auxiliary melodies; 99.

Q: NIL

Radha, beloved of Krishna; 117, 118, 119.
Raga, male melodies; 99.
Raghu, 129.
Raghuvamsa; 94.

Ragini, female melodies; 99.
Rahula; 46.
Rajah; 13, 75.
Raja Ram Mohan Roy; 52, 53.
Rajas, activity; 39, 91.
Rajasthan; 17, 73, 113.
Rajendra Chola Deva I; 7.
Rajnitisastras; 93.
Rajput; 7, 8, 15, 16, 18, 73.
Rajput school of painting; 113.
Rajtarangini; 96.
Raka; 79.
Rakhi Purnima, a festival; 130.
Rakshasa, a demon; 32.
Raktabija, a form of Durga; 129.
Raktadanti, a form of Durga; 129.
Rama; 14, 32, 34, 50, 90, 129, 130.
Ramachandra, a name of Rama; 24.
Ramakrishna Mission; 132.
Ramakrishna Paramahansa, a saint; 27.
Ramalila; 103, 130.
Ramananda, a teacher; 25, 43, 50.
Ramanuja, a philosopher; 25, 43, 50.
Ramayana; 24, 25, 32, 34, 90, 95, 130.
Ramdas, Guru; 50, 51.
Rameshwaram; 34, 108.
Ramnavami, a feast; 130.
Ram Ram, a form of greeting; 71.
Ramzan; 50, 123.
Ranade, Mahadev Gobind; 53.
Ranjit Singh; 52.
Rasalila dance; 103.
Rathas; 108.
Ratirahaya; 115.
Ravana, the demon king of Lanka; 24, 31, 32, 90, 103, 130.
Ravana Vadha; 95.
Ravi-var, Sunday; 123, 125.
Ravi Varma; 113.
Rawlinson; 95, 120, 132.
Realisation; 41.
Rebek, a musical instrument; 50.
Rele, Dr. V. G.; 40.
Rig Veda; 22, 87, 94.
Rikhikesh; 35.
Rishabha, a musical note; 99.
Ritusamhara; 94.
Rohini, a star; 127.
Romaka, a system of astronomy; 96.
Roman Catholic; 21, 22.
Roman empire; 6, 15.
Romans; 7.
Rudramala temple; 107.
Rudrayamala, a *Tantra*; 91.
Rugviniccaya; 96.

Sabara, a dance; 103.
Sabaraswami; 39.
Sabroan, battle of; 52.
Sacrifices; 85.
Sadharana Samaj, a sect; 53.
Sagar, an island; 34.
Sagara, a king; 34.
Sahidharis, a sect of Sikhs; 53.
Saka era; 124.
Saktas, a sect; 27, 91.
Sakti, a goddess; 27, 28, 29, 30.
Sakuni, a gambler; 89.
Sakyamuni, a name of the Buddha; 45, 46.
Salagrama, a sacred stone; 29, 83.
Salivahan, a king; 124, 131.

Salwar; 73.
Samadhi; 39.
Samavartana; 78, 81.
Sama Veda; 87, 88. 92.
Samayacharika Sutras; 92.
Sāmayamatrika; 121, 22.
Samudragupta; 95.
Samvarta, a law giver; 91.
Samvat, a year; 124.
Sanatanists; 54, 55.
Sanchi; 105, 110.
Sandhyas, prayers; 28.
Sani, Saturn; 125, 126.
Sani-var, Saturday; 123, 125.
Sankara; 26, 27, 41, 47.
Sankha; 91.
Sankhini, a type of woman; 114, 115.
Sankhya, a system of philosophy; 38, 39, 49.
Sankranti; 123, 127.
Sankrant Vrata; 127.
Sanskaras, ceremonies; 78, 80.
Sanskrit; 87, 88, 96, 97.
Sanyasa, renunciation; 12, 13.
Sanyasin; 42, 43.
Saptak; 99.
Saptami, a day of the lunar month; 123.
Saptapadi; 83.
Saptarshi Kala, an era; 124.
Saptarshis, seven sage; 13, 124.
Sarada Act; 62.
Saradatilaka, a Tantra; 91.
Sarasvatas, a sub-caste of Brahmins; 13.
Sarasvati, a goddess; 13, 23, 99, 100, 131.
Sari; 73, 74.
Sarinda, a musical instrument; 100, 101.
Saringi, a musical instrument; 100, 101.
Sarn-gadhara-paddhati; 92.
Sasruta; 96.
Satapatha; 88.
Sati; 53, 127.
Saturn; 123, 125.
Satva, refinement; 39.
Satyanarayana Puja; 127.
Satyartha Prakash; 54.
Saunders, K.; 95.
Sauraspathas, a sect; 28.
Savitri; 127.
Sects; 25-28.
Selucus Nicator; 4, 5.
Serpent worship; 30, 31.
Seven Pagodas; 109.
Seven Sages; see Saptarshis.
Shadj, a musical note; 99.
Shadow play; 61.
Shadvimsa; 88.
Shah Jehan; 51, 113.
Shaivas; 25, 26.
Shaivism; 26, 27, 43.
Shakuntala; 94, 95, 111.
Shami, a sacred tree; 129.
Shasha, a type of man; 114, 115.
Shashtav, godling; 32.
Shashti, a goddess; 79, 123.
Shashtipurthi; 83.
Shatatapa; 91.
Shishupala; 24, 95, 118.
Shiva, a god; 3, 25, 26, 30, 32, 33, 129.
Shivaji; 8.
Shivapurana; 91.
Shivaratra or Shivratri, a festival; 129.
Shraddhas, funeral ceremonies; 11, 83, 84.
Shravan or Shravana, a month; 123, 130, 131.

Shravan Belgola; 4, 48.
Shrotriyas, a sub-caste of Brahmins; 13.
Siddhartha; 45.
Siddhas; 28.
Sidhapur; 107.
Sikh; 8, 49-52, 73, 97.
Sikha, a lock of hair; 80.
Sikhara of a temple; 107.
Sikhism; 49-52.
Siksha, a Vedanga; 92.
Simantam, a ceremony; 78.
Simantonnayana, a ceremony; 78.
Simha, Leo; 123.
Sind; 16, 52, 97.
Sindhi; 97.
Sinivali, a goddess; 79.
Sisodia, a Rajput clan; 16.
Sita; 16, 90, 95.
Sitar, a musical instrument; 100.
Skanda, a goddess; 79.
Skanda, a Purana; 91.
Smartha, a sect; 25, 28.
Smartha Sutras; 89.
Smasana, cremation ground; 84.
Smriti; 88, 89.
Solanki, a Rajput clan; 16.
Solar reckoning; 123.
Soma, a plant; 31, 86.
Soma sacrifice; 86.
Somadeva; 96.
Somakrant, a king; 124.
Soma-var; Monday; 119, 125.
Somnath temple; 107.
Somnathpur temple; 107.
Song of Songs; 117.
Song of the Sanyasin; 42, 43.
South India; 7, 66, 108.
Spirit worship; 32.
Sri, a Raga; 99.
Sribhasya; 43.
Sridhara; 38, 96.
Srimandir; 106.
Srinagar; 35.
Srirangam; 35, 108.
Sruti; 87, 88.
Stupa; 105.
Subhadra; 34.
Subrahmanya; 24.
Suddha Swaram, sharp note; 99.
Suddhi movement; 54, 55.
Suddhodhana; 45.
Sudra, the menial caste; 1, 10, 11, 12, 17-19, 20, 21.
Sudraka; 95.
Suffism; 117.
Suklapaksha, bright half of the lunar month; 123.
Sukra, Venus; 125.
Sukraniti; 111.
Sukra-var, Friday; 123, 125.
Sun, worship of; 25, 28.
Sunga dynasty; 5.
Superstitions; 75, 76, 76, 77.
Supreme Being; 22, 23, 24.
Surapala; 96.
Surpanakha, a female demon; 32.
Suryamati, a queen; 96.
Surya temple; 107.
Sutra, a literary form; 37, 91.
Suttas, a branch of Buddhist literature; 93.
Svar, a mystic syllable; 79.
Swami Narayana; 25
Swetambaras, a Jain Sect; 48, 49.

GLOSSARY AND INDEX

Syamarahasya, a *Tantra*; 91.
Syria; 47.
Syrian Christians; 18.

Tabla, a musical instrument; 100.
Tagore, Devendranath; 53.
Tagore, Dr. Rabindranath; 97.
Tailangas; 13.
Taittiriya; 88.
Talwandi; 50.
Tamas, grossness; 39.
Tambura, a musical instrument; 100.
Tamil; 13, 97, 98.
Tandava Lakshanam; 101.
Tandya; 88.
Tanjore; 100.
Tansen, a musician; 100.
Tantras; 27, 86, 91.
Tara, a goddess; 110.
Taranga of Katha; 120.
Tathas, musical scales; 99.
Tatvachintamani; 38.
Tavernier; 16.
Tej Bahadur, Guru; 51.
Telugu; 13, 98.
Thendan, an evil spirit; 32.
Theosophy; 53.
Thirthankar or Thirthankara; 48, 49, 107.
Thiruvalluvar; 98.
Thiruvasakam; 98.
Thiya, a sub-caste of Sudras; 18.
Thomas, Apostle; 7.
Thrayodasi, a day of the lunar month; 123.
Thretayuga; 1, 90.
Thugs; 27.
Thyagaraja, a musician; 100.
Tibet; 47.
Thithi, a division of time; 123.
Toga; 72.
Totayam; 102.
Tree, worship; 30, 31.
Trishati; 96.
Tripitaka; 93.
Tritiya, a day of the lunar month; 123.
Trojan war; 16.
Tukaram, a Vaishnava saint; 44.
Tula, Liba; 123.
Tulsi, a sacred plant; 31.
Tulsidas; 44, 97.
Turban; 73.

Udayana; 38.
Uddisa; 91.
Ujjain; 6, 94, 95, 96, 124.
Ulladahs; 18.
Uma, a goddess; 27.
United Provinces; 73, 74.
Upanayanam, a ceremony; 16, 80, 81.
Upanishads; 23, 40, 41, 88.
Upaveda; 96.
Urdhvabhus, a sect; 26.
Urdu; 97.
Urvasi, a nymph; 94.
Usanas; 91.
Ushas, goddess of the dawn; 22, 87.
Utkalas, sub-caste of Brahmins; 13.
Uttara Mimamsa, a system of philosophy; 41, 42.
Uttara Ramacharita; 95.

Vachaspati; 39.
Vagbhatta; 96.
Vagdana; 82.
Vairagya, renunciation; 39.
Vaisakh or Vaisakha, a month; 123, 128.
Vaiseshika, a system of philosophy; 38.
Vaishnava; 24, 25, 34, 35, 98, 117, 130.
Vaishnavism; 24, 25, 44, 108, 118, 119.
Vaisya; 1, 16.
Vaitarani, infernal river; 10.
Vallabhacharya, a teacher; 24.
Valmiki, author of the *Ramayana*; 90, 97.
Vamamargis, a sect; 27, 28.
Vamana, dwarf incarnation of Vishnu; 24.
Vamanapurana; 91.
Vaman Dwadasi, a feast; 131.
Vanaprastha; 11, 12.
Vandana Slokam; 102.
Vanik, a trader; 16.
Var or Vara, a week; 123.
Varaha, boar incarnation of Vishnu; 24.
Varahamihira; 96.
Varahapurana; 91.
Vardhamana, a name of Mahavira; 47, 48, 49.
Varnashrama Dharma, caste system; 10.
Varuna, sea god; 124, 130.
Vasanta Panchami, a feast; 131.
Vasantsena; 95.
Vasishta, a legislator; 91.
Vasishta, a sage; 19.
Vat Purnima, a feast; 127.
Vat Savitri, a feast; 127.
Vatsyayana, a commentator; 38.
Vatsyayana, author of *Kamasutra*; 114-117, 119.
Vedas; 10, 12, 22, 23, 46, 54, 85, 87.
Vedangas; 92.
Vedanta, a system of philosophy; 40, 41, 43.
Vedantasamgraha; 43.
Vedantin; 41.
Venus; 123, 126.
Verities; 46.
Vetal; 124.
Vichitravirya, a prince; 89.
Videha, an ancient kingdom; 47.
Vidyapathi; 119.
Viharas; 106.
Vijaynagar; 8, 120.
Vijnanabhikshu; 39.
Vikramaditya; 95, 124.
Vikram era; 124, 127.
Vikramorvasi; 94.
Vimala temple; 107.
Vimana; 107.
Vimba, a fruit; 114, 118.
Vina, a musical instrument; 100.
Vinaya; a branch of Buddhist literature; 95.
Vindhyas; 13.
Vipala, a time division; 123.
Virgil; 16.
Visakhadatta; 96.
Vishishta Advaita, a system of philosophy; 43, 44, 54.
Vishnu; 1, 2, 23, 24, 43, 44, 118, 126.
Vishnupurana; 91.
Vishu, New Year Day of Malabar; 76.
Vishwamitra, a king; 19, 94.
Vithoba, a form of Vishnu; 35.
Vivaha, a ceremony; 78.
Vivekananda, Swami; 27, 42, 132.
Vrata; 126-128.
Vriddhachanakya; 93.
Vrinda; 96.

Vrindavan; 34.
Vrischika, Scorpio; 123.
Vrisha, a type of man; 114, 115.
Vrishabha, Taurus; 123.
Vyakarana, a *Vedanga;* 92.
Vyasa, a sage; 21, 41, 89.

Westerners; 14, 21.
Western India; 107.
White Huns; 6.
Widow; 62.
Williams, Monier; 31, 78, 87, 88, 133.
Wilson; J.; 11.
Women, status of; 61, 62.

X : NIL

Yaga, sacrifice; 85.

Yagnavalkya; 91.
Yajur Veda; 85, 87, 88.
Yakshas, mythical beings; 32.
Yakshis; 32.
Yama, a law giver; 91.
Yama, god of death; 35.
Yamapuri, court of Yama; 35.
Yaska; 92.
Yasodhara; 45.
Yavanapura, city of Greeks; 96.
Yoga, a conjunction; 123.
Yoga, a system of philosophy; 39, 40.
Yogi; 39, 40.
Yudhishtira, a king; 89.
Yuga, an age; 1, 123.

Zamindars; 61.
Zanana, women's apartments; 58, 67, 69.
Zodiac; 123.